W9-BNH-235

A CHRONOLOGY OF WESTERN ARCHITECTURE

Doreen Yarwood

Facts On File Publications
New York, New York ● Oxford, England

© Doreen Yarwood 1987
First published 1987

copyright © 1987 by Doreen Yarwood

First published in the United States of America by
Facts on File Publications, 460 Park Avenue South,
New York, New York 10016

Library of Congress Cataloging-in-Publication Data

Yarwood, Doreen.
    A Chronology of Western Architecture.

    Includes index.
    1. Architecture — History.   I. Title
NA200.Y37   1987   709   87-13652
ISBN 0-8160-1861-8

Printed in Hong Kong

10 9 8 7 6 5 4 3 2 1

CONTENTS

INTRODUCTION

The scope of this book is wide. The time-span extends from the early beginnings of a European building form in about 2000 BC to the present-day adoption of what we call modern architecture all over the world. Geographically the book is concerned with western Europe and North America. A number of books are available which cover – to a greater or lesser degree – a similar scope, but here an attempt has been made to handle this vast quantity of historical material in a different manner from that normally adopted.

The most usual way of presenting such a complex history of building forms is by dividing up the material into architectural movements: classical, Romanesque, Gothic, Italian Renaissance etc., and to consider these movements specifically – describing the styles, the architects, sometimes the building materials – but with less emphasis upon the reasons behind such developments. What is often omitted is the relationship in time within the different movements; for example, the fact that two centuries separated the emergence of the Renaissance in Florence, with Brunelleschi's Foundling Hospital in the 1420s, from the adoption of the style in, for instance, England, Germany or Spain; a delay caused not only by reasons of geography and communication but also religion, national character and economic development. Similarly, in more recent times, a considerable, though less extended, delay occurred between the rise of advanced building techniques in the USA (in the 1880s) and their wholehearted adoption after World War II in countries such as Britain.

To present in an easily assimilated form both the detail and the overall pattern of architectural development, this is primarily a picture book: a visual presentation of a visual art form. The landscape (horizontal) format of an A4 page has be used in order to show at a glance, on 105 double spreads, the comparative building styles over the whole area of Western civilization at any given date.

The early civilizations – Minoan, Greek, Etruscan, Roman, Byzantine and Pre-Romanesque – are handled in long periods of time; three or four double spreads being devoted to each extensive period. From AD 1100 to the present day the material is presented in 50-year spans, three, four or five double spreads being allocated to each half century. The date of the period and the style is printed as a heading. The countries and areas concerned are listed in the left margin of the left-hand page and the drawings extend across both pages to represent that period and those countries. There are 1056 illustrations in total.

While the illustrations show the detail of individual buildings, town planning schemes and the work of specific architects, the two text columns on each spread are intended to give a general account of the major trends in design for the half-century concerned and attempt to explain the reasons – social, political, climatic, nationalistic and technological – for such trends. For ease of reference an index is given, as is also a glossary of terms with a figure reference to illustrations.

By this method of presentation the reader may see at a glance, in pictures and text, that for instance, in the half-century 1550-1600 in Rome, architects had moved on in style from Renaissance to Mannerist and were experimenting with baroque in Jesuit church design. In the Veneto, Palladio was adapting ancient Roman building forms to the needs of his sixteenth-century clients. Michelangelo and others were exploring the possibilities of ideal town planning in city centres, while de l'Orme, Bullant and Lescot in France, Herrera in Spain and de Torralva in Portugal were introducing the Renaissance style, yet Flemish and German Mannerism was still dominant in these areas, as it was in Elizabethan England.

On each double spread there is also a column giving a note of contemporary world-wide events and personalities. This column is not intended primarily to be informative. It intentionally lists names and happenings which will be familiar to many readers, in order to provide a connecting link of interest between what is occurring in the realm of building and the wider world beyond. From many of these discoveries, theories and events stemmed the reasons behind architectural developments.

This book should be treated as an introduction to the subject. It presupposes no previous knowledge of building or architectural history on the part of the reader, whether adult or school student; only a background knowledge and general interest in the arts, travel and social history.

Doreen Yarwood
East Grinstead 1987

THE BRONZE AGE IN MAINLAND AND ISLAND GREECE   2000 – 1100 BC

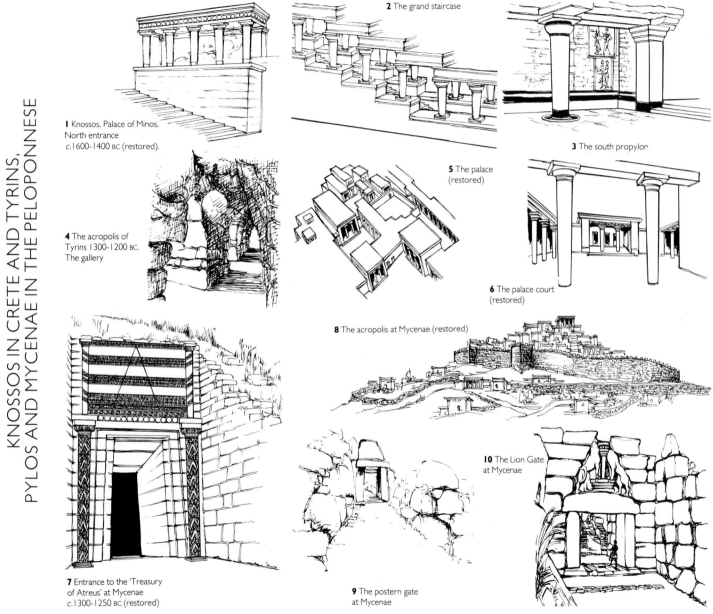

1 Knossos, Palace of Minos, North entrance c.1600-1400 BC (restored).

2 The grand staircase

3 The south propylon

4 The acropolis of Tyrins 1300-1200 BC. The gallery

5 The palace (restored)

6 The palace court (restored)

8 The acropolis at Mycenae (restored)

7 Entrance to the 'Treasury of Atreus' at Mycenae c.1300-1250 BC (restored)

9 The postern gate at Mycenae

10 The Lion Gate at Mycenae

The earliest civilization in Europe to develop a high art form, to build palaces, harbours and towns, and produce a written language, was in Crete soon after 2000 BC. The means and knowledge to do this derived from Asia and Egypt, and were transmitted from about 2500 BC from the Bronze Age centres in the interior of Asia Minor to the coastal area of Troy and, from thence, to the islands of the Aegean and, later, the mainland of the Peloponnese. In Troy, excavation has revealed extensive citadel building of the years c. 2700-1200 BC.

The style of construction and decoration evolved in the island of Crete in the Middle Bronze Age lasted about six centuries. The Cretans were a maritime people who established close commercial contact with the people of Egypt and the Near East, strongly influencing the developing Cretan culture. This may be seen in excavated palaces at Knossos, Phaistos and Mallia – particularly at Knossos where Sir Arthur Evans brought in architects and artists to reconstruct parts of the palace (**1-3**).

The Cretans built harbours to shelter their great navy which gave protection to their palaces laid out inland. The palace layout was asymmetrical and had a multiplicity of rooms. These were generally flat-roofed and, according to Homer, the roofs were utilized for sleeping or drying foodstuffs on. An important feature of design was a central courtyard – the idea taken from Egypt and Mesopotamia – but the Cretan version was more rectangular, being twice as long on the north/south axis as on the east/west, to gain maximum sunshine in winter.

Walls were of dressed stone slabs at base and above were of timber and adobe (sun-dried brick). They were plaster-faced and painted with coloured frescoes. Windows

6

and doorways were timber-framed. Supports were columns and square pillars; the columns were of wood, decoratively painted, and with the shafts tapering towards the low stone base (**14**). The capitals, precursors of the later Greek Doric design, comprised a square abacus above a cushion moulding. Pillars were of masonry. The richly carved and painted decoration displayed linked spirals with rosettes, as in Egypt (**11**). At Knossos the palace was fitted with an elaborate drainage system of earthenware pipes; there were also bathrooms and water closets.

With the collapse in Crete about 1400 BC of the Minoan civilization a new culture arose on the mainland in the Peloponnese in maritime principalities at, notably, Mycenae, Tyrins and Pylos. These peoples built strongly fortified citadels protected by thick walls constructed from immense blocks of stone, each weighing several tons (**4, 8-10**). Only in Hittite Asia Minor, at that time, were such colossal stones handled. Later, the Greeks called this building form 'cyclopean', attributing it to the mythical Cyclopes (**15**).

The Mycenaeans were more advanced as engineers, building megalithic vaulted galleries and chambers (Tyrins), great lintel-spanned gateways surmounted by triangular relieving stones (Lion Gate, Mycenae) and interior corbelled squared-stone roofing (tholos tombs, Mycenae). The palaces, within the city walls, were not dissimilar to the Cretan ones, being flat-roofed and using the same type of materials, column and pillar supports, and decorative means, but the Mycenaean great hall in the centre of the palace was much larger – the *megaron*, as Homer called it (**4, 5**).

11 Minoan ornament, Knossos, c.1500

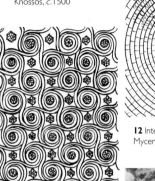

12 Interior of domed chamber, Mycenae, c.1320

13 Capital (restored), Palace of Nestor, Pylos, c.1300

14 Column, Palace of Minos, Knossos, c.1600

16 Detail, doorway column, 'Treasury of Atreus' (see 7)

15 Cyclopean walling, Citadel of Tyrins, c.1280 BC

17 Detail ornament (see 7)

18 Detail ornament (see 7)

BC

2000–1100   Movement of building materials and means of construction utilized the earth ramp, sledges pulled by slaves, rockers and the lever. The power of the lever was utilized throughout antiquity, though the principle was formulated later – by Archimedes

3000 onwards   Development of understanding of hydraulics in China, Arabia, Mesopotamia and Egypt. Dams, reservoirs, irrigation schemes and canal systems

c. 2750   Sumerian numeral system developed. Used for commercial accounting, measurement and the calendar. Based upon a scale of 60, and acceptance of a year of 360 days; which survives in our division of angular degrees, hours and minutes into 60 sub-units

c. 2700   Building of the true arch and vault in Mesopotamia, in brick and stone, based on centering

c.2600   Earliest masonry construction (Egypt)

2500–1800   Zenith of Indus Valley culture in India. Advanced urban planning on grid plan. Elaborate public drainage system for streets and buildings. Wheel-turned, fired decorative pottery

1550–1500   Glass vessels being made in Mesopotamia and Egypt

1450–1300   Hittite empire flourishes in Syria and Anatolia. Massive architectural construction, especially defensive encircling citadel walls, as in contemporary Mycenae

1350–1300   Wrought iron being manufactured from smelting of iron ore in Asia Minor and Egypt

1303–1223   In Egypt, building of great hypostyle hall at Karnak and temple at Abu Simbel

GREEK TEMPLES   520 – 350 BC

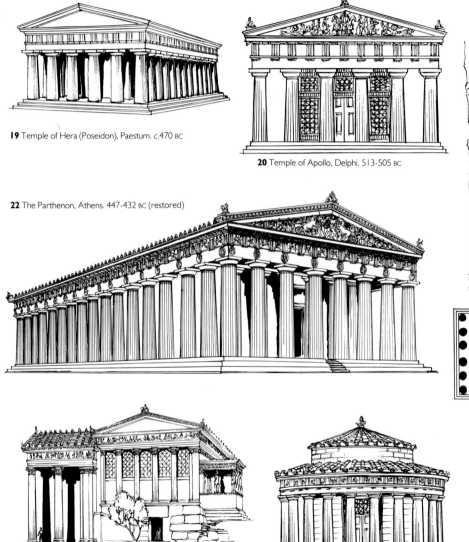

19 Temple of Hera (Poseidon), Paestum. c.470 BC

20 Temple of Apollo, Delphi. 513-505 BC

22 The Parthenon, Athens. 447-432 BC (restored)

21 Interior view of Temple of Hera, Paestum, showing upper tier of columns inside naos

NAOS   PRO NAOS

23 Ground plan. Temple of Hera, Paestum

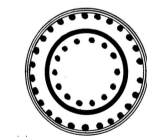

24 The Erechtheion, Athens. Ionic order, 421-405 BC

25 Tholos, Delphi. c.375 BC (restored)

26 Ground plan. Tholos, Epidauros, c.350 BC (restored)

Several centuries – a Dark Age period – passed between the collapse of the Bronze Age Mycenaean culture and the rise of the Hellenic one. When the new architecture evolved in the seventh century BC it was different from its predecessors. The Greeks were strongly influenced by commercial contact with their neighbours: Egypt, Assyria, Persia. Their massive Doric structures had much of the Egyptian monumentality about them, as had their colour and ornament something of Assyrian richness.

The prime feature of Greek architecture is its intellectual quality. The Greeks did not develop great variety in design, nor did they show exceptional structural inventiveness. They achieved – to an immensely high degree – a standard of perfection for the designs which they adopted, reaching a zenith in the fifth century BC.

Greek architecture belongs to three chief periods: the archaic, up to about 480 BC, the fifth and fourth century classical, and the Hellenistic, reaching into the Christian era. Ancient Greece extended its domain beyond the mainland and adjacent islands to all lands bordering the Mediterranean Sea. In general, the Doric style was characteristic of mainland Greece and the Ionic of Asia Minor, nearby islands and North Africa.

Greek architecture is primarily a post-and-lintel form of construction. The Greeks were reluctant to adopt more daring structural techniques; this was particularly so in their attitude to building arches and vaults. The principle of erecting the true arch by means of mutually supporting wedge-shaped blocks of stone or brick had been understood two millennia before in Egypt and Mesopotamia, but the Greeks tended to confine their use of it to structures

THE GREEK ORDERS   520 – 330 BC

such as tombs, which they tunnel-vaulted.

In early times they built with sun-dried bricks, terracotta and wood, thatching the roofs. During the seventh century BC they began to build in cut stone. An important reason for this was the invention, earlier in the century, of roofing tiles and, since these were much larger and heavier than modern tiles, a stone structure was required to support them. From the sixth century onwards most important buildings were of stone and, after 500 BC, marble was increasingly used in areas where it was available, particularly in mainland Greece. Elsewhere, as in southern Italy, the limestone might be coated with marble stucco.

The Greeks rarely used mortar. They fitted their blocks with meticulous care and, because of the earthquake hazard, used metal dowels and cramps set in molten lead to hold the blocks in position. Early columns were monolithic. From the sixth century they were more often in superimposed drums which had been turned by lathe. Column flutes were carved at top and bottom, then completed after erection. Roofing construction was of timber, covered by terracotta or marble tiles. The low pitch, suited to the climate, gave to the end pediments their elegant proportions. Inside, the ceiling was of coffered marble or stone.

The most important Greek buildings were temples built not to house worshippers (who remained outside round an altar) but the representation of the deity. At first the design was based upon the megaron of the Minoan palace: a rectangular hall with columned porch in front. The Greek preference for symmetry led to a porch at each end and the enclosing, by walls and a colonnade, of the central chamber (naos) which housed the

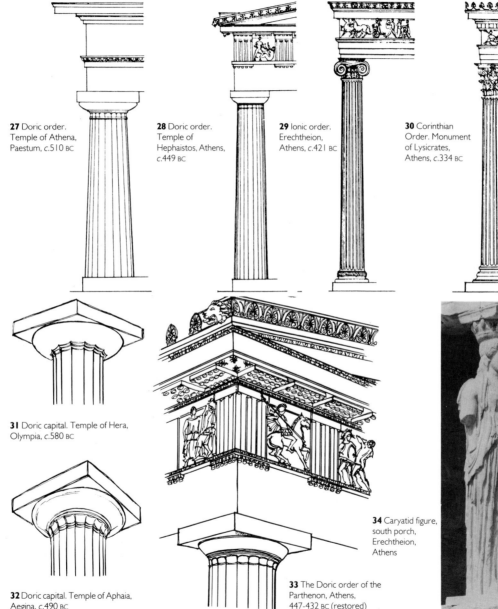

27 Doric order. Temple of Athena, Paestum, c.510 BC

28 Doric order. Temple of Hephaistos, Athens, c.449 BC

29 Ionic order. Erechtheion, Athens, c.421 BC

30 Corinthian Order. Monument of Lysicrates, Athens, c.334 BC

31 Doric capital. Temple of Hera, Olympia, c.580 BC

32 Doric capital. Temple of Aphaia, Aegina, c.490 BC

33 The Doric order of the Parthenon, Athens, 447-432 BC (restored)

34 Caryatid figure, south porch, Erechtheion, Athens

BC

800–480   Growth of the Greek city-state civilization – the archaic period. Overseas colonization in the Mediterranean area

Early sixth century   Introduction of silver coins for the first time at Aegina and Corinth. Smaller value than the seventh-century electrum coins from Lydia. A coin money basis for the economy developed

Sixth century   Development of kiln design for firing pottery in Greece

Sixth century   Pythagorus, born in Samos; Greek sage and philosopher

526   Anaximanes dies. A Greek philosopher born in Miletus. He believed that air was the primary element and the first principle of the universe. It could become fire, water, earth or stone

Fifth century   Cotton, of Indian origin, grown in the Nile valley from this time

Fifth century   Hippodamos of Miletus. A Greek town planner. Credited (erroneously) by Aristotle with the invention of the grid street plan for cities. Hippodamos was concerned with the laying out of Piraeus

500–404   Zenith of the Greek city-state culture. Highest standard in the arts and architecture. Classical period

480   Battle of Thermopylae

Fifth century   Development of a Greek empire based upon Athens. 461-29 Pericles in power there.

TOWN PLANNING AND BUILDING IN GREECE AND TURKEY

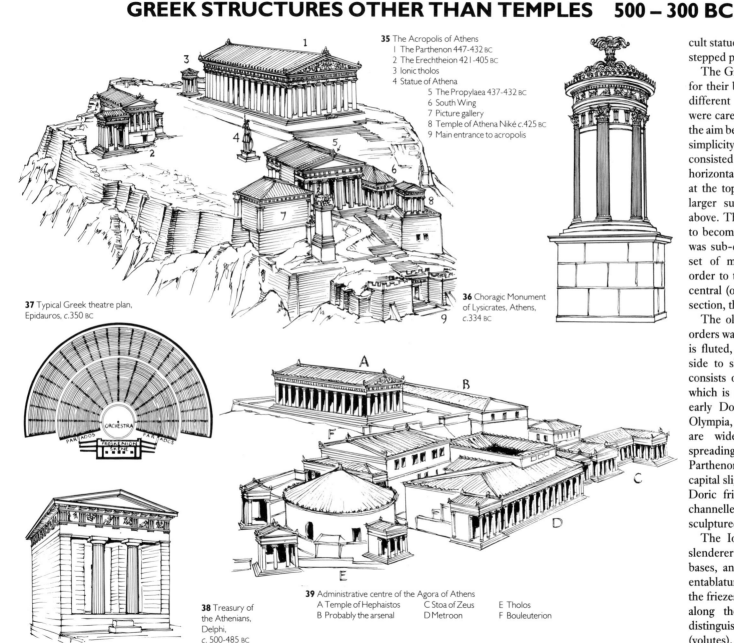

35 The Acropolis of Athens
1 The Parthenon 447-432 BC
2 The Erechtheion 421-405 BC
3 Ionic tholos
4 Statue of Athena
5 The Propylaea 437-432 BC
6 South Wing
7 Picture gallery
8 Temple of Athena Niké c.425 BC
9 Main entrance to acropolis

36 Choragic Monument of Lysicrates, Athens, c.334 BC

37 Typical Greek theatre plan, Epidauros, c.350 BC

38 Treasury of the Athenians, Delphi, c. 500-485 BC

39 Administrative centre of the Agora of Athens
A Temple of Hephaistos
B Probably the arsenal
C Stoa of Zeus
D Metroon
E Tholos
F Bouleuterion

cult statue. The building was erected upon a stepped platform (**19–26**).

The Greeks developed a system of orders for their building construction. In these the different parts, mouldings and ornament were carefully prescribed and proportioned, the aim being to create structures of apparent simplicity, perfection and beauty. Each order consisted of vertical columns supporting horizontal lintels. Each column was finished at the top with a capital, which provided a larger surface area to support the lintel above. The lintels over each column joined to become a continuous entablature, which was sub-divided horizontally into an upper set of mouldings (cornice) projecting in order to throw rain clear of the building, a central (often decorated) frieze and a lower section, the architrave (**27–34**).

The oldest and most used of the Greek orders was the Doric. It has no base. Its shaft is fluted, the shallow flutes rising on each side to sharp edges (arrises). The capital consists of a square block (abacus), below which is a cushion moulding (echinus). In early Doric buildings – at Paestum and Olympia, for example – the column shafts are wide and the capitals large and spreading. In later work – for instance, the Parthenon – the shaft is slenderer, and the capital slighter and more subtly curved. The Doric frieze is ornamented by vertically-channelled triglyphs alternating with sculptured metopes (**27, 28, 31–3**).

The Ionic and Corinthian orders have slenderer columns standing upon moulded bases, and flutes separated by fillets. The entablatures are less deep than the Doric and the friezes are often sculptured continuously along the length. The Ionic capital is distinguished by two front-facing side scrolls (volutes). The Corinthian capital is bell-

GREEK ORDERS AND ORNAMENT 600 – 300 BC

shaped and enriched by leaves and small volutes; it has a four-faced abacus (29, 30).

Many Greek cities were built on hill tops, and the slopes of such natural defences were reinforced by fortified walls. Within the walls of such an acropolis (literally 'city upon a hill') were erected the most important buildings; as in, for example, the Athenian Acropolis (35).

By the fifth century, where a city was planned on a new and flatter site, the streets often crossed one another at right angles, creating uniform building plots. This grid concept is believed to have originated much earlier in the Near East, and was developed in seventh-century Ionian Greece (Smyrna, for instance); it is often called Milesian, after the city of Miletus in Asia Minor, laid out in this way from 470 BC.

In such fifth- and fourth-century cities the centrally placed agora was an open meeting place. Erected here were business and audience halls, sometimes circular structures (tholoi), the council house for administration (bouleuterion), a concert hall (odeion) and, particularly, various stoas (39). A stoa was a long, low colonnaded structure which provided shade and shelter for people to meet, to shop and carry out their business. Secular buildings had more windows than temples and carried more ornamentation as shown on p. 10.

40 Aeolic type capital. Larisa early sixth century BC

41 Ionic capital. Temple of Artemis, Ephesos, c.550 BC

42 Ionic capital. Erechtheion, Athens, c.421 BC

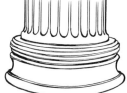
43 Ionic. base. Temple of Athena Niké, Athens, c.427 BC

44 Corinthian capital. Monument of Lysicrates, Athens, c.334 BC

46 Egg and dart ornament

47 Leaf and dart ornament

48 Bead and reel ornament

49 Centaur and Lapith, metope, Parthenon, Athens, c.445 BC

45 Corinthian capital. Tholos at Epidauros, c.350 BC

50 Doorway detail. Erechtheion, Athens

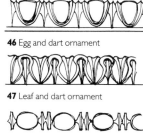
51 The Greek acanthus spinosus leaf

52 Entablature. Tholos at Epidauros

53 Anthemion (honeysuckle) decoration

Establishment of Periclean democracy

Fifth century Pheidias, Greek sculptor of the classical period, born in Athens before 480. Worked in several Greek cities. In 447 appointed by Pericles to oversee the decoration of the great building programme on the Acropolis of Athens. Designed the sculpture on the Parthenon (architect Ictinus). Carved himself the great statue of Athena Parthenos 447-432. Died c. 430.

c. 485–430 Herodotus, born Halicarnassos (now Bodrum, Turkey). Greek historian. Responsible for the first history of Western civilization

c. 470–399 Socrates, Greek philosopher and moralist

c. 460–*c.*370 Democritus. Greek philosopher; developed the idea of the atomic theory – that the universe is made up of minute particles (atoms) moving in empty space (void)

c. 460–377 Hippocrates. Greek physician born on the island of Cos. 'Father of medicine'

c. 455–400 Thucydides. Greek historian born in Athens. The first to write a history of contemporary events

428–348 Plato, philosopher. Born in Athens. Founded the Academy there, which lasted 800 years until closed by the Emperor Justinian

384–322 Aristotle. Greek philosopher and scientist, born in Macedonia. Became tutor to the boy Alexander

THE ETRUSCANS 700 – 200 BC

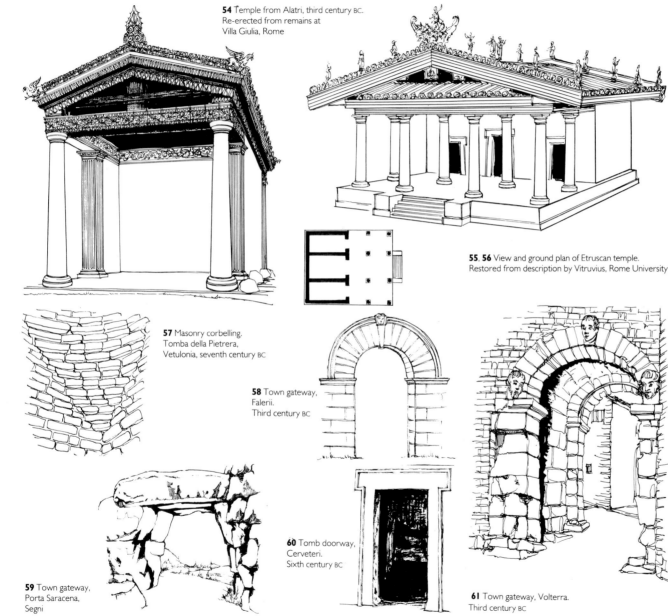

54 Temple from Alatri, third century BC.
Re-erected from remains at
Villa Giulia, Rome

55, 56 View and ground plan of Etruscan temple.
Restored from description by Vitruvius, Rome University

57 Masonry corbelling.
Tomba della Pietrera,
Vetulonia, seventh century BC

58 Town gateway,
Falerii.
Third century BC

59 Town gateway,
Porta Saracena,
Segni

60 Tomb doorway,
Cerveteri.
Sixth century BC

61 Town gateway, Volterra.
Third century BC

The cultural history of ancient Italy differed from that of the Aegean area. Before the coming of the Etruscans there was no advanced form of art and architecture. From the later seventh century BC the Greeks colonized Sicily and southern Italy, but it was the Etruscans who introduced a high culture to the central area of the peninsular.

The Etruscans (named Etrusci or Tusci in Greek or Latin) called themselves the Rasenna. It is believed that they migrated to central Italy from Asia Minor or possibly further east, in the eighth century BC; remaining dominant and independent until the third century BC, after which they were Latinised under Roman rule.

The Etruscans lived an urban life in fine cities and were capable of a high standard in building and the visual and literary arts. Over five centuries they developed their own art and architecture, which were derived from Greek and oriental sources, but adapted to their needs in Italy. Greek influence was particularly strong upon their culture. Remains are not extensive and no complete buildings survive intact; there are, though, many examples of walling, gateways, arches and tombs.

They were great builders and masons. In their stone walling they used large blocks, often polygonal, without cement. Later they constructed arches with radiating voussoirs – though they were not the inventors in Europe of this type of construction: the Greeks had been building in this way from the fifth century. In their tombs the Etruscans skilfully constructed high vaults of dressed stone, some corbelled out, pointing the way towards the later, pendentive method of covering a square-walled building with a circular-based domed covering (**57**). By the sixth century they had mastered advanced timber construction. They used sun-dried bricks widely, their bricks being of Lydian proportion, thin and measuring about 12 x 18in. Like the Minoans, they often combined brick bases with an upper structure of timber.

Early Etruscan towns were built on hills, surrounded by low walls. By the fifth century higher fortress-walling with city gates was being constructed to protect the towns from Roman attack (58–61). The Etruscans introduced the Greek rectangular town plan to Italy. Though little domestic building survives, much has been learned of its style from the tomb interiors decorated by painting, terracotta and metal.

The temple was important in Etruscan life, and temples were built in the centre of towns. Foundation remains show the ground plan, but reconstruction of the superstructure has to be more speculative. There appears to have been a colonnaded pronaos in front with a wide inter-columniation. The entablature and columns were usually of wood. Temple design differed from the Greek pattern in that the building was erected on a podium with front approach steps. The temple also was colonnaded. Ornamentation was by rich terracotta work (54–6).

Versions of the Doric and Ionic order were used, the columns fluted. The Doric capitals were large and simple, the Ionic ones of the Aeolic type. Vitruvius also refers to a variation on the Doric order which he calls Tuscan; this has an unfluted column shaft and stands on an Ionic-type base (62–6, 68).

62 Pier. Tomb at Cerveteri, third century BC

63 Aeolic (Ionic) capital, Cerveteri. Sixth century BC

64 Capital. Temple in Rome, fifth century BC

65 Doric column. Tomb at Cerveteri, sixth century BC

66 Tuscan pillar. Cerveteri, third century BC

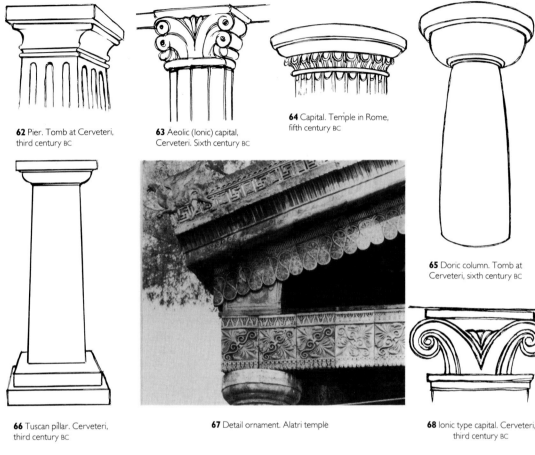

67 Detail ornament. Alatri temple

68 Ionic type capital. Cerveteri, third century BC

69 Antefix of terracotta. Capua, sixth century BC

70 Antefix, Ardea, c.500 BC

71 Detail ornament. Alatri temple

BC

Ninth and eighth centuries
Zenith of power in the Phrygian Kingdom. Indo-European people of fabulous wealth living in Anatolia. Origin of Greek legend of King Midas

753 Traditional date for the founding of Rome. The first of the monarchs, Romulus, held to have reigned 753–716

***c.* 700** The date of an Etruscan wooden bowl made by turning on a lathe. This is the most ancient machine tool, believed to be in use long before this

691 Great aqueduct built by Sennacherib, the Assyrian King, to bring water 50 miles to the capital at Nineveh. An impressive work of hydraulic engineering

700–546 The great period of the Lydian Kingdom in western Anatolia. The first people to use coined money, made of pieces of electrum, which is an alloy of native silver and gold. Coins stamped by the state to guarantee uniformity of weight and quality. A kingdom famous for its riches, ruled over 560–546 by King Croesus

604–562 Babylonian Empire under King Nebuchadnezzar II spread in Syria, Palestine and Egypt

610–*c.* 545 Anaximander. Philosopher and astronomer, born at Miletus. First Greek to make a map of the known world

587 Destruction of Jerusalem and captivity of the Jews

13

TEMPLE, CIVIC AND DOMESTIC BUILDING IN GREECE, ITALY AND TURKEY

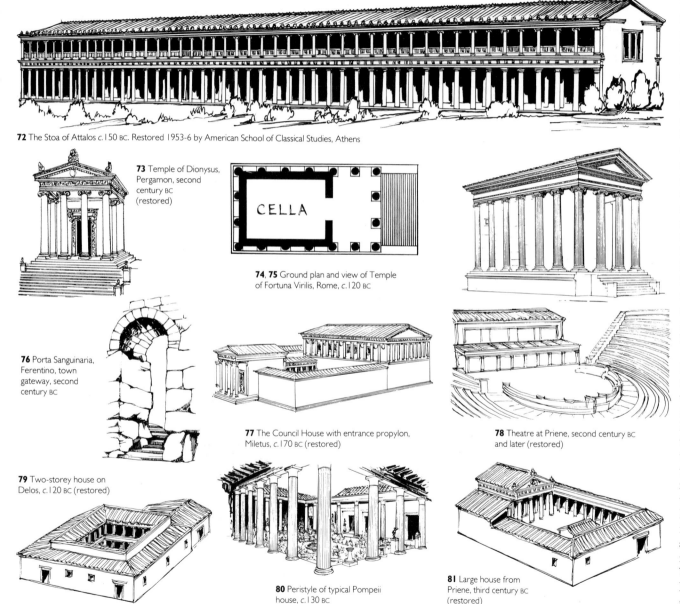

72 The Stoa of Attalos *c.*150 BC. Restored 1953-6 by American School of Classical Studies, Athens

73 Temple of Dionysus, Pergamon, second century BC (restored)

CELLA

74, 75 Ground plan and view of Temple of Fortuna Virilis, Rome, *c.*120 BC

76 Porta Sanguinaria, Ferentino, town gateway, second century BC

77 The Council House with entrance propylon, Miletus, *c.*170 BC (restored)

78 Theatre at Priene, second century BC and later (restored)

79 Two-storey house on Delos, *c.*120 BC (restored)

80 Peristyle of typical Pompeii house, *c.*130 BC

81 Large house from Priene, third century BC (restored)

The Hellenistic age dates from the time of the victories of Alexander the Great. His conquest of the Persian Empire, completed in 330 BC, brought a new prosperity to the Greek cities of Asia Minor. Some of these were enlarged, others rebuilt on fresh sites. Alexander's campaigns resulted in a blending of the purer Greek form of art and architecture with ideas on construction, function and ornament which stemmed from a Greek Empire greatly extended towards, and influenced from, the east. In architecture there appeared a greater variety of buildings for different purposes. The character and proportions of the orders changed: columns were slenderer, taller and spaced further apart and entablatures became narrower. There was a marked increase in rich decoration (**83–6**). The Corinthian order was now used. The Greeks remained cautious in their use of the arch and vault, but by the second century BC, both semicircular and segmental arches were being more widely employed.

Town planning, especially in the Hellenistic cities of Asia Minor, had become more important. The grid pattern of streets was widely adopted and the areas for religious, civic and private building carefully laid out. Priene was rebuilt near the mouth of the River Meander about 334 BC. Because the town was not of great importance under the later Roman rule, few alterations were made to adapt it to Roman needs, so much of the Hellenistic building has survived. Pergamon was an imposing hillside city, and full advantage was taken of this dramatic site: approached from the sea the effect was magnificent. Alexandria, founded in 331 BC by Alexander, had, not surprisingly, an Egyptian influence on its plan. This could be seen in its broad principal avenue flanked by colonnaded buildings.

In a Hellenistic town the agora had now acquired a greater importance; large cities possessed several. Usually these market places were bounded on three sides by stoas, which had become more elaborate. Larger examples were two-storeyed and later followed a custom not familiar in the classical period of Greece; two orders appeared on the front colonnade, Doric on the ground storey, Ionic above; as in the rebuilt Stoa of Attalos II of Pergamon in the agora of Athens. The wide stoa now needed an internal colonnade to support the roof, which was usually in the Ionic order with tall column shafts. Behind this colonnade shops and offices were built against the rear wall (**72**).

Temple design was also changing. The building was taller, its doorways larger and more elaborately decorated (**73–5**). There were also administrative council houses (**77**), meeting halls, libraries, gymnasia and public baths. These baths, like the early Roman ones at Pompeii, included dressing rooms and latrines, as well as chambers provided with different air and water temperatures.

A quantity of remains of Hellenistic domestic building survives in, for example, Priene, the island of Delos, and at Pompeii. Houses were inward-looking, few window and door openings breaking the blank outer walls. Inside were one- or two-storeyed colonnaded courts. Rainwater was collected from the roofs to drain into cisterns in the courts. Stone was now more often used for the lower walls, the upper storey being of sun-dried brick and timber. Floors were mosaic-covered, walls painted. Bathrooms were rare, but latrines were provided (**79–81**).

82 Atlantes figure supporting seats. Odeon, Pompeii, c.80 BC

83 Anthemion and bead-and-reel ornament. Athenian tholos

84 Ionic capital. Temple of Artemis, Sardis, c.300 BC

85 Corinthian capital. The Olympeion, Athens, c.170 BC

86 The porch order, Tower of the Winds, Athens, c.40 BC. This octagonal building is the only surviving Greek horologium. On each side at the top (**87**) is a relief of a directional, personified wind. It originally had sundials and a water clock

87 The sculptured 'winds', Tower of the Winds

BC

337–323 Alexander's empire. He destroyed the Persian Empire, occupied Egypt and marched to India

c. **280** The earliest true lighthouse (pharos) built at Alexandria, designed by Sostratus of Cnidos. One of the wonders of the ancient world, it was over 276ft high and contained large mirrors of polished metal which enabled the light to be seen at a distance of over 30 miles

c. **287–212** Archimedes of Syracuse. Greatest of ancient exponents of mechanics and one of the outstanding mathematicians of all time. His researches included work on the fundamental principles of the lever, the screw, the pulley, and upon gravity

146 Greece subjected to Roman rule

First century Hero of Alexandria. Greek mathematician, scientist and engineer, who wrote theoretical treatises on optics, mechanics, geometry and pneumatics, and devised many ingenious contrivances including a water clock, hydraulic organ, syringe, steam engine and engines of war

58–51 Julius Caesar conquers Gaul

47–30 Egypt becomes a Roman province

Late first century Marcus Vitruvius Pollio, Roman architect and engineer, wrote his treatise *De Architectura*, in 10 volumes. This is the only surviving written account of contemporary Hellenistic and early Roman architecture

Late first century Invention of glass blowing in Syria

IMPERIAL ROME   27 BC – AD 476

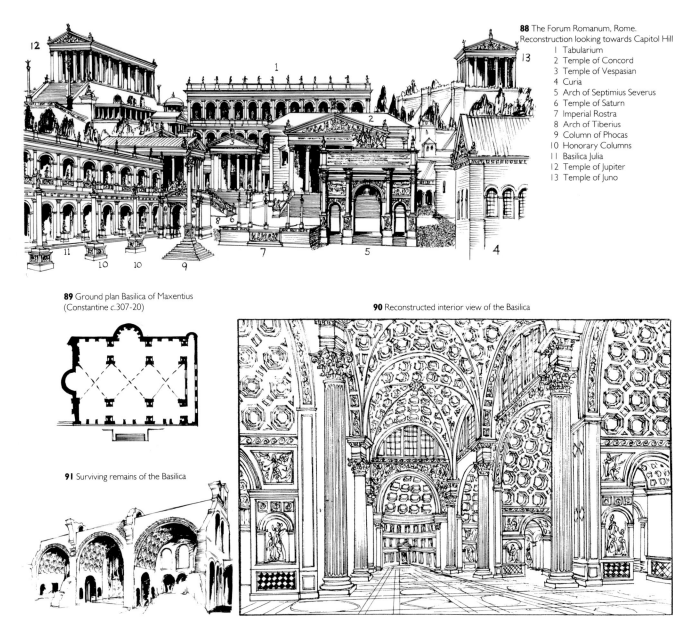

88 The Forum Romanum, Rome.
Reconstruction looking towards Capitol Hill
1 Tabularium
2 Temple of Concord
3 Temple of Vespasian
4 Curia
5 Arch of Septimius Severus
6 Temple of Saturn
7 Imperial Rostra
8 Arch of Tiberius
9 Column of Phocas
10 Honorary Columns
11 Basilica Julia
12 Temple of Jupiter
13 Temple of Juno

89 Ground plan Basilica of Maxentius
(Constantine c.307-20)

91 Surviving remains of the Basilica

90 Reconstructed interior view of the Basilica

Over almost five centuries of Imperial rule the Romans adapted and extended the classical form of architecture which they had inherited from the Greeks. The classical language of the orders and ornamentation survived, but was relegated more and more to sculptural decoration. The vastly greater complexity of the needs of peoples living in the cities of many countries, in climatic conditions as widely diverse as Britain or Egypt, Spain or Syria, demanded new materials and modes of construction. Concrete was the material which made possible the imaginative spatial handling of massive interiors, utilizing the curves of arch and vault (pp. 16, 17, 19, 21). In these designs, by the second century AD, the Romans were, as in earlier Hellenistic times (pp. 14-15), deriving many of their ideas from the eastern provinces of their empire. It was this complex, sophisticated architecture which evolved from so many sources that was later revived in Renaissance and baroque Europe.

Towns were being planned and built all over this empire. The ideal plan was considered to be the symmetrical grid system with encircling town walls; these punctuated by fortified gateways where the principal streets made their exit.

The forum was the Roman equivalent of the Greek agora (pp. 10, 11), but under the empire life in the larger cities had become much more complex, and the older idea of a market and business meeting place with temples and stoas was outmoded. The Roman forum covered a much larger area. It was laid out axially and, among its magnificent buildings, included basilicas, temples, libraries, triumphal arches and colonnades of shops and markets (88). Important cities possessed several fora; in

Rome itself certain emperors built new ones: the forum of Trajan, entered through a triumphal arch, was characteristic.

The basilica was one of the most important Roman civic buildings. This type of structure was an ancient one, its name deriving from the Greek *basilikos* and referring to a royal apartment. By Roman times the basilica had become a multi-purpose building: it was simultaneously a hall of justice, a business centre and a social meeting place. The structure was of rectangular plan with an apse at one or both ends. The interiors of earlier basilicas were covered by timber roofing, supported upon colonnades which divided the chamber into 'nave and aisles'. Later versions, such as the great Basilica of Maxentius, were roofed with concrete vaults which rested upon a few, very large concrete piers: in this example the piers were each 14ft in diameter (89–91).

Public bathing establishments (called *thermae* from the Greek *thermos* = hot) were an institution in Roman life. In the towns, many people lived in overcrowded conditions and the baths provided cheaply a place where one could relax and meet socially or for business purposes, bathe, receive massage or medical treatment, eat and drink, be entertained, or take part in athletic sport. An integral part of life, in the city of Rome alone there are estimated to have been over 800 thermae.

Public bathing establishments were well-known in Hellenistic times and early Roman baths were built at Pompeii and Herculaneum. The later and larger thermae of Rome were immense and complex establishments. The main central area of the Baths of Caracalla, for example, covered 270,000sq.ft. Characteristically there was a vast vaulted central hall (183 x 79ft) lit by

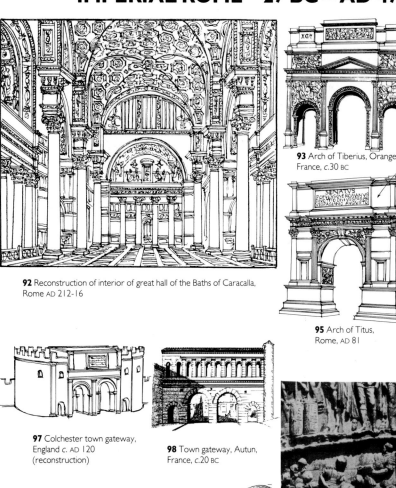

92 Reconstruction of interior of great hall of the Baths of Caracalla, Rome AD 212-16

93 Arch of Tiberius, Orange, France, c.30 BC

94 Arch of Augustus, Rimini, Italy, 27 BC

95 Arch of Titus, Rome, AD 81

96 Arch of Constantine, Rome, AD 312-15

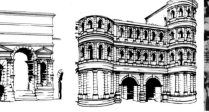

97 Colchester town gateway, England c. AD 120 (reconstruction)

98 Town gateway, Autun, France, c.20 BC

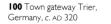

99 Porta Maggiore, Rome, AD 52

100 Town gateway Trier, Germany, c. AD 320

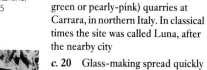

101 Detail, Trajan Column, Rome, AD 114

BC

First century Iron plough-shares began to be used in Britain. Possible Roman influence

First century State postal and messenger service well established in the Roman Empire. Organized in combination with passenger trans-port service. Transportation by ox-wagon, or faster carts hauled by horses or mules

First century Roman invention (described by Vitruvius) of the vertical water-wheel. A development from the earlier Greek design where the wheel was horizontally placed. The Roman water-wheel, used widely for grinding corn, was much more efficient

c. 25 The opening up and development of the famous white marble (sometimes marked with green or pearly-pink) quarries at Carrara, in northern Italy. In classical times the site was called Luna, after the nearby city

c. 20 Glass-making spread quickly from Syria and Egypt to Italy and Spain. Glass craftsmen from the Middle East brought their skills to Europe and established manufactur-ing centres where contact was maintained with the areas of origin. By the second century AD glass-making was being carried out at Trier and Cologne in Germany, and later expanded to northern France, Belgium and Britain.

27 BC–14AD Gaius Julius Caesar Octavianus ruled as Augustus, the first Roman emperor

AD

14 Official School of Greek

PALACES, FLATS, VILLAS: IMPERIAL ROME 27 BC – AD 476

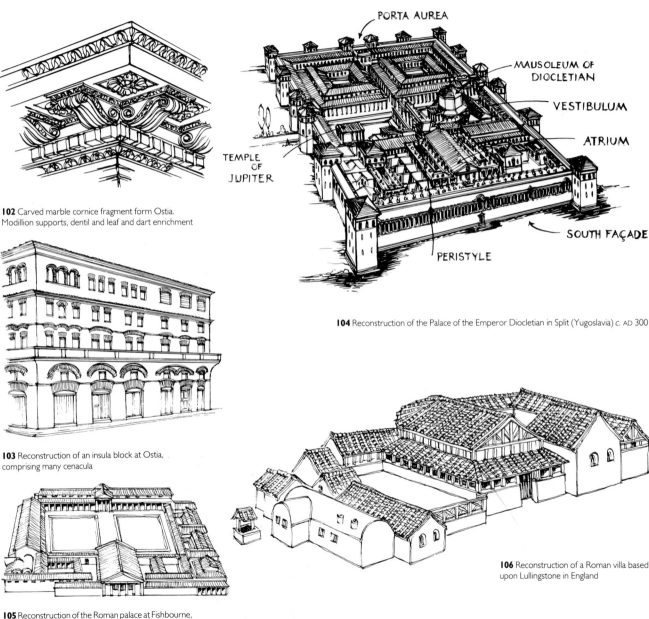

PORTA AUREA

MAUSOLEUM OF DIOCLETIAN

VESTIBULUM

ATRIUM

TEMPLE OF JUPITER

SOUTH FAÇADE

PERISTYLE

102 Carved marble cornice fragment form Ostia. Modillion supports, dentil and leaf and dart enrichment

103 Reconstruction of an insula block at Ostia, comprising many cenacula

104 Reconstruction of the Palace of the Emperor Diocletian in Split (Yugoslavia) c. AD 300

105 Reconstruction of the Roman palace at Fishbourne, near Chichester in England c. AD 80

106 Reconstruction of a Roman villa based upon Lullingstone in England

clerestory windows. Adjoining was a tepidarium (cool room), a circular, domed caldarium (hot room) and the frigidarium containing a cold water open air swimming pool. Such thermae were among the architectural wonders of the Roman Empire (**92**).

Equally adventurous and lavish, both in scale and in arched and vaulted construction, were the great palaces of the empire. The Palatine Hill in Rome was the favoured site for these elaborate schemes, which would comprise richly decorated interiors of audience chamber, banqueting hall, temple, basilica, theatre and baths; all buildings set out in magnificent gardens with fountains and lakes. Nero's Golden House was one such palace, Hadrian's Villa at Tivoli another. In Split in Yugoslavia there survive extensive remains of the Emperor Diocletian's palace, built AD 300-5, which is more a complete town than just a residence (**104, 105**).

More normal-scale domestic building was of three main types: the domus (town house), the insula (apartment block) and the villa (country house). The layout and design of the domus was derived from its Greek prototype, and evolved further from the Hellenistic house pattern of Priene and Delos (pp. 14, 15). This was the town house for the middle class or well-to-do families. It had a narrow street façade, its centrally placed entrance often flanked by shops. The rectangular site extended well back from the street. As in Pompeii the house was inward-looking towards courtyards, which were open to the sky, where rainwater was collected from the sloping roofs of the compluvium (open central square) into the impluvium (a receptacle below). Rooms were arranged round the atrium and colonnaded garden courts (peristyles) so shade or sun could be enjoyed at all seasons and time of day.

With a rapidly increasing urbanization of a growing population, the majority of city-dwellers lived in flats. Such a flat (*cenaculum*) would be in an apartment block (*insula*) which in Pompeii was generally only two-storeyed and constructed of brick and timber. Later *insulae*, considerable remains of which may still be seen at Ostia Antica (the port of Rome), were built of concrete and brick and rose to four or five storeys. In the city of Rome it is believed that some 40,000 *insulae* lined the streets and squares. Life in a *cenaculum* was overcrowded and lacked many basic amenities (**103**).

The rural villa was a larger, spreading layout. It was a self-sufficient unit comprising farm buildings and accommodation for slaves, servants, artisans and family. It would include buildings and areas for baking, storage, wine and textile making, as well as all farming needs (**106**).

The rectangular Roman temple continued to follow the Greek post-and-lintel form – there were no arches and vaults here – but the trend initiated by the Etruscans, and followed up in Hellenistic times, for a deep podium base and a specifically aligned front entrance was confirmed. The Maison Carrée at Nîmes is characteristic (**111, 112**).

The increasing use of concrete as a structural building material led to a more daring development of circular temples. Here, the Pantheon in Rome is the supreme example. In continuous use, first as a temple, later as a church, this remarkable building has survived, its interior a masterpiece of construction and lighting effect. The only source of daylight is the central unglazed oculus. The concrete, coffered dome (142 ft diameter) supported on concrete walls

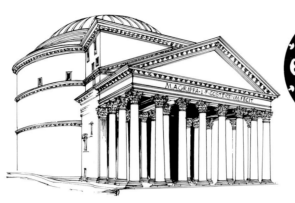

107, 108, 109, 110 Exterior view, ground plan and detail of Corinthian capital and base from the portico at the Pantheon, Rome, AD 120 onwards

111, 112 Corinthian capital and entablature detail and general view, Maison Carrée, Nîmes, France, AD 1–10

113 Doorway with bronze doors. Temple of Romulus, Forum Romanum, Rome, AD 307

Medicine founded in Rome. Aulus Cornelius Celsus was the author of, amongst other works, the most complete medical encyclopaedia of the time. He also wrote a history of early medicine

c. 29 Crucifixion of Jesus Christ

43–51 Invasion of Britain

c. 50 Quarries in Egypt founded by the Emperor Claudius to work the imperial porphyry. This was so-called because of its purple colouring. It was widely used in Rome as a decorative veneer

64 Great fire of Rome

c. 70 A Roman mechanical reaper was in operation: it was described by Pliny. It comprised a wooden wheeled cart with a blade to cut the corn, and was pushed by a draught animal. The description bore a marked resemblance to early-nineteenth-century reapers

23–79 Pliny (the Elder), soldier, lawyer, writer. His *Naturalis Historia* in 37 volumes was an encyclopaedia of the science known at his time

79 Eruption of Vesuvius, which buried the twin cities of Pompeii and Herculaneum in ash. Pliny (see above) died in this eruption

77–84 Conquest of Britain reached Scotland

40–103 Sextus Julius Frontinus, Roman soldier, engineer and super-intendent of the Aqueducts of Rome. In AD 97 he wrote an important work on hydrodynamics related to Rome's water supply

c. 55–c. 118 Cornelius Tacitus, great Roman historian. Authority on

THE ROMAN ORDERS AND METHODS OF BUILDING

114 The Roman Doric order. The Colosseum, Rome, AD 70-82

115 The Roman Ionic order. The Temple of Fortuna, Virilis, Rome, c.120 BC

116 The Roman Corinthian order. Temple of Castor and Pollux, Rome, AD 6

117 The Roman composite order, The Arch of Titus, Rome, AD 81

118 Detail of 115. Cornice mouldings carved with egg and dart and dentil ornament. Sculptured frieze. In the Ionic order capital egg and dart ornament appears between the side volutes

CORNICE CYMA RECTA MOULDING

EGG-AND-DART

DENTIL ORNAMENT

FRIEZE

ARCHITRAVE

BEAD-AND-REEL ORNAMENT

EGG-AND-DART ORNAMENT

VOLUTE

119 Detail of Composite capital, as in 117

120 Scroll ornamentation

121 The Roman Doric order. The Baths of Diocletian, Rome, AD 298-305

reinforced by brick relieving arches, diminishes in thickness from 20ft at base to 5ft at crown (**107-10, 125**).

The trabeated form of construction of classical architecture had been developed by the Greeks, who carried this to the highest possible standard of artistic perfection. The length of each lintel had determined the intercolumniation, that is, the distance between one column of the order and the next. The contribution of the Romans was in the development of the arcuated form of classical construction. The Greeks had built chiefly one- or two-storeyed structures: the Romans up to four or five. The more complex needs of the Roman way of life, with the greater variety of building forms required for a much larger population, led their architects and engineers to experiment more extensively with the arched rather than post-and-lintel type of construction.

The Romans continued to use the Greek system of orders but, as the structure was basically arcuated, the orders became purely decorative. Their proportion could be varied as the intercolumniation was no longer governed by structural requirements, so the need for the strict relationship between different parts of an order, established by the Greeks, had become invalid. The Romans utilized five orders: Doric, Ionic and Corinthian derived from Greece, Tuscan from the Etruscans and a fifth order, the Composite, whose capital – as the name suggests – was a blend of two designs: the Ionic and the Corinthian (p. 9). The Romans used several different orders to ornament one building, one per storey, lining up the columns one above the other. The Flavian Amphitheatre (later called the Colosseum) is the classic instance of this custom: it displays four different orders on its exterior walling (**131, 133**).

BUILDING METHODS AND CONSTRUCTION: IMPERIAL ROME 27 BC – AD 476

The Roman form of arcuated construction utilized the arch built with radiating voussoirs and supported upon massive piers, rather than slender columns. This type of structure could then carry a vaulted ceiling which was more permanent and fireproof than the Greek timber roofing method. The Romans also built domed roofs of semi-circular section, as in the Pantheon, but the full potential of this type of covering was only realized later in Byzantine architecture (**90, 92, 124, 125, 127, 129** and p. 16).

The Romans used a variety of building materials, but the two which made this type of construction possible were brick and concrete. Kiln-burnt bricks had been introduced in Hellenistic times. Roman bricks were thin, large and very hard. These were used for facing and for bonding courses for the concrete of which the vaults, arches and piers were made (**122, 128**).

Concrete had long been utilized as a bonding and covering material, but it was the Romans who developed it as a structural one. By the second century BC, they were experimenting with a volcanic earth found near Vesuvius and named pozzolana, after the town of Pozzuoli there. Pozzolana is a volcanic ash, available in quantity in Italy, containing alumina and silica, which combines chemically with lime to produce a hard, durable substance. The Romans mixed it with an aggregate of broken stone, marble, brick and lava, and poured it over wood centering or into brick compartments, to produce massive supporting piers and vault spans of a magnitude not equalled until the steel structures of the nineteenth century. The interiors of these large buildings were then faced with a wide variety of coloured marbles and mosaics (**89, 92, 125**).

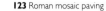

122 Stone and brick walling at Ostia, Italy. Opus reticulatum

123 Roman mosaic paving

124 Coffered vault, Basilica of Maxentius

126 Roman pantile roofing, Cirencester, England

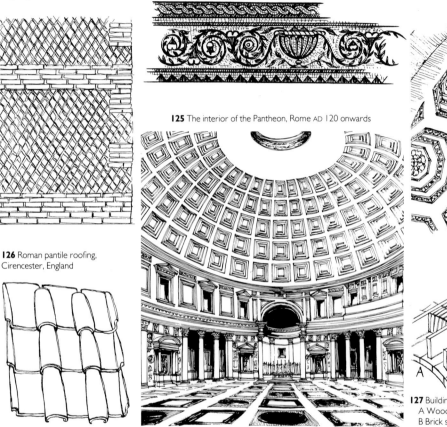

125 The interior of the Pantheon, Rome AD 120 onwards

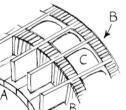

127 Building a brick and concrete vault
A Wood centering
B Brick structure C Concrete infilling

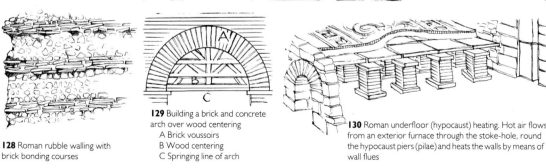

128 Roman rubble walling with brick bonding courses

129 Building a brick and concrete arch over wood centering
A Brick voussoirs
B Wood centering
C Springing line of arch

130 Roman underfloor (hypocaust) heating. Hot air flows from an exterior furnace through the stoke-hole, round the hypocaust piers (pilae) and heats the walls by means of wall flues

the political and social history of early Britain and Germany

First century Preparation of parchment (made from animal skins) was gradually perfected and it became the chief writing material under the Roman Empire

First century Cultivation of flax developed extensively in the Po valley in Italy, where the soil was suitably damp and fertile. Flax was also grown in Spain, Gaul and the Baltic coastal regions
Silk was imported from China via the 'Old Silk Road'

c. **117** Roman Empire reaches its greatest extent

First and second centuries
Chief period of construction of the great network of Roman roads throughout the empire, from Britain to Carthage and Spain to the Persian Gulf. By the third century the pace of construction had slowed. Some roads were paved with stone, some sanded or gravelled and some, especially in African and Syrian desert areas, were unmetalled

Second century Cast iron. According to Pausanias, Theodorus of Samos discovered how to melt, and so pour, iron into moulds to make statues

122–8 The 77 miles of fortified wall traversing the north of England, from Wallsend in the east to Bowness in the west, were constructed on the orders of the Emperor Hadrian, in order to protect the province of Roman Britain from northern invaders

129–200 Galen, one of the most renowned physicians of the classical world

THE ENGINEERING ACHIEVEMENT: IMPERIAL ROME 27 BC – AD 476

131 The Colosseum, Rome AD 80. An elliptical structure measuring 615 x 510ft on the exterior, the amphitheatre was built to accommodate 50,000 spectators. Above the foundations (some 40ft in depth of brick and concrete) the construction was of a framework of travertine stone blocks, supported upon a travertine block platform. The rest of the building was of tufa blocks and concrete; marble was used for seating

132 A characteristically Roman theatre ground plan

133 Detail of the third storey of the Colosseum

It was not only in the making and use of concrete that the Romans achieved such high standards, knowledge of which was lost in the west after the fifth-century collapse of the Empire in Rome, not to be rediscovered until the Renaissance or even later. This also applied to the building of road systems, to the making of glass for window glazing, to underfloor and cavity wall space heating by currents of hot air (**130**), and to the transportation over immense distances of water supplies for public baths, toilets and fountains. The Romans attached great importance to the plentiful supply of good water for these purposes. In Rome alone, it has been estimated, over 340 million gallons per day were needed from the 11 great arched aqueducts which crossed the Campagna to supply the city. According to Vitruvius, a fall of six inches for every 100ft was considered desirable, and often long detours had to be made to avoid a too sudden descent.

Considerable remains of many of these aqueducts survive in parts of Europe (**138, 140**), as do also Roman bridges. The oldest surviving bridge in Rome over the River Tiber is the Pons Fabricius (**136**). Dramatic, large-scale examples include Hadrian's Alcántara Bridge over the River Tagus, and those at Salamanca and Mèrida, all in Spain (**137, 139**).

Entertainment in classical times, by drama or spectacle, was usually held in the open air. The Greek theatre was generally hollowed out from a hillside; spectators sat on rows of seats round the semicircular auditorium, looking down upon the chorus and actors performing on a circular area, the orchestra, which means literally 'dancing place' (**37**).

As time passed and the technique of drama changed, a scene building was erected

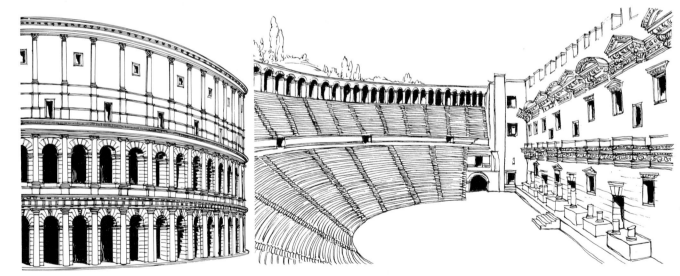

134 The Theatre of Marcellus, Rome 13-11 BC (conjectural restoration)

135 The theatre at Aspendos, Turkey, AD 161-80. A rare example in the preservation of the stage building comprising the two-storeyed façade and the proscenium upon which the play was performed

in front of the orchestra to contain dressing rooms and scenery. In the Hellenistic theatre, as at Priene, a raised stage for the actors was built in front of the scene building (the proscenium) (78).

The Romans often adapted existing Greek theatres, but new Roman theatres (like amphitheatres) were generally built on flat ground and the tiers of seats were supported upon concrete vaulting. Under these vaults were corridors lit by outer arcades. The whole theatre was surrounded by an arcaded wall enriched by orders (134). The amphitheatre was built for displays and competitive activities. It was oval in plan, and much larger than the theatre. Several theatres and amphitheatres survive in good condition and are still used for operatic and other performances as at, for example, Verona (Italy), Nîmes (France), Pula (Yugoslavia), and Aspendos (Turkey) (135).

136 Pons Fabricius, Rome 62-21 BC. Spans half of the River Tiber to the Isola Tibereina in the centre of the river

137 Bridge at Alcántara over the river Tagus, Spain AD 105-6

138 Aqueduct at Segovia, Spain, which still carries the city's water supply. *Temp.* Augustus

139 Ponte dei Cappuccini, Ascoli Piceno, River Tronto

140 The Pont du Gard, France, 20-16 BC. An aqueduct built to carry water 31 miles to the town of Nîmes. The section shown here crosses the River Gard 160ft above the stream. The main road on the first stage is still in use

286 The Roman Empire had become so large it was difficult to govern and defend. The Emperor Diocletian divided it into two parts, east and west, along a north-south line extending from the Danube to the southern Adriatic. He remained emperor in the east, and established Maximian in Rome to govern the west

313 Emperor Constantine I (the Great) issued his Edict of Milan, which gave to Christians freedom of worship on an equal basis with other religions. In 325 the emperor himself professed Christianity, which then became the official religion of the empire

324 Constantine temporarily re-united the empire and moved the capital to Byzantium, a city which was later re-named Constantinople (now Istanbul) after him

395 The empire permanently divided, with two emperors, one in the eastern capital at Constantinople, the other in the western at Milan (later at Ravenna)

407 The Roman army withdrawn from Britain

410 Visigoths sack Rome

419 Visigothic kingdom established in Spain

431 Vandals create a kingdom in North Africa

455 Vandals sack Rome

476 Deposition of the last Roman Emperor in the west (Romulus Augustalus) by the barbarian king Odovacar

FOURTH-CENTURY EARLY CHRISTIAN CHURCHES IN ROME

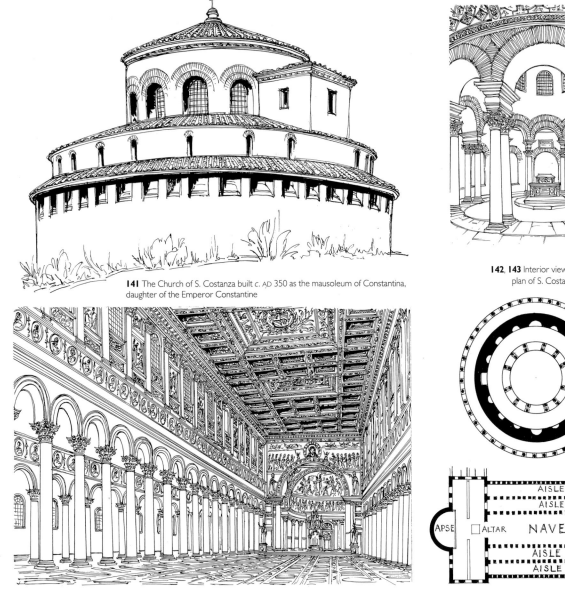

141 The Church of S. Costanza built *c.* AD 350 as the mausoleum of Constantina, daughter of the Emperor Constantine

144 Interior, S. Paolo-fuori-le-mura (St Paul-without-the-walls). Begun AD 385. Rebuilt after a fire of 1823

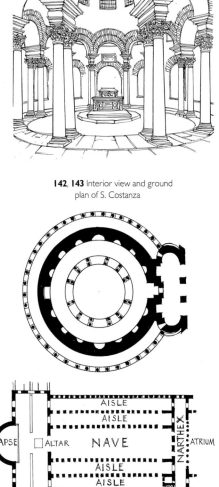

142, **143** Interior view and ground plan of S. Costanza

145 Ground plan, S. Paolo

There was no Christian architecture before AD 200; believers gathered together to meet in each others' homes and used the courtyard fountain for baptism. During the third century Christians became far more numerous, including important citizens in their numbers. This led to a period of persecution when large gatherings were prohibited, but by AD 260 the authorities tolerated – if not legalized – Christian activities, and purpose-built structures began to be erected. These buildings were simple, their style based upon Roman domestic architecture (pp. 18, 19). They were Christian community houses which contained rooms (among other purposes) for meals, for meeting and for services for funerals, baptism and confirmation.

In AD 313 the Roman emperor Constantine issued the Edict of Milan, which gave to Christians the legal right to practise their religion openly on an equal basis with other religions and, after AD 325, Christianity became the official religion of the empire. From this time onward Christian churches were built for the purpose of worship, and a form of Christian architecture developed. Until his death in AD 337 many of the more important churches were inaugurated by Constantine himself: S. Peter's Basilica in Rome was the greatest of these, built to house the shrine of the Apostle Peter. The basilica, completed in AD 329, was 391ft long and 208ft wide. Standing in the huge apse, covered by a *baldacchino*, was the monument to St Peter. The adjacent transept (an unusual feature at this time) accommodated the crowds who came to pay homage to the memoria of the apostle enshrined there. This basilica was replaced during the Renaissance by the cathedral now standing on the site (p. 120).

FOURTH- AND FIFTH-CENTURY EARLY CHRISTIAN CHURCHES

When the form of the Christian church was being developed, it was clear that a different type of design was required from that of the classical temple (pp. 8, 19), which had evolved to house not the worshippers, but a representation of the deity. Christians needed a building which would be dignified, yet practical. It had to contain a sanctuary for the clergy where Mass would be said, a lay part for the congregation (the nave), a forecourt (atrium) where postulants and unbelievers could assemble and, in later instances, a martyrium to shelter the relics or graves of the martyr to whom the church was dedicated.

The form of structure chosen was the Roman basilica (pp. 16, 17) and, from this, evolved the Christian basilican church. In the time of Constantine there was no standard design of basilica; variations were incorporated according to local needs and wishes. Some large examples in important towns such as Rome, Constantinople, Milan, Trier and in the Holy Land were complex designs (146, 150) which might possess more than one hall, or were multi-aisled and had several apses. Others were simple and unpretentious.

As time passed a more standard form of basilica evolved, particularly in the west – in Italy, France, England and Germany – while adaptations were made to the standard pattern in Dalmatia, Sicily, Greece and the coastal regions of Asia Minor, to conform to local needs and influences.

The most usual western basilican design is oblong in plan. It has an apse at one of the shorter sides and a narthex at the opposite one. The apse contained the altar from the beginning, but this was not then necessarily facing the east. The narthex extended along the whole width of the end of the church. It

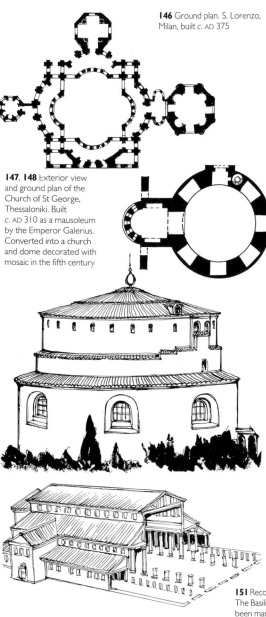

146 Ground plan. S. Lorenzo, Milan, built c. AD 375

147, 148 Exterior view and ground plan of the Church of St George, Thessaloniki. Built c. AD 310 as a mausoleum by the Emperor Galerius. Converted into a church and dome decorated with mosaic in the fifth century

149 Mosaic pavement from the early church of c. AD 320 in the nave of the eleventh-century Cathedral of Aquileia

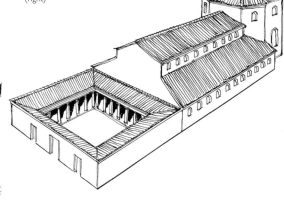

150 Reconstruction of the fourth-century Church of the Nativity at Bethlehem showing the atrium (left), basilica (centre) and martyrium (right)

151 Reconstruction of the Emperor Constantine's Lateran Basilica in Rome as in c. AD 320. The Basilica Constantina, now the Cathedral of Rome, S. Giovanni in Laterano, has since been many times altered and added to

330 The decayed city of Byzantium rebuilt by the Roman Emperor Constantine and officially dedicated on 11 May as New Rome. The name Byzantium continued to be used and the term 'Byzantine' was coined by later scholars to describe the culture of this eastern branch of the empire, from the sixth century until the city's fall in 1453. The popular name for the city, however, was Constantinople; that is, the city of Constantine. Under Turkish rule the city became the capital of the Ottoman Empire. Its Turkish name was Istanbul, a name by which it is still known

Fourth century Silk weaving (the yarn imported from China) developed in Constantinople

Fourth century Weaving of cloth still carried out on the Roman type of vertical loom, which was an advance upon the Greek type as the warp was stretched by being wound round a beam at the bottom, instead of being merely weighted in grouped threads

Fourth century Adoption by Roman cavalry of the padded riding saddle, introduced from the Orient

Fourth century Development of the Roman water-mill. Shortage of labour led to the wider adoption of water power for grinding corn and, later, other operations such as sawing wood or marble

410 Rome sacked by the Visigoths (a Germanic people who had originated in Scandinavia) under Alaric. Within a few years the Visigoths had moved northward into Gaul, and established a kingdom in the area of present day southern

ROME, RAVENNA, CONSTANTINOPLE, THESSALONIKI

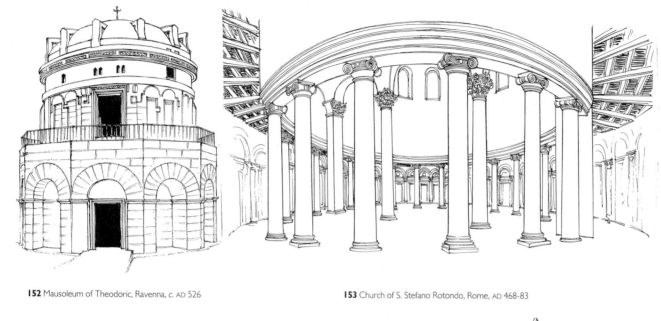

152 Mausoleum of Theodoric, Ravenna, c. AD 526

153 Church of S. Stefano Rotondo, Rome, AD 468-83

154 Church of S. Sabina, Rome, AD 422–32

155 Mausoleum of Galla Placidia, Ravenna, c. AD 425

156 The Orthodox Baptistery, Ravenna, c. AD400-50

was an ante-room, colonnaded along three sides, and gave on to an open court, the atrium (**145**). The basilican interior is divided lengthwise by colonnades which create nave and aisles. Some examples (the Basilica Constantina for instance) possessed further colonnade divisions, making five aisles instead of three (**151**). In some designs the columns carried an entablature (for example, S. Maria Maggiore in Rome, **160**). In others (S. Sabina in Rome, **154** and S. Demetrios in Thessaloniki) the colonnade was arcaded. Above this (where the medieval triforium is usually to be found) was a solid wall pierced in the upper part by round-headed clerestory windows. The roof was of timber, open or ceiled, and placed no strain upon the walls: vaulted coverings of Roman type were rare.

Early Christian churches were of brick and concrete, with some stone, and were plain on the exterior. Inside was glowing colour and ornamentation in varied marbles, mosaic (**159**), painting and gilding. The architectural style was Roman classical and columns, capitals and bases had often been taken from Roman buildings and re-used. Some churches were very richly decorated internally. Santa Maria Maggiore in Rome (**160**), which retains much of its original character, gives such an impression of richness in its Ionic marble colonnade and mosaic and gilded apse.

By the fifth century the Roman Empire had been permanently divided, its eastern capital in Constantinople and, in AD 402, the western one moved to Ravenna on the Adriatic coast of Italy. Here, the fleet moored at adjacent Classe provided protection against the successive waves of invaders which attacked the west during the succeeding 150 years. During the fifth century the basilican church was developed in Ravenna. As in S. Apollinare Nuovo (159, 161), there is a wide, high nave with arcaded colonnades separating it from the aisles and, above the colonnades, richly coloured mosaics emit a softly shimmering light. Most Ravenna basilicas possessed narthex, atrium and an octagonal baptistery but, in the fifth century, no towers: these were added later. It was accepted by the end of the fifth century that the Christian church should be aligned on an east/west axis, with the altar placed at the east end.

Apart from those on basilican lines, a number of Early Christian churches were centrally planned; these were developed from the Roman mausoleum concept (147, 148). Two particular examples survive in Rome, that of S. Costanza, built c. AD 350 on a concentric double circle plan with central dome and sloping outer roofs (141–143) and S. Stefano Rotondo, built AD 468–83 (153). The interior of S. Costanza is in good condition with mosaics (restored) and a colonnade of coupled Composite columns. The brick walls have niches originally with mosaic covering. S. Stefano has an inner ring of Ionic columns carrying an entablature and, across the circle, is a pierced dividing wall supported on two Corinthian columns. The outer walls are decorated with fresco paintings.

157 Capital, Church of the Acheiropoietos, Thessaloniki, c. AD 460

158 Capital, Church of St John Studios, Constantinople, c. AD 465

159 Mosaic decoration of nave arcade representing the 'Three Kings' c. AD 550. Church of S. Apollinare Nuovo, Ravenna. Built c. AD 490

160 Church of S. Maria Maggiore, Rome. Built c. AD 432, remodelled 1587

161 Capital, S. Apollinare Nuovo, c. AD 490

France and Spain. The Visigothic kingdom in Spain survived until it was conquered by the Moors in 711

Fifth century Early development, especially in France and Spain, of the cultivation of apples and pears suited to the making of cider and perry

Fourth–Sixth century Glass-making continued in the Rhineland, Italy and Belgium

489 The Ostrogoths (another branch of the German tribes) moved into Italy under their leader Theodoric the Great (c. 454–526). The Ostrogoths became allies of Rome and Theodoric was recognized as ruler of Italy, subject to the Eastern emperor. Theodoric died in the western capital Ravenna (152).

509–10 Clovis united the factions of the Franks and, becoming King over them all, extended their territory to cover much of what is now France

Sixth century In China, printing on paper by means of wood or metal blocks and, later, by movable type made of earthenware or wood

EARLY BYZANTINE ARCHITECTURE 527 – 563

CONSTANTINOPLE

RAVENNA

163 S. Irene, Constantinople, begun 532

162 S. Sophia, Constantinople, 532-7. Dome reconstructed 563

164 S. Vitale, Ravenna, completed 546-8

165 S. Apollinare in Classe, near Ravenna, 432-49

After the collapse of the western part of the Roman Empire, Constantinople, in the east, became the capital of a Byzantine Empire which, though its fortunes fluctuated over the centuries, survived until the Turkish conquest of 1453.

The art and architecture of this empire reflected the changed geographical emphasis from a centre in Rome in the west to one in Constantinople, situated athwart Europe and Asia. There were two important periods of building activity during this long era, the first in the sixth century under the patronage of the Emperor Justinian and the second during the eleventh to the thirteenth century, when the empire extended from the Euphrates to the Danube. To the earlier period belong the churches of Ravenna, the Istrian peninsular and the great buildings of Constantinople, including S. Sophia; to the later, the Cathedral of St Mark in Venice, and the Greek and Balkan churches and monasteries. Even after 1453 Byzantine architecture lingered on, richer and more decorative than ever, in the ecclesiastical edifices of Romania, Bulgaria and Russia.

Surviving remains of Byzantine architecture are largely ecclesiastical; little secular building exists above ground level, though archaeological studies have yielded information which seems to indicate a design of domestic architecture which has much in common with later Roman building. Important and particularly interesting from the few structures to be seen are fortifications, notably the walls and gates of Constantinople and, in the same city, the numbers of underground cisterns. A magnificent example of these is the one called 'a thousand-and-one columns', which is believed to have been the work of Anthemios of Tralles, one of the architects of S. Sophia (172).

Byzantine church architecture reflects influence from east and west. From a blend of these two very different building styles Byzantine architects evolved their own form of structure and decoration, which varied considerably from area to area but which was adapted to serve the needs of rapidly expanding Christian communities.

In the time of Justinian (527-65) church structure was derived from the form of the basilica, as in the fourth and fifth centuries, blended with a cruciform arrangement or a centrally-planned octagon or square and, most often, was surmounted by a dome or domes. In general the basilican plan was to be preferred in the west, and in Italy basilicas of Early Christian type continued to be built during much of the sixth century. Examples include S. Apollinare in Classe (171) and Grado Cathedral (174) in the Veneto, Parenzo (Poreč) Cathedral (175) in the Istrian peninsular and S. Lorenzo-fuori-le-mura in Rome. Of centrally planned design, stemming from the circular structures of S. Costanza (141-3) and S. Stefano Rotondo (153), are the octagonal examples of S. Vitale in Ravenna (164, 170) and S. S. Sergius and Bacchus in Constantinople (173).

In Constantinople a trace of the basilican form remained, but the trend was towards a large central dome supported on square piers over a square space and the columns, which divided nave from aisles and carried galleries, no longer supported the side walls and roof. The church of S. Irene is an example of this (163).

The outstanding building of Justinian's reign was without doubt S. Sophia in Constantinople (162, 166, 168); this church is to Byzantine architecture what the

166 Ground plan, S. Sophia, Constantinople

167 Capital, S. Sophia

168 Interior, S. Sophia

169 Capital, SS. Sergius and Bacchus, Constantinople, c.535

170 S. Vitale, Ravenna

171 Capital, S. Apollinare in Classe

527–565   Justinian I Emperor of the eastern Roman Empire

531–579   Zenith of the Sassanian Empire in Persia under Chosroes I

570–1   Birth at Mecca of Mohammed, prophet of Allah, founder of the religion of Islam

610-632   The Word of God as revealed over these years to Mohammed later recorded in the Koran. Accepted version 646

622   First year of the Muslim calendar. Mohammed leaves Mecca for Medina

628   Mecca becomes the religious capital of Islam and a place of pilgrimage

632   Death of Mohammed. Succeeded by the reign of the caliphs

632–634   Abu Bakr became the first caliph to reign

632–700   From the Arabian peninsular the Arabs gradually invaded and conquered large areas of the Byzantine Empire, for example:

636–641   Syria

637   Sassanian empire

641–642   Egypt

635–650   Persia

634–c.700   North Africa

641   Upper Mesopotamia

674   Muslim attacks on Constantinople repelled

680   Bulgarians establish themselves over large area south of the River Danube

717–741   Muslim attempts to

CONSTANTINOPLE

THE RAVENNATE AND ISTRIA

172 Binbirdirek Cistern (the Cistern of the Thousand-and-One Columns), Constantinople. Sixth century

173 Gallery capitals, S. Sophia, Constantinople

174 Baptistery, Grado Cathedral, the Ravennate, c. AD 450

175 Poreč (Parenzo) Cathedral, Istria (now Yugoslavia) c.550

Parthenon is to Greek. S. Sophia was the prototype for the Byzantine style, incorporating trends from both east and west, but creating something new, imaginative and truly magnificent. It was built on the site of two earlier churches of S. Sophia, Constantine's of AD 335 and Theodosius's of AD 415. It was begun in 532 and was built in the incredibly short time of just under six years; its architects were Anthemios of Tralles and Isodorus of Miletus. The immense church covers an area of 241 x 221ft; its dome, supported on four massive piers, is over 100ft in diameter and soars to 180ft above the floor. East and west of the dome are hemicycles each covered by semi-domes, thus creating a vast oval nave, an open space under the airy central dome which gives the unique impression of a light, floating architecture which is the chief quality of S. Sophia.

The interior was superbly and richly decorated. All wall surfaces, piers and floors were faced with coloured marble. The columns were of coloured veined marble, the capitals of white. The arches, vaults and domes were adorned with the glowing richness of mosaic. Despite damage from earthquake, transformation into a Turkish mosque, with the added minarets and buttresses and the plastering over of the mosaic enrichment, S. Sophia survives remarkably well: its mosaics are once more visible. Its design influenced that of many smaller churches but it has never been equalled on the same scale. Here is one of the great architectural feats of the world.

The outstanding contribution of Byzantine architects to architectural construction was their development of the dome supported on four piers which stood at the corners of a square plan. The dome is the most typical feature of Byzantine architecture, as vital to its design as orders were to the Greek or the steeple to the Middle Ages. The basis for Byzantine dome construction, the use of the pendentive, was derived from eastern building techniques rather than from the west.

The Romans had covered buildings of circular form with domes, as in the Pantheon, for example (**107, 125**). This is a straightforward constructional problem, erecting a dome of circular section upon circular walling. They had often covered square forms with groined vaults as in their baths (**92**) and it is thought that they also knew how to build a domical vault over a square space. This is a domical form made of four webs separated by groins which rise to a point; it is not a true dome and its design lacks flexibility of proportion.

The essential problem in building a dome of circular section upon a drum, also of circular section (which can contain windows to light the interior) over a square, is to transform the square base into a circle, upon which the drum may be supported. This may be achieved in two different ways: by the use of the squinch or the pendentive. Both methods derive from Asia, the former from third- and fourth-century Persia, and the latter, it is believed, from Syria or Asia Minor. In squinch construction an arch, or series of arches, are built across the upper angles of the square to transform the square base to an octagonal one, and so more easily support a circular base. This method was extensively employed in the Byzantine period and later in both east and west.

The pendentive is a more ambitious and imaginative, as well as more successful, solution. It was widely used in the best Byzantine building from S. Sophia in

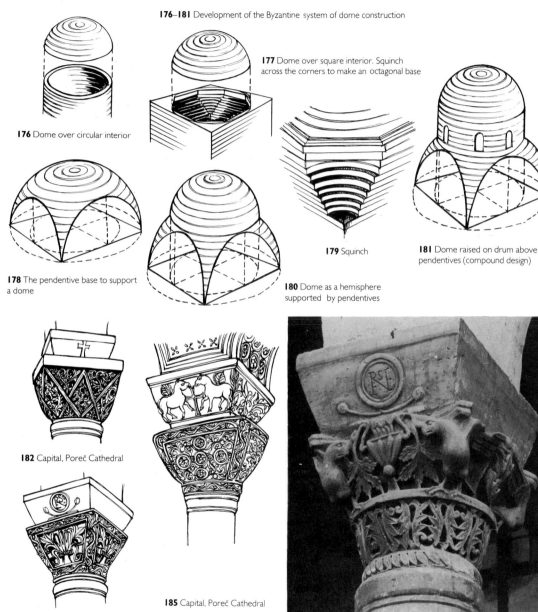

176–181 Development of the Byzantine system of dome construction

176 Dome over circular interior

177 Dome over square interior. Squinch across the corners to make an octagonal base

178 The pendentive base to support a dome

179 Squinch

180 Dome as a hemisphere supported by pendentives

181 Dome raised on drum above pendentives (compound design)

182 Capital, Poreč Cathedral

184 Capital, Poreč Cathedral

185 Capital, Poreč Cathedral

726–823 Iconoclastic controversy. Years of persecution of the orthodox Byzantine Christians by the emperors of the time in Constantinople, for venerating holy images (icons)

c.750 Byzantine Empire greatly reduced in area. Lands lost to the Arabs, Slavs, Lombards. Constantinople controlled only Asia Minor, southern Italy and part of Greece

762 Baghdad established as the capital of the Abbasid caliphs. Within a few years the city had become an important Arab cultural and commercial centre

c.776 Abu-Musa-Jābir-ibu-Haiÿan, Arabian alchemist and chemist at the peak of his achievement

786–809 Reign of Hārūn-al-Rashid, patron of learning, as fifth caliph of the Abbasid Empire. Very important years for this empire

813–833 Al-Mamum continued the standard of patronage of the arts and sciences begun by his father Hārūn. The great works of antiquity were translated into Arabic. This enabled the Muslim world to study the science, philosophy and literature of Greece and Persia. Among such translations were works by Aristotle, Plato, Euclid and Hippocrates

867 Byzantine empire, under Emperor Basil I, began the reconquest of its lost lands. By 1056 it had retaken Armenia, Georgia, Dalmatia, Bulgaria, Crete, Cyprus, Phoenicia and Palestine

BYZANTINE ARCHITECTURE   600 – 1200

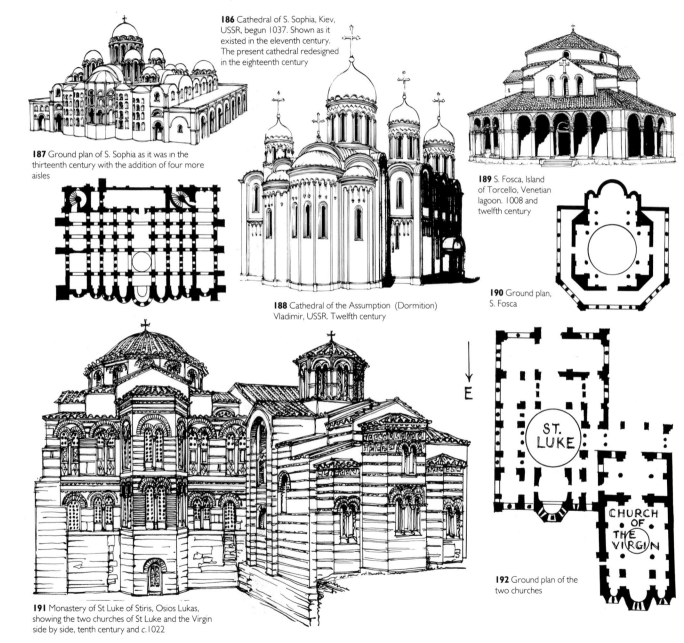

186 Cathedral of S. Sophia, Kiev, USSR, begun 1037. Shown as it existed in the eleventh century. The present cathedral redesigned in the eighteenth century

187 Ground plan of S. Sophia as it was in the thirteenth century with the addition of four more aisles

188 Cathedral of the Assumption (Dormition) Vladimir, USSR. Twelfth century

189 S. Fosca, Island of Torcello, Venetian lagoon. 1008 and twelfth century

190 Ground plan, S. Fosca

191 Monastery of St Luke of Stiris, Osios Lukas, showing the two churches of St Luke and the Virgin side by side, tenth century and c.1022

192 Ground plan of the two churches

ST. LUKE

CHURCH OF THE VIRGIN

E

Constantinople onwards, and has been the basis of dome construction in the west from the Italian Renaissance to the present century. In the pendentive method a lower, larger dome, of a diameter equal to the diagonal of the square space to be covered, is constructed to a height where it forms a complete circle within the walls of the square. This circle then provides the basis for supporting the actual dome and drum. As the lower dome is too large to fill the square space it is cut off in vertical planes formed by the four walls of the square. The remaining spherical triangles are called pendentives. In such structures the weight of the dome is transmitted via the pendentives to the piers at the corners of the square and not to the arches between, so providing a stable structure. Byzantine domes are visible externally, where they are generally tiled (**176, 181**).

The chief building material for Byzantine churches was brick, though stone was used widely on some Greek islands, and in Armenia, Georgia and Syria. On the exterior, brickwork was decoratively banded and patterned. Inside marble and mosaic facings were used. The wall core was generally of concrete and/or rubble.

Classical forms and mouldings appeared in window and doorway design. Windows were small and filled with alabaster or marble sheets and, sometimes, glass. Byzantine capitals were of greatly varied design. Classical capitals were adapted; Ionic and windswept acanthus leaf decorated Corinthian styles, for example. The most characteristic Byzantine capital was the basket shape, decorated, deeply incised and drilled in leaf and geometrical scroll forms. Many capitals were surmounted by an impost block (dosseret), which provided a

BYZANTINE ARCHITECTURE 600 – 1200

broader surface-support for the arcade or entablature above. Such impost-blocks were to be seen chiefly in Greece and Italy and much less often in Constantinople (**167, 169, 182-5, 193-7**).

In the tenth and eleventh centuries, in the second period of building expansion, the Justinian type of church had been largely replaced by a considerable variety of plans, though the style of architecture, particularly in eastern Europe, was much more uniform. Most of the churches, notably in Greece and Serbia, were small. Among the plans then currently being used was the Greek cross design of cruciform church, which had short arms, each often terminating in an apse, with a central dome over the crossing. There was also the octagonal variant on this, which might or might not be cruciform. Of Armenian origin, the domes of such churches were generally supported on squinches, providing an octagonal base. The monastery churches of St Luke of Stiris (**191**) and of Daphni (**198**) are of this type.

The most common and the classic form of Byzantine church of the tenth century onwards was the cross-in-square plan. Such churches were small but tall. The short arms of the cruciform church were enclosed in a square, which was subdivided to form nine bays. A dome upon a drum, and supported by pendentives, rose over the crossing, and barrel vaults covered the four arms. The corners of the square between the arms of the cross were domed or vaulted. There are many examples of this type of church, mainly to be seen in Greece, Serbia, Sicily and Constantinople.

In the eleventh century there was a trend towards a multiplicity of domes in Byzantine churches, and this was particularly so in Russia. With their conversion to Christianity

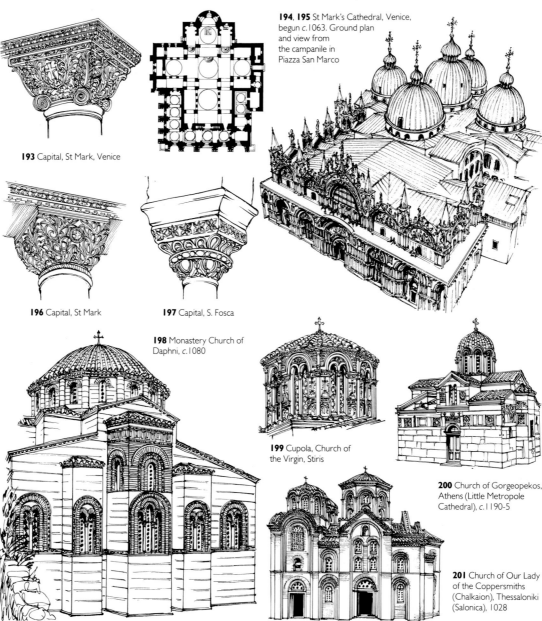

193 Capital, St Mark, Venice

194, 195 St Mark's Cathedral, Venice, begun c.1063. Ground plan and view from the campanile in Piazza San Marco

196 Capital, St Mark

197 Capital, S. Fosca

198 Monastery Church of Daphni, c.1080

199 Cupola, Church of the Virgin, Stiris

200 Church of Gorgeopekos, Athens (Little Metropole Cathedral), c.1190-5

201 Church of Our Lady of the Coppersmiths (Chalkaion), Thessaloniki (Salonica), 1028

Late ninth century Arabic numerals, derived from the Hindu in India, adapted for use in Muslim commerce

Tenth century Abu Bakr al-Rāzi, great Persian physician, practising in Baghdad. Known especially for his medical treatises, for example, one on measles and smallpox

976 Earliest manuscript written in Latin uses Arabic numerals (from Spain)

965–1020 Ibn-al-Haitham, notable Muslim physicist specializing in optics. His studies upon lenses and the understanding of the human eye influenced, through Latin translation, western scientists such as Kepler

Tenth–eleventh century Highest point of achievement in the development of (classical) Arabic science. Important centres of study include Baghdad, Cairo, Antioch and Cordova. Scientific disciplines of algebra, chemistry, alchemy, astronomy, mathematics, medicine and optics

1037 Seljuk Turkish Empire founded

1055 Seljuk Turkish conquest of Baghdad

1099 Crusaders of the First Crusade capture Jerusalem

1056–1453 Slow decline of the Byzantine empire in face of Turkish advance. A rise of western culture; for example, Norman conquest of Bari, capital of Byzantine southern Italy in 1071

c.1123 Death in Nishapur, Persia of Omar Khayyam, Persian poet,

LATE BYZANTINE ARCHITECTURE   1200 – c.1520

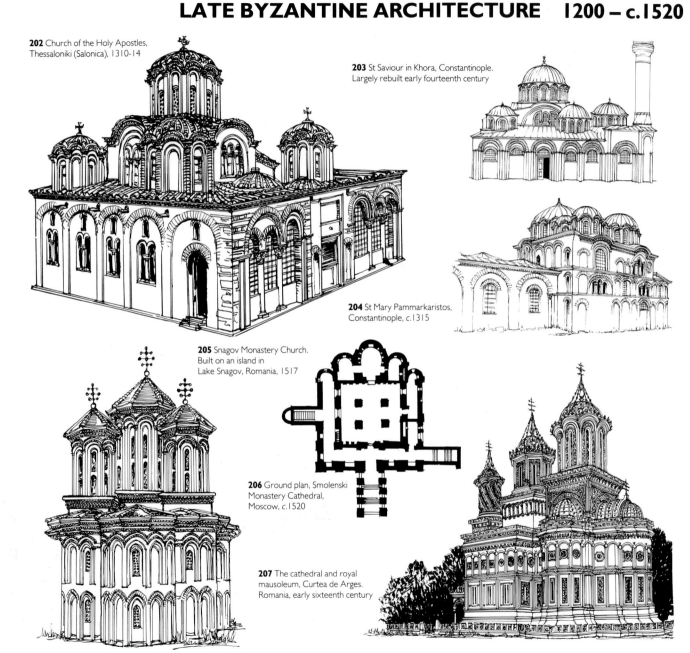

202 Church of the Holy Apostles, Thessaloniki (Salonica), 1310-14

203 St Saviour in Khora, Constantinople. Largely rebuilt early fourteenth century

204 St Mary Pammarkaristos, Constantinople, c.1315

205 Snagov Monastery Church. Built on an island in Lake Snagov, Romania, 1517

206 Ground plan, Smolenski Monastery Cathedral, Moscow, c.1520

207 The cathedral and royal mausoleum, Curtea de Arges. Romania, early sixteenth century

at the end of the tenth century the Russians were basing their ecclesiastical architecture upon Constantinople, and many churches were being built and decorated by Byzantine craftsmen. The Byzantine style was introduced at first to three chief centres: Kiev, Novgorod and Vladimir (**188**). The Cathedral of S. Sophia in Kiev, begun 1037, was the first great Byzantine church in Russia. It was a Greek cross-domed basilica, its plan based on Constantinople pattern, but with a large central dome and 12 smaller ones to represent Christ and His Apostles. Originally it had five aisles, each terminating in an apse; later four more were added (**186, 187**).

In the west, in Italy, the eleventh-century pattern of Constantinople strongly influenced the Veneto area. S. Fosca on the island of Torcello is a typical Greek cross octagon (**189, 190**), while the magnificent Cathedral of St Mark in Venice (**194, 195**) is of Greek cross plan, with five domes, one over the crossing and one over each arm. This was the third church to be built on the site. It is richly ornamented with mosaic, painting and gilding – though some of the mosaics and the façade gables are fifteenth-century Gothic additions.

The plan and layout of Byzantine church architecture changed only marginally after 1200. Decoration, both inside and out, became more ornate, domes more numerous, surmounting tall drums. The interiors were also taller but became narrower. Characteristic, for example, are the monastery churches of Greece, the Aphendiko (**208**) and the Pantanassa (early fifteenth century) at Mistra and the church of the Holy Apostles at Thessaloniki (Salonica, **202**) and Gračanicá church in Serbia (**211**). In eastern Europe Serbia, Romania, Bulgaria

LATE BYZANTINE ARCHITECTURE   1200 – c.1520

and Russia continued to build in this cultural tradition even after 1453. Many of these churches are large, lofty, complex in design and richly ornamented (**205, 206, 210**).

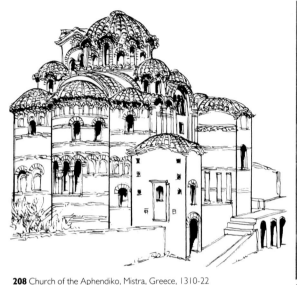

208 Church of the Aphendiko, Mistra, Greece, 1310-22

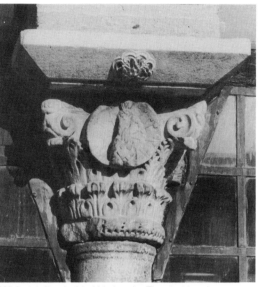

209 Capital, Church of the Holy Apostles, Thessaloniki

210 Cozia Monastery, Olt Valley, Romania, 1387-8

211 Monastery Church, Gračanicá, Serbia, (Yugoslavia), 1321

mathematician and astronomer. Known in the west particularly for his collection of quatrains, the Rubaiyat of Omar Khayyam. Omar made important contributions to mathematics, particularly algebra, in the classifying and solving of equations. He was also astronomer royal and produced a series of astronomical tables. In conjunction with other scholars he attempted a reform of the Muslim calendar

1138–1193   Saladin, Kurdish emir from Syria, later Sultan of Egypt and Syria. By 1183 had unified Egypt, Syria and Mesopotamia and, in 1187, defeated the Crusaders and captured Jerusalem

1145–95   Building of the great Crusader castle, Krak des Chevaliers, in Syria

1204   Fourth Crusade. Constantinople attacked and sacked. Frankish emperor established as head of a newly founded Latin Empire

1261   Constantinople re-taken for the Byzantine Empire and Latins expelled

1326   Bursa taken by Ottoman Turks. Becomes the first capital of the young empire

1453   Ottoman conquest of Constantinople

PRE-ROMANESQUE ARCHITECTURE 660 – 800

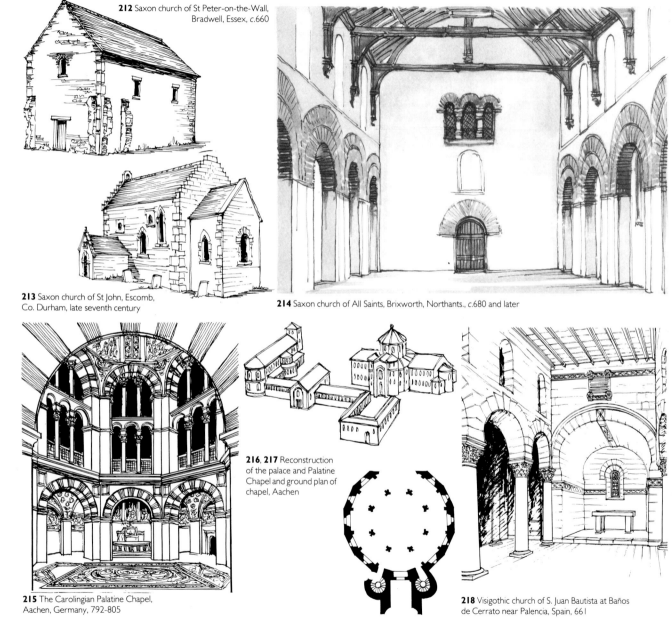

212 Saxon church of St Peter-on-the-Wall, Bradwell, Essex, c.660

213 Saxon church of St John, Escomb, Co. Durham, late seventh century

214 Saxon church of All Saints, Brixworth, Northants., c.680 and later

215 The Carolingian Palatine Chapel, Aachen, Germany, 792-805

216, 217 Reconstruction of the palace and Palatine Chapel and ground plan of chapel, Aachen

218 Visigothic church of S. Juan Bautista at Baños de Cerrato near Palencia, Spain, 661

While the Byzantine Empire, with its capital in Constantinople, was being established, the countries of western Europe had been plunged into chaos. With the departure of the Roman legions which had protected the states of empire, the civilized ordered life of the preceding centuries had been disrupted. In Britain, France, Germany and Spain the countryside and life of its people steadily returned to what it had been before the coming of the Romans. Roads became overgrown, buildings were damaged or destroyed and a more primitive way of life was resumed. The arts – literature, painting, sculpture, architecture – were lost and for some time destruction was general.

From about 450 to 650 are the years of the 'Dark Ages', when most building was primitive and of materials which did not last. Archaeological research has increased our knowledge of the buildings of this time, but remains are few. Even in the seventh and eight centuries the majority of building was of impermanent materials – timber, wattle and daub, air-dried brick – and has not survived. But the most important buildings were wholly or partly of stone, and considerable remains are to be found, chiefly in Ireland, England and Spain. Architectural style and structure varied greatly in these areas, influenced from different sources, which included late Roman and Byzantine work, Scandinavian timber structures, Celtic monasticism and Lombard and Visigothic forms.

The monastic way of life had evolved in Egypt, where monks pursued solitary lives as hermits in caves and huts. The movement spread westwards and northwards and monks began to establish communities. During the sixth and seventh centuries monasteries were built in Ireland, where they flourished. The monks then took their gospel to Scotland and northern England, founding monasteries at, for example, the Island of Iona and at Lindisfarne. The monks, seeking a contemplative life, built small cell-like structures of wood or stone, containing simple rooms on isolated, often island sites. Remains of such monastic building in Britain are fragmentary, but several dry masonry examples survive in Ireland. Notable are the Gallerus Oratory in Co. Kerry (**224**), the building called Columba's House at Kells (**226**) and the church on St Madara's Isle (**225**).

The remains of seventh- and eighth-century Christian building in England are mainly of small churches and monasteries. They are of two main types which derived from the two areas of Christian influence: those in the south which followed the Roman Christian pattern stemming from St Augustine and those in the north which had close ties with Celtic monasticism. The southern churches, all in Kent and Essex, are on basilican plan with an eastern apse and, often, a western narthex. The rectangular interior was divided into nave and cell-like chapels by an arcade or wall with openings. The ruined church at Reculver was one of these (**221**) as was the Church of S.S. Peter and Paul in Canterbury. Of especial interest because it has been less altered or restored is the little Church of St Peter-on-the-Wall at Bradwell (**212**), the walls of which are built mostly of re-used Roman material.

The early Northumbrian churches were of simpler design. Tall and narrow, they consisted of aisleless nave and rectangular chancel, like the Escomb church in Co. Durham (**213**). Even the great seventh-century monastic churches of Jarrow and Monkwearmouth were of this type (**219**).

219 Saxon church of St Peter, Monkwearmouth, Co. Durham, c.675

220 Saxon crypt, Hexham Abbey church, Northumberland, c.675. Built of stone from Roman Corbridge

221 Ground plan, Saxon church at Reculver, Kent, c.670

222 Doorway, Brixworth Church

223 Brixworth Church

224 The Gallerus Oratory, Dingle, Co. Kerry, Ireland, seventh century

225 Church, St Madara's Isle, Co. Galway, Ireland, c.700

226 S. Columba's house, Kells, Co. Meath, Ireland, c.800

227 Ground plan of Visigothic church of S. Pedro de la Nave, Spain, seventh century

228 Carved capital, S. Pedro de la Nave

229 Doorway, S. Juan Bautista, Baños de Cerrato

415–711 Visigothic rule in Spain

428–751 Merovingian dynasty dominant in the area covered by much of modern France and a little to the east of it

*c.***466–511** Clovis I, King of the Franks who, uniting the two branches of the Frankish tribes, established their pre-eminence among European barbaric peoples

*c.***480–547** St Benedict founded in 520 the great Monastery of Monte Cassino in Italy, the mother-house of the Benedictine Order. Here St Benedict composed the rule which became the basis of monasticism in Western Europe

*c.***609** St Augustine, first archbishop of Canterbury, died. As prior of the Benedictine Monastery of St Andrew in Rome, Augustine was chosen by Pope Gregory to bring the Christian message to England. With a group of monks St Augustine landed on the Kentish coast in 597, from where he established his ministry at Canterbury

650–70 Sutton Hoo ship burial. Grave of an East Anglian King in a wooden ship laden with treasure. Archaeological find of 1939

673–735 Bede (the Venerable), Anglo-Saxon monk of Jarrow, leading scholar and writer. His *Ecclesiastical History of the English People* (written in Latin) was his most important work, and is a primary source for early Anglo-Saxon history.

GERMANY

SPAIN, FRANCE AND DALMATIA

230 S. Michael's Church, Fulda, c.820, Carolingian

231 The Carolingian Minster, Mittelzell, Island of Reichenau in Lake Constance, 819, enlarged tenth century

232 Interior of Carolingian church of S. George, Oberzell, Reichenau. 836 and later

233 Asturian church of S. Maria de Naranco, near Oviedo, Spain, 848

234 Asturian church of S. Miguel de Liño, near Oviedo, Spain, 842-50

235 Church of S. Donato, Zadar, Yugoslavia, c.820. Dalmatian church in the Lombard style

After the synod of Whitby, in 664, Northumbrian monasticism began to follow the Roman rite. By 700 an energetic church building programme was under way, and these new structures followed the basilican plan. Those at Hexham (**220**), York and Ripon were notable examples.

The most impressive extant church of this period is All Saints at Brixworth (**214, 222, 223**). It is a large building (nearly 100ft in length), constructed of ragstone and re-used Roman bricks. It was built as an aisled basilica with eastern apse, polygonal on the exterior and rounded within. Badly damaged in Viking raids, the church was partly rebuilt in the tenth and eleventh centuries.

Visigothic architecture had become established in northern Spain before the Muslim invasion, flourishing from about 450-720. Most examples of seventh-century work have been greatly altered, but surviving churches show an interesting, yet different, Christian style. Particularly fine is S. Juan Bautista at Baños de Cerrato (**218**), a three-aisled stone basilica with timber roofing to the nave and a stone barrel vault covering the sanctuary. Interesting is the characteristic Visigothic use of the horseshoe arch, deriving not from the later Arab culture but from Syria or Persia; also the re-use of Roman capitals and columns alongside Visigothic versions.

The most important influence in the ninth century was Carolingian architecture, which evolved under the patronage of Charlemagne, who had become King of the Franks in 771. On Christmas Day in 800 the Pope crowned Charlemagne Emperor of a new Holy Roman Empire. Under Charlemagne monasticism flourished and many ambitious palace and monastic architectural schemes were built. This

PRE-ROMANESQUE ARCHITECTURE 800 – 900

represented a new Constantinian age of Christian architecture (p. 24), displaying the richness and robustness of the classical architecture of the later Roman Empire. But Carolingian work was not merely a copy of its prototype, it also reflected Byzantine influence from Constantinople (p. 29) and gradually established characteristics of its own, suited to climatic and social needs of a people living north of the Alps.

Remains of Carolingian architecture are not extensive and most of the impressive layouts have been lost as at, for example, S. Riquier near Abbeville in France; built 790-9 and known to us from drawings and descriptions. The abbey church here showed the basis of later German Romanesque design, having two transepts each flanked by round towers and with two further towers over the crossings. The choir terminated in an apse, the nave in a westwork, which was a characteristic German method of designing the west end of a Romanesque church; this had a vaulted entrance hall with chapel above. Of this pattern, Corvey Abbey Church on the Weser (873-88) survives only partially altered.

The outstanding surviving instance of Charlemagne's building programme is the Chapel Palatine (now part of the cathedral) at Aachen (215, 217). Of Byzantine derivation, from S. Vitale in Ravenna (164), it is octagonal inside, but has 16 sides on the exterior. Here was the seat of Charlemagne's court and the site of his palace in Germany. The palace, based upon the Lateran Palace in Rome, was a grand scheme with immense great hall, long colonnades and a courtyard which held seven thousand people (216).

Among notable instances of surviving Carolingian building in Germany is the gatehouse of the Monastery of Lorsch, built

236 Gateway, Monastery of Lorsch, Germany, c.800

237 Detail of gateway. Ionic capital

238 Ground plan, S. Michael, Fulda

239 The crypt, S. George, Oberzell

240 Window, Church of S. Miguel de Liño

241 Oratory, Germigny-des-Près, France, 806

242 Ground plan of oratory

243 Window opening, Church of S. Maria de Naranco

c.735–804 Alcuin of York, influential teacher, scholar and theologian, preceptor of the palace schools of Charlemagne at Aachen 782-96

c.742–814 Charlemagne, King of the Franks and, from 800, Holy Roman Emperor

754 Carolingian dynasty which ruled in Western Europe, mainly in France, Germany and Italy, until the early tenth century

711–10th century Muslim expansion in Spain – by 929 – controlled almost all the peninsula, under a caliphate

Eighth century Development and manufacture of Cordovan leather, originally from the mouflon sheep and using both tanning and tawing methods. This was high quality leather which became internationally famed. It might be silvered or gilded, and was embossed. A special product in bright red was obtained by dyeing with kermes

782 Construction of Offa's Dyke. Built by order of King Offa of Mercia and largely marked the boundary between England and Wales

849–99 Alfred the Great, Anglo-Saxon King (871-99) who, during the Danish wars, came to an agreement with the Danes to divide the country of England

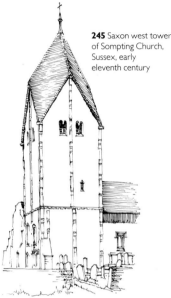

245 Saxon west tower of Sompting Church, Sussex, early eleventh century

244 Saxon church of Deerhurst, Gloucestershire, early tenth century

246 Saxon crypt, Repton Church, Derbyshire, tenth century

247 Ottonian church, S. Cyriakus, Gernrode, Germany, 961 and later

248 Lombard style church at Romainmôtier, Switzerland, c.1000

c.800, its stone façade patterned in red and white and decorated by classical half-columns and pilasters (**236, 237**); the three churches on the Island of Reichenau in Lake Constance, which were part of a monastic centre established there in 724 (**231, 232**); and the monastic burial Chapel, S. Michael's Church in Fulda (*c*.820), which is a centrally planned building of Roman type based upon the Holy Sepulchre Church in Jerusalem (**230, 238**). In France, near Orléans, a Palatine palace and church was erected at S. Germigny-des-Près in 806. The church here (poorly restored) was built on a characteristic late Byzantine plan of cross-in-square (p. 33); it had a central dome, barrel vaulted arms of the cross and vaulted corners of the square (**241, 242**).

In the period up to the year 1000 Carolingian architecture in Germany under the Ottonian emperors moved further towards the Romanesque forms; for example, in the stone convent church of S. Cyriakus at Gernrode (**247**). The Lombard style of Italy, also moving towards a full Romanesque, as at the basilican church of S. Vicenzo in Prato, Milan, *c*.833, was seen as well further afield at, for instance, the Swiss church at Romainmôtier (**248**) and at Zadar (Yugoslavia), in the church of S. Donato, which is an early example to have an ambulatory with radiating chapels (**235**).

In Spain the Moorish occupation had been completed, leaving only a small Christian area centred on Oviedo on the north coast. Here evolved an Asturian style, partly derived from Visigothic design, partly influenced by Carolingian. The churches of S. Maria Naranco and S. Miguel de Liño are typical, both displaying the round, not horseshoe, arch (**233, 234, 240, 243**). By 900 refugees coming north from Muslim-

PRE-ROMANESQUE ARCHITECTURE   900 – 1000

occupied Spain settled near León, and here developed an architectural style which was part Christian, part Arabic. Called Mozarabic, it shows late Roman character-istics blended with Arabic arches, brickwork and decoration. The monastic church of S. Miguel de la Escalada is a fine example (**252, 255**).

In England, after the Viking raids, the Saxons in the tenth and eleventh centuries rebuilt many of the monasteries and churches, often in more permanent materials than before. Such churches now had towers, a number of which survive: Earl's Barton (**250**), Sompting (**245**) and Barton-on-Humber (**249**), for example. The characteristic features of Saxon building can be seen in a number of examples in England: pilaster strip decoration derived from timber building design, the distinctive quoins, the triangular window heads and the baluster shaft window and belfry openings (**244-6, 249-51**).

249 Saxon tower, Church of Barton-on-Humber, Humberside, tenth century

250 Saxon tower, Church at Earl's Barton, Northamptonshire, c.1000

251 Nave window, Saxon church at Worth, Sussex, tenth century

Ninth century   Viking raids on England

912–1002   Ottonian dynasty of German emperors

927   Dedication of the first abbey church of Cluny in Burgundy. Cluniac reforms of monasticism

987   Establishment of the Capet dynasty in France

991   Danegeld first levied. This was a land tax which raised large sums of money for the Anglo-Saxon kings of England to buy off invaders from Scandinavia

252 Mozarabic church of S. Miguel de la Escalada, near Léon, Spain, c.913

253 Capital, S. Miguel de la Escalada

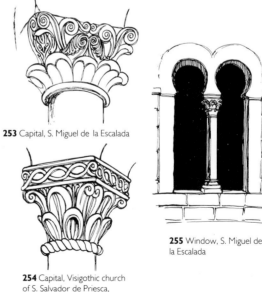

254 Capital, Visigothic church of S. Salvador de Priesca, Villaviciosa, Spain, 921

255 Window, S. Miguel de la Escalada

41

EARLY ROMANESQUE ARCHITECTURE   1000 – 1100

ENGLAND

FRANCE

256 Nave, Gloucester Cathedral, 1090-1100. Later vault

257 The White Tower, Keep of the Tower of London, 1078-90

258 St John's Chapel, the White Tower, c.1080

259 S. Etienne, Caen, the west front, begun c.1066. Spires later

260 La Trinité, Caen, the west front, begun 1063

261 Interior, La Trinité

The Romanesque architectural style evolved during the eleventh century. There were many variations upon this style, the differences being due chiefly to climate and availability of materials, but also to the fact that Europe was still divided and controlled in small areas, each responding to its own form of government and local needs: only England at this time presented a more or less single unified area, under the control of the Norman Kings.

As the name Romanesque suggests, the architectural character was based upon that of the later Roman Empire. Thus, almost universally, the structure was arcuated, using the Roman round arch and, where vaulting was constructed, the continuous form of the barrel or tunnel vault, creating groined vaulting at intersections.

The Romanesque style evolved from several major sources, and developed a character of its own to suit the requirements of eleventh-century life. The regional variations of the style depended upon which of the earlier sources exerted the strongest influence. The chief sources were the blend of Carolingian and Lombardic designs, established under the Holy Roman Empire, the architectural form originating in Normandy and the surviving buildings of the Roman Empire. In general, the architectural style of the Holy Roman Empire was the dominant influence in Germany, northern Italy, eastern France and parts of Scandinavia; Norman architecture was predominant in north-west France, in England, parts of Scandinavia and in southern Italy and Sicily; while the tradition of Roman architecture was strongest in the areas closest to what had been the important centres of empire and where the greatest number of buildings survived; that is, south-

EARLY ROMANESQUE ARCHITECTURE 1000 – 1100

east France and central Italy. A wealth of such buildings also existed in southern Spain, but due to the strength of Muslim control Romanesque design developed only in the north of the country.

Most eleventh-century building in Europe was wholly or partly of timber, and little has survived. Only the most important structures were erected in permanent materials – stone, brick, marble, mosaic – and it is this work which exists, in considerable quantity, though often altered and/or restored in later ages. The overriding influence in the Middle Ages was a religious one, so the greatest quantity of extant building is of churches, cathedrals and monasteries. The Church was the dominant influence on medieval life, providing for the community succour and refuge, education and medical assistance, and teaching the principles of Christian living. In return each member of the community, which was no longer a slave state, was expected to contribute his skill and labour towards the immense task of erecting the great cathedral and monastic churches.

The dominant power behind the movement in church building lay with the monastic orders, which developed their own individual style of Romanesque architecture to conform to the needs of the order. These styles tended to transcend frontiers so, for example, one Benedictine church was similar to others, whether in France, England or Italy. The famous prototype for the Benedictine Order was the mother church at Cluny in Burgundy. Built originally in 927 and replaced in 955, the third church (begun in 1088) was the greatest of all the monastic churches of this time. 443ft in length, it was five-aisled and had double transepts and seven towers. A fragment only survived the destruction of

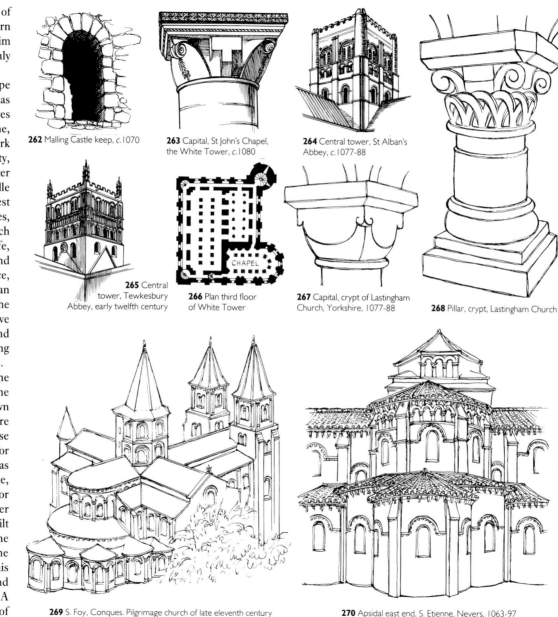

262 Malling Castle keep, c.1070

263 Capital, St John's Chapel, the White Tower, c.1080

264 Central tower, St Alban's Abbey, c.1077-88

265 Central tower, Tewkesbury Abbey, early twelfth century

266 Plan third floor of White Tower

267 Capital, crypt of Lastingham Church, Yorkshire, 1077-88

268 Pillar, crypt, Lastingham Church

269 S. Foy, Conques. Pilgrimage church of late eleventh century

270 Apsidal east end, S. Etienne, Nevers, 1063-97

CHAPEL

GERMANY

NORWAY, FRANCE AND BRITAIN

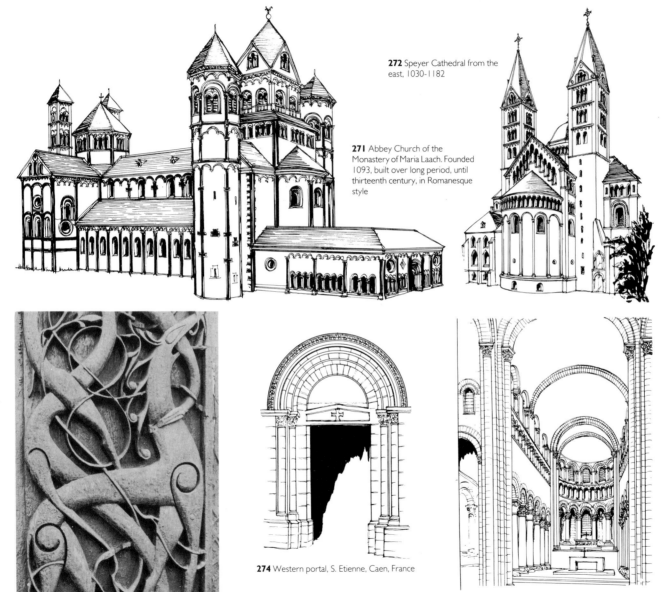

272 Speyer Cathedral from the east, 1030-1182

271 Abbey Church of the Monastery of Maria Laach. Founded 1093, built over long period, until thirteenth century, in Romanesque style

273 Carved detail, Urnes stave church, Norway. 1060, re-used on later building

274 Western portal, S. Etienne, Caen, France

275 Choir, Basilica of S. Benoît-sur-Loire, France, c.1080-1130

most of the building, in the early nineteenth century.

Knowledge of the architectural features of style was dispersed partly by the monastic orders and partly by the great pilgrimages. The cult of relics was important and imposing churches were built to house such relics. Pilgrims travelled immense distances on foot, or horseback across several countries, to pay homage to such relics and churches were erected along these routes to give shelter to the pilgrims. The most famous of these pilgrimages was to the great church of St James at Santiago de Compostela in north-west Spain (**284, 291**), said to contain the remains of the apostle. Pilgrims to Santiago came from many countries, notably England, Germany, Italy and France, and pilgrimage churches lined all the routes (**269, 282, 283, 290, 292**). Such churches tended to follow similar architectural patterns due to their similar needs. They were large to accommodate the pilgrims, generally having long aisled and galleried naves, wide transepts and a large sanctuary. Aisles and galleries were carried round the whole building. The whole church was usually tunnel-vaulted, the crossing being covered by a dome with lantern above. The church at Santiago itself set a pattern for the others. The exterior is now in baroque style but the Romanesque interior largely survives.

In northern Europe, further away from the southern dependence upon the ancient Roman model, new themes were being developed to create the Romanesque style. By the early decades of the eleventh century such ideas were crystallizing in Germany and in France. The Early Christian and Byzantine churches had been richly and colourfully decorated in the interior but the outside had been plain and simple. In the Rhineland area of Germany, in particular, the design of the exterior was becoming as striking and decorative as that of the interior. Both were being clearly articulated and designed to present a specific and dramatic handling of architectural shapes. On the exterior, tall towers flanked the end of the western arm, and probably also the transepts (which might be double); these, together with lanterns over the crossings, lent a majestic appearance to the silhouette. Inside, the arms of the Latin cross were articulated vertically by shafts marking the bays which extended from floor to roof, while horizontal string courses divided the wall area into three parts: ground floor arcade, triforium arcade and clerestory windows above (271, 272, 276, 277).

Church design became more complex. The worship of many different saints brought a need for more altars and more chapels. For this purpose the eastern arm of the church was designed in a radiating plan, where an ambulatory extended round behind the main altar, and from this led several radiating chapels so that the main eastern apse became multi-apsidal. The church of St Martin at Tours in France (rebuilt *c*.997) was a very early example of this; then the theme was more fully exploited in the third abbey church at Cluny. This had five chapels leading from the ambulatory.

A further variant of northern Romanesque architecture in Europe was initiated by the Normans. These men were of Viking stock, descendants of those Northmen (Norsemen) who had given their name to the part of north-west France to which they had come from Scandinavia soon after 900. They were energetic fighting men, who adapted to the Latin culture and the French language, then

276 Trier Cathedral from the west, 1016 onwards

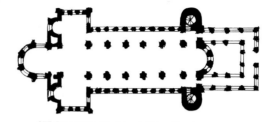

277 Ground plan, Maria Laach Abbey Church

278 Capital, S.S. Peter and Paul, Niederzell, 1050

279 Capital, S. Michael, Hildesheim, *c*.1030

280 Keep and mound, Cardiff Castle, Wales, eleventh century

281 Nave, abbey church of Mont S. Michel, France, 1022-1135

Duke William of Normandy. Reigned as King 1066-87

Eleventh century Mould-board introduced into the design of heavy agricultural ploughs in Europe. This was a device for guiding the furrow slice and turning it over. The wheeled plough was in general use for heavy work. Oxen most widely employed for ploughing rather than horses

Eleventh century Fulling mills operating in Europe to felt and thicken woollen cloth

Eleventh century By this time Italian craftsmen were making furniture of high quality. They practised inlaying and veneering and made mortise-and-tenon and dove-tail joints

Eleventh century Christian re-conquest of Spain began to take effect

Eleventh century Knowledge of brick-making spread to southern France from northern Italy, where it had continued since Roman times

Eleventh century Rapid development of water power. Water mills constructed for grinding corn, and tanning leather, plus various textile processes such as fulling and irrigation. Monasteries built near rivers in order to provide power for all needs

Eleventh century Expansion of urban and commercial life in Italy and establishment of important city-states: for example, Milan, Florence, Genoa, Venice

1065–1109 Alfonso VI succeeded to the Christian thrones of Castile,

SPAIN

ITALY

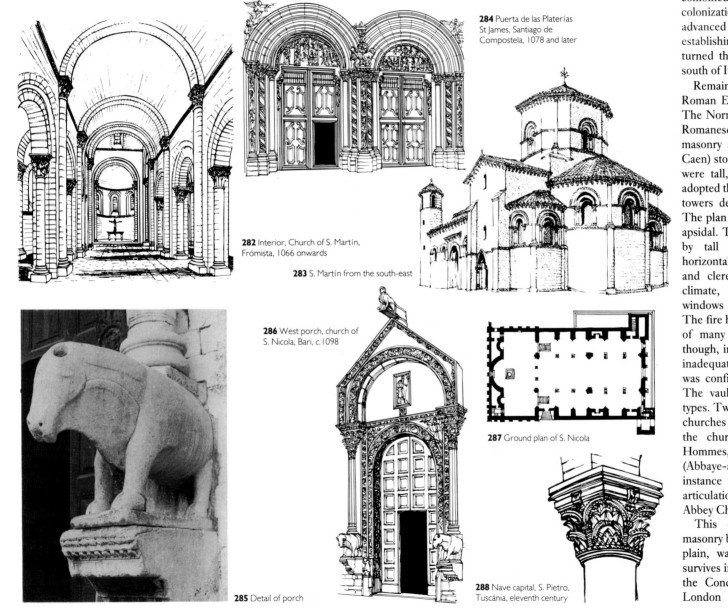

284 Puerta de las Platerías St James, Santiago de Compostela, 1078 and later

282 Interior, Church of S. Martín, Frómista, 1066 onwards

283 S. Martín from the south-east

286 West porch, church of S. Nicola, Bari, c.1098

287 Ground plan of S. Nicola

285 Detail of porch

288 Nave capital, S. Pietro, Tuscánia, eleventh century

combined their abilities in the arts of war and colonization with those of administration and advanced political thinking. After establishing themselves in Normandy they turned their attention to England and the south of Italy.

Remains of buildings dating from the Roman Empire were scarce in Normandy. The Normans began to establish their own Romanesque style, learning the arts of masonry and utilizing the local (especially Caen) stone. The churches which they built were tall, monumental and austere. They adopted the plain, lofty west façade with twin towers derived from the German pattern. The plan was cruciform, the east end being apsidal. The interior was clearly articulated by tall shafts into bays and divided horizontally into ground arcade, triforium and clerestory. Because of the northern climate, roofs were steeply pitched and windows larger than those further south. The fire hazard led to the early replacement of many timber roofs by stone vaulting though, in the eleventh century, because of inadequate knowledge and experience, this was confined to the narrower aisle spans. The vaulting was of tunnel and groined types. Two of Duke William of Normandy's churches in Caen survive fairly unaltered: the church of S. Etienne (Abbaye-aux-Hommes, **259**, **274**) and that of La Trinité (Abbaye-aux-Dames, **260**, **261**). A clear instance of the characteristic interior articulation can still be seen in the nave of the Abbey Church of Mont-S-Michel (**281**).

This church plan, the monumental masonry building style, massive and severely plain, was brought to England where it survives in, for instance, the White Tower – the Conqueror's Keep of the Tower of London – (**257**, **258**, **263**, **266**) and

EARLY ROMANESQUE ARCHITECTURE 1000 – 1100

Colchester Castle, as well as considerable parts of several cathedrals and abbey churches. These include Winchester, Lincoln (316), Gloucester (256), Canterbury (318), Exeter (317) Cathedrals and Tewkesbury and St Alban's Abbey Churches (264, 265). Most impressive of all Norman work in England is Durham Cathedral, almost all in the Romanesque style, and superbly sited on rock above the winding River Wear (310).

In Italy, as in southern France, links with the Roman tradition were never entirely severed, and the classical form of ornament – capitals, columns and arches – prevailed. In church design the early Christian basilican plan was largely adhered to, with its rectangular shape, apsidal termination to the sanctuary and interior roofing of wood rather than stone. Domes and lanterns were more usual than towers, particularly over the crossing of a cruciform church, and the bell tower was usually slender, tall and separate from the church structure (294). Inside the triforium stage was rare in Italy, as indeed, it was also in central areas of France and Germany as in, for example, S. Michael at Hildesheim and the Abbey Church of Maria Laach (271, 277) or S. Madeleine at Vézelay. Within this general framework Romanesque architecture in Italy is most varied, the northern work being Lombardic with decorative exterior arcading, the central area noted for its rich use of marble facing (293) and the south dominated by the Norman style interlaced with Byzantine and Saracenic features (285, 286, 287).

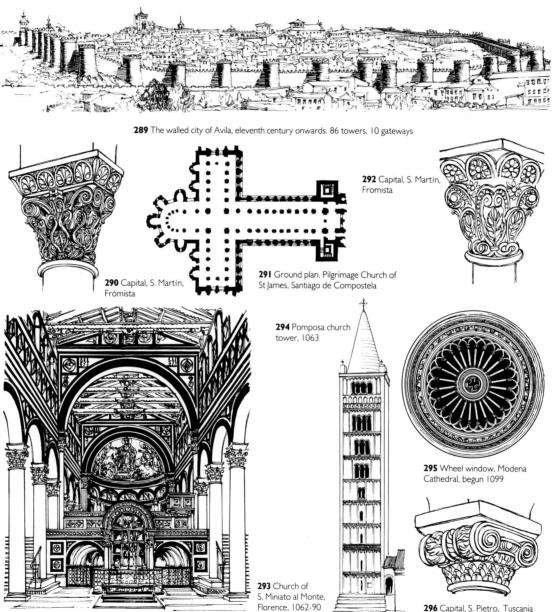

289 The walled city of Avila, eleventh century onwards. 86 towers, 10 gateways

290 Capital, S. Martín, Frómista

291 Ground plan. Pilgrimage Church of St James, Santiago de Compostela

292 Capital, S. Martín, Fromista

293 Church of S. Miniato al Monte, Florence, 1062-90

294 Pomposa church tower, 1063

295 Wheel window, Modena Cathedral, begun 1099

296 Capital, S. Pietro, Tuscania

Léon and Galicia (Spain). Married Constance of Burgundy, who encouraged the Benedictine mother house at Cluny to build accommodation for the pilgrims *en route* to Santiago de Compostela

*c.*1070–83 The Bayeux Tapestry (*Tapisserie de la Reine Mathilde*) worked in coloured wool on a strip of linen 231ft long and 19½in wide. The embroidery was commissioned by Odo, Bishop of Bayeux, half-brother of William I. It depicts both Norman and English life and events in 1066 and is an historical record of eleventh-century style and behaviour, illustrating building, costume, armour, ships and military weaponry

*c.*1080 Tide-mills constructed: for example, at Dover

1085–6 Domesday Book. A written record (in Latin) of the economic resources of Britain in land, population, livestock and equipment, established in a survey commissioned by William I for the purpose of accuracy in taxation

1086 Cistercian Order founded at Citeaux, near Dijon in France

1088 Traditional date for the founding of the law school at Bologna University (Italy). Medical and theologian faculties were established here in the thirteenth century and a faculty of mathematics in the fourteenth

1095 Pope Urban II's appeal at Clermont in France for the First Crusade

1099 Crusaders took Jerusalem by storm

ITALY

ITALY AND SPAIN

297 Trani Cathedral, Apulia. Begun 1094

298 Bronze door panel by Niccolò and Guglielmo. S. Zeno Maggiore, Verona, c.1140

299 Palatine Chapel, Palermo, Sicily, 1132-89

300 The Parma Cathedral group – cathedral, bell-tower, baptistery – Parma, Italy, 1117 to thirteenth century

301 Monastery Church of S. Maria, Ripoll, Spain. Façade c.1140-60, restored nineteenth century

During the twelfth century Romanesque architecture and ornament matured. As experience and knowledge of building in masonry increased, walling became less massive and openings for windows and doorways larger. Attempts were made to stone-vault wider and higher spans; a matter of urgency to counteract the loss of timber roofing through fire. The extreme plainness of the early Romanesque work began to be offset by richer ornamentation in carved and sculptural decoration, as well as marble and mosaic facing and coloured glass.

The Church used such decorative forms to inform a largely illiterate population of the Bible story and of the Christian ethic. The focal centre for such informative as well as artistic decoration was the western façade, particularly the great doorways with their carved tympana illustrating such themes as Christ in Majesty or the Last Judgement. Surrounding such tympana were elaborately carved voussoirs and the multi-shafted flanking sides of the doorways, with their richly and variably ornamented capitals. France is particularly rich in such doorways as, for example, at the Abbey Church of Vézelay, Autun Cathedral and the churches of S. Pierre at Moissac and S. Trophîme in Arles (**349, 350, 353**).

Mouldings in eleventh-century work were cut very simply with shallow hollows, chamfers and fillets, and were generally sparingly decorated. By the year 1100 the mouldings were being cut more deeply in rolls, rounds and hollows; and being profusely and decoratively carved. Such carving in Normandy and in Britain was mostly geometric in character; for instance, the chevron or zig-zag was especially to be seen in the deeply recessed mouldings of round-arched windows and doorways at, for example, Durham and Lincoln Cathedrals (**310, 316**) or Iffley Church, Oxon (**360, 364**). Also in common use was the billet, lozenge and cable ornament. Twelfth-century Romanesque decoration was, in general, richly and deeply carved and most varied in form. Capitals, voussoirs and tympana displayed all kinds of floral, animal and human subjects as well as representations of devils and monsters and complete Biblical scenes. This type of bold sculptural ornament was especially characteristic of France (**320**), Italy (**306**), Germany (**326**) and Scandinavia (**329, 330**). In Britain it was comparatively rare, apart from the Kilpeck school of sculpture seen in Kilpeck church (**311**). The most typical sculptural carved ornament in Britain was the beak-head design, where the heads of birds, beasts and humans were carved in a hollow moulding so that their beaks or tongues overlapped into the adjacent round moulding (**316**).

Glass-making had been widely practised to a high quality under the Roman Empire. After the collapse of the western part of the empire, knowledge of making glass had died out in many parts of Europe – but survived in some areas, notably Italy, the Rhineland of Germany and in northern France. Coloured glass was used in ecclesiastical building from early Romanesque times; the earliest extant examples are the eleventh-century windows in Augsburg Cathedral in Germany and in Le Mans Cathedral in France. The pieces of glass made up a translucent mosaic, depicting, as in the case of the sculptured porticoes, the Bible's teaching. These pieces were held together by lead strips which also stressed the outline drawing of the pictorial design.

Glass was coloured by adding different

302 S. Ambrogio, Milan, 1080 onwards

303 Wheel window of marble plates. West front, Troia Cathedral, twelfth century

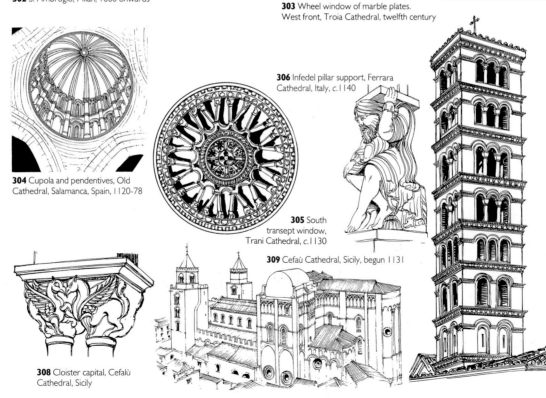

304 Cupola and pendentives, Old Cathedral, Salamanca, Spain, 1120-78

305 South transept window, Trani Cathedral, c.1130

306 Infedel pillar support, Ferrara Cathedral, Italy, c.1140

309 Cefaù Cathedral, Sicily, begun 1131

308 Cloister capital, Cefalù Cathedral, Sicily

c.1055–c.1140   In Spain, the gifted poet Judah ben Samuel Halexi

1090–1140   Building of the priory church at Lindisfarne

1090–1153   St Bernard, the Cistercian monk, who left the mother house at Citeaux to found a monastery at Clairvaux in the Jura, which became the leading Cistercian house

1090–1160   Building and decorating of the west front of Lincoln Cathedral. Work begun under Remigius

Early twelfth century   Rebuilding of Old St Paul's Cathedral in London, after a fire had destroyed the Saxon building in 1087

Early twelfth century   Construction of Castle Rising in Norfolk – keep and earthworks

1100   First mention of a 'Master of Oxford', referring to the university

c.1100   Construction begun of Stavanger Cathedral in Norway. Built in an Anglo-Norman style

1110–1130   The construction of the crypt of Canterbury Cathedral, with its unusual (for England) carved capitals depicting foliage, animals and human figures

1122   Concordat of Worms in Germany. A solemn agreement between the Roman Catholic Church and the sovereign civil state which, in this case, settled the investiture struggle between Pope and Emperor

c.1123–1190   Frederick I (Barbarossa), King of Germany and Holy Roman Emperor. In 1189

ENGLAND

FRANCE

310 Nave and choir from the west, Durham Cathedral, England. 1093-1133

311 South doorway, Kilpeck Church, England, c.1140

312 Nave from the west. Ely Cathedral, c.1150

313 Nave, Abbey Church of S. Madeleine, Vézelay, c.1104-32

314 Autun Cathedral, c.1120-40

315 Cathedral of S. Front, Périgueux, 1120-50

metallic oxides to the ingredients for white glass and, even at this early date, a considerable variety of shades was obtained. This was partly due to the impurity of the oxides used, and partly depended upon how high a temperature was attainable during manufacture. There were three chief methods for making coloured glass. The most usual was by fusion of the materials, – soda ash, lime and sand – and in this the glass was coloured all through. Alternatively, the coloured pigment could be burnt on to one surface of the glass only. A third means was by flashing; this more highly technical method involved blowing bubbles of coloured glass, then dipping and blowing them with white glass, resulting in a coloured glass showing through the white which produced an attractive, subtle effect.

Most of the countries of Europe were still fragmented and in consequence the style of Romanesque architecture varied considerably from one area to another; this was especially so in Italy and France. There were three very differing interpretations in Italy. In the north, notably in the Po valley and in the area centred on Milan, the Lombard style prevailed, characterized by exterior arcaded decoration, the early Christian form of basilican-plan church with western narthex and atrium, and the cathedral group composed of three separate buildings: church, lofty bell tower and octagonal baptistery. The projecting portico was typical, its supporting columns often resting upon the backs of animals, usually lions or bulls (**286**); above was often an ornamental wheel window (**295**). Important examples include the cathedral groups at Parma (**300**, Cremona and Ferrara (**306**), the cathedrals of Modena and Piacenza, and the churches of S. Ambrogio, Milan (**302**), S. Zeno,

Verona (298) and S. Michele, Pavia.

Tuscan Romanesque was typical of central Italy, its influence extending from northern Tuscany south to Naples. Here the arcaded exterior decoration was the chief characteristic, as seen so vividly in the Pisa Cathedral group (p. 55). This is an area of great mineral wealth, particularly in white and coloured marbles and volcanic materials. Brick was extensively used for construction and this was then faced and ornamented with marble and mosaic, giving a colourful rather than plastic effect to the decoration. Buildings in Florence and Lucca show this particularly as in, for instance, the twelfth-century façade of the church of S. Miniato al Monte (293).

The third region, southern Italy and Sicily, produced an unique form of Romanesque architecture, which is an exciting blend of different cultures illustrating the turbulent history of this area. The Greeks had colonized the region (p. 9) and it was later dominated by the Byzantine culture from Constantinople, whose best craftsmen were Greek. The area was then held under Muslim domination, and finally conquered by the Normans – a different branch of the same Normans who conquered England in 1066. It was the Normans who built the magnificent cathedrals of Apulia and Sicily in the eleventh and twelfth centuries – Trani (297, 305), Troia (303), Molfetta (333), Bitonto (334, 342), Canosa, Cefalù (308, 309), and Monreale (339, 340). The buildings have much in common with the massive solidity of English Norman churches, but the Italian examples are wider and lower, more colourful, and decorated with carved sculpture, marbles and glittering mosaics. They also show Saracenic influence in their arches and vaults.

316 Beakhead and chevron ornament, west portal, Lincoln Cathedral. 1130-40

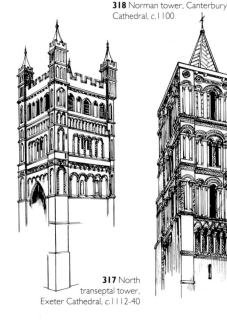

318 Norman tower, Canterbury Cathedral, c.1100

317 North transeptal tower, Exeter Cathedral, c.1112-40

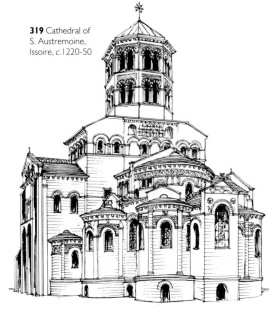

319 Cathedral of S. Austremoine, Issoire, c.1220-50

320 Capital 'Sins of Babylon', S. Pierre, Chauvigny, c.1120

Frederick led the Third Crusade to the Holy Land

1125–1137 Building of the west front of Rochester Cathedral, after completion of the nave

1126–1139 Building of Rochester Castle keep

1127 Roger II united the two Norman Kingdoms of Apulia and Sicily to become the Kingdom of the Two Sicilies

1128 Commencement of the building of the new abbey church at Dunfermline in Fife, Scotland

1128 Building begun of Kelso Abbey, Roxburghshire in Scotland

1130 Norman nave of Leominster Priory Church, Herefordshire, consecrated by Robert de Bethune, Bishop of Hereford

c.1130 Building of the round church at Cambridge, the Holy Sepulchre Church

1130–1150 Urnes stave church built on the banks of Luster Fjord in Norway. Believed to be the oldest surviving stave church. Carvings from an older church (273) are incorporated into the north wall

1133 Nave and aisles of Durham Cathedral completed and both stone vaulted. This nave vault, one of the earliest ribbed vaults in Europe, still stands today

1133–89 Under the rule of Henry II the Frankish jury system was adapted to create English Common Law and the foundation of this jury system was laid

c.1138 Foundation of Jedburgh

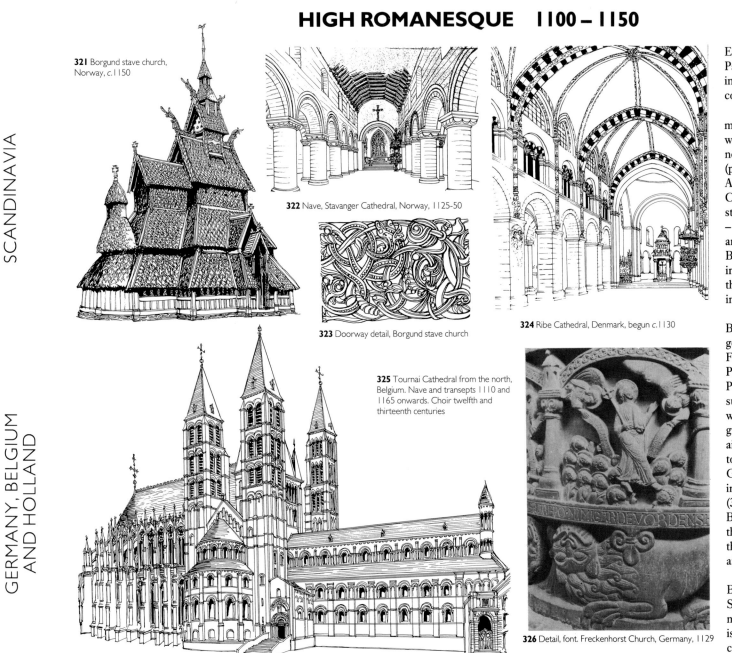

HIGH ROMANESQUE   1100 – 1150

321 Borgund stave church, Norway, c.1150

322 Nave, Stavanger Cathedral, Norway, 1125-50

323 Doorway detail, Borgund stave church

324 Ribe Cathedral, Denmark, begun c.1130

325 Tournai Cathedral from the north, Belgium. Nave and transepts 1110 and 1165 onwards. Choir twelfth and thirteenth centuries

326 Detail, font. Freckenhorst Church, Germany, 1129

Especially characteristic of this is the Palatine Chapel in Palermo, a truly unique interior, vividly patterned and glowing with colour (**299**).

In France the areas which produced the most distinctive and differing Romanesque work were, apart from Normandy and the north (p. 46) and Provence in the south (p. 56), Burgundy, Aquitaine, Poitou and the Auvergne. In Burgundy the influence of Cluny (p. 50) was strong, but the general style also owed a great deal to ancient Rome – as can be seen in the classical pilasters and articulation of Autun Cathedral (**314**). Burgundy is also rich in examples of imaginative and vigorous sculpture, of which the abbey church at Vézelay (especially its inner portal) is so remarkable (**313**).

In the western and central parts of France Byzantine forms of construction dominated general design. In parts of Anjou (at Fontevrault for instance), in Aquitaine at Périgueux and Angoulême, in Poitou at Poitiers and, similarly at Solignac, domes supported on pendentives or domical vaults were more common than timber roofs or groined vaults. Many such churches were aisleless, or the aisles were of a similar height to the nave and choir, so producing the German 'hall church' pattern (p. 92). In the impressive church of S. Front at Périgueux (**315**) – as elsewhere in this region – the Byzantine Greek cross plan, with domes over the crossing and all four arms, prevailed over the more usual Romanesque 'Latin cross' aisled design.

In the volcanic region of the Auvergne, Byzantine influence is shown – as in the Sicilian cathedrals at Monreale and Cefalù – more in decoration than construction. This is in the use of polychrome inlay of lava and coloured stone in diaper and striped designs.

The cathedrals at Le Puy and Issoire are superb examples of this, as is S. Pierre at Chauvigny (**320**).

The mast or stave wooden churches of Norway are now unique in Europe. They were built during the whole of the Middle Ages from the eleventh century onwards. Only a handful of the many hundreds constructed now survive (**449**).

The method of construction of these churches is unusual; each part of the building is self-supporting. The walls – the stave screens – do not take weight but rest – as prefabricated, self-contained units – upon timber ground sills. Supporting vertical poles – the masts – are fixed to these and the sills, and, in turn, with the aid of cross beams at the top, support the roof which is shingled on the exterior.

The whole church is tall, narrow and dark, but very decorative. Most of the good surviving examples are in the north, such as the churches at Borgund (**321**) and Urnes (**273**), both near the Sognfjord.

327 Husaby Church, Sweden, c.1150

328 Lund Cathedral, Sweden, c.1140

329 Corbel, Lund Cathedral, Sweden

330 Doorway capital, Stavanger Cathedral, Norway

331 Freckenhorst Abbey Church, Germany, 1116-29

332 St Mary's Church, Maastricht, Holland. East façade, c.1150

Abbey, Roxburghshire, Scotland

c.1140–1150 Carisbrooke Castle on the Isle of Wight built upon a motte

c.1140–1150 Building of the abbey church at Malmesbury

1148 Collapse of the Second Crusade

Twelfth century Development of the craft of cloth weaving in Flanders, centred upon Bruges and Ghent

Twelfth century Horse traction-harness had been developed and was in use in Europe

Twelfth century Canal systems with lift-locks being constructed in Flanders and Holland

SOUTHERN ITALY AND SICILY

SPAIN AND PORTUGAL

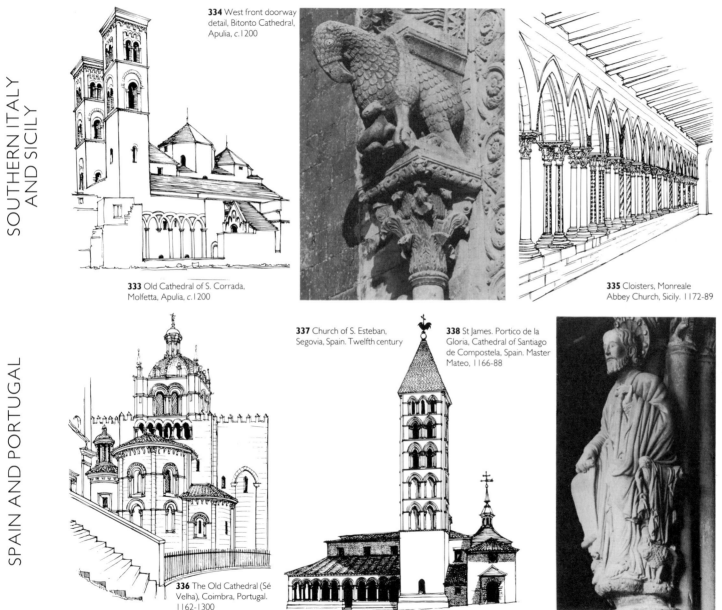

334 West front doorway detail, Bitonto Cathedral, Apulia, c.1200

333 Old Cathedral of S. Corrada, Molfetta, Apulia, c.1200

335 Cloisters, Monreale Abbey Church, Sicily. 1172-89

337 Church of S. Esteban, Segovia, Spain. Twelfth century

338 St James. Portico de la Gloria, Cathedral of Santiago de Compostela, Spain. Master Mateo, 1166-88

336 The Old Cathedral (Sé Velha), Coimbra, Portugal. 1162-1300

The war of reconquest against the Moors had begun in the Iberian Peninsular in 718, and by 1085 Christian Spain had forced a Muslim retreat as far south as Toledo. Because of the earlier Muslim dominance, and the remoteness of the area from the rest of Europe, new architectural ideas had been slow to penetrate and most eleventh-century Romanesque architecture had been plain and utilitarian. Exceptions to this were the pilgrimage churches built along the northern coastal route to Santiago (p. 44); these were mainly of French monastic origin, mounted by the Cluniac Order: S. Martìn, Fròmista, begun in 1066, is typical (**282**, **283**, **290**, **292**).

By the second half of the twelfth century a later, more mature Spanish Romanesque style was evolving, which continued well into the following century. There were a number of spheres of influence current, which resulted in stylistic variations from region to region. Christian building was limited to the northern half of the peninsula, but the more southerly of these areas were influenced by Muslim methods of construction and decoration which were, at this time, still of a higher standard of workmanship and design that that of purely Christian architecture.

Due to maritime trade with Italy from Catalonian ports, north-east Spain was strongly influenced by Lombard design. This can be seen in the bell towers, arcaded decoration and Roman detail of ornament and capitals, as in Perpignan Cathedral and the Abbey Church at Ripoll (**301**). A more mature Romanesque character is evidenced further south in central Spain in the churches of Segovia: S. Estebàn and S. Millàn are striking examples (**337**, **346**). In the north-western part of the peninsula there was a strong French influence as, for instance, at Zamora, where the central cupola is roofed in fish-tail design, in a similar manner to French buildings in Poitiers, Angoulême and Fontevrault (344 and p. 52). A few surviving Portuguese examples of Romanesque ecclesiastical building also show French influence as at, for instance, the Old Cathedral of Coimbra, though this building displays also Muslim and Byzantine features (336).

In eleventh- and twelfth-century Tuscany the area around the cities of Pisa and Lucca became an outstanding centre for art and architecture; artists and craftsmen were attracted there from all over Italy by the high quality of the work produced. The characteristic church of the region is noted for its decorative arcading which ornaments the exterior façades in rows of galleries one above the other (p. 47).

The most famous example of this type of work is the cathedral group in the Piazza dei Miracoli at Pisa. The four separate structures – baptistery, cathedral, bell tower and cemetery building – though constructed over the long period of 1063–1350, are all in a Romanesque style which displays a close affinity with classical Rome, and presents a homogeneous group built of gleaming white and coloured marble (347, 348).

The Pisan group is so superb that it overshadows the other contemporary work in the area, but only a little less magnificent are the three churches in Lucca: the cathedral, S. Michele and S. Frediano (351).

It was about the middle of the twelfth century, while countries such as Spain and Italy were creating buildings in a mature Romanesque form, that the first structures appeared in what we now term the Gothic style. This was in the small area surrounding the city of Paris called the Île de France.

339 Apsidal east end of Monreale Abbey Church, begun 1174. Limestone inlaid with black lava marble shafts

340 Cloister capital, Monreale

341 Nave capital, S. Pietro, Tuscania, southern Italy. Late twelfth century

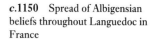

342 West porch, Bitonto Cathedral, c.1200

343 Portal, Old Cathedral, Coimbra, Portugal

344 Central cupola, Zamora Cathedral, Spain, c.1174

345 Wheel window, Meira Abbey Church, Spain. Late twelfth century

346 S. Millan, Segovia, Spain, c.1200

c.1150 Spread of Albigensian beliefs throughout Languedoc in France

1152 Severe earthquake in northern Syria

1154 Accession to the English throne of the Angevin Henry II, first of the Plantagenet kings

1157–60 Frederick Barbarossa's break with the Papacy

c.1160 Building begun of Laon Cathedral in France

1163 Commencement of building of the Cathedral of Notre Dame in Paris

1167 Formation of the Lombard League; a coalition of 16 cities in northern Italy which banded together to oppose the attempt of Frederick I (Barbarossa) to assert imperial authority over the communes

1170 Murder by four knights of Archbishop Thomas à Becket in Canterbury Cathedral

1174 William of Sens commissioned to rebuild the choir of Canterbury Cathedral after its destruction by fire

ECCLESIASTICAL ARCHITECTURE 1150 – 1200

347 The Cathedral group, Piazza dei Miracoli, Pisa. Baptistery 1152-1278, Cathedral 1063-1270, Bell tower (*Torre Pendente*) 1173-1350

348 Doorway capital detail, west façade, Pisa Cathedral, *c.*1270

350 West portico, Abbey Church of S. Gilles-du-Gard, *c.*1170

349 West porch, S. Trophîme, Arles, 1170-80

In general European Gothic architecture emerged gradually from the Romanesque, and the dates at which this happened varied greatly from country to country – 1135-40 in the Île de France, about 1175 in England but the late thirteenth century in Germany, and only a little earlier in Spain and Italy.

It is never easy to pinpoint precisely the birth of a new movement. Certainly the first buildings which characterized the Gothic style appeared near Paris, but it cannot be stated as categorically that if they had not been constructed here they would not have been created elsewhere. The Gothic style evolved because constructionally it became necessary, and this need sprang from the urgent problem of finding a means of roofing large churches with permanent fire-proof materials, so that the devastating fires to which timber roofs were heir would no longer destroy so much fine building.

Romanesque vaulting, like that of classical Rome, was of the tunnel-and-groined type. Construction was based on the round arch, and this form is insufficiently flexible for vaulting the differing heights and spans of nave, choir and aisles. To construct higher and wider vaults it was necessary to build ribbed quadripartite vaults, as had been done early in the twelfth century at Durham Cathedral (**310**). Such vaults are lighter in weight than groined vaults, since the ribs are constructed first over centering and a thinner infilling is added afterward. There is only a limited range of variations to the round arch, from stilted to segmental, and these proved inadequate for a complex vaulting system.

These difficulties were solved by the adoption of the pointed arch, which the French so aptly call the *arc brisé*; the broken arch. Such arches can be tall and narrow, equilateral (as when the width equals the height) or broader still. This flexibility made possible the development of ribbed vaulting over higher and higher spans.

The three chief characteristics of Gothic architecture are the pointed arch, the ribbed vault and the concomitant abutment system. None of these factors was new. The pointed arch, in particular, had long been used in Arab lands and had been introduced into areas of Europe subject to their influence – such as Spain, Sicily and Provence. It had also been used in construction elsewhere in, for example, Cistercian abbey churches – where it was preferred for its austere, clean lines – but was employed, without comprehension of its constructional possibilities, as an arcade supported on heavy Romanesque columns. This can be seen in such abbeys as Fountains or Rievaulx, and in Spain at Poblet or Meira, where a pointed arch continuous vault was also constructed. What was new in Gothic was the fusion of these constructional features into an original style of lofty and delicate complex stone structures, a style which evolved and advanced over a period of 400 years, adapting to the aesthetic and practical needs of the Christian Church of the time.

The likeliest reason for the initiation of the new architectural style in northern France was that here was an area which was comparatively peaceful and economically stable. A very early instance was the Abbey Church of S. Denis, built in the decade from 1135 by the Abbé Suger. Now in a Paris suburb, most of the church has been restored or rebuilt, but part of the original choir exists (355). Sens Cathedral, of similar date, has common features with S. Denis. The world-famous cathedrals of the Île de France area – Paris, Laon, Reims, Chartres – were all

351 S. Michele, Lucca, Tuscany, begun c.1140, façade c.1239

352 Palazzo Loredan, Venice, late twelfth century

353 Detail, S. Gilles-du-Gard

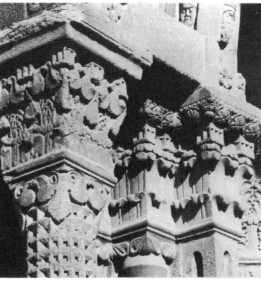

354 Portal detail, Cathedral of Le Puy, twelfth century

1174–84 The mason William the Englishman working on the rebuilding of the Canterbury Cathedral choir in the new Gothic style, part of this time under the direction of William of Sens

Twelfth century Sericulture flourished in Italy and Sicily. Lucca in Italy became the chief centre of the European silk industry

c.1180 Earliest recorded use of a windmill in western Europe, in Normandy. These early designs were post-mills

1180 Accession of Philip II to the French throne

c.1184–90 Approximate date of death of William of Tyre, archbishop of Tyre from 1175, and known especially for his history in 23 volumes *Historia rerum in partibus transmarinis gestarum*; this is an important source for the history of the Latin Kingdom 1127-84 and of the French crusaders of the years 1095-1184

1187 Sultan Saladin defeated the Christian armies at Hattin and took the ports of Jerusalem, Jaffa, Acre and Beirut

ECCLESIASTICAL ARCHITECTURE 1140 – 1200

FRANCE

355 Choir, Abbey Church of S. Denis, Paris, 1140-4

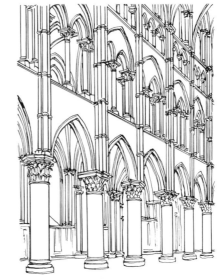

356 Jamb figure sculpture, central portal, façade, Chartres Cathedral, c.1150-5

357 Nave, Laon Cathedral, from 1170

ENGLAND

358 Orford Castle, Suffolk, c.1165

359 Trinity Chapel, Canterbury Cathedral, 1175-84

360 South doorway, Iffley Church, Oxon, c.1170

begun by the second half of the twelfth century. Collectively, and individually, they represent a contribution to the establishment of the Gothic style comparable to that of the Parthenon to Greek architecture and S. Sophia in Constantinople to Byzantine. These cathedrals were the prototypes for the whole evolution of northern Gothic architecture (356, 357, 361).

The equivalent pacesetter in the Gothic style in England is the choir of Canterbury Cathedral. This, the first Gothic structure in Britain, was mainly the work of a Frenchman, William of Sens, so-called after the town of his birth where he had watched the erection of the Gothic cathedral. Canterbury Cathedral was seriously damaged by fire in 1174 and William was asked to rebuild the choir. This he did in the new style. He directed operations until a fall from the scaffolding crippled him and he returned to France. The work was completed by another William, called 'the Englishman' to differentiate him. Canterbury Cathedral choir represented a revolutionary break with architectural tradition in England. Its clustered piers with slender column shafts and foliated capitals, its clerestory lancet windows, its ribbed high vault and its precise and lofty articulation are totally Gothic, with no hint of Romanesque ancestry (359).

The chief remains in secular architecture are castellar. There are many surviving tower keeps, a number in fair condition, of both shell and donjon or rectangular design. These castles were massively built with walls – some 15-20ft thick at base – into the thicknesses of which were constructed passages, garderobes and bedchambers. Wide flat buttresses strengthened the corners and faces. In Britain extant shell keeps include Cardiff (**280**, Windsor (Round Tower), York (Clifford's Tower), Lincoln, and Carisbrooke on the Isle of Wight. Rectangular keeps are more numerous. Among notable examples are the Tower of London (White Tower **257, 258**), Dover, Castle Hedingham (Essex), Rochester, and Castle Rising (Norfolk). Beaugency and Loches (Loire) are impressive French keeps of this type.

During the twelfth century a number of keeps were built on polygonal design, or with the square corners rounded off; this was to obviate the drawback of the rectangular keep, which was the corner blind spot suffered by the castle defenders. Provins Castle (Seine) was an early example of this. In England, Henry II's royal castle at Orford in Suffolk was a prototype of the new design. The central area was for living accommodation, and the three great towers for military and service use (**358**).

Comparatively few walled towns of this early date survive unaltered in Europe. A famous example is Carcassonne in France, which was a Roman town then, successively, Visigothic, Arab and Frankish. Most of its 53 towers and surrounding walls, which date from the twelfth and thirteenth centuries though to the nineteenth century, saw an extensive restoration by Viollet-le-Duc (**384**). Àvila in central Spain was an important town in the Middle Ages. Its city walls (86 towers) and 10 gateways built of granite are the most complete in Europe. Building of this fortification was begun in the eleventh century (**289**).

German Romanesque architecture, which had developed early from the Carolingian and Ottonian traditions (pp. 38-40) reached maturity during the twelfth century. The dramatic skyline of towers and lanterns,

361 Tympanum Sculpture, central doorway, façade, Chartres Cathedral, *c.*1150-5

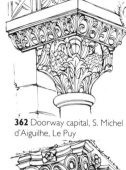

362 Doorway capital, S. Michel d'Aiguilhe, Le Puy

363 Capital, west portal, S. Trophîme, Arles

364 Doorway detail, Iffley Church

365 Great cellar (cellarium), Fountains Abbey, Yorkshire, *c.*1150-80

1189-92 Third Crusade to the Holy Land. An army of 100,000 men led by the elderly Emperor Frederick Barbarossa. The Emperor drowned in a mountain river on 10 June 1190

1190–2 Personal glory won by Richard I of England (*Coeur de Lion*) in the Third Crusade

1193 Death of Saladin

1194 Building of Chartres Cathedral in France begun

1195 Death of Herrad von Landsberg, Alsatian Abbess of Hohenburg (Odilienberg). A woman of great learning and author of *Hortus Deliciarium*, a book in which she had compiled the sum of current knowledge in art, history, geography, theology, philosophy and astronomy

Late twelfth century Growth of the Hanseatic League centred on Lübeck (Germany); a medieval confederation of German cities and merchant guilds for trade in the Baltic coastal region which, by the fourteenth century, had expanded to include Scandinavia, Poland, Holland and Belgium

366 Kalundborg Church, Denmark, late twelfth century

368 Round church at Bjernede, Denmark, 1150-75

367 S. Gereon, Cologne, Germany, east end, c.1160

369 Church of the Apostles, Cologne, Germany. East end, c.1190-1200

370 Mainz Cathedral from the north-east, Germany. 1085-1239. Central tower, 1361

371 Worms Cathedral from the south-west, Germany, c.1170-c.1230

already established, evolved further. Another characteristic of German design was to build an apse at the west end of the church as well as at the east. This deprived masons and sculptors of the opportunity to provide (as was so in France and England) a richly ornamented western portal, so the main entrance became a lateral transeptal one. The cathedrals of Worms, Speyer and Mainz are like this (**272, 370, 371**). Circular towers are not common in European Romanesque architecture, except in northern Italy, but were often constructed on German cathedrals, as at Worms and Mainz. The helm type of roof covering to the square or polygonal tower was another feature of German churches. This was particularly so in the Rhineland area as at, for example, the Church of the Apostles in Cologne (**369**).

In some parts of Germany, notably further south as at Regensburg, some churches boast richly sculptured Romanesque portals, of the kind to be seen in France and northern Italy, which represent biblical scenes, animals and monsters depicted in high relief. The Schottenportal on the church of S. Jakob in the city is a fine example (**374, 375**). The Romanesque portal on the Gothic Minster in Basel is similarly sculptured (**372**).

In the Low Countries, Dutch Romanesque architecture has much in common with German, though churches are generally less tall; St Mary's Church in Maastricht is characteristic (**332**). Tournai Cathedral in Belgium is a magnificent example of medieval architecture which, although altered and added to in later ages, remains one of the finest Romanesque buildings in Europe (**325**). The choir is in Gothic style, but the long nave remains Romanesque, while the apsidal transepts are in a transitional form, as are the five towers. The exterior, largely built of black Tournai marble, is an impressive structure.

In Scandinavia, wood continued to be the predominant building material during the Middle Ages (p. 53). Masonry was used for very important ecclesiastical structures, especially in the south where designers were strongly influenced by foreign sources – France, Germany, England, Italy. Lund Cathedral in Sweden (328, 329), Stavanger Cathedral in Norway (322) and Ribe Cathedral in Denmark (324) are characteristic. Some churches followed the German fortified west front design; Husaby, for example (327). Kalundborg Church in Denmark is unusual in that it is centrally planned on the Greek cross pattern: a Scandinavian version of a Byzantine theme (366). Round churches, based on eastern European pattern, were typical of parts of Denmark, especially the Island of Bornholm (368).

372 Detail, Galluspforte, Basel Minster, Switzerland, late twelfth century

373 Font, Löderup Church, Sweden, late twelfth century

374 Church of S. Jakob, Regensburg, Germany (Schottenkirche), c.1180

375 Detail of Doorway (Schottenportal)

Late twelfth century In Europe the armoured suit of chain mail began to be reinforced by additional defences of quilted fabric, hardened leather or metal plates at knees, shins, elbows and chest

1198 Founding in Acre of the Order of Teutonic Knights who, at that time, dedicated themselves to the tending of the sick in Palestine

1198 Innocent III becomes Pope. He imposed a high level of papal power and authority

c.1200 Making of inlaid paving tiles developed in France

ECCLESIASTICAL ARCHITECTURE   1200 – 1250

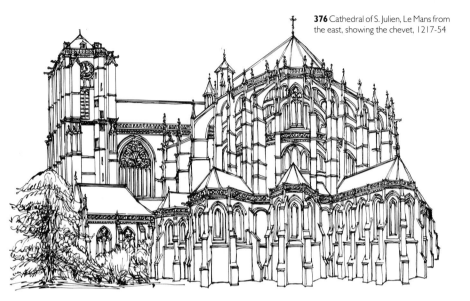

376 Cathedral of S. Julien, Le Mans from the east, showing the chevet, 1217-54

377 Jamb figure, central portal of façade, Reims Cathedral, c.1240

378 Virgin on trumeau of central portal of façade, Reims Cathedral, thirteenth century

379 Bourges Cathedral interior, early thirteenth century

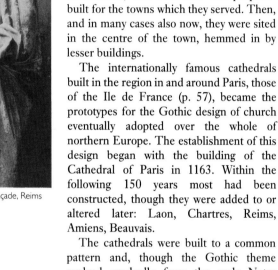

380 West front Amiens Cathedral, 1220-88

In northern and central France a stupendous number of cathedrals and large churches were constructed during the thirteenth century. The majority of these, unlike their English counterparts, were not monastic foundations, but were new and purpose-built for the towns which they served. Then, and in many cases also now, they were sited in the centre of the town, hemmed in by lesser buildings.

The internationally famous cathedrals built in the region in and around Paris, those of the Ile de France (p. 57), became the prototypes for the Gothic design of church eventually adopted over the whole of northern Europe. The establishment of this design began with the building of the Cathedral of Paris in 1163. Within the following 150 years most had been constructed, though they were added to or altered later: Laon, Chartres, Reims, Amiens, Beauvais.

The cathedrals were built to a common pattern and, though the Gothic theme evolved gradually from the early Notre Dame of Paris to the later Beauvais, so giving a different character to each building, the general features were similar. The cathedrals are cruciform, with slightly projecting transepts, and have an apsidal termination to the eastern arm. All are lofty, with high vaults supported by flying buttress schemes. Numerous chapels are set in or project from the walls, particularly so round the eastern apse; so creating the characteristic French chevet, of which Le Mans Cathedral with its 13 chapels is such a notable example. In this type of design there is an interior ambulatory extending round behind the high altar, so giving access all round the church – at least at choir and triforium levels. Between the bays are set semicircular chapels, lending to the exterior an appearance of a gladiolus corm growing its smaller new corms round its base. This is shown clearly in the ground plan of Le Mans (383). Between the chapels springs a forest of flying buttresses (376, 381).

By the thirteenth century masons were becoming more knowledgeable and experienced. They still worked empirically and often over-compensated for safety, building thicker walls and vaults than were actually necessary. They were erecting immense structures and each new building, as time passed, was larger, taller and of greater complexity than its predecessors. As a proportion of total building activity, collapses were not common and, when they occurred, the masons learned from the mistakes made. The outstanding among them travelled great distances in Europe, building, teaching and influencing those in the areas which they visited. French vaults were particularly high and each success led to the next one being higher still; so that the nave of Notre Dame, Paris is 115ft high, Reims 120ft, Amiens 144ft and the choir of Beauvais 157ft (the nave was never built).

The cathedrals were intended to have several towers, most crowned with spires, but few – apart from the western ones – were built, and even fewer of the spires. Partly this was due to the cost, but mainly it was because French cathedrals were so lofty that experience showed that adding towers, especially over the crossing, was too great an engineering hazard. At Beauvais, for example, a 500ft spire collapsed in 1573. An exception is Laon Cathedral, where five towers were built out of the seven planned; there is also the earlier example of Tournai Cathedral in Belgium (p. 60).

381 Apse flying buttress, Reims Cathedral, 1210

382 Circular window, plate tracery, Chartres Cathedral, 1196-1216

383 Ground plan, Le Mans Cathedral

384 Outer walls and towers, Carcassonne, thirteenth century. Restored nineteenth century

1200–25   Rediscovery of the works of Aristotle. His complete works translated into Latin. One of the leading scholars in this task was Robert Grosseteste, Chancellor of Oxford University (1215-21) and Bishop of Lincoln (from 1235)

1204   Sack of Constantinople

1204   King John of England founded the naval dockyard at Portsmouth

1200–30   Flowering of German epic poetry as in, for example, the *Niebelungenlied* (the story of Siegfried and Brunhilde), Gottfried von Strassburg's *Tristan* and Wolfram von Eschenbach's *Parzifal*. The Minnesingers (aristocratic travelling minstrels) were noted exponents of the presentation of popular poetry and song. Famous among them were Walter von der Vogelweide and Reinwar von Hagenau

*c.*1200–59   Matthew Paris, English medieval historian. Historiographer at monastery of St Albans for the *Chronica Majora*, a record of English history kept at the monastery

1207–31   St Elisabeth of Hungary, who spent her short life in humble service to the poor at Marburg in Germany. She was canonized in 1235

*c.*1210   Roger Bacon born near Ilchester. Became a Franciscan friar and a pupil of Robert Grosseteste. A philosopher and scientist who helped to lay the foundations of the modern approach to science

1208–65   Simon de Montfort. Anglo-French baronial leader

ECCLESIASTICAL ARCHITECTURE   1200 – 1250

GERMANY AND SCANDINAVIA

ENGLAND

385 Trondheim Cathedral, Norway, from the east, 1183-1248

386 Church of S. Quirin, Neuss, Germany. West front begun c.1209, tower c.1230

387 The prophets, St George's choir, Bamberg Cathedral, Germany. 1220-30

388 The crossing, Wells Cathedral, 1192-1230

389 Ripon Minster, west front doorway, 1220-30

390 Detached tower, West Walton Church, Norfolk. Thirteenth century

391 Thirteenth-century broach spire

The Ile de France cathedrals are storehouses of magnificent craftsmanship. The rapport between masons, carpenters, glaziers, painters and metalworkers was complete and satisfying – but no craftsman was of more vital importance than the sculptor. Carvers and modellers enjoyed freedom of expression, and were presented with an immense architectural canvas upon which to experiment and design. In this field French sculptors were supreme. The principle vehicle for this sculptural and architectural expression was the Gothic western façade, in a pattern set in the Ile de France cathedrals (**380**). It was a twin-towered façade, with triple portico at the base spreading across the whole width of the elevation; above was a galleried band of sculptured figures, surmounted by the great central circular widow (**382**). In these cathedrals the whole façade was symbolically sculptured, but it was the portals which were the focus of the design. Here, jamb and trumeau figures, tympanum scenes and archivolt groups all played their part in relating the Bible story from Old and New Testaments. The style of the sculpture developed rapidly between 1150 and 1250; the earlier work represented at Chartres evincing a formal approach with vertical emphasis, especially in the figure drapery (**356**), while the Virgin and Child on the trumeau of the central portal at Reims illustrates a softer, more naturalistic feeling (**377, 378**).

The cathedral interiors present a stone framework for the carving and coloured glass. All the cathedrals have fine glass, but Chartres is most justly famed for its magnificent glasswork. In contrast to the heavier, more solid Romanesque cathedrals, the Gothic interior is characterized by tall,

64

slender-shafted piers soaring upwards to finish in tiny foliated or moulded capitals (**397**). The nave and choir arcades are lofty, with pointed arches. Above are the arcaded triforium and large clerestory windows. The vault is of simple quadripartite ribbed design with ridge rib. Some cathedrals have three aisles, some five (**379**).

England was the only other European country to be building almost entirely in an established Gothic style in this century. English Gothic architecture is only rarely sculptural. Carved decoration was confined mainly to capitals and tympana: the decoration is architectural rather than sculptural. Nonetheless, the English work is as fine, in its way, as the French. Apart from the ornamental treatment, the English Gothic cathedral differs from the French chiefly in its proportions. The English nave and choir are wider and lower than their French counterparts. With the exception of Westminster Abbey – which with an internal height of 103ft, was strongly influenced in its building by French practice – the English examples are less than two-thirds the height of the French. Compare, for example, Lincoln Cathedral, with a height of 74ft and Wells at 67ft with Amiens at 144ft. The difference which this makes in appearance to the interior may be seen by studying the drawing of Wells (**388**) and Bourges (**379**). These proportions are also notable in their effect upon the exterior western façades. At Ripon Minster and Peterborough Cathedral (**400**), for instance, the design is wider and lower than at Amiens (**380**). The portals are architecturally handled, not sculptured, and there is no emphasis on flanking towers (**389**). Only at Wells and Lincoln are sculptured façades developed, and these are screens bearing little relationship to the form of the building behind them.

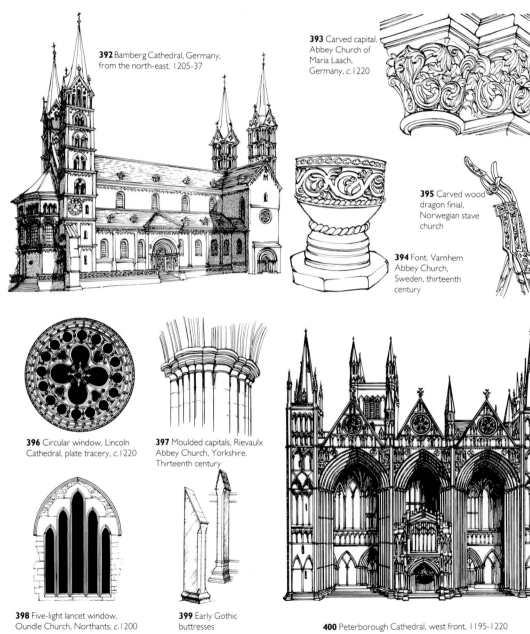

392 Bamberg Cathedral, Germany, from the north-east. 1205-37

393 Carved capital. Abbey Church of Maria Laach, Germany, c.1220

395 Carved wood dragon finial, Norwegian stave church

394 Font. Varnhem Abbey Church, Sweden, thirteenth century

396 Circular window, Lincoln Cathedral, plate tracery, c.1220

397 Moulded capitals, Rievaulx Abbey Church, Yorkshire. Thirteenth century

398 Five-light lancet window, Oundle Church, Northants, c.1200

399 Early Gothic buttresses

400 Peterborough Cathedral, west front, 1195-1220

1209   A university established at Cambridge

1215   Signing of Magna Carta by King John at Runnymede

1212–50   Frederick II Holy Roman Emperor and King of Germany and Sicily. Born in Italy, but his capital was at the then great city of Palermo in Sicily. Frederick undertook the modernization of southern Italy and Sicily. He established a new legal code, sponsoring and encouraging science and medicine. In 1224 he founded the University of Naples, the first state university of western Europe

1220–50   Expansion of the Hanseatic League into a trading union of nearly a hundred towns as far afield as Riga, Tallinn and Novgorod

1231–5   Pope Gregory IX formally established and defined the procedures of the medieval Inquisition

c.1225–74   St Thomas Aquinas born in southern Italy. Joined the Dominican order 1243. Outstanding scholar, philosopher and theologian. Canonized 1323

c.1235   Villard de Honnecourt, architectural designer and mason from the Cambrai area of northern France, prepared his textbook for teaching his students on the subjects of masonry, figure sculpture, carpentry, architectural draughtsmanship and geometry. This book survives and is preserved in the National Library in Paris. The book is a priceless record of a mason's work in the thirteenth century and illustrates the many buildings which its author visited. It also

ECCLESIASTICAL ARCHITECTURE   1200 – 1250

ITALY AND YUGOSLAVIA

SPAIN AND PORTUGAL

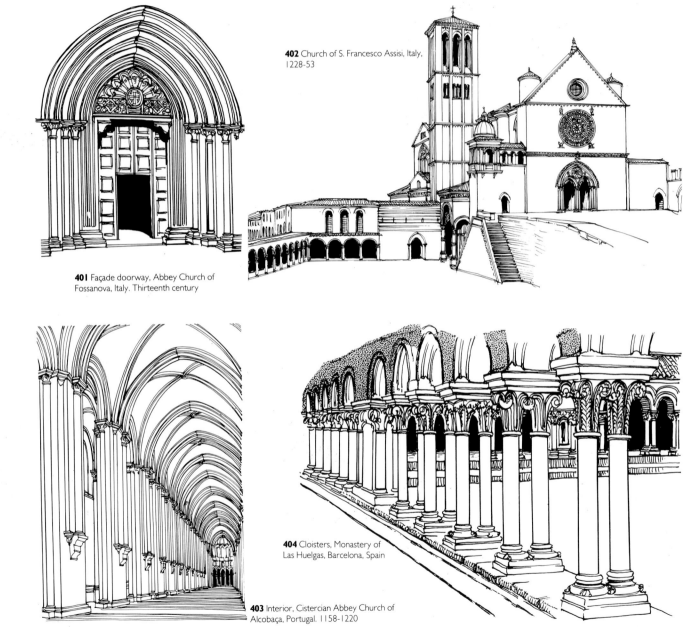

401 Façade doorway, Abbey Church of Fossanova, Italy. Thirteenth century

402 Church of S. Francesco Assisi, Italy, 1228-53

404 Cloisters, Monastery of Las Huelgas, Barcelona, Spain

403 Interior, Cistercian Abbey Church of Alcobaça, Portugal. 1158-1220

Due to the lower vaults, the English needed to employ less elaborate abutment at this date (**399**). The eastern arm of the cathedral was commonly square, and there was no chevet with its concomitant flying buttresses. Furthermore, due to the lower vaults, the English found it safe to build tall towers (**390**), many with spires. Most of the spires of this century were of broach type, where pyramidal buttresses (broaches) were built up the sides of the spire, supported at base upon squinches inside the corners of the towers (**391**).

English vaults, unlike the French, were generally designed with a longitudinal ridge rib, where decorative bosses concealed its junction with ribs rising from the vaulting shaft. Where French vaults of this period were usually quadripartite, in England tierceron ribs were being introduced as at Lincoln Cathedral (p. 70). Windows at this time were mostly of lancet form, that is, tall lights covered by a pointed arch, and employed singly or in groups of three, five or seven encompassed under one arch (**398**). Circular windows of plate tracery were also characteristic, as in France (**382, 396**).

In most other European countries building, both ecclesiastical and secular, continued in the Romanesque style. An exception to this was in Norway, where the larger stone churches showed a marked English influence. This was largely because the mountain barrier between Norway and the rest of Scandinavia was so formidable to early medieval travellers that the access for trade purposes by sea to Britain was easier. The most important Gothic building of this time in Norway was Trondheim Cathedral, which, though extensively rebuilt in later ages, retains some of the early medieval characteristics. The steeples, in particular, show English influence (**385**).

ARCHITECTURE   1200 – 1250

South of the alps the monastic Orders, influenced by Burgundian France, were also building in early Gothic style, as may be seen in the interior of the Cistercian abbey church at Alcobaça in Portugal (**403**), and a not dissimilar Cistercian abbey church in Italy at Fossanova (**401**, **407**). Probably better known is the Franciscan double church at Assisi (**402**). Here the exterior is of simple Gothic design, but the interior is more characteristically Italian in its colourful mosaic and fresco decoration.

In Germany the Romanesque architectural style had been so successfully adopted that it lingered on for much of the thirteenth century. Bamberg and Naumburg Cathedrals are examples of this (**386**, **387**, **392**, **393**).

In Spain, Italy and Yugoslavia buildings were mainly Romanesque (**404**, **408**, **409**, **410**, **411**) and were also, in many instances, strongly Roman influenced. For castle building in Italy, the Emperor Frederick II incorporated ancient Roman military symmetry into the ultra-modern medieval concept of a concentric defence system (p. 75-6), as can be seen, for instance, in his Castel del Monte in Basilicata. The principal doorway here is of classical design (**405**, **406**).

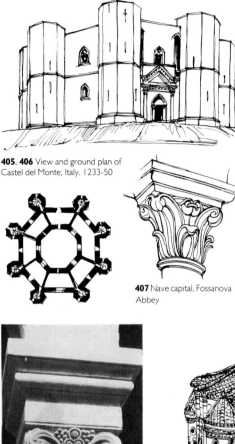

405, **406** View and ground plan of Castel del Monte, Italy. 1233-50

407 Nave capital, Fossanova Abbey

408 Porch column support. Trogir Cathedral, Yugoslavia *c.*1240

demonstrates the extensive travelling undertaken by masons, leading to a rapid exchange of ideas and knowledge

*c.*1250   Early mention and illustration of a screw-jack, for lifting loads (from de Honnecourt's book)

Thirteenth century   Returning crusaders introduced into western Europe a knowledge of modern castle building and fortification, eastern science and arts, and a variety of beautiful colourful fabrics greatly prized by the aristocratic classes

409 Cloister capital. Poblet Monastery, Spain. Thirteenth century

410 Central cupola. Collegiate Church of S. Maria, Toro, Spain, *c.*1250

411 Cloister capital, Poblet Monastery

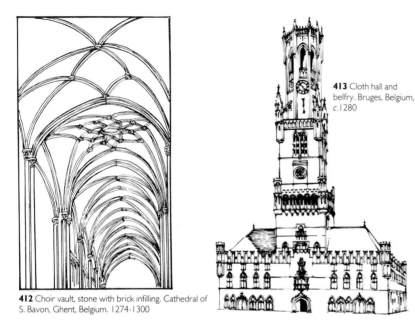

412 Choir vault, stone with brick infilling. Cathedral of S. Bavon, Ghent, Belgium. 1274-1300

413 Cloth hall and belfry. Bruges, Belgium, c.1280

414 Tympanum, façade central portal. Strasbourg Cathedral, France. 1276-1318

415 Angel in the Annunciation, façade central portal, Reims Cathedral. 1250-60

416 Church of the Jacobins, Toulouse, c.1300. Hall church in brick and stone.

Although in the second half of the thirteenth century the Gothic style was beginning to be established generally in Europe, only in France and England were its forms being built with confidence; a confidence which stemmed now from wide experience. In the Ile de France the cathedral pattern was fully developed, and the great churches of the area were being completed. The high vaults, the twin-towered western façades and flying buttress schemes were integrated into a single, yet elaborate, design. Particularly typical were the eastern chevet with its chapels, and forest of flying buttresses, and the superb giant rose windows illuminating the upper part of the transept façades (**418**, **421**). The sculptural decoration had also reached a zenith of artistic and technical quality; Reims Cathedral exemplifies this superb craftsmanship (**415**).

Elsewhere in France, regional differences are apparent. In Normandy, for instance, though the church plan and arrangement of its parts are similar to the buildings of the Ile de France, the style is simpler, almost austere, as is evinced at Coutances Cathedral (**419**), where the tall steeples are more English than French in their height and severity. In the south-east, Alsace, on the other hand, the variation is due to the proximity of German influence. Strasbourg Cathedral is characteristic. Though basically a German cathedral, mainly built by Germans, it clearly owes a great deal to the influence of French cathedral design. The western façade, of thirteenth-century date, is traditionally French – with its triple portal and magnificent rose window above – but its openwork stone tower (only one was ever built) is of classic German type, and was designed by Urich d'Ensingen. Sadly, considerable damage was done to the rich

ECCLESIASTICAL ARCHITECTURE 1250 – 1300

façade sculpture during the French Revolution – but this has been excellently restored (414, 417).

In the later twelfth century, early Gothic church architecture in England was strongly influenced by the French prototypes – but, by 1250, design and form were showing a fundamental divergence from the Continental version. The narrow strip of sea between Britain and France was sufficient to impede the easy passage of ideas. Britain was isolated from Continental thought, and was evolving national characteristics in architecture. One major difference (as discussed on p. 65) was in the building of lower, wider structures, with consequently less need for elaborate flying buttress systems. Another notable variation is in the square eastern termination.

In France a thirteenth-century cathedral was designed as one unified scheme. Though building may have continued over a very long period, the original concept was carried through. In England the approach was in sections, one part evolving from those already built or being built. Partly this was due to the fact that the country possessed such a wealth of large Romanesque churches that these were only gradually Gothicized, but this was not the complete answer because Salisbury Cathedral, the supreme example of the thirteenth-century Early English style, was built almost entirely in a single building operation between 1220 and 1258, yet shows the same characteristics as, for example, Lincoln or Wells.

One feature resulting from this type of building approach was the development of a double transept; a second was the square eastern end. Both were developments suited to ecclesiastical and artistic convenience. The gradual establishment in England of the

417 Rose window of west façade. Strasbourg Cathedral, France. 1277

418 East end, Amiens Cathedral, France. 1258-70

419 Apse flying buttresses. Coutances Cathedral. Thirteenth century

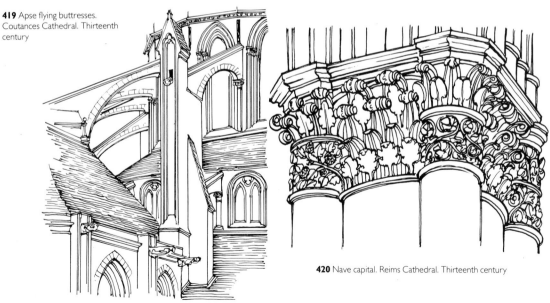

420 Nave capital. Reims Cathedral. Thirteenth century

c.1206–1280 Albertus Magnus, Dominican monk and an outstanding scholar of the Middle Ages. Albertus wrote widely on many subjects – philosophy, theology and the natural sciences. He pioneered studies of the experimental sciences

Thirteenth century The remainder of the famous Icelandic sagas, and also the great Icelandic poetry, mythology and history which had been handed down orally since the tenth and eleventh centuries, were written out on vellum

c.1220–1284 Nicola Pisano, Italian sculptor from the south who, with his son Giovanni Pisano (c.1250-1314) of Pisa, adapted the classical tradition of Tuscan sculpture with the current Gothic phase and blended the two into an original proto-Renaissance style. Nicola designed and carved the marble pulpit in the baptistery at Pisa (1259), and subsequently the pulpit in Siena Cathedral (1265-9). Giovanni assisted his father at Siena, and also worked with him on the façade of the Pisa baptistery. He is best known for his façade of Siena Cathedral, designed and carried out when he was architect in charge there (1287-96), and his superb pulpit in Pisa Cathedral (1302-10), which is an inspired marriage of classical and Gothic forms

Thirteenth century Brick-making and clay-tile-making were being practised in the Low Countries. By the end of the century, knowledge of these crafts had permeated the whole Baltic coastal region from Holland to Russia. This wide coastal plain was flat and partially wooded, and contained little

ECCLESIASTICAL ARCHITECTURE   1250 – 1300

421 Cathedral of Notre Dame, Paris, from the south-west. 1180-1330

422 Church choir, Rievaulx Abbey, Yorkshire, England, c1230-60

424 Geometrical tracery. Chapter house, Salisbury Cathedral, c.1270-80

423 Tierceron vault, nave, Lincoln Cathedral, c.1240-60

425 South transept. York Minister. Completed c.1260

square termination instead of the French chevet came about by first building transepts east of the main transepts, and then extending the central arm further east as a square-ended Lady Chapel; a design characteristic of Salisbury, and elsewhere (**426**).

In England Gothic architecture progressed through several phases between the thirteenth-century lancet or Early English style* and the later fifteenth-century designs. These different phases may be recognized from their decorative ornament, their window tracery, the form of arch used and the design of stone vaulting. English vaulting, particularly in the earlier years, is more varied than Continental versions. In the mid thirteenth century, French vaults continued to be largely of the quadripartite type without a ridge rib, while in England the intermediate rib, called a tierceron, had been introduced: an early example is the nave vault at Lincoln Cathedral (**423**). Tierceron ribs extend from the vault-springing to the ridge rib where the junction is covered by a decoratively carved boss. This type of vault is more decorative than the French version, but marks the division of the church into bays less clearly.

Window tracery is one of the principal features of Gothic architecture. Romanesque windows had been small and narrow, partly for defensive reasons and partly because of the fear of weakening the wall too greatly (p. 169). During the early thirteenth century, with improved security and the increased skill and experience of the

*In 1817 Thomas Rickman designated the various styles of Gothic architecture in England. His terms were Early English (c.1180-1275), Decorated (c.1275-1375) and Perpendicular (c.1375-1530) (see p. 169).

builders, window openings became larger and lancet designs, arranged singly or in groups, were built (p. 66 and **398**). From these lancet designs evolved tracery. When a group of lancets were encompassed under one arch they created a space above – the spandrel – which was an awkward feature of design. This was overcome by piercing the solid stone spandrel into carved circular or quatrefoil shapes. This earliest form is called plate tracery (**382, 396**). The stonework is comparatively solid and the pierced holes are cusped.

From plate tracery evolved bar tracery. In this the volume of glass was larger, and the volume of stonework smaller; dividing up the increasingly elaborate designs with bands or bars of stone. Window openings then became wider, and were divided vertically by stone mullions, so creating a larger window head which was designed in geometric form; the bars shaping circles, trefoils and quatrefoils. The earliest instances of bar tracery were at Reims Cathedral in France (built between 1210 and 1220), and these were soon followed by more elaborate four-light designs at Amiens Cathedral. In the second half of the century English windows with geometrical tracery were being designed, as at Salisbury Cathedral (**424**).

Colour was an integral part of Gothic architecture, walls and carved stonework being painted in bold colour schemes, though little remains of this today. What does survive in quantity, however, is the richness of the coloured window glass, to be seen at its best in the superb-quality craftsmanship at Chartres Cathedral in France and León Cathedral in Spain (**433**). Thirteenth-century glass, at least until the last quarter of the century, is noted for its glowing colours and sparkling appearance:

426 Salisbury Cathedral, England, 1234-58. Tower and spire 1334-80

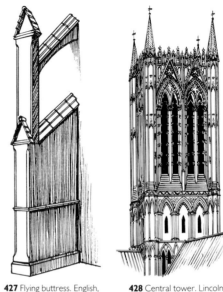

427 Flying buttress. English, thirteenth century

428 Central tower. Lincoln Cathedral, c.1240-1311

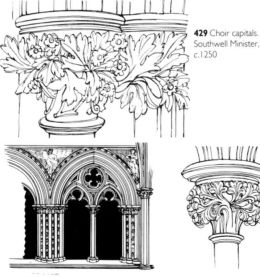

429 Choir capitals. Southwell Minister, c.1250

430 Triforium. Angel choir, Lincoln Cathedral, c.1260-80

431 Capital detail from 430

432 Choir capital. Lincoln Cathedral, c.1250

building stone. Brick was the ideal permanent material for construction and, as time passed, builders became expert in developing a Gothic style suited to it

*c.*1240–1302 Giovanni Cimabue was the thirteenth-century leader of the Florentine school of painting, which was developing a new style which interpreted the current thought of Humanism and the Renaissance

*c.*1255–1319 Duccio di Buoninsegna, with the Lorenzetti brothers and Simone Martini (*c.*1283-1344), led a similar movement in the Sienese school of painting

*c.*1254–1324 Marco Polo, the Italian traveller and first European to cross the Continent of Asia, recorded his journeyings in the book *The Travels of Marco Polo*; this was originally entitled *Description of the World*. His journey across the mountain and desert terrain of Asia lasted three and a half years, until he reached Shangtu, the summer capital of Kublai Khan. Polo then made further journeys, including one to Peking. His book covers a much wider spectrum than just an account of his travels; it deals with scientific inventions and discoveries, such as gunpowder and oil, and information upon animal and plant life as well as local customs and forms of government

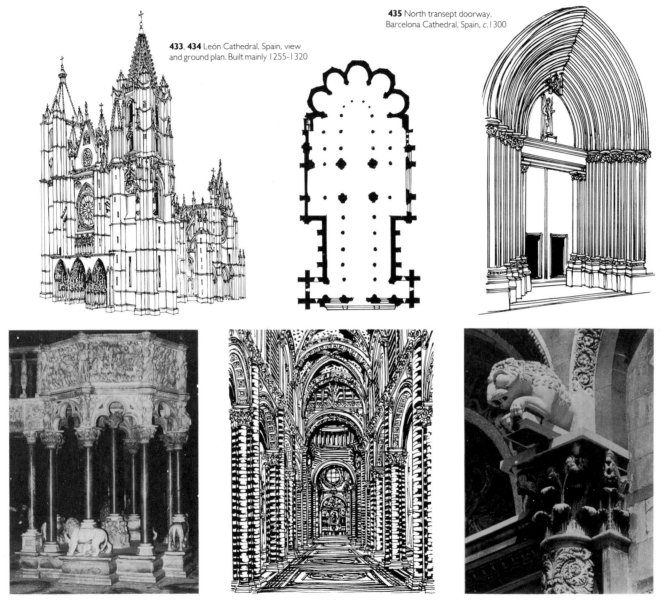

435 North transept doorway. Barcelona Cathedral, Spain, c.1300

433, **434** León Cathedral, Spain, view and ground plan. Built mainly 1255-1320

SPAIN AND ITALY

ITALY

436 Pulpit. Siena Cathedral. Nicola Pisano, 1265-9

437 Siena Cathedral interior, 1245 onwards

438 Doorway capital detail. Façade, Pisa Cathedral, c.1270

both Canterbury and Lincoln Cathedrals contain some of this work.

The years 1260-1325 are also renowned for the quality and the beauty of grisaille glass. This is largely in monochrome, usually silvery grey, hence its name, from French *gris* (grey). Several reasons have been advanced for the lack of colour used in this type of glass. One suggestion is that it was an economy measure, another that it stemmed from Cistercian influence, as evidence of the chosen austerity of this monastic order. The best grisaille glass is the most decorative; it is drawn in an almost three-dimensional manner. A famous, large and particularly fine English example is that of the Five Sisters Window (*c*.1250) in York Minster: each of these five lancets is 50ft high.

A greater variety and richness is to be seen in the capitals of the later thirteenth century. Magnificently carved examples showing great vitality appeared early in Reims Cathedral (**420**), but in England it was not until the early Gothic work was merging into that of the mid-term Decorated period that the vigorous, richly carved capitals were produced. Most of these are foliated, the stiff-leaved designs where the stalks stand apart from the capital bell giving way later to foliage falling in heavy clusters. Most famous and characteristic are the vine leaf capitals of Southwell Minster and those of the Angel Choir in Lincoln Cathedral (**429**, **430**, **431**, **432**).

Between 1250 and 1300 the Gothic style was gradually being adopted in those areas of Europe where Romanesque forms had lingered late; in Italy, Spain and the German-speaking regions. Italian Gothic architecture is very different from that of other European countries. Its form was governed by the climate – so unlike that of northern Europe – and even more by Italian traditions and available building and decorative materials. The classical tradition of ancient Rome, which had so strongly influenced and controlled Italian Romanesque work, continued to dictate to the Gothic style. The pointed arch was adopted, and also Gothic ornament, but most churches remained basilican in form, roofed with timber more often than stone vaults. A tall nave arcade was built, but rarely a triforium. The west front was in fact literally a façade, a vehicle for decoration bearing little relationship to the form of the church behind it. Sculpture was more often in relief than in the round, or even replaced by pictorial mosaic.

The best known Gothic work of the later thirteenth century is in Tuscany and the area round the expanding empire of Venice. Buildings were of brick rather than stone, sheathed in dazzling white and coloured marbles enriched by mosaic. Domes or lanterns were preferred to towers and spires, though most cathedrals possessed the characteristically Italian tall, separate campanile. The cathedrals of Florence, Siena and Orvieto are typical of the finest work. In all of these the marble veneer creates an essentially classical feeling imposed upon Gothic architecture: a surprisingly successful blend of two such different architectural styles (**437, 438, 483, 484**). In some of the craftsmanship, that of Nicola Pisano for example, the classical features look forward to the Renaissance, rather than back to ancient Rome (**436**).

Less richly ornamented, but fine examples of high quality Italian Gothic architecture, are some of the churches of the northern Veneto region; for instance S.S. Giovanni e Paolo in Venice (**441**) and the Basilica of

439 Palazzo Pubblico, Siena, Italy. 1288-1309

440 Basilica of S. Antonio, Padua, Italy. 1232-1307

441 Church of S.S. Giovanni and Paolo, Venice. 1234-1390

442 Castello Nuovo, Naples. 1279-82

Thirteenth century   First colleges founded at Oxford and Cambridge, to provide food and maintenance for scholars who needed these. At Oxford, Balliol dates from 1261, Merton 1263 and Peterhouse at Cambridge from 1284

Thirteenth century   Knowledge of the technique of tin-glazing earthenware had been brought to Spain from the Middle East, where it was made from this time. In this process tin oxide was added to the glaze, so making it white and opaque; virtually an enamel. The white ware provided an ideal surface for painting designs in colour. The island of Majorca became a centre for this ceramic industry, from where the products were exported. This gave rise to the name of the ware as majolica or maiolica

Thirteenth century   Knowledge and practice of wood-panelled construction reached Germany and the Low Countries. This panel-and-frame type of construction was used to line walls and to make furniture

Thirteen century   Lustre ceramic ware introduced into Spain from Egypt

SCANDINAVIA

GERMANY

443 Skara Cathedral, Sweden, c.1300

444 The nave. Trondheim Cathedral, Norway. 1235-90

445 Interior, Uppsala Cathedral, Sweden. 1270-1315

446 St Mary's Church, Lübeck

447 St Mary's Church, Lübeck. 1251-1302

S. Antonio in Padua. Despite its late date, this basilica shows considerable Byzantine influence, as in its many domes supported upon pendentives (**440**). Medieval Italy also produced a wealth of civic architecture of similar form, for the seats of government of wealthy city states of the peninsula. The Palazzo Pubblico in Siena, with its immensely tall tower, castellated roofline and Gothic fenestration, is typical (**439**), as is also the later Palazzo Vecchio in Florence (**480**).

Gothic design was retarded in Spain, chiefly due to Moorish domination, and the earlier Gothic work naturally developed in the north of the country. By the mid thirteenth century builders here felt their Romanesque work to be outdated, and began to adapt themselves to Gothic. But the process of change did not come, as in England, as a natural evolution from Romanesque architecture, but as an import of fully developed French Gothic. The monastic orders spread their influence south and west from France, and French masons were invited to create imposing cathedrals in northern Spain. The most outstanding and the most French of these is that of León, built largely in the thirteenth century on Ile de France pattern, and most closely based upon Reims Cathedral. León Cathedral is designed on Latin cross plan, with single aisled nave and double choir; the chevet of which has five chapels and double-arched flying buttresses. The glass and sculpture make it the Spanish equivalent of Chartres (**433, 434**).

Medieval Germany was not a nation but a group of states which covered much of central Europe. Architecturally the German influence extended from the Baltic coast to the Alps, and from Alsace to modern

Hungary. The building pattern of the northern part was dominated by the Hanseatic League (**446, 447** and pp. 57-58). Elsewhere, in the region now comprising East and West Germany, Gothic development was different from that of England and France. Romanesque architecture had been so well suited to the needs and character of the peoples that there was a reluctance to change. Builders adopted the Gothic vault and the pointed arch but little else: Bamberg Cathedral is a notable example (**392**).

Soon after the House of Hapsburg came to power in 1273, Gothic architecture was developed in Germany but, as in Spain, this was as a fully developed import from France, largely on the Ile de France pattern. Many large churches adopted the French façade design, although in Germany there was sometimes only one centrally placed tower, rather than the two flanking ones. A particularly German characteristic was the decorative fretwork stone spire (seen at Strasbourg, p. 68) and often, as at Regensburg, of a much later date (**452**).

During the thirteenth century the design of castle building was revolutionized. The earlier tradition of a central strongpoint, the keep, was abandoned in favour of a concentric system consisting of rings of walls, one built inside the other, and defended along their whole length by fortified towers. These mural towers were designed to provide covering fire against the attacker from every point of the compass. No part of the structure was then weaker than another. There were most commonly three such lines of defensive walls, each entered via a fortified gatehouse.

The Crusaders brought this concept of concentric castle building to Europe. The

448 Haakonshalle Bergen, Norway. Thirteenth century and later

449 Stave construction. Lom Church, Norway. Thirteenth century

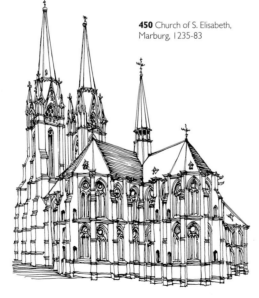

450 Church of S. Elisabeth, Marburg, 1235-83

452 Façade. Regensburg Cathedral, 1275-1330. Spires, nineteenth century

451 Tympanum of S. Elizabeth, Marburg

1256 Augustinian monastic order formed by the consolidation of several groups under the rule of St Augustine

1274 Second Council of Lyons recognized the 'orders four' and forbad lesser mendicant groups to receive novices

Thirteenth century Twisting mills developed in Italy (Lucca) for the reeling and throwing of silk. Before long they were powered by water-wheels

Thirteenth century Horizontal frame weaving loom introduced into Europe from Arabic contacts in Sicily and Spain. This type of loom was fitted with a shedding mechanism which could lift and lower warp threads; it was operated by treadles

1286–1287 Spectacles first made in Italy. These had convex lenses which assisted the elderly (suffering from presbyopia) to read. No provision was made for sufferers from myopia (short-sightedness) until the mid sixteenth century

CONCENTRIC CASTLE BUILDING AND TOWN DEFENCES 1250 – 1300

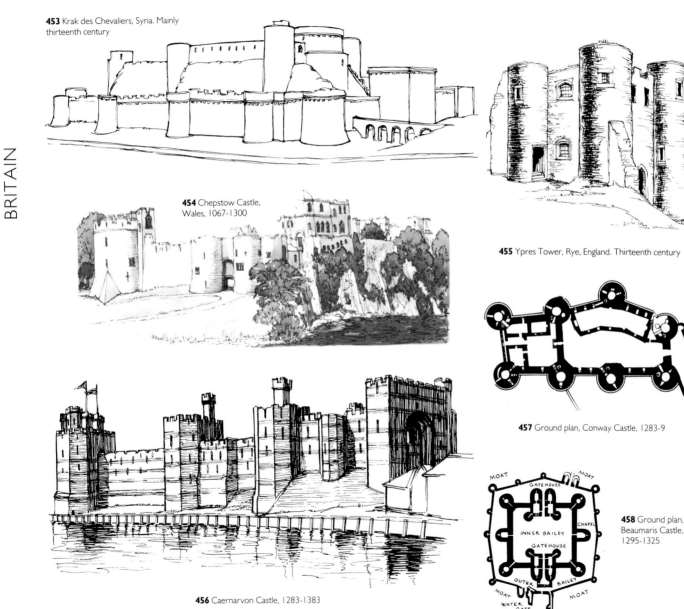

453 Krak des Chevaliers, Syria. Mainly thirteenth century

454 Chepstow Castle, Wales, 1067-1300

455 Ypres Tower, Rye, England. Thirteenth century

457 Ground plan, Conway Castle, 1283-9

458 Ground plan, Beaumaris Castle, 1295-1325

456 Caernarvon Castle, 1283-1383

idea was an eastern one; it had been put into operation as early as AD 400 to protect the city of Constantinople. The theme was adopted widely further east, and copied by the Crusaders in their defence of areas in the Middle East. The best known and largest of such Crusader Castles was Krak des Chevaliers in Syria (**453**). It was begun in the twelfth century, with further walls added during the thirteenth. It was unsuccessfully besieged many times, only finally surrendering in 1271.

In Europe the earlier keep castles were adapted to the concentric plan (**454**, **461**). Defensive walls were built encircling the keep, which was retained for accommodation purposes and as a final strongpoint. There was a considerable area of land between the encircling walls, which was used for garrisoning and stables, for cattle, bakehouses, smithy, armoury and other necessary structures. Such castles housed several hundred workers and soldiers. The Tower of London was one of the first castles to be so adapted.

Many new castles were built in Britain between 1275 and 1350, on concentric plan. Some of the best known were built by Edward I (they were often called Edwardian castles), to consolidate his domination of Wales and Scotland. Harlech, Beaumaris and Caerphilly are notable examples (**458**, **462**). Frederick II's castle at Prato is a fine Italian example.

The thirteenth century was also a time of laying out new towns or adapting older ones, and providing them with an up-to-date defensive wall and gate system (**442**, **460**). The idea of a symmetrical layout on classical pattern with a grid system of streets was revived, particularly in Italy and France. The town of Aigues Mortes in the South of

France is a particularly fine example. Built from 1272 at the mouth of the river Rhône near Montpellier, it has retained a great deal of the original building work (**459**).

In Britain a number of rather less symmetrically planned castles were built as part of town defences. Two well known examples are Caernarvon and Conway, both in North Wales. Both occupy commanding defensive sites; Caernarvon is almost encircled by the river estuary and Conway is sited on land rising steeply from the harbour's edge. In both castles the outer walls with mural towers are built on a roughly rectangular plan (**455, 456, 457**).

459 Town walls and gateway, 'Porte de la Reine', Aigues Mortes, France. Thirteenth century

460 Muiden Castle, Holland. Thirteenth century

*c.*1290–1295   The spindle-wheel (spinning wheel) introduced into Europe from the east. Known as the great wheel on account of its size, this was operated by hand in two successive movements, the first to wind the thread, the second to twist it. There was no treadle. The spinster stood, turning the wheel with her right hand and drawing out the fibre with the left. The spindle was rotated by means of a driving band from the large wheel

461 Constable's Gate, Dover Castle, 1230 and later

462 Great gatehouse and outer gate. Harlech Castle, 1286-90

HIGH GOTHIC ARCHITECTURE   1300 – 1350

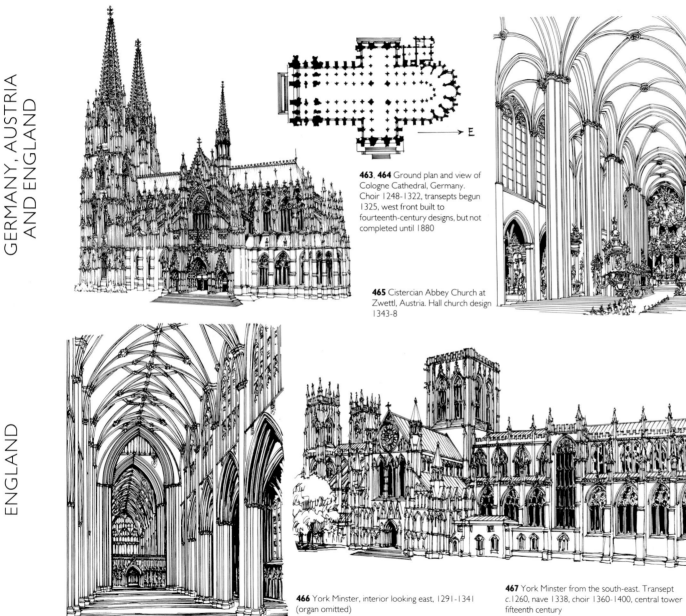

463, **464** Ground plan and view of Cologne Cathedral, Germany. Choir 1248-1322, transepts begun 1325, west front built to fourteenth-century designs, but not completed until 1880

465 Cistercian Abbey Church at Zwettl, Austria. Hall church design 1343-8

466 York Minster, interior looking east, 1291-1341 (organ omitted)

467 York Minster from the south-east. Transept c.1260, nave 1338, choir 1360-1400, central tower fifteenth century

By 1300 Gothic architecture had become the established building style throughout western Europe, but it was a style which manifested itself in very different guises. Such variations partly derived from the wealth or poverty of the regions concerned, partly from the building materials readily available, and also from the natural character of the people – but the strongest determining factor was the climate.

In northern Europe where the air temperature was lower, the sunlight less strong and the winters darker, the emphasis was on height, with steeply pitched roofs to throw off rain and snow, and large window openings to admit maximum daylight. Interior roofing was of stone or brick, because of the greater hazard of fire in a climate which demanded artificial heating and lighting, both using the naked flame. South of the Alps and the Pyrenees, where the sunlight was brighter and rain and snow less damaging, roofs were flatter and window and door openings smaller. Decoration was more likely to be two-dimensional – by paintings, mosaic or marble facing – than by three-dimensional sculpture. The horizontal rather than vertical emphasis was paramount here, a factor partly derived from the lower pitch of the roofs, but also from the classical tradition – which had never completely died out in these regions after the collapse of the Roman Empire. Interior roofing in these lower buildings was still more often of timber, rather than vaulting in more permanent materials.

In northern Europe – apart from the Baltic coastal regions – the French Gothic pattern, established in the twelfth century in the Ile de France, was the basis of Gothic design. Gradually this original, pure and highly disciplined style evolved to become more elaborate and decorative. Knowledge of structure in masonry was extending quickly, and with this came confidence to erect buildings which were mere shells of stone, taller and larger and pierced by openings of greater size and ornamental complexity. Heavy piers and columns were replaced by slender, lofty piers encircled with clustered column shafts, some terminating in small moulded or foliated capitals (472), others rising to the vault springing (466, 479).

One of the most impressive examples of this evolution is Cologne Cathedral in the German Rhineland. Of immense size, it measures 468ft long and 275ft wide; its nave vault rises to 150ft, nearly the height of Beauvais (p. 63). Cologne Cathedral is French in inspiration, its eastern arm with chevet of seven chapels separated by double-arched flying buttresses closely modelled on Amiens (p. 62): it is imposing both in scale and detail. Only the eastern arm is medieval. The choir was consecrated in 1322 and the transepts and nave were begun soon after, but the money ran out and work on the nave, though based upon fourteenth-century designs, was not carried out until the nineteenth century. Here, the western steeples show the characteristically German style of openwork stone carving (463, 464).

In England also the second, more decorative, style was replacing the first phase of Gothic design. Window openings were larger, and stained glass richer. The tracery of the window head was more elaborate, at first in geometric form based on circles (471, 476), but developing into more flowing reticulated and curvilinear designs (468, 475).

The tierceron stone vaults evolved to greater complexity, as at Exeter Cathedral, and soon the lierne vault was introduced.

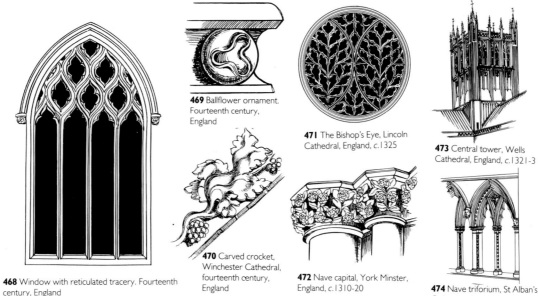

469 Ballflower ornament. Fourteenth century, England

471 The Bishop's Eye, Lincoln Cathedral, England, c.1325

473 Central tower, Wells Cathedral, England, c.1321-3

470 Carved crocket, Winchester Cathedral, fourteenth century, England

472 Nave capital, York Minster, England, c.1310-20

474 Nave triforium, St Alban's Cathedral, England

468 Window with reticulated tracery. Fourteenth century, England

475 East window of choir, Carlisle Cathedral, c.1350

476 Geometrical tracery, east window of choir, Ripon Cathedral, c.1300

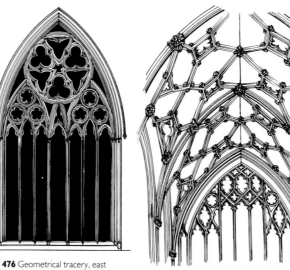

477 Lierne vault, choir, Wells Cathedral, c.1329

1265–1321 Dante Alighieri, Italy's greatest poet, best known as the author of *La Divina Commedia* (The Divine Comedy), which was begun about 1306. The work is a narrative poem written in the first person which describes the poet's journey through the world of the dead. This is in three sections: *Inferno* (hell), *Purgatorio* (purgatory), *Paradiso* (paradise). The poem frequently alludes to the political, social and cultural events of Dante's time

c.1266–1337 Giotto di Bondone, outstanding and original Italian painter of the Florentine School and, at the end of his life, while architect to Florence Cathedral, designer of the campanile; work was begun in 1334, but only the lower part had been built when Giotto died

Early fourteenth century
Wheelbarrow adopted for general building work

Early fourteenth century
Technical invention leading to the use of gunpowder in firearms in western Europe. Metal-barrelled guns produced. Cannon were in use by 1325

1313–1375 Giovanni Boccaccio, Italian poet, writer and humanist. One of the most important contributors to early Renaissance literature. His famous work, the *Decameron*, is a collection of one hundred tales thought to have been written over a number of years and begun c.1348

HIGH GOTHIC ARCHITECTURE   1300 – 1350

FRANCE AND ITALY

SCANDINAVIA

478 Albi Cathedral, France, begun 1282

479 Vendôme Abbey Church, France, begun 1306

480 Palazzo Vecchio, Florence, Italy, 1298-1344 (restored sixteenth century)

481 Turku Castle, Finland. From late thirteenth century, restored

482 Interior of choir, Turku Cathedral. Thirteenth and fourteenth centuries

This was a different structural form for, whereas the tierceron ribs all extended from the vault springing to the ridge rib, the lierne ribs might extend in any direction from the structural ribs and might join any other rib. The name aptly was derived from the French verb *lier*, 'to tie'. Lierne vaults became very complex as time passed as at, for example Wells, York, Gloucester and Winchester Cathedrals (**477**). (For other decorative and structural English work of this period, see **466, 467, 469, 470, 472-474**).

In Scandinavia Gothic architecture developed fairly late. In the southern areas of Denmark and Sweden the Baltic influence of brick building was strongest, while much of the Norwegian building continued to be in timber. However, the most important ecclesiastical structures in all four Scandinavian countries – whether constructed in stone or brick – were influenced by a more developed northern Gothic style, incorporating features from France, England and Germany. Characteristic is the interior of Trondheim Cathedral in Norway (**444**), Skara, Uppsala and Linköping Cathedrals in Sweden (**443, 445, 485**) and the interior of Turku Cathedral in Finland (**482**).

Very different forms of Gothic architecture may be seen in south-west France, Catalan Spain, northern and central Italy (p. 73), southern Germany and Austria, and in the Baltic Coastal regions. There is a common denominator to several of these varied designs: an opening up of the interior space and an abandonment of the previously formal parallel divisions of nave and flanking aisles. Some of the thirteenth-century Italian churches evidenced this trend earliest, as at the aisleless S. Francesco in Assisi (p. 67) and the concept developed further in north-

HIGH GOTHIC ARCHITECTURE 1300 – 1350

east Spain, where it crystallized into the Catalan Gothic type of church characterized by a wide aisleless nave with chapels set between the buttresses: Barcelona Cathedral, begun in 1298, is largely of this type.

Catalan Gothic church design also influenced areas in south-west France, where Albi Cathedral, begun in 1282, is a most impressive and original example. Built of warm pinkish brick on massive lines, the exterior resembles a formidable rounded fortress, lacking any semblance of Gothic articulation. Inside, the cathedral is a rectangular hall, 60ft wide and 100ft high. The great buttresses project inwards some 15ft, and between them are set the tall, narrow windows. All round the building chapels are inserted between the buttresses into the immense wall thickness (478).

The same open trend may be seen in the German *hallenkirche*. The idea of the hall interior was an older one, probably deriving from monastic apartments such as refectories or dormitories and, in Germany, such hall churches stemmed from Romanesque building in central and southern areas. Whereas the Gothic church of northern and French origin was an import into Germany, the hall church was indigenous; though it was also to be seen in south-west France as in, for example, the Church of the Jacobins in Toulouse (416).

Early hall churches in Germany were simply aisleless interiors but, from the late thirteenth century, these developed into aisled interiors where the aisles rose to the same height as nave and choir, creating a lofty, light hall. Such churches might be richly ornamented in their carved capitals, doorways and window tracery, but were structurally simple. Nave and choir could

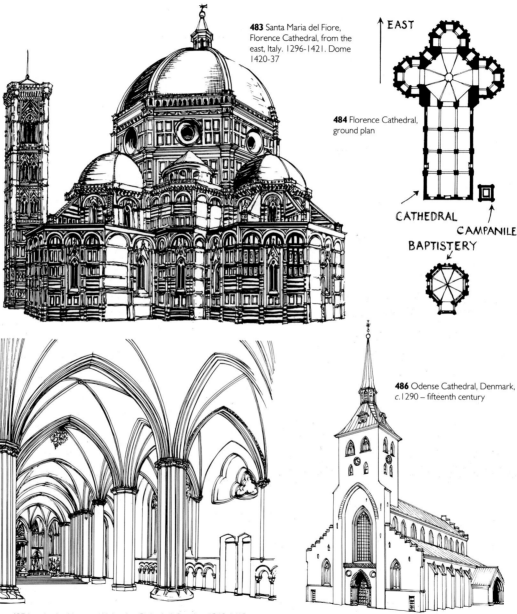

483 Santa Maria del Fiore, Florence Cathedral, from the east, Italy. 1296-1421. Dome 1420-37

484 Florence Cathedral, ground plan

EAST

CATHEDRAL
CAMPANILE
BAPTISTERY

485 Interior looking east, Linköping Cathedral, Sweden. 1260-1412

486 Odense Cathedral, Denmark, c.1290 – fifteenth century

1314 Battle of Bannockburn, in which Robert the Bruce, Earl of Carrick and King of Scotland, defeated the English King Edward II – and so secured an independence for Scotland from the English throne which lasted until the union of the crowns in 1603 under James VI of Scotland, who became also James I of England

1315–1353 The establishment and expansion of the Confederation of territories in Switzerland

c.1325 Forged iron firearms first made in Germany. By about 1350 bronze arms were replacing these

c.1340 The Luttrell Psalter. Illuminated manuscript of the East Anglian School, fascinating to the historian for its vivid depiction of contemporary life

Fourteenth century Spinning wheel (the great wheel) widely used. The spinster stood to operate this large wheel, turning the wheel with her right hand and drawing out the fibres with her left. The spindle, mounted horizontally on bearings, was rotated by means of a driving band, from the wheel. The two operations, of spinning the thread then winding it on to the spindle, had to be done separately and consecutively

1346 Successful employment of the English longbow at the Battle of Crécy

HANSEATIC BRICK-BUILDING AREA   1300 – 1350

GERMANY AND THE LOW COUNTRIES

SCANDINAVIA AND THE LOW COUNTRIES

487 Hanover Town Hall, thirteenth century (left) and Marktkirche, fourteenth century (right)

488 Geometrical tracery, Mechelen Cathedral, Belgium. Begun 1341

489 Cathedral of S. Rombaut, Mechelen (Malines), Belgium. Begun 1341

490 Aarhus Cathedral, Denmark, thirteenth and fourteenth centuries

have no triforium or clerestory, so were lit by exceptionally tall aisle windows. Tall, slender piers supported vaults of quadripartite or lierne design, which extended unbroken across the whole church roofing – with little to obstruct the interior vistas. The Church of S. Elisabeth in Marburg is an early hall church (p. 75). During the fourteenth and fifteenth centuries this form of church design spread across the entire German-speaking area of Europe, and was particularly to be seen in southern Germany and Austria (465).

The Gothic architecture of the fourteenth and fifteenth centuries in the Baltic coastal region displays a unity of style which cuts across the geographical frontiers of several present day countries. The 1200 miles of this European coastline bordering the North and Baltic Seas extends from Bruges in Belgium in the west to Novgorod in the USSR in the east. There are two chief reasons for this similarity in building style over this wide coastal belt: the control and wealth of the Hanseatic League, and the paucity of building materials.

The League (the word is derived from *hansa*, the old high German word for guild) was originally a German federation, chiefly concerned with trade and its protection from the piracy rife in the early Middle Ages. By the mid thirteenth century Lübeck and Hamburg in Germany were co-operating commercially, and before long other German towns – Stralsund, Soest, Dortmund, Wismar and Lüneburg – had joined, after which the League incorporated towns as far distant as Utrecht in Holland, Bruges in Belgium, Danzig (Gdansk) in Poland and Novgorod in Russia. Its influence spread to Scandinavia, to London, to Cracow and to Cologne.

HANSEATIC BRICK-BUILDING AREA 1300 – 1350

This Baltic plain possessed little building stone and was only partially wooded. Brick was the building material which was developed, and was used almost universally for permanent structures. This constrained the builders of Gothic design, for brick is unsuited to constructing tall spires, finials and flying buttresses – or to carving ornament. In the early Middle Ages, therefore, buildings were large and barn-like; the walls, vaults and piers all plain.

By about 1300 the desire for more decorative forms grew and builders became ingeniously adept at handling the brick material to meet this need. Polychrome brick was introduced to give variety by colour; black, yellow and white bricks were laid to produce patterns in the walling. Ceramic polychromy was used for roof tiling. Builders also became expert at providing some plasticity to the surfacing, making panels, recesses and stepped gabling. Even brick window tracery, in a simple form, was created, though, where it was available, stone was used for such tracery as well as for carved capitals and doorway decoration.

Of the Baltic region only Belgium in the Low Countries possessed outstanding examples of the French style of Gothic architecture, as in Brussels and Mechelen (Malines) Cathedrals (**488, 489**). Elsewhere the Baltic brick style prevailed (**412, 446, 447, 486, 487, 490-494**).

491 Choir and ambulatory, Grotekerk, Brouwershaven, Isle of Schouwen, Duiveland, Holland. Early fourteenth century

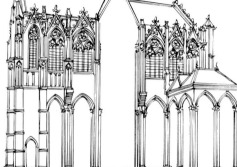

492 Utrecht Cathedral, Holland. Begun 1254 (nave demolished)

493 Løgumkloster Abbey Church, Denmark, c.1300-50

494 Convent Church at Ystad, Sweden. Fourteenth century

1348–1350 The Black Death in Europe. The terrible epidemic of bubonic plague, brought in merchant ships from the east, which killed about one third of the population of western Europe

1349 Edward III established the Order of the Garter, a pattern to be followed by all later orders of chivalry

LATE GOTHIC   1350 – 1400

ITALY

ITALY AND PORTUGAL

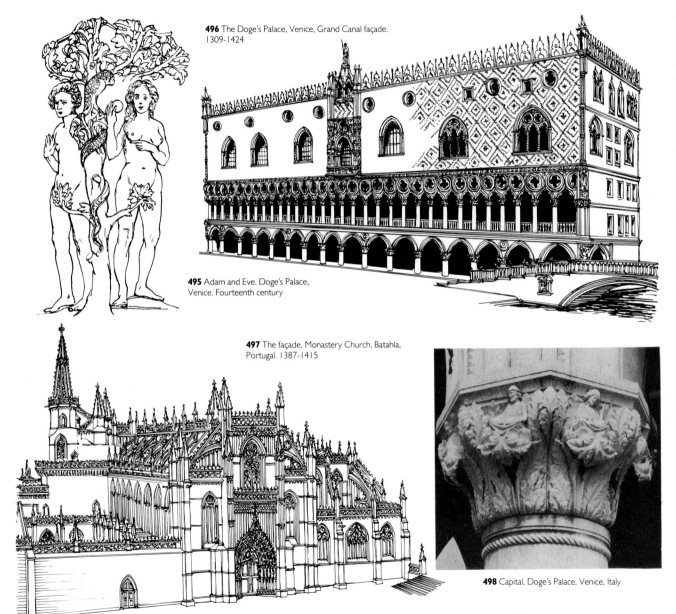

496 The Doge's Palace, Venice, Grand Canal façade. 1309-1424

495 Adam and Eve. Doge's Palace, Venice. Fourteenth century

497 The façade, Monastery Church, Batahla, Portugal. 1387-1415

498 Capital, Doge's Palace, Venice, Italy

The trends apparent in the first half of the fourteenth century continued and intensified. The structure of Gothic architecture became more complex; as did also the decoration, which displayed greater richness and sophistication. With increasing confidence, masons pierced the walls with larger window and doorway openings, the window heads being enriched with a greater variety of tracery design.

Nowhere was the new complexity of form and ornament more clearly illustrated than in English building. The simple geometric forms of tracery had been gradually replaced by curvilinear ones made up from bars of stone, interlacing ogee and other flame-like shapes. By the end of the century these were beginning to give way to the more rectilinear panel tracery of the Perpendicular Gothic style – as can be seen at Westminster Hall in London (**516**). The coloured window glass also acquired a greater richness in both line and shade. The early-fourteenth-century discovery that a yellow stain could be produced by applying a solution of silver was by now fully developed. This gave a clear, transparent film on the glass, and could be varied from pale yellow to deep orange. Applied to blue glass, vivid shades of green could be obtained.

Although the English stone vaults were never as lofty as their Continental counterparts, they were being constructed to a greater height by the late fourteenth century and their variety of form was unsurpassed. Tierceron and lierne vaults continued to be built and, about 1360, the peculiarly English form of the fan vault appeared in the cloister of Gloucester Cathedral (**508**). The fan vault evolved in response to a desire for a design which would accommodate the ribs of different curves as

they sprang from the capital. The radiating ribs of the fan are of equal length and the bounding line is in the shape of a semicircle. The whole group of ribs is made into an inverted concave cone. The radiating ribs are then crossed by lierne ribs, so that the complete surface is panelled and cusped in stone. The fan vault is basically a design of the later fifteenth century, the Gloucester Cloister being a small-scale prototype.

As vaults were constructed to be higher and more complex, English builders at last followed their Continental colleagues by utilizing more and more the appropriate abutment; that is, by constructing flying buttress reinforcement on the exterior of the building. A stone vault exerts an outward and downward thrust upon the walls and this has to be counteracted by the abutment system, which provides strengthening from the exterior face at a point where the greatest pressure is to be expected. Trial and error had established this to be just below the springing line of the vault on the interior wall face. The flying buttress had been evolved, primarily in thirteenth-century France, to produce such strengthening at the critical point. The system serves a dual purpose: the counter thrust at a given place on the exterior wall surface conveys the vault pressure away from the building and down to the ground and also, by means of a heavy pinnacle above, helps to offset the vault thrust (**503, 513**).

A wealth of ecclesiastical building survives from this period of Gothic architecture in England. Of the cathedrals, the west fronts of Exeter and of York are outstanding (**507, 514**) and there are many graceful towers; for example, the central tower at Worcester (**515**). Extant also is quality workmanship in many parish churches. St Patrick's Church in Patrington (**509**), near the coast of North

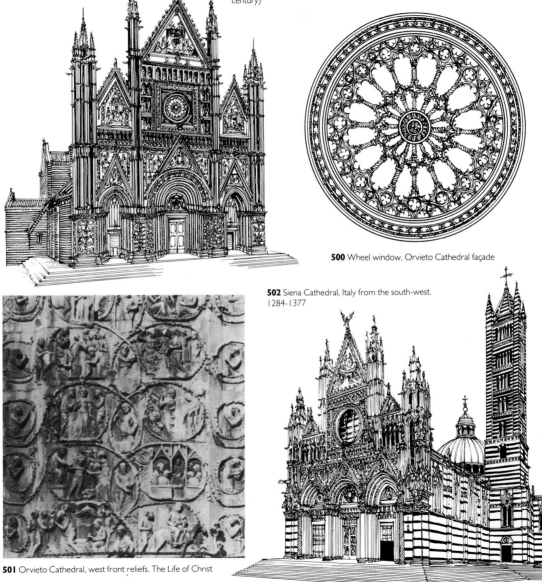

499 West front, Orvieto Cathedral, 1290-1600 (restored nineteenth century)

500 Wheel window, Orvieto Cathedral façade

501 Orvieto Cathedral, west front reliefs. The Life of Christ

502 Siena Cathedral, Italy from the south-west. 1284-1377

1304–1374 Petrarch (Francesco Petrarcha), Italian poet, humanist and man of letters. Famous lyric poet. As a humanist, Petrarch led the movement towards recovery of the classical manuscripts, encouraged revival of Greek studies and made critical editions of the work of classical authors

1337–1453 Hundred Years War. A name coined in France in the 1820s for the series of conflicts in which England and France were engaged during these years

Mid fourteenth century In the wool trade, the introduction of the institution of the Staple. This established a corporate company of merchants – the staplers – who handled the wool at a fixed place where English goods for export had to be collected, taxed and sold; the Staple

1358 Jacquerie – a French peasant uprising – named from the common soubriquet for the word peasant in France – Jacques Bonhomme – which took place in the summer of that year in areas around Paris. Contemporary accounts record that about 20,000 peasants were killed in the savage suppression of the rebellion

1316–1378 Charles IV, King of Bohemia, elected King of the Romans in 1334. Charles (baptised Wenceslas), ruled 1346-1378, as one of the last of the powerful emperors of the Holy Roman Empire. He expanded his Kingdom of Bohemia and brought new and vigorous life to the empire. He founded the University of Prague and, as patron of the arts and

LATE GOTHIC   1350 – 1400

BELGIUM AND ENGLAND

ENGLAND

503, 504, 505 Antwerp Cathedral, Belgium, 1352-1422. View from south-east, ground plan and interior of transept

506 Bruges Town Hall, Belgium. Late fourteenth century

507 West front, York Minster, c.1291-1474

508 Gloucester Cathedral cloister fan vault, c.1360

509 Church of St Patrick, Patrington, Humberside. Late fourteenth century

Humberside, is unequalled as a late-fourteenth-century building for its fine proportions, lofty steeple and interior carving. In the same area Kingston-upon-Hull, founded as a port by Edward I, boasts the magnificent Parish Church of Holy Trinity, which was built largely during the fourteenth century; the first instance of the use of brick for the construction of a major church in Britain.

Numbers of secular buildings have also survived from these years. In castle construction the quadrangular plan began to supersede the Edwardian concentric layout between 1370 and 1380. Bodiam Castle in Sussex (**510**) still presents the shell of such a great castle, its outer walls in good condition and lapped by the waters of the moat. The barbican is in ruins but, entering through the well-preserved gatehouse, one steps into a quadrangular court surrounded by substantial remains of buildings which include the great hall, chapel, private chambers and kitchen.

The great achievements in the Italian version of Gothic architecture continued to be in Tuscany and the Veneto. The characteristics described on p. 78, decoration being provided by colour in mosaic and varied marbles rather than three dimensional sculpture, as in France, the almost classical forms and motifs, the timber roofs rather than stone vaults, domes in preference to steeples and brick buildings sheathed in marble rather than stone, continued to be used. The late-fourteenth-century work, however, on the great cathedrals, particularly Siena and Orvieto, showed a more extensive use of Gothic forms than the earlier building. For example, Giovanni Pisano's façade of Siena Cathedral, which had been completed under

LATE GOTHIC   1350 – 1400

his direction to just above the triple portal by 1300, displayed chiefly classical and Renaissance features. The upper part of the façade, built between 1360 and 1377, finished in gleaming white marble pinnacles and crockets, comes as near to the Gothic style as can be seen in Italy. This applies in only a somewhat lesser degree to the façade of the cathedral of the hill, in the hill city of Orvieto (499-501).

In Venice much of the richly carved Gothic work in the canal façades of the palaces dates from the fifteenth century, but the Doge's Palace (495, 496), begun in the ninth century, was largely built in its present form between 1309 and 1424. The façade fronting the Molo, the entrance to the Grand Canal, dates from the last quarter of the fourteenth century. In glowing pink-patterned brickwork and brilliant white marble carving and arcading, this elevation is the essence of Venetian Gothic design at its best; a unique blend of Byzantium, the Orient, classical Rome and north European Gothic. The lower gallery is constructed with pointed arches supported on short columns, with ogee arches under circles filled with quatrefoils. The depth of the two galleries is equalled by the solid wall of patterned brickwork above, which is pierced only by a few wide-arched windows. The balance and the contrast of materials and treatment is unusual and particularly pleasing.

Apart from the thirteenth-century Gothic building in northern Spain, which was very much based on the French model, as at León Cathedral (p. 74), and the Catalan forms of Barcelona and Gerona Cathedrals which have much in common with Albi Cathedral in south-east France (p. 81), the bulk of important Spanish and Portuguese Gothic

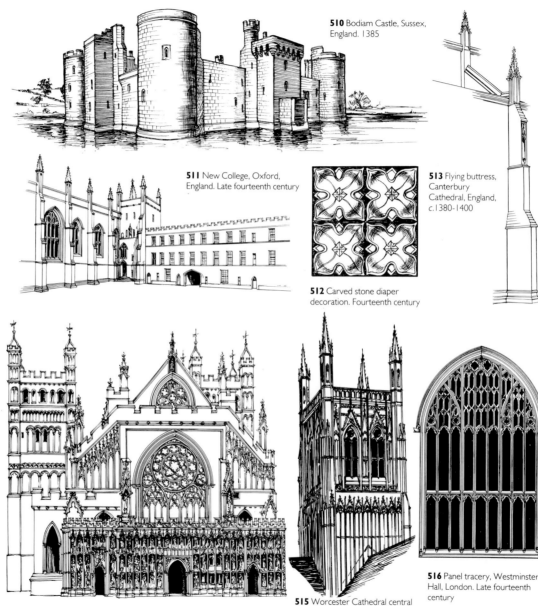

510 Bodiam Castle, Sussex, England. 1385

511 New College, Oxford, England. Late fourteenth century

513 Flying buttress, Canterbury Cathedral, England, c.1380-1400

512 Carved stone diaper decoration. Fourteenth century

514 Exeter Cathedral from the west, 1328-77 (Norman tower)

515 Worcester Cathedral central tower, c.1365-74

516 Panel tracery, Westminster Hall, London. Late fourteenth century

architecture, rebuilt much of the city (including the Karlstein Castle and S. Vitus's Cathedral) in the up-to-date fashionable style, employing French and German builders. He also commissioned the Charles Bridge over the river Vltava. He patronized men of letters and invited Petrarch to Prague

1330–1384 John Wycliffe, Oxford priest, philosopher and reformer who strongly attacked in his writings the ecclesiastical hierarchy and, in particular, the religious orders for their pursuit of wealth and power. In 1379 he also began to question the doctrine of transubstantiation. His supporters and sympathizers were known as Lollards, a term sub-sequently applied more generally to those critical of the wealth, power and doctrines of the Church

c.1337–c.1405 Jean Froissart, the French priest and writer whose *Chronicles* present a vivid picture of fourteenth-century life, especially the traditions of chivalry. The work entitled *Chroniques de France, d'Angleterre, d'Ecosse et d'Espagne*, is in four sections, covering the years 1325-1400. For the earlier years Froissart relied on the accounts of others, such as the chronicler Jean le Bel

c.1340–1400 Geoffrey Chaucer, English poet, who was the leading exponent of literature in medieval England. His best known work is the *Canterbury Tales*, which is a collection of stories narrated by a group of pilgrims who were travelling from London to the shrine of St Thomas à Becket in Canterbury Cathedral and who, in their trades and professions,

LATE GOTHIC   1350 – 1400

517 Central porch, Regensburg Cathedral, Germany, c.1482

518 The Frauenkirche, Nuremberg, Germany, (hall church), 1354-61

519 Doorway, Frauenkirche

520 The choir, Prague Cathedral, Czechoslovakia. 1344-85

521 Portal, Coronation Church of S. Matthias, Budapest, Hungary. Fourteenth century

522 Church of Our Lady of the Sands, Wroclaw, Poland. Fourteenth century

building was late, mainly fifteenth- and early-sixteenth-century. During much of the Middle Ages the French influence on Gothic design in the Iberian Peninsula was perpetuated by the builders working for the monastic Orders. This was an imported style and, until later in the fifteenth century, did not develop into an indigenous form. A late-fourteenth-century example is the abbey church founded in 1387 at Batahla in Portugal (**497**), the building of which continued well into the fifteenth century. The earlier work follows French Cistercian style, the façade is reminiscent of English Perpendicular Gothic and the richer, later work is a blend of western European forms of the time. The low pitched roofs are characteristic of Gothic building in Mediterranean areas, where there is little need to thaw off snow and ice. None of these forms yet coalesced to create a national Portuguese style.

Belgium was a wealthy area during the Middle Ages, particularly from the fourteenth century onwards. During this century, while France was being drained by constant warfare, the artistic centre of this part of Europe moved from Paris to Belgium, where Brussels and Antwerp especially were able to attract artists of fame and quality. At this time architectural style was mainly northern French. Important buildings were constructed in stone and have lofty towers and spires, and a great richness of sculptural and carved decoration. The influence from the Ile de France may be seen primarily in church design, in the eastern chevet, the width of the building with double or triple aisles, and in the high vaults. A number of façades, such as those at Brussels and Antwerp Cathedrals, possess the characteristic French twin towers with portals below;

though others, for example, the Cathedral of S. Bavon in Ghent, show a German influence in their single western tower and spire.

The most impressive Gothic cathedral in Belgium is at Antwerp (503-5). This is a richly ornamented building, begun in 1352 at the east end, the nave completed in 1474. Though the twin western towers are on French pattern, only the north one was capped with a spire, which rises to 400ft above ground level. The whole cathedral shows a particularly French influence, more so than any other in Belgium. Apart from the façade, this may be seen in the chevet, the transept portals and the triple aisles. The strange lantern over the crossing is a relic of the Spanish occupation. The cathedral is best viewed from an upper storey of nearby buildings, as shown in 503.

Much fourteenth-century German Gothic building still showed its French origins, but by the later decades the work of the area under German influence was developing a character of its own. The single-towered west façade was one such feature, to be seen in the elegant, lofty steeples of Ulm Minster (begun 1377) and Freiburg Minster. Ulm resembles a parish church on an immense scale, particularly at the west end where the characteristic openwork spire (not added until the nineteenth century) rises to 529ft. The exterior of the building is richly carved as in, for instance, the ornamental buttresses and the fenestration: the triple porch is especially magnificent. The glory of the interior is in the superbly carved choir stalls. Freiburg Minster is slightly smaller. It had been begun as a Romanesque basilica in 1200, and was eventually completed at the west end by the mid fourteenth century. The 380ft tower and spire on this façade is an early example of this German type of open tracery.

523 Vault of the Church of the Holy Cross, Schwäbisch Gmünd, Germany. 1351

524 Cistercian Abbey Church at Vadstena, Sweden. Begun c.1368

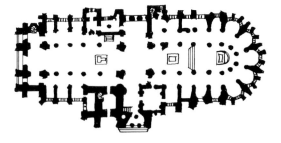

525, 526 View of choir and ground plan of S. Vitus's Cathedral, Prague, Czechoslovakia. 1344-85

were representative of the changing society of the day

Fourteenth century   Gradual and limited revival of brick-making in England

1350–1400   Development of plate armour, which extended to cover the whole body. The plates were worn over the chain mail, particularly to protect the breast and back. The weight of such a suit of armour was tremendous

1370   Iron needles without an eye but with a closed hook termination made in Germany

1379   Foundation of New College, Oxford by William of Wykeham, Bishop of Winchester

1381   The Peasants' Revolt, led by Wat Tyler, over various social grievances of the peasants, but specifically the heavy poll tax levied by the government of Richard II. The Archbishop of Canterbury was beheaded by Wat Tyler's men on Tower Hill and, after Richard's concessions, Wat Tyler was slain in retribution at Smithfield

1382   Foundation by William of Wykeham of a grammar school at Winchester, to provide a better education for the secular clergy (Winchester College)

Late fourteenth century Gradual superseding in England of the French language by English given a tremendous impetus by Geoffrey Chaucer and other writers; for example, William Langland's religious allegory *Piers Plowman* (1362-98)

Late fourteenth century Adoption in Europe of the tower

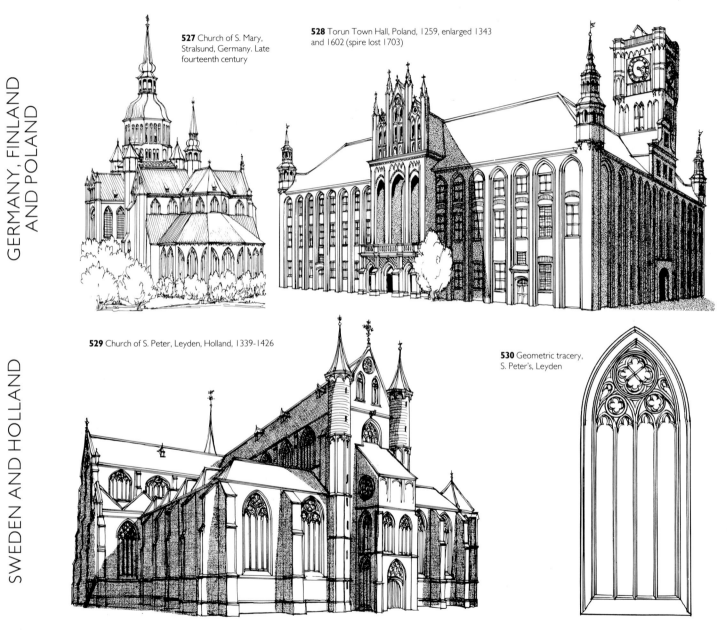

527 Church of S. Mary, Stralsund, Germany. Late fourteenth century

528 Torun Town Hall, Poland, 1259, enlarged 1343 and 1602 (spire lost 1703)

529 Church of S. Peter, Leyden, Holland, 1339-1426

530 Geometric tracery, S. Peter's, Leyden

GERMANY, FINLAND AND POLAND

SWEDEN AND HOLLAND

A smaller, richly ornamented church of about 1355 is the Frauenkirche at Nuremberg, seriously damaged in the last war but its exterior now fully restored. Its ornamental façade, which is fronted by an elegant, carved porch, rises to a finialled stepped gable (**518, 519**).

In contrast to Germany, there was no strong Romanesque tradition in neighbouring Czechoslovakia and Gothic architecture, spread by the monastic orders, was soon accepted and established. Due to the troubled times in this area of central Europe, little survives of early Gothic building; the great Czech surviving monuments of the Middle Ages are of the richer, more decorative work of the fourteenth and fifteenth centuries, and the chief city of Prague, despite later energetic reconstruction in baroque style, retains much of this Gothic heritage. S. Vitus's Cathedral (**520, 525, 526**) is the outstanding example of this work here. it was designed and begun by Matthias of Arras, who came to Prague in the 1340s from the court of the Popes at Avignon so, not surprisingly, his contribution was of French Gothic pattern.

The architect died in 1352 and his place was taken by Peter Parler, from Cologne, who was invited to come from Schwäbish Gmünd, where he had been assisting his father, Heinrich Parler, designer of the Church of the Holy Cross there (**523**). It is interesting to compare in the cathedral choir, both on the exterior and interior, the traditionally French lower work by Matthias and the more innovatory upper part by Parler. In particular, the vault (**520**) closely resembles an English lierne vault (at York Minster, for instance) though there is no written evidence that Parler actually visited England. Peter Parler was a member of an architectural family, and work on the cathedral and the

Charles Bridge, in Prague and S. Bartholomew's Church in Kolín (1360-78) was to a certain extent a family affair.

Brick construction continued and developed in countries bordering the Baltic coastline. Builders became remarkably adept at handling the material and in decorating it more richly and with greater variety as time passed. In Holland, the large, spreading church of S. Peter in Leyden is characteristic (529, 530) as is S. Mary in Stralsund in Germany (527). The town hall in this city is a remarkable example of decorative ingenuity (531).

Many fine buildings were erected in Poland. Particularly impressive is the immense town hall in Torun (528) and the many fine churches in such towns as Gdansk, Cracow, Chelmo and Wroclaw. In Wroclaw (the pre-war German city of Breslau) is the Church of Our Lady of the Sands, now restored after war-time damage. Like a number of Polish medieval churches this one has the unusual Piast vaults, which are tripartite but then subdivided to make nine panelled compartments (522).

In Sweden from the fourteenth century the Church became richer and more influential. The great cultural influence came from the monastic settlements, the most active of which was the Cistercian Order. After the Reformation these buildings fell into disuse but, as in England, some were retained as parish or cathedral churches. They were nearly all altered in the seventeenth and eighteenth centuries, then restored to their medieval appearance in the nineteenth or twentieth. Among such churches are the Cistercian Abbey Church at Vadstena (524) and the Dominican S. Mary at Sigtuna (535): both are hall churches characteristic of the area of Hanseatic influence.

531 Stralsund Town Hall, Germany. Late fourteenth century

532 Decorative brick gable in Hanseatic style. Pernaja Church, Finland. Late fourteenth century

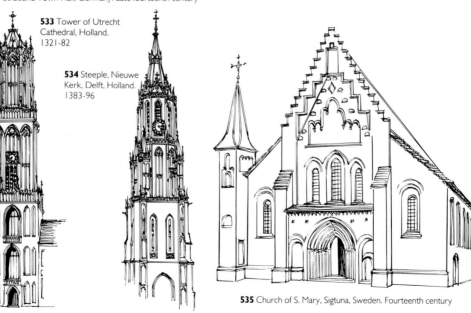

533 Tower of Utrecht Cathedral, Holland. 1321-82

534 Steeple, Nieuwe Kerk, Delft, Holland. 1383-96

535 Church of S. Mary, Sigtuna, Sweden. Fourteenth century

form of windmill. This had a cap which contained the shaft on which the sails turned, and it was only the cap which needed to be turned. The body of the windmill, now stationary, could therefore be made from the more durable materials of brick or stone – instead of wood, which had been normal for earlier post mills. Such solid mill bodies also provided greater wind resistance

Late fourteenth century The tall blast furnace was developed to produce cast iron. In this, which had evolved from the thirteenth-century Catalan forge, the iron took longer to penetrate to the bottom of the furnace and, in so doing, absorbed more carbon content; so rendering its melt-point some 350°C lower than that of pure iron. This made it possible to liquidize the metal, which could then be poured into moulds. This cast iron lacked the tensile strength of wrought iron, but was stronger in compression

1397 Union of Kalmar in Sweden, where the Scandinavian kingdoms of Norway, Sweden and Denmark were united under the sovereignty of Eric of Pomerania

536 Font, Stavanger Cathedral, Norway

537 Cathedral of S. Jan, 's Hertogensbosch, Holland. 1419-1529

538 Town Hall, Brussels, 1402-50 (restored)

539 Archivolts, West doorway, Antwerp Cathedral, Belgium. 1422-74

540 Town Hall, Bourges, France. Fifteenth century

After 1400 a much greater richness was apparent in decorative forms and, in structure, designs became more complex and sophisticated. There was also a greater variety in Gothic expression, as each area of Europe developed differently. In England the Perpendicular style evolved, leading to more complicated vaulting systems and larger windows which contained more ambitious tracery patterns. In Spain and Portugal ornament became richer and vaults more complex. As time passed and trade expanded, particularly in the Hanseatic areas of northern Europe, countries became wealthier; this was evidenced architecturally in the building of many large, imposing parish churches in Germany, the Low Countries (**537, 542**), northern France (**543**) and England.

The hall type of church (the *hallenkirche*), which had been adopted in several of the areas under German influence from the early fourteenth century, was further developed to create many magnificent church interiors containing slender, tall columns and piers, elongated, traceried aisle windows and complex and very beautiful vaulting systems. The pattern had been set by the superb interior of the Church of the Holy Cross at Schwäbisch Gmünd in Germany (**523**), the mid-century design of Heinrich Parler, father of Peter the master mason of Prague Cathedral (p. 90). Others followed, erected over a wide area: S. Martin at Landshut, S. Lawrence in Nuremberg and S. George at Dinkesbühl (**549**), all in Germany; the Cathedral of S. Stephen in Vienna (**554**), and the varied and numerous instances in the broad Hanseatic area from Holland to Poland, including Scandinavian examples such as S. Mary at Helsingør (**541**).

From the late fourteenth century, through the fifteenth and well into the sixteenth, the civic edifices – guild halls, cloth halls, town halls – were becoming more elaborate and more imposing, testimony to the increasing wealth and importance of the medieval trading nations: in Italy, England, Germany and along the entire Hanseatic coastline. The cloth halls of Bruges and Ypres have already been referred to (413) and the town hall of Bruges is illustrated in 506. From the first half of the fifteenth century came the French town hall at Bourges (540) and the imposing town hall of Brussels which (restored) still dominates the Grande Place in the centre of the city (538). Germany lost many of her finest medieval civic buildings during World War II, especially in the northern Hanseatic towns; the old town hall in Brunswick is a welcome survivor (545), as is the decorative example at Stralsund (531).

Gothic architecture in Spain and Portugal, apart from in the extreme northern area as at Léon, developed on different lines from the original French pattern of the Ile de France. In many instances the German influence was stronger, as at Burgos Cathedral, where the interior vaulting designs and the western towers were the work of German master masons. Hans of Cologne, for example, was responsible for the characteristic openwork spires of these towers in 1486 (553). The later central lantern, the octagonal *cimborio*, possesses a magnificent eight-pointed star vault of German type, and in Portugal the octagonal Founder's Chapel in Batahla Abbey Church is covered by a superb star vault carried on an octagonal drum (558).

Fifteenth-century Gothic work in Spain was moving towards the rich all-over decoration prevalent in the following

541 S. Mary's Church, Helsingør, Denmark. Hanseatic brickwork. Fifteenth century

542 Church of S. Pierre, Louvain, Belgium from the east. 1425-97

543 Church of S. Pierre, Caen, France 1309-1540. Eastern apsidal chapels, Renaissance design, 1528-45

544 Château at Sully-sur-Loire, France. Fourteenth and fifteenth centuries

1400–1405 Owen Glendower led the last effective Welsh revolt against the English Crown. He was proclaimed Prince of Wales and, by 1405, with the aid of the English Percy family, was in control of Wales; but his success was short-lived

1404 Foundation of the University of Turin

Early fifteenth century Under the Ming dynasty in China were produced great compendia of learning. The chief of these was the *Yung ho Ta Tien*, which was intended to summarize all knowledge gained prior to 1400. Over 3000 scholars were employed in creating this vast work, which comprised more than 20,000 volumes

1409 Foundation of Leipzig University

1410 The atlas of Claudius Ptolemy of Alexandra of 150 AD, the only Greek map to survive, was translated into Latin. This led the way to a revival of cartography as a science in Europe

Early fifteenth century Bethlehem Hospital in London, which had been founded in 1247 as a church priory dedicated to St Mary of Bethlehem, became a hospital for the insane and was later known as 'Bedlam'

1411 Building of the Guildhall in the City of London

c.1386–1466 Donatello, leading Florentine Renaissance sculptor. Among his best-known works are: *David* (1408), *St George* (1415-17), scenes of figure sculptures for the

GOTHIC 1400 – 1450

GERMANY AND ENGLAND

ENGLAND

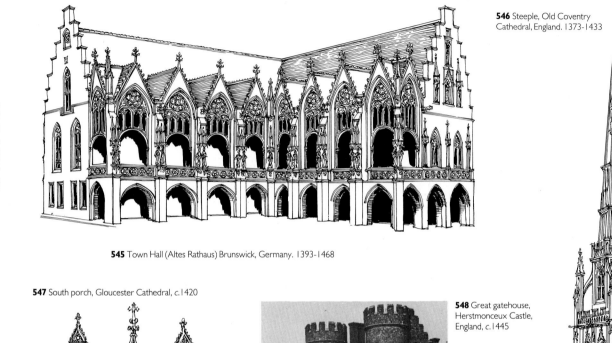

545 Town Hall (Altes Rathaus) Brunswick, Germany. 1393-1468

546 Steeple, Old Coventry Cathedral, England. 1373-1433

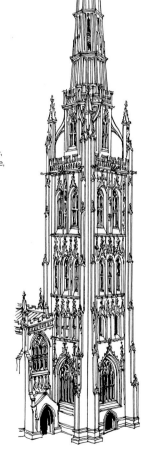

547 South porch, Gloucester Cathedral, c.1420

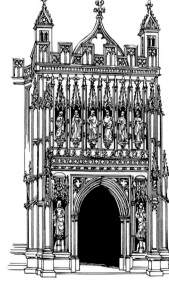

548 Great gatehouse, Herstmonceux Castle, England, c.1445

century, absorbing in its especially Spanish form derived from both German themes and its Moorish heritage. Toledo Cathedral, for example, is based on the French model but, built over the very long period of 1226-1452, it became less French and more Spanish as time passed. The richly sculptured, almost plateresque Puerta de los Leones is a notable example of this.

Many secular fortified buildings survive from the fifteenth century. These include castles, town walling and gateways. The château of Sully-sur-Loire is a French example (544); the town walls and bars (gateways) of York are notable stone structures, while German Hanseatic remains such as Lübeck's Holstentor (restored) (550) present fine instances of Baltic patterned brickwork. But it is Spain which is more noted for its medieval castles than any other country. Castile, the large area in the centre of the peninsula, had so many that it was named from them (*castillo*). Medieval castles are there in all styles, Gothic to Moorish to Renaissance. Characteristic are the immense structures of Castillo de la Mota at Medina del Campo, Olite Castle near Pamplona and Castle Coca, an immense mass of pinkish brick towers and turrets set within a deep enclosing moat (562).

It was about 1420 in Italy when the concepts and ideals of the Renaissance were first expressed in architecture. The word itself, whether in Italian, French or Spanish, means rebirth; and the movement was, literally, a rebirth of the tenets and the arts of the ancient classical world of Rome, though it represented more than mere eclecticism in art. The Renaissance put forward a new philosophy and a questioning of medieval dogma and society; it refers to nothing less than man's emergence into the modern world from the medieval one.

Medieval society had largely ignored the remains – architectural, artistic and literary – of the classical cultures. Dissatisfaction with the medieval answers to man's curiosity about himself, his history and his world led to a rediscovery and renewed study of what had gone before the Roman Empire embraced Christianity. The beginnings of a new comprehension came in Italy – as a natural corollary, because in Italy most remained of antique Roman art and architecture. Despite the despoliation of the great classical structures for use as quarries for building material during the Middle Ages, a great deal had survived.

It is natural to question why such a movement should arise in the fourteenth century (for this is when the Renaissance began in the literary field) and, even more, why it should have arisen at all.

Since the disintegration of the ancient classical world, mankind had emerged from barbarism into a society dominated by Christianity. This religion, in western Europe, became the foundation of all human life, with all intellectual thought and experience, and therefore learning, in the hands of the Church. Fourteenth-century Italy (and later France, Germany, England) began to produce men of high intellectual stature and knowledge who questioned, not the importance of Christianity, but the unimportance, so far accepted, of man. In their studies of the literature of Greece and Rome they discovered a conception of man as an individual human being, important in his own right. Even though this meant conflict with the established ecclesiastical ruling that man's life on earth should be subjugated to his future life after death, these

549 St George's Church, Dinkiesbühl, Germany, hall church design. 1448-92

550 Holstentor (town gateway) Lübeck, Germany. Fifteenth century

552 Canterbury Cathedral. 1348-1497

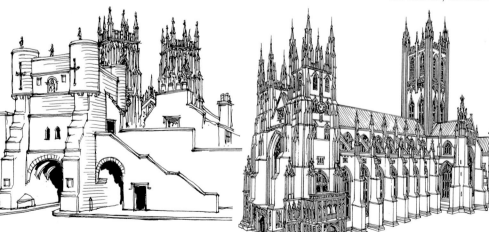

551 Bootham Bar (town gateway), city walls and Minster, York. Fifteenth century

Florence Cathedral companile (1416-39) and the dancing *putti* reliefs for the cathedral cantoria (1433-9), the outdoor pulpit for for Prato Cathedral (1433-8), and the Gattamelata equestrian statue at Padua outside the Basilica of S. Antonio, which was a portrait of the Venetian *condottiere* Erasmo da Narni and reintroduced the classical Roman theme of so honouring the heroic figure

Early fifteenth century
Illuminated book of hours *Très Riches Heures du Duc de Berry*, named after the duke who died in 1416. An invaluable source material for French dress of the period

*c.*1380–1455 Lorenzo Ghiberti, Italian sculptor, known especially for his bronze doors on the Baptistery of Florence Cathedral. The north doors were carried out 1404-24 and the east doors ('Porta di Paradiso') between 1425 and 1452

*c.*1390–1441 Jan van Eyck, leading painter of fifteenth-century Flanders, and a master of panel painting in oils, using alternate layers of opaque tempera and oil glazes

1401–*c.*1428 Masaccio (born Tommaso Guidi), notable Italian Renaissance painter and exponent of tonal and linear perspective

1404–1453 Constantine XI, the last Christian Emperor (Roman Emperor of the east) in Constantinople. He died in the defence of the city against the victorious Turks

1418 Rediscovery of the Portuguese islands of Madeira by the Portuguese navigator Joas Gonçalves

GOTHIC 1400 – 1450

553 Burgos Cathedral, Spain, from the south-west. Begun 1220. Façade towers 1442-58

554 S. Stephen's Cathedral, Vienna, from the south-west. 1304-1491

555 Base. Founder's Chapel, Batahla Abbey Church, Portugal. 1415-34

556 Carved foliated capital, England. Fifteenth century

557 Carved stone gargoyle, Thaxted Church, England. Fifteenth century

scholars found themselves compelled to explore further the concepts of Humanism.

In Italy the Renaissance began in the literary field, with the studies and writings of men such as Dante, Boccaccio and Petrarch. The works of the classical scholars were revived and circulated. Man's thoughts and experiences were recounted in the new literature. Sculpture also was an early field of exploration, evincing a new and freer naturalism in the human form, as seen in the works of Donatello (**567**) and Ghiberti (**614**). Painters followed: Cimabue and Giotto, for example. Architecture came late to the field; the first Renaissance architect was Brunelleschi, his work dating from the 1420s. In all the arts, a fundamental difference between medieval work and that of the Renaissance is to be seen in the human, natural and vigorous forms. Christianity, though still a most important basis for art, was not now depicted in such a hieratic manner, nor was it the only subject. All of man's life and experience with Christian background became the artist's inspiration, together with nature in all its forms.

Two vital characteristics of the Renaissance were the change of status of artists in the community, and their versatility. The Renaissance began in Tuscany – in Florence – where, under Medici patronage, poetry, painting, sculpture and architecture flourished and the artist became one of the most important members of the community. He was in demand by men of wealth and position to write, to build palaces and churches, and to decorate these according to taste and means. The artist, in turn, recognized this and was sensible of his value. At the same time the best artists were extremely able, versatile and cultured men.

None excelled at only one art or craft. Many were painters, sculptors and architects and some wrote or were goldsmiths, bronzeworkers, mathemeticians or ceramicworkers. Thus, the first Renaissance architect of Florence Cathedral was Giotto, a painter. Alberti was scholar, writer, mathematician and architect (568).

Filippo Brunelleschi (1377-1446) was the first Renaissance architect. He had been both goldsmith and sculptor, had studied mathematics and spent some time in Rome making measured drawings of ancient Roman buildings. His early work, like the Foundling Hospital in Florence, begun in 1419, was Tuscan and Romanesque in derivation. Nevertheless, such designs showed the new classical approach, a desire for symmetry, proportions carefully related in one part to another, and the adaptation of the new-found science of perspective to architecture.

In his commission to build a dome to the unfinished medieval cathedral of Florence (571), Brunelleschi had to bring all his knowledge of mathematics and of the structures of ancient Roman vaults. The practical problems at this date (1404) were considerable; how to construct a dome to span the 138ft diameter space. This was too great a distance to support on available timber centering. Brunelleschi, like all classical architects, knew that a hemispherical dome would be aesthetically most desirable. He dared not build one on the existing octagonal drum, which had no external abutment; so he compromised and proceeded step by step. His dome is a pointed one, constructed on Gothic principles, with ribs supporting a lighter infilling. It is taller than a hemisphere to offset the thrust. To retain his exterior and

558 Vault. Founder's Chapel, Batahla Abbey Church, Portugal. 1415-34

560 Fifteenth-century pier base. England

561 Carved stone finial, England. Fifteenth century

559 Nave buttress, Winchester Cathedral, England, c.1394-1450

562 Coca Castle, near Segovia, Spain. Brick

Zarco, who founded Funchal in 1421. The islands had been known to the Romans, when they were called *Purpurariae Insulae*. The word Madeira comes from the Portuguese name for wood, the term associated with the luxurious afforestation of the islands

*c.*1400–1455   Fra Angelico, a Domenican friar, one of the great painters of religious subjects of the Italian Renaissance. Born Guido di Pietro and known in his lifetime as Giovanni da Fiesole

*c.*1412–1431   Joan of Arc. In 1429 she successfully led the French in a series of engagements against the English armies. In Rouen, burned at the stake 30 May 1431

*c.*1420–*c.*1481   Jean Fouquet, French painter of illuminated manuscripts and miniatures, who was responsible for helping to introduce the Italian Renaissance style of painting into France

1423   Death of Sir Richard Whittington, three times elected mayor of London

1431–1432   The Azores discovered by the Portuguese navigator Gonçalo Velho Cabral

1400–1477   Establishment of the State of Burgundy which, during these years, rivalled both England and France in wealth and power. This was evidenced in costume and the visual arts

ITALY: GOTHIC TO RENAISSANCE 1400 – 1450

563, **564**, **565** Milan Cathedral. View from the east (1387-1410), ground plan and interior of nave (fifteenth century)

construct a suitable, lower, interior form, he made two domes, one inside the other; a practice followed by many later architects; for example, Sir Christopher Wren at St Paul's.

In his basilican churches Brunelleschi sought symmetry, a control and unity of space; and achieved a great breadth and feeling of light not to be found in medieval churches. S. Spirito, 1436 (**572**) and S. Lorenzo , from *c*.1420 (**566**) are examples of this. Like so many Renaissance architects, Brunelleschi was fascinated by the concept of the centrally planned church. Used by both Greeks and Romans in temple design, this is the ultimate form of classical metaphor. Brunelleschi's unfinished but surviving Church of S. Maria degli Angeli, 1437, was the first of such Renaissance buildings. It has 16 sides and, inside, eight chapels open out of an octagonal central area, which is covered by a dome. His Pazzi Chapel, 1433, in the Church of S. Croce, is more sophisticated. The beautiful ceramic work on the interior is by Luca della Robbia.

Only in the north, in the great east/west valley carved out by the river Po, geographically subject to some German and Austrian influence, had Italy ever adopted a form of Gothic architecture which had any affinity with that of northern Europe. The principal example of this is Milan Cathedral, begun in 1385 and, like Cologne, completed at its west end in the nineteenth century. It is very much a German product, since so many of its artists and craftsmen came from north of the Italian alpine border. Despite this, the vast cathedral retains Italian characteristics. These can be seen in the insistence upon a geometrically based design, in the emphasis upon the horizontal rather than vertical elements, in the brick construction sheathed

566 Interior. Church of S. Lorenzo, Florence. Architect: Brunelleschi, from 1420

568 Façade entablature. Church of S. Francesco, Rimini, 1446. Architect: Alberti

567 Exterior pulpit, Prato Cathedral, 1434-8. Architect: Michelozzo. Sculptor: Donatello

ITALY: GOTHIC TO RENAISSANCE 1400 – 1450

all over in white marble and the proportions, which are wide and low rather than upwardly soaring (563-5).

Also Gothic in detail but Italian in the emphasis placed on the horizontal line and the decorative medium of mosaic and coloured marble facing are the richly ornamental palace façades of Venice. Fronting the Grand Canal is the classic instance of this, the Ca' d'Oro (1421-36), which displays delicate white marble ogee arches and tracery, and elegant balconies (569, 570).

1448 Demonstration by Johann Gutenberg in Mainz, Germany that printing from movable type was practicable. His '42-line' Bible followed, accepted as the first important printed work from a printing press

569 Palazzo Ca' d'Oro, Venice, 1421-36

570 Palazzo Franchetti, Venice, c.1430

571 The dome of Florence Cathedral, 1420-36, lantern 1461. Architect: Brunelleschi

572 Interior, church of S. Spirito, Florence, 1436. Architect: Brunelleschi

1450 – 1500

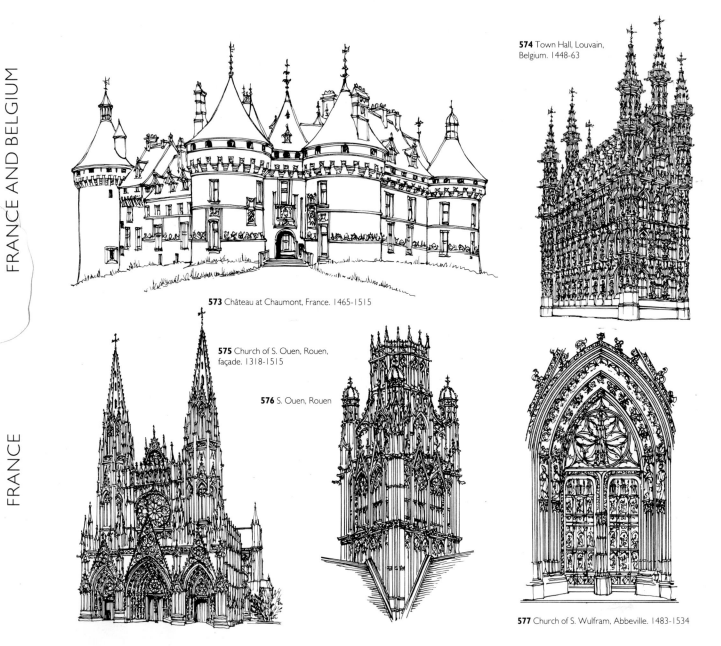

573 Château at Chaumont, France. 1465-1515

574 Town Hall, Louvain, Belgium. 1448-63

575 Church of S. Ouen, Rouen, façade. 1318-1515

576 S. Ouen, Rouen

577 Church of S. Wulfram, Abbeville. 1483-1534

These were the years of the rich, high-quality decoration which characterized the late Gothic workmanship in France and Belgium. Fifteenth-century work is described as *flamboyant*, a term which refers to the ogival curves of the window tracery, which resemble upward leaping flames. The rose windows of the façade at Rouen Cathedral and those of the west and the south transept façades at Amiens Cathedral (**581**) are superb examples of this type of work.

Fifteenth-century stained glass shows a greater sophistication in the handling of colour and more stylized, formal way of designing the floral motifs. A technique of abrasion was developed, in which portions of the colour areas could be abraded by an iron tool or a whetstone; this expanded the colour palette as well as giving a modelled effect. After 1450 designs became more complex and leadwork was kept to a minimum, in order not to obscure the pattern. Stylized diaper designs and heraldic motifs were widely employed. In floral decoration, the flowing seaweed pattern replaced the earlier, traditional oak, vine and ivy.

Apart from window tracery, the French *flamboyant* period of late Gothic architecture was characterized by the rich though not crudely ornate carving on the towers, and the delicate flying buttresses and the doorways. The ogee curve was much in evidence. Many churches survive from this time in France. In Rouen, at the Cathedral, the Tour de Beurre rises 252ft on one side of the façade (**579**). The tower is so-called because money was provided for its erection from payments for dispensation given, permitting consumption of butter during Lent. There are two other beautiful churches in *flamboyant* style: S. Maclou and S. Ouen, both superbly carved (575, 576). In Abbeville is that remarkable classic of the *flamboyant*, S. Wulfram, largely built 1488-1534 but never finished and, later, damaged during World War I (577). S. Pierre in Louvain in Belgium is a fine late Gothic example (542), as is also S. Pierre in Caen in France, to which eastern apsidal chapels were added in a Mannerist Renaissance style early in the sixteenth century (543). In civic building, the town hall in Louvain is particularly richly ornamented (574).

In domestic architecture, French châteaux of the later fifteenth century show the beginnings of the transformation from fortress to palace. They are still encircled by moats or set by lakes or rivers, and they display machicolations and crenellation – but spacious accommodation is now disposed around the impressive courtyards. The château at Chaumont is a classic instance of this trend (573).

In towns, the larger houses (hôtels) were developing a characteristic style, suited to a more limited site but also containing reasonably spacious accommodation arranged around a central courtyard. Such hôtels, built for well-to-do merchants or church dignitaries, were three-storeyed with dormers in the high-pitched roofs. The entrance doorway led into a medieval stairway in the centre of the courtyard façade. A fine surviving example is the house of Jacques Coeur in Bourges (578). Similar examples in Paris are the Hôtel de Sens and the Hôtel de Cluny, both late-fifteenth-century and both retaining finialled dormers and *flamboyant* tracery (580).

Contemporary work in England was very different. Here, the Perpendicular Gothic style was firmly established and changed only slowly, to reach its final form in the Tudor

579 Tour de Beurre, Rouen Cathedral, France. 1485

578 House of Jacques Coeur, Bourges, France, Courtyard. 1443-51

580 Dormer window, Hôtel de Sens, Paris. 1475-1507

581 Rose window, west front, Amiens Cathedral, *flamboyant* tracery, c.1500

582 Courtyard entrance, Hôtel de Cluny, Paris. 1483

1451 Glasgow University founded by Pope Nicholas V

1450s Revival of the Vatican Library (founded in the fourth century by Pope Damasus I) under Pope Nicholas V. Great improvements were made by his librarian Giovanni Tortelli of Arezzo

1452 The great Renaissance genius of Italy, Leonardo, born at Vinci. A man of wide vision, a keen observer, an indefatigible inventor and instigator, he was unique even in this age and country of outstanding talent: as engineer, designer, scientist, philosopher and painter

1453 Constantinople fell to Sultan Mehmet II. End of the Christian Empire and the eastern section of the Roman Empire

1453 The great Byzantine church of S. Sophia converted into a mosque by the victorious Turks

1453 End of the Hundred Years' War between England and France

1455 Alfonso Borgia became Pope Calixtus III

1435–1488 Andrea del Verrocchio, Florentine sculptor, painter and goldsmith of the Italian Renaissance. Like Donatello, Verrocchio was primarily a sculptor and his equestrian statue in Venice of the military commander Bartolommeo Colleoni is one of his best known works

1458 The Parthenon temple on the Acropolis Hill in Athens converted into a mosque by the Turks

1445–1510 Sandro Botticelli, one of the leading painters of the

583 Magdalen College, Oxford, England, c.1490-1509

584 Basel Minster, Switzerland. Fifteenth century

585 Nave fan vault, Sherborne Abbey Church, England, c.1475-1500

587 Stoneacre. Timber-framed house, c.1480

588 Carved stone brattishing. Late-fifteenth-century ornament

586 King's College Chapel, Cambridge. 1446-1515

589 The timber-framed Mermaid Inn, Rye, England, c.1500

Gothic of the time of Henry VIII. By the second half of the fifteenth century the overall panel type of decoration was fully developed, extending all over the building, inside and out: the roof and walls were panelled in stone, the windows in stone and glass. Carving was restrained and largely confined to the cusping of the panelled form, with its stress upon the vertical and horizontal line. The exception to this was the vault design, where the last phase of English Gothic vaulting – that peculiarly English form, the fan vault – had evolved.

From the prototype of the fan vault, seen in the cloisters of Gloucester Cathedral as early as the mid fourteenth century (**508**), the complex, sophisticated designs such as those in Sherborne Abbey Church (**585**) and Kings' College Chapel Cambridge (**586**) had evolved. The fan vault was developed in response to the desire for a vault which would accommodate ribs of different curves as they sprang from the capital. The radiating ribs of a fan are of equal length and the bounding line is in the form of a semicircle. The whole group of ribs is made into an inverted concave cone. The radiating ribs are crossed by lierne ribs and the whole surface is then, like the windows, walls and buttresses, panelled and cusped.

The English window tracery of this period is as different from the French *flamboyant* as it could possibly be. It is a panelled form of tracery in which the whole window area – the head encompassed at first in an obtuse arch and later a four-centred one – is divided by numerous mullions and one or more transoms, giving a large number of smaller rectangular-shaped lights. The west window of St George's Chapel, Windsor is a fine late-fifteenth-century example (**593**).

Supreme amongst English architecture

built entirely in Perpendicular Gothic style are the chapels: that at Eton College (1441), King's College, Cambridge (1446-1515) and St George's Windsor (1475-1509). In all these structures the ground plan is rectangular and simple. There are many large windows separated by finialled flying buttresses (a feature at last fully embraced by English builders), leaving a small area of wall between. At each end of the building is an enormous multi-light window. The fan-vaulted interiors are light, rich and elegant (586, 593). Apart from the chapels, as in France, many churches of this period survive. These include such beautiful examples as St Botolph, Boston, Louth Church, St Mary Redcliffe, Bristol, Lavenham Church, St John, Glastonbury and St John, Cirencester (592).

Ornately carved timber-framed buildings also survive in England in quantity from this time. They include inns, houses, guild and town halls. Timber was also used extensively for roofing, and the timber-trussed roof was the equivalent in wood of the stone vault. As the centuries passed it similarly developed into a more refined, sophisticated and complex design. In England the later fifteenth-century timber-trussed roof had evolved from the early medieval tie and collar beam designs into the beautifully carved hammerbeam form, to be seen at its most magnificent in Westminster Hall in London (c.1395) and in the great hall at Eltham Palace (1475-1500).

In the Iberian peninsula late Gothic work was characterized by elaborate surface decoration. This plateresque ornament, as it is called, was so named in a later period as a term of disapprobation, referring to its affinity with silverwork (*platería*), which was a major Spanish industry at the time. The use

590 Hollola Church, Finland, c.1480

592 Church of St John the Baptist, Cirencester, c.1400-1500

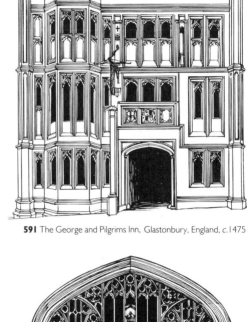

591 The George and Pilgrims Inn, Glastonbury, England, c.1475

593 Panel tracery, St George's Chapel, Windsor, c.1485-1509

Florentine Renaissance, born Alessandro di Mariano dei Filipepi in Florence. His two famous allegories, painted for the Medici villa at Costello, *Primavera* (1477-8) and *Birth of Venus* (1485-8), both now in the Uffizi Gallery in Florence, are his best known works

1453 The English expelled from France with the exception of Calais

1471 Birth at Nuremberg of Albrecht Dürer, the great artist of the Renaissance in northern Europe, known especially for his outstanding contributions to the graphic arts in imagery and in the developing techniques of woodcutting and engraving

1473 Birth at Torun in Poland of Nicolaus Koppernigk – the name was later latinized to Copernicus – the founder of modern astronomy. He established the heliocentric concept that the earth is not, as previously believed, the centre of the universe but is a planet revolving about the sun in the company of other planets and that it is the sun which is the centre of such a system

1474 Translation by William Caxton of *Recuyell of the Historyes of Troye*. Caxton then joined Colard Mansion in Bruges in printing the work, the first book published in the English language. A few years later Caxton printed, among other books in his Westminster premises, Chaucer's *Canterbury Tales* and Malory's *Morte D'Arthur*

1475–80 The adoption in northern Europe of linenfold panelling, where a representation of material folded vertically appears in wall panelling.

SPAIN AND PORTUGAL

SPAIN

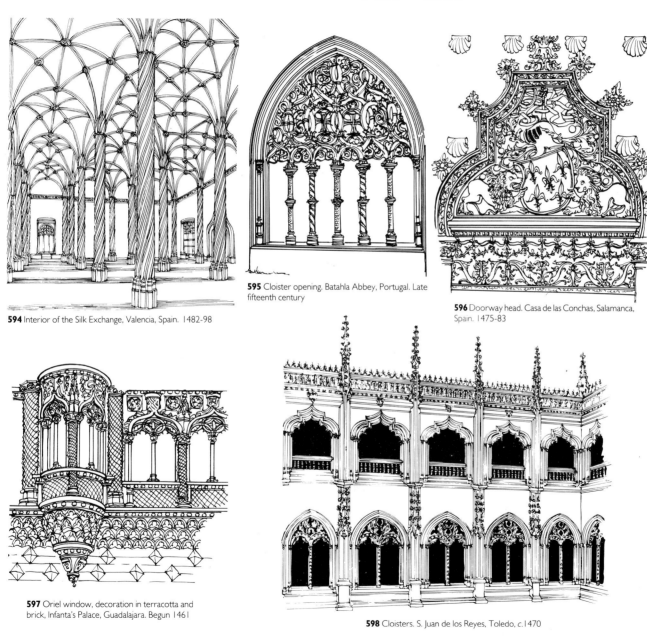

594 Interior of the Silk Exchange, Valencia, Spain. 1482-98

595 Cloister opening. Batahla Abbey, Portugal. Late fifteenth century

596 Doorway head. Casa de las Conchas, Salamanca, Spain. 1475-83

597 Oriel window, decoration in terracotta and brick, Infanta's Palace, Guadalajara. Begun 1461

598 Cloisters. S. Juan de los Reyes, Toledo, c.1470

of the word plateresque emphasizes the entirely surface character of the decoration, which had only a minimal relationship to the architectural form beneath. As it was applied all over doorways, portals, or even whole façades, it tended to blur the architectural articulation with a carpet of ornament. Motifs were of Gothic inspiration and included plant, bird, animal and human forms as well as heraldic themes, all in fairly high relief. This type of excessive decoration continued well into the sixteenth century, only the motifs changing, from Gothic to Renaissance, as time passed. Notable examples of fifteenth-century date include the west portal of the church of S. Cruz at Segovia, the façade of the College of S. Gregorio in Valladolid and the façade of S. Pablo in the same city (**596, 597, 599, 601**).

The Manoeline style represents, to a certain extent, the Portuguese equivalent to Spanish plateresque. It is so-called after Dom Manoel I who reigned 1495-1521, during the period when Portugal was establishing her new sea routes and her great navigators were exploring the world. Manoel was a patron of the arts and helped to encourage the rich decoration of buildings. The style, like plateresque, is essentially of surface decoration. Aptly, the motifs carved were often of marine origin – sea shells, twisted ropes, seaweed – intermingled with oriental forms. The cloister openings at Batahla Abbey are of this type of design (**595, 600**).

Hall churches continued to be built in Germany and further east in Austria and Czechoslovakia. S. Jakob in Brno and S. James in Kutna Hora are typical (**604**).

A number of countries which were building in late Gothic styles developed their own, individual designs of vaulting. While England was building fan vaults, the Spanish and Portuguese were designing elaborate vaults of a different type, based on an extrapolation of earlier vaulting forms as in, for example, the Silk Exchange at Valencia (**594**). In Czechoslovakia an intricate type of vault which displays plaited swirls evolved. The palace interiors of the Vladislav Hall of Prague Castle show this clearly (**606, 608**), as do the slightly later vaults in the church of S. Barbara at Kutna Hora (**625**).

Building styles in the country which is now Yugoslavia are naturally very mixed, as the modern state comprises a blend of a number of very different cultures. In the fifteenth century in the south the Byzantine influence was paramount, but along the Adriatic coastline the architecture was dominated by the Venetian Republic. A mixture of Romanesque and Gothic forms can be seen in the Ćipiko Palace at Trogir (**609**) and in the Cathedral of Šibenik (**607**). In Dubrovnik the local authorities began a new palace for the rectors. Though restored, this is still an interesting building, especially the carved capitals of the loggia (**610-612**).

In Italy the other great fifteenth-century Renaissance architect, Leon Battista Alberti (1404-72), was continuing in the tradition begun by Brunelleschi. Alberti was born in Genoa. He was more of an academic than Brunelleschi; a writer, with an intellectual and mathematical approach to classicism. He also had studied the ruins surviving from the Roman Empire, and was also a sculptor. His famous books on architecture spread Renaissance ideas and classical designs throughout Italy and into western Europe.

Alberti's church architecture reflects his personality. His façade to S. Maria Novella in Florence (**622**), where he solved the

599 Façade portal, plateresque ornament, College of S. Gregorio, Valladolid, Spain, *c.*1492

600 Cloister detail, Batahla Abbey, Portugal

602 Cloister. S. Juan de los Reyes, Toledo

601 Façade detail. Church of S. Pablo, Valladolid, *c.*1460

Such folds were produced by a moulding plane and the ends were then finished by a hand carver

*c.*1480 Flyer mechanism for the spinning wheel first appeared in an illustration, though it seems to have originated earlier than this. The advantage of the incorporation of the flyer and bobbin was that it enabled the spinster to undertake the two processes of twisting and winding on the thread as a continuous operation, rather than having to stop spinning in order to wind on a spun length of thread. A flyer of this type is illustrated by Leonardo da Vinci in one of his sketchbooks (*Codice Atlantico*)

1483 Tomas de Torquemada nominated Inquisitor General of Spain by the Catholic Monarchs King Ferdinand of Aragon and Queen Isabella of Castile; his appointment was confirmed by the Pope. Torquemada was a Dominican Prior in Segovia. He established an efficient and just organization to run the Inquisition

1485 Yeomen of the Guard constituted as a corps by Henry VII

1486 First printed edition of the volumes of *De Architectura*, written by Marcus Vitruvius Pollio in the first century BC

1487 The Star Chamber – court of civil and criminal jurisdiction – re-established by Henry VII at Westminster

1487 Discovery of the Cape of Good Hope by the Portuguese navigator Bartolommeo Diaz

Late fifteenth century
Developments in shipbuilding and

1450 – 1500

CZECHOSLAVAKIA AND YUGOSLAVIA

603 Town Hall and houses in the Market Square, Tabor, Czechoslavakia. Late fifteenth and early sixteenth centuries. Restored 1878

604 Interior. Church of S. Jakob, Brno, Czechoslovakia. 1480-1500

605 Convent Church in the Market Square, Tabor. Late-fifteenth and early-sixteenth-century work

606 Detail of Vaulting. Vladislav Hall

607 Wheel window façade Šibenik Cathedral, Yugoslavia. 1440-1540

centuries-old problem of reconciling the differing heights of nave and aisles in façade design by the insertion of giant side scolls, is a mathematical solution; the church façade was a prototype which influenced the design of many later churches. The treatment is typically Tuscan in its coloured marble veneer, but correctly classical in proportion and detail. Alberti's S. Francesco at Rimini has a different but equally finely detailed and articulated façade. Probably his finest work is S. Andrea in Mantua; certainly far ahead of its time in the handling of the crossing dome, the coffered barrel vaults and aisleless nave. Here is a proto-baroque method of dealing with space enclosure, not seen again until Vignola's II Gesú (p. 122).

Italy was a country of many city-states, controlled by rich merchants and church families. These wealthy men built palaces in the city centres, which still needed protective fortification, and comprised living, office and warehouse accommodation. Florentine palaces are the prime instances and the most characteristic. The street fronts are rusticated and fortified in appearance with few, small openings on the lower floors (used for shop and warehouse quarters), while classical windows lit the living accommodation above. The strongly projecting cornice was usual. The ground plan is square and inside opens into a courtyard, which contrasts with the exterior in the delicate lightness of its arcades and colonnades. Most Florentine palaces of this time are astylar (no façade orders) but Alberti's Palazzo Rucellai (**613**) set a new pattern with its superimposed pilastered orders, giving an articulation to such elevations not emulated for a number of years. Other palaces in Florence include the Medici-Riccardi (1444-60) by Michelozzo, the Strozzi (1489) by da Maiano, the Gondi (1490-8) by da Sangallo and the vast Pitti Palace (begun 1458 and enlarged *c*.1550) designed possibly by Brunelleschi or Alberti. This is perhaps the most typical and impressive façade of all, with its tremendous rusticated length a tribute to the wealth of Florentine merchants.

Venetian palaces of this date are not so very different from the Gothic Ca' d'Oro (569), though classical fenestration and detail slowly began to replace the medieval, as in the Palazzo Vendramin-Calergi (623). One of the finest of the fifteenth-century examples is the Ducal Palace at Urbino, set high on a hill top giving magnificent views. The courtyard, in particular, is elegantly proportioned in pure Renaissance style (616).

A different type of early Renaissance work was developed in Lombardy and the Po valley (p. 73). Due to the Gothic tradition, the Renaissance building style was decorative rather than structural, and in this shared a common factor with later development in Germany, Flanders and England. Typical of such north Italian buildings is the façade of the Certosa di Pavia (615) and the Colleoni Chapel at Bergamo (617). These are both elaborately decorated marble-faced structures in rich colour and good craftsmanship, but the Renaissance decoration is only of surface character while the construction remains medieval.

The Italians pioneered the concept of town planning in city centres. They had a long tradition of urban living and this led them, as early as the thirteenth century in Todi, to group civic buildings and the cathedral round the principal square of the town

In the fifteenth century revival of interest

608 Plaited, swirling vaulting. Vladislav Hall, Prague Castle, Czechoslovakia. 1487-1500

609 Čipiko Palace façade, Trogir, Yugoslavia. Fifteenth century

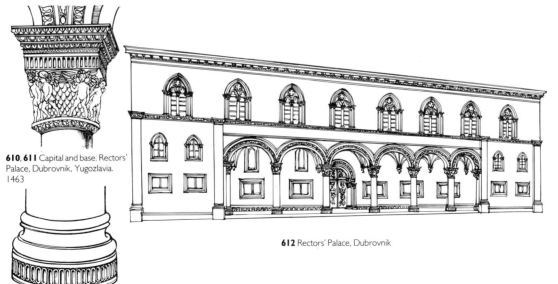

610, 611 Capital and base. Rectors' Palace, Dubrovnik, Yugozlavia. 1463

612 Rectors' Palace, Dubrovnik

design made necessary by the long voyages being undertaken by the European explorers and navigators of the time. The three-masted merchantman (carrack) was a strongly-built ship with a bow and poop swept up fore-and-aft to a high deck, with a lower waist in the centre. These ships could sail well with variable wind direction

Late fifteenth century Increased use of water-wheels to power industrial needs. This led to the development of industry in and around towns where running water was available

Late fifteenth century Increase of mechanization in mining industries. Examples included the crank and connecting rod system. Rails were installed to run small trucks on to different parts of the mine

Late fifteenth century Improvements in the design of lock gates, which led to an extensive development of canal systems

1492 Under the patronage of Ferdinand and Isabella, Christopher Columbus sailed from Palos in the south of Spain across the Atlantic Ocean, reaching the Bahamas two months later

1493 Publication of the Nuremberg Chronicle, a work which contained some 2000 woodcuts depicting views of cities and portraits

1494 Publication of *Summa de aritmetica, geometria, proportioni e proportionità*, an account of mathematical research of the period, by Luca Pacioli, a Franciscan monk and Italian mathematician. The book

1450 – 1500

613 Palazzo Rucellai, Florence, Alberti. Begun 1446

614 Detail panel from bronze doors 'Gate of Paradise' (east). Baptistery, Florence Cathedral, Lorenzo Ghiberti. 1425-52

615 Façade entablature. Certosa di Pavia, G.A. Amadeo. 1481

617 The Colleoni Chapel, Bergamo, G.A. Amadeo. 1470-6

616 Ducal Palace, Urbino, the courtyard, Laurana. 1465-79

in planning towns specifically on an architectural and social basis, not only expediency, came with the Renaissance rediscovery of the schemes that had been developed under the Roman Empire. The new town centre of Pienza was an early experiment on these lines. Pienza was the creation of Pope Pius II (elected 1458) who planned a rebuilding of his own village and called it after himself. A small town between Arezzo and Orvieto, it appears to have altered little since Pius II's day. The centre of the town is planned round a piazza with cathedral, town hall and palaces (618, 621). The town hall is still rather medieval in appearance though with classical detail, but the Palazzo Piccolomini bears a resemblance to Alberti's Palazzo Rucellai in Florence.

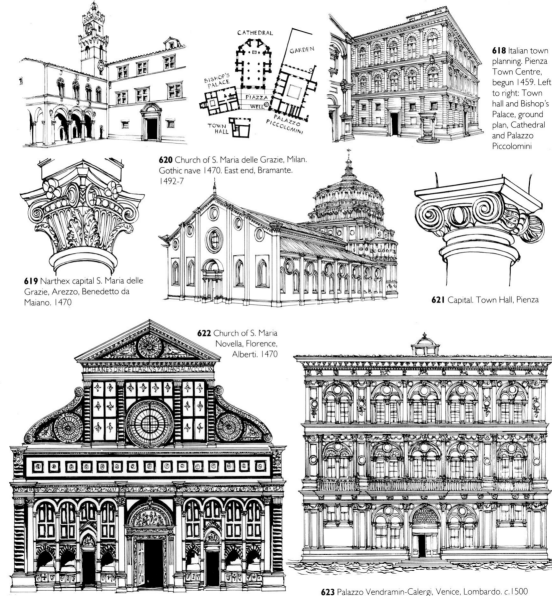

618 Italian town planning. Pienza Town Centre, begun 1459. Left to right: Town hall and Bishop's Palace, ground plan, Cathedral and Palazzo Piccolomini

620 Church of S. Maria delle Grazie, Milan. Gothic nave 1470. East end, Bramante. 1492-7

619 Narthex capital S. Maria delle Grazie, Arezzo, Benedetto da Maiano. 1470

621 Capital. Town Hall, Pienza

622 Church of S. Maria Novella, Florence, Alberti. 1470

623 Palazzo Vendramin-Calergi, Venice, Lombardo. c.1500

also contained an account of the systems of double-entry bookkeeping

1495–8 The painting of *The Last Supper* by Leonardo da Vinci

1497 First voyage to India, made via the Cape of Good Hope by the Portuguese navigator Vasco da Gama. He reached Calicut, a town which gave its name to the cotton fabric 'calico', long imported from there

1497 and 1498 Voyages by the Italian explorer John Cabot from Bristol to North America, where he visited Maine and Newfoundland

1498 Savanarola, the Italian friar and religious reformer, was publicly hanged and his body burned in the Plazza della Signoria in Florence: his ashes were scattered into the river Arno

1499–1500 Voyage of the Italian explorer Amerigo Vespucci across the Atlantic Ocean and his discovery and exploration of the coast of South America

LATE GOTHIC 1500 – 1550

624 Hampton Court Palace, England. Base Court showing Anne Boleyn's gateway and, behind on left, the great hall. 1520-36

625 Vault. Church of S. Barbara, Kutná Hora, Czechoslovakia. Early sixteenth century

628 Chimneystack, Hengrave Hall. 1525-38

629 The Feathers Inn Ludlow. Timber-framed building. 1520-30

627 Hall lantern, Horham Hall. 1502-20

626 Interior. Bath Abbey, 1501-39. Designed Robert and William Vertue

English architecture entered its final Gothic phase in this half-century; the style was a continuation of the Perpendicular, as was evidenced in the stone fan vaults, the hammerbeam timber-trussed roofs, the panelled window tracery and the use of the four-centred arch. The shape of the arch became rather flatter in Tudor times as can be seen in door and window heads and, especially, in fireplace design.

Most of the building during the sixteenth century was in the civic, university and domestic sphere (627-9, 632-4); so many churches had been constructed during the Middle Ages that few new ones were erected. Only additions or alterations were made to existing buildings, generally in the form of porches, chapels or enlarging the fenestration.

After the Dissolution of the Monasteries and the consequent reapportionment of lands and wealth, many new and large country houses were built. Henry VIII pointed the way in the Palace at Hampton Court, which he took over from Cardinal Wolsey, who had acquired the site in 1514 and built a large house to his own initial design – one suited to a leading churchman. In the fashion of the day the rooms (over 1000 of them) were laid out round quadrangular courts to accommodate the guests and the 500 or so members of Wolsey's household. Henry retained the collegiate layout, but enlarged Wolsey's great house into a palace, building a new and magnificent hall, the interior roofed by James Nedham in hammerbeam style (624).

Ecclesiastical architecture of this time is represented by two fine buildings: Bath Abbey (626, 631) and the Henry VII chapel at Westminster Abbey. The beautiful fan-vaulted chapel at Westminster contains an isolated example of Italian Renaissance work erected in England prior to the seventeenth century. This is the tomb of Henry VII and his queen, the work of Pietro Torrigiano in 1518. It represents Henry VIII's only success in attracting Italian craftsmen to England to design in the new Renaissance style. Such craftsmen preferred to work in France at the Court of Francis I. It was nearer to Italy, the climate was less intemperate and the language more comprehensible. After Henry's break with the Roman Catholic Church, England's tenuous links with Renaissance Italy were broken and when the Renaissance did finally come, in Elizabethan times, it was of quite different form, derived from the Mannerism of Flanders and Germany (p. 126-7).

Spain and Portugal also continued to build in Gothic style during these years, but this was a very different form from that in England. Characteristic are three great cathedrals, those at Seville, Salamanca and Segovia. Seville Cathedral is of immense size. It was built over a long period and, both in its decoration and layout, showed Moorish influence. The ground plan was dictated by its being built on the site of a Moorish mosque; the slender and beautiful bell tower had been its minaret. Its name 'giralda' (from girar = to turn) refers to the later, Renaissance revolving bronze figure which crowns the belfry.

Segovia and Salamanca are more representative of Spanish late Gothic building. Both are sixteenth-century structures with richly ornamental vaults, window openings and towers, and display a wealth of plateresque all-over decoration (**637**). Similar rich ornamentation in Gothic form may be seen in the central lantern (cimborio) at Burgos Cathedral (**641**) and in

630 Façade. Church of S. Barbara, Kutná Hora, Czechoslovakia. Early sixteenth century

631 West front, Bath Abbey, England. 1501-39

632 Carved and panelled oak door. 1515-30

633 Gateway decoration. St John's College, Cambridge. Early sixteenth century

634 Gateway. Christ Church, Canterbury. 1517

1501 Marriage of Arthur, Prince of Wales, to Catherine of Aragon, linking up the crowns of England and Spain

1502 John Fisher became first professor of Divinity at Cambridge. Induced Erasmus to come to Cambridge

1504 At Nuremberg Peter Henlein, a young locksmith, working under the supervision of an abbot in the cathedral, made the first portable timepiece. This first 'watch' took two years to make. It was made of iron in a drum shape and was spring-driven

1505 Christ's College, Cambridge founded by Lady Margaret Beaufort

1508–9 Sebastian Cabot, Italian explorer and son of John Cabot, voyaged in search of Cathay by way of a Northwest Passage. He travelled by way of Iceland and Greenland to Labrador, then turned south down the North American east coast as far as Virginia, before setting sail for England

1509 Accession of Henry VIII of England

1510 John Colet, Dean of St Paul's Cathedral, founded St Paul's School in London for the free education of poor children. The school statutes stated that the curriculum should include Greek and Latin, together with moral and religious instruction

1511 Hospital of St John, Cambridge, converted into St John's College

1498–1512 Active political life of the Florentine Niccolò Machiavelli, when he served in the chancellery of the Florentine Republic. With the

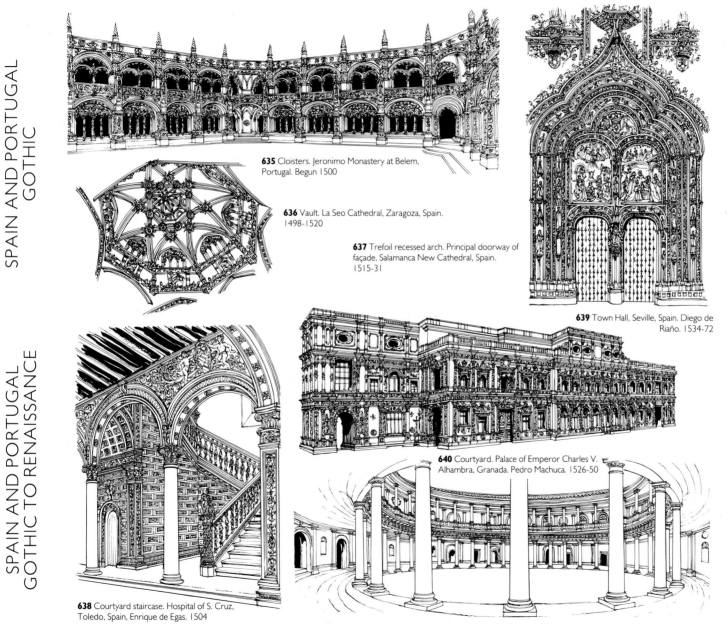

635 Cloisters. Jeronimo Monastery at Belem, Portugal. Begun 1500

636 Vault. La Seo Cathedral, Zaragoza, Spain. 1498-1520

637 Trefoil recessed arch. Principal doorway of façade, Salamanca New Cathedral, Spain. 1515-31

639 Town Hall, Seville, Spain. Diego de Riaño. 1534-72

640 Courtyard. Palace of Emperor Charles V. Alhambra, Granada. Pedro Machuca. 1526-50

638 Courtyard staircase. Hospital of S. Cruz, Toledo, Spain, Enrique de Egas. 1504

the vaulting of La Seo Cathedral in Zaragoza (**636**).

The Portuguese equivalent (Manoeline) decoration is well represented in the Templar's Monastery at Tomar. There are seven cloisters in this monastery, of which one is a fine Gothic example (**645**). In the chapter house of the church there is a window displaying superb Manoeline ornamentation. Designed by Diogo de Arruda, its frame is composed of a wealth of marine decoration (**643**). The last great Gothic building enterprise in Portugal is the Jeronimo Monastery at Belem near Lisbon. Its hall church displays riches of fine ornamentation in its fenestration, portals and lierne vaults. As at Batahla (p. 104), the cloisters are the glory of the monastery. These are two-storeyed, with traceried and cusped openings, and have lierne vaults roofing each storey. There is infinite variety in the carved decoration of column and pier shafts (**635, 642**).

Spain is rich in examples of buildings which are influenced decoratively or entirely by Renaissance ideas, but only a minority of these are in pure classical style. There are three principal stages in Renaissance development in the architecture of the years 1500 to 1700. The Renaissance is evidenced in the early work in an essentially surface decorative form; a plateresque treatment, which differs from the Gothic plateresque of the late fifteenth century only in the motifs used. The façade of the University of Salamanca is a superb example of this (**644**), and it is interesting to compare it with the façade of the New Cathedral in the city (**637**) and the slightly earlier work at Valladolid (**599, 601**).

One of the most successful architects in this type of plateresque work of the early

sixteenth century was Enrique de Egas (d. 1534). He built the great Hospicio de los Reyes Catolicos in Santiago de Compostela (1501-11). This fine building is now one of Spain's luxury hotels; its façade looks on to the main square, adjacent to the cathedral. The architect's masterpiece is the Hospital of S. Cruz de Mendoza in Toledo, begun in 1504. The entrance portal is a beautiful plateresque feature. But, behind this, Egas designed the interior court and staircase in a much purer, Italianate style: this is a very early example of such work in Spain (638).

Another exceptionally early instance of more strictly Roman classicism is the circular courtyard of the Alhambra Palace at Granada, commissioned by the Emperor Charles V and designed by Pedro Muchaca (1527-50). This is a two-storeyed classical colonnade, based upon designs from the Emperor Hadrian's second-century villa at Tivoli. The architecture of this courtyard is plain, almost severe, and in great contrast to both the contemporary Spanish plateresque and the Moorish palace in the Alhambra.

The second stage of Renaissance development in Spain is still plateresque in decoration, but evinces a tentative understanding of classical principles and construction. Characteristic is the town hall in Seville (639). Particularly interesting is the work of Diego de Siloé (1495-1563). He is known especially for his Escalera Dorada in Burgos Cathedral (1524) which, in its symmetry and handling, indicates his debt to Michelangelo's Laurenziana Library in Florence (p. 117). De Siloé worked for many years on the partly-built Gothic Granada Cathedral. The resulting interior is, therefore, a blend of Gothic and classical forms presenting, for instance, crossing piers of the Corinthian order, on pedestals

641 Cimborio, Burgos Cathedral, Spain. Early sixteenth century

642 Cloister detail, Jerail Monastery, Belem

644 University of Salamanca, capital, plateresque decoration. 1516-29

643 Chapter House window, Convent of Christ, Tomar, Portugal. Manoeline decoration. Diogo de Arruda. Early sixteenth century

645 Cloister capitals, Convent of Christ, Tomar

return of the Medici to Florence in 1512, Machiavelli retired from public life and, until his death in 1517, lived quietly, writing his political, historical and literary works; for example, *The Prince*, 1513, *The Discourses*, 1519, *The Art of War*, 1519-20, and *The Florentine History*, 1525

1513 The Spanish explorer Juan Ponce de León discovered Florida and took possession of the land in the name of Ferdinand of Spain. He landed near the coast of St Augustine. Because it was April, he called it *Pascua Florida* (Flowery Easter)

1515 Thomas Wolsey made a Cardinal. Henry VIII also made him Lord Chancellor of England

1518 Thomas Linacre, physician to Henry VIII, founded the College of Physicians and was its first president

1500–1519 Last years of Leonardo da Vinci. His works at this time included a great mural in the Palazzo Vecchio in Florence, the *Mona Lisa*, and a tremendous number of maps and notebooks full of anatomical, architectural, mathematical and mechanical studies

1500–1520 Second half of the short life of Raphael (Raffaello Sanzio), Italian painter and architect. Notable are: 1507-8, Madonna portraits in Florence; 1509-17, The Vatican Stanze in Rome; 1517-20, Sistine Chapel Tapestry Cartoons, Palaces in Rome and Florence, Villa Madama; 1514-20, Architect of St Peter's Basilica

DENMARK AND BELGIUM

646 Egeskov Manor House, Kvaerndrup, Denmark. 1545

BELGIUM, YUGOSLAVIA POLAND

647 Town Hall, Oudenaarde, Belgium. 1525-9

648 Sponza Palace (Custom House and Mint) Dubrovnik, Yugoslavia. 1516-21

649 Maison des Francs-Bateliers, Ghent, Belgium. 1531

supporting classical entablatures and a medieval lierne vault.

The wealth of the merchants and guilds continued to be reflected in the richly ornamented civic buildings of Belgian towns (647, 649). The constructional style was still medieval, but the decorative motifs were changing towards a Mannerist form of Renaissance design.

In classical architecture Mannerism is a term which may be used to indicate a rigid form of academic classicism but, more commonly, it refers to the use of classical forms and motifs in a manner different from that traditionally accepted. This might be as a result of an architect of brilliance and originality wishing to vary the usual way of designing, and thus intentionally breaking some of the antique and Renaissance rules in order to create a new effect. This was what a number of sixteenth-century Italian architects, such as Michelangelo, Romano and Vignola did, in fact, do (pp. 117, 122). Alternatively, as in the case of sixteenth-century Flanders, Germany and England, the effect was due to an imperfect understanding of the classical orders, which led to them being utilized incorrectly and decoratively, rather than structurally. This was the case in Belgium where, as in the episcopal palace in Liège (650), the design is medieval, with Gothic arches and dormers, but the arcade is carried on bulging columns ornamented by strapwork and topped by a Mannerist version of Ionic capitals. Another instance is the palace of justice in Bruges, where there are superimposed orders with strange capitals, Gothic-style fenestration with rich banded decoration between, and tall gables with high relief animal and human sculptural ornament.

The domestic architecture of Denmark

also evidenced a reluctance to abandon the medieval and semi-fortified aspect but, here again, Renaissance features in gabling and decoration began tentatively to be introduced. The romantically-sited brick manor house of Egeskov is one such example (**646**).

In Italy, by 1500, the Renaissance had become fully established: at this period in Rome began the High Renaissance style. The architect who was instrumental in introducing this purer Roman classical form was Bramante (born Donato d'Agnolo Lazzari 1444-1514). Bramante came from Urbino, where he had watched the building of the ducal palace (**616**). He began working as an architect in Milan where he designed three cloisters for the Monastery of S. Ambrogio. The Doric cloister (1497-8) is the most mature, and shows clearly his appreciation of the Urbino palace and the purity of his Roman style.

Like Brunelleschi, Bramante was particularly interested in the classical concept of the symmetry of the centrally planned building. He had studied Brunelleschi's work, and also the drawings of Leonardo da Vinci. He reconstructed the tiny ninth-century church of S. Maria presso S. Satiro; then went on to build the east end of the Gothic church of S. Maria delle Grazie, in the form of a polygonal drum with three subordinate apses. Bramante's S. Maria (**620**) inspired many other architects to design centrally planned churches, a classic instance of which is S. Maria della Consolazione in Todi. It is a completely symmetrical square building with an apse on all four sides, surmounted by a drum and dome (**655**).

Bramante moved from Milan to Rome at the beginning of the new century, where he

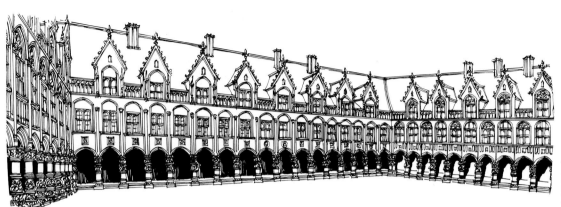

650 Courtyard. Episcopal Palace, Liège, Belgium. 1525-32

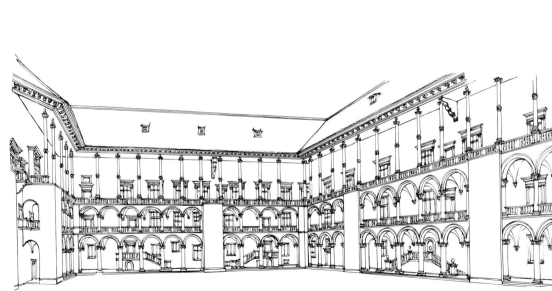

651 Central courtyard, Royal Palace, Cracow, Poland, Bartolommeo Berrecci. From 1506

ITALY

ITALY

652 Chapel in courtyard of S. Pietro in Montorio, Rome Chapel is called 'Il Tempietto', Bramante. 1500-02

653 Interior, Mantua Cathedral, Giulio Romano, c.1545

654 'Dawn'. Tomb of Lorenzo dei Medici, S. Lorenzo, Florence. Michelangelo. Begun 1531

655 Centrally planned church of S. Maria della Consolazione, Todi, c.1520. Style of Bramante

worked on the new Basilica of St Peter, in the Courts of the Vatican and on a small building which became famed as the perfect model for the centrally planned Renaissance structure: a fame out of all proportion to its size. This was a little temple (the Tempietto, **652**) built in the courtyard of S. Pietro in Montorio to mark the supposed site of St Peter's crucifixion. In a typically Renaissance attitude, the temple combined both Christian and pagan influences. It commented upon a Christian event, yet its inspiration was the circular temple of the antique world. The Tempietto is austerely plain, using the Tuscan order. It is perfectly proportioned, each part relating harmoniously to the others.

In 1503 the newly elected Pope Julius II faced the problem of what to do about the almost 1200-year-old Basilica of St Peter, founded by the Emperor Constantine but now in a seriously dilapidated condition. Courageously, the Pope decided to demolish and rebuild. He commissioned Bramante to design a contemporary basilica. The Bramante St Peter's was a vast, domed and completely symmetrical building on Greek cross plan, with apses terminating each arm of the cross (**658**). The Pope laid the foundation stone in 1506 but, when Bramante died in 1514, little had been achieved and the only source of what the façade would have looked like is the foundation medal (**661**).

The towering genius of sixteenth-century Italy was Michelangelo Buonarroti (1475-1564). Probably more has been written about him than any other artist. Even in his lifetime he commanded idolatry from his patrons, the public and his fellow artists. Painter, sculptor, architect; Michelangelo excelled as all these. He came to architecture in his

HIGH RENAISSANCE 1500 – 1550

forties, working in Florence. His architecture there, as elsewhere, has a sculptural quality, a three-dimensional forcefulness and chiarosuro, the antithesis of Alberti's and Bramante's academic classicism.

Of particular interest in Florence is his New Sacristy in the Church of S. Lorenzo where, in his Medici Mausoleum Chapel, he was responsible for the building and the sculpture (654). In his Laurenziana Library, also in the monastery of S. Lorenzo, Michelangelo began to break away from the High Renaissance concept into Mannerism. His work was always original and personal, but here he broke the classical rules with intention to improve his design; this is especially visible in the recessed, coupled columns bearing no load and flanked by blind windows. The entrance hall here is tall and narrow and a feeling of tension and power is produced by the recessed columns. The entrance hall and the ordered and controlled library schemes complement one another in disciplined austerity.

The greater part of sixteenth-century architecture in Italy was in town palaces and country villas, especially in Rome. Many talented architects (who were also artists in other fields) designed such buildings, which were masterpieces of interior decoration in sculpture, painting and mosaic. Some architects designed in classical Renaissance/ Roman style; for example, Antonio da Sangallo (656). But many moved from this approach in their early work to develop an original Mannerist style later: Raphael (Raffaello Sanzio 1483-1520), Baldassare Peruzzi (1481-1536) and Giulio Romano (1499-1546) were among these (653, 657). In the Veneto Sansovino (1486-1570) was the principal architect in Venice, while

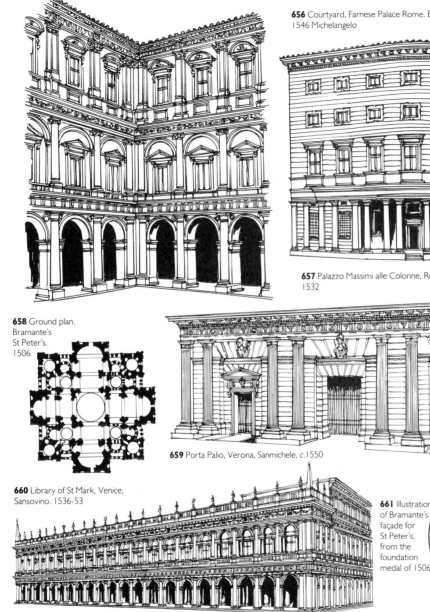

656 Courtyard, Farnese Palace Rome. Before 1514 da Sangallo, after 1546 Michelangelo

657 Palazzo Massimi alle Colonne, Rome, Baldassare Peruzzi. From 1532

658 Ground plan. Bramante's St Peter's. 1506

659 Porta Palio, Verona, Sanmichele, c.1550

660 Library of St Mark, Venice, Sansovino. 1536-53

661 Illustration of Bramante's façade for St Peter's, from the foundation medal of 1506

sealed the conquest of the Inca Empire of Peru with the capture of the royal capital Cuzco

c.1489–1534 Correggio (Antonio Allegri). Outstanding Italian painter

1478–1535 Sir Thomas More, English statesman, philosopher and scholar. His most famous work was *Utopia*, which describes an ideal state. More was beheaded in 1535 for refusing to acknowledge Henry VIII's repudiation of papal authority

c.1469–1536 Desiderius Erasmus, Dutch classical scholar, Renaissance humanist and church reformer

1483–1546 Martin Luther, German Augustinian friar who initiated the Protestant movement

1493–1541 Paracelsus (born Theophrastus Philippus Auroleus Bombastus von Hohenheim). Swiss physician, alchemist and important contributor to the development of the sciences of medicine and chemistry. His medical therapy was based upon the curative power of nature, believing that every disease had a remedy

1498–1543 Hans Holbein the Younger, German Renaissance painter, born in Augsburg but spent much of the last 15 years of his life in England. He painted many court and other dignitaries, including Henry VIII and several of his wives

1546 Cardinal College, Oxford, founded by Wolsey in 1525, became Christ Church

1546 Henry VIII founded Trinity College, Cambridge

1500–1550 Michelangelo Buonarroti (1475–1564). Italian

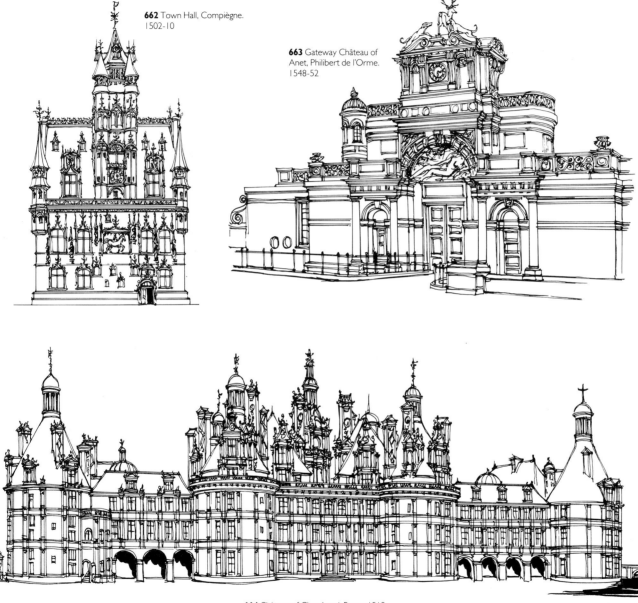

662 Town Hall, Compiègne. 1502-10

663 Gateway Château of Anet, Philibert de l'Orme. 1548-52

664 Château of Chambord. Begun 1519

Sanmichele (1484-1559) worked chiefly in Verona (**659**, **660**). Outside Italy the Venetian Republic extended its influence down the eastern seaboard of the Adriatic (**648**) while, much farther away, there was an early import of the Italian Renaissance which stemmed from Italian artists working in Poland (**651**).

France was the only major European country outside Italy to build in true Renaissance form before the seventeenth century. Even here, however, it was not until after 1550 that such work was to be seen. In the earlier sixteenth century the buildings erected were basically Gothic in structure and classical only in detail. Ecclesiastical and civic buildings were, especially, treated in this way; they lagged behind domestic work, and it was the early seventeenth century before purer forms replaced Mannerist designs. The church of S. Etienne du Mont in Paris and the town hall in Compiègne are examples (**662**).

Though France had close contacts with Italy in the early sixteenth century, and though French designers took easily to using Italianate decorative forms such as orders, scrolls and *putti*, the medieval tradition of building persisted. Architecture was slow to follow classical lines, until the second half of the century when architects like de l'Orme and Lescot, influenced by the work of Italians in France, such as Sebastiano Serlio in his château at Ancy-le-Franc (**668**) and Rosso and Primaticcio at Fontainebleau (**667**), adopted the new style (**663**).

Most of the best architecture of the years 1500-1550 was in palaces and châteaux where wealthy patrons wished to build in the latest mode. The king, Francis I, pointed the way. He established a great court, determined to model his culture on the

GOTHIC TO RENAISSANCE   1500 – 1550

Italian pattern. He attracted many Italian artists and craftsmen to France, even the great Leonardo da Vinci. At Blois, Fontainebleau and Paris, Francis built on Renaissance lines. Others followed suit and French architects, having understood and developed the new style, took to it with pleasure. French Renaissance work is more academic and less plastic than the Italian, but it is of high quality.

The Francis I range at the château of Blois, with its famous staircase – classical in appearance and decoration, though constructed on a double spiral in medieval manner (**665, 669**) – and the extant rebuilding work of the years 1500-1550 at Fontainebleau – are characteristic of the more Italianate approach. On the other hand, picturesque châteaux such as Amboise, Azay-le-Rideau and Chambord, though surface-decorated with Renaissance motifs, remained consistently medieval in fortification and Gothic in construction and layout (**664, 666**).

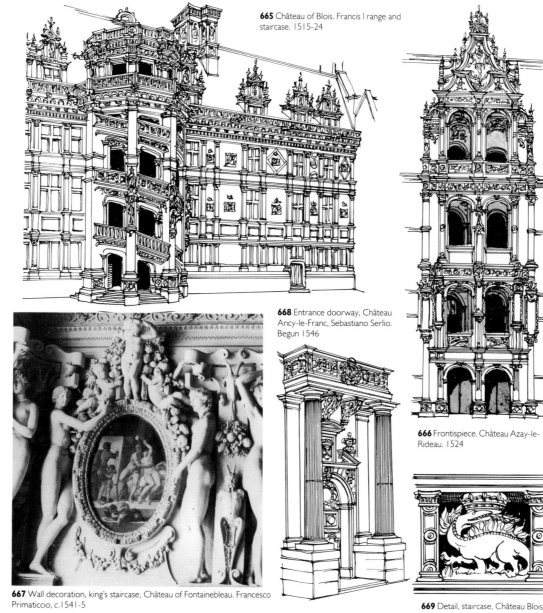

665 Château of Blois. Francis I range and staircase. 1515-24

668 Entrance doorway, Château Ancy-le-Franc, Sebastiano Serlio. Begun 1546

666 Frontispiece. Château Azay-le-Rideau. 1524

667 Wall decoration, king's staircase, Château of Fontainebleau. Francesco Primaticcio, c.1541-5

669 Detail, staircase, Château Blois

painter, sculptor, architect, carried out in these years the major part of his work, for example:
1498-1500 *Pietà*, St Peter's Basilica, Rome
1501-4 Colossal statue of David, Florence
1504 Mural, Palazzo Vecchio, Florence
1508-12 Sistine Chapel ceiling, Rome
1513-16 Moses. Church of S. Pietro in Vincoli, Rome
1520-34 The Medici Mausoleum Chapel, Florence
1523 Laurenziana library, S. Lorenzo, Florence
1535-50 *The Last Judgement*, Sistine Chapel
1545 Julius tomb. S. Pietro in Vincoli
1546 Campidoglio, Rome
1547-64 Architect of St Peter's Basilica, Rome

1514-64 Andreas Vesalius, Belgian anatomist who became famous for his anatomical demonstrations in Padua. He published several anatomical works, notably one beautifully illustrated by woodcuts made by Jan Stevenszoon van Calcar, a pupil of Titian, which was printed in Basel in 1543

c.1480–1576 Titian (Tiziano Vecellio), greatest master of the Venetian School of Painting

1517–90 Ambroise Paré, a French surgeon who instigated new methods of healing the wounds of war casualties

RENAISSANCE 1550 – 1600

ITALY

670, 671, 672 Basilica of St Peter, Rome. Exterior view of the west end. Michelangelo: 1547-64. Michelangelo's ground plan; interior of transepts and crossing, Michelangelo 1547-64. Bernini's baroque baldacchino omitted

673 The Cour Carrée, Louvre, Paris. Range left of clock pavilion by Pierre Lescot, 1546-55. Sculpture largely by Jean Goujon. Restored nineteenth century

FRANCE

Michelangelo took over, as Prefect of Works, surveyorship of St Peter's Basilica in Rome in 1547. He spent the last 30 years of his life in the city, and regarded St Peter's as his most important commission, refusing any salary and working on the building until his death at the age of 89. He greatly admired Bramante's plan and, with modifications, retained it, though reducing the area (and so the cost) and simplifying the small compartments into fewer, larger ones (**671**).

Much of the building as it is seen today is the work of Michelangelo. As primarily a sculptor, he first made a clay model of his intended basilica, then translated this into wood. His church is vast, but so perfectly proportioned that the size is not apparent until one compares the height of a human being with one of the great piers. On the exterior Michelangelo used the Corinthian order in giant pilaster form, each 100ft high and surmounted by a 32ft high attic. The whole forms a podium upon which the great drum and dome rest. There are three apses, one at the choir – the west end, because the new St Peter's was built on the same alignment as the old, which had been erected before it was customary to orientate a church towards the east (p. 25) – and one to each transept. The central dome is cozened by its four smaller domes situated between the crossing arms (**670**).

When Michelangelo died the basilica was largely complete, except for the west end of the nave and the dome above the drum. The giant dome, of 137ft span, was completed 1587-90 by Giacomo della Porta and Domenico Fontana. Like Brunelleschi's dome at Florence Cathedral (p. 97) it is constructed with a double shell, the outer one rising to be slightly taller than the hemisphere planned, and so not concentric

RENAISSANCE 1550 – 1600

with the inner dome for the same reasons as at Florence; that is, the safety of the structure.

The interior of St Peter's (672) is also mainly by Michelangelo. Architecturally it is simple in its coffered and panelled barrel vaults, and vast crossing dome rising from pendentives which are supported on four great crossing piers. Despite the lengthening of the nave arm into a Latin cross plan in the seventeenth century (p. 135), the design of the basilica interior is remarkably homogeneous. That this is so in a building begun in 1506 and not completed until 1612 is in no small part due to the overriding genius of Michelangelo.

The most influential architect at this time in the Veneto was Andrea Palladio (1508–80). His work, like that of Alberti and Michelangelo, profoundly affected architects of other nations and in other ages as well as that of his own. This was apparent in the Palladian movement in Holland in the 1620s and 1630s (p. 129) and in early-seventeenth-century England in the influence upon Inigo Jones (p. 131) and, a century later, the Burlingtonian School (p. 135-4).

Palladio endeavoured to pattern his work clearly on the ancient Roman prototypes – where necessary adapting the forms to the different building needs of his day, as in church design, for example. He made hundreds of drawings of Roman monuments in Rome and as far afield as Dalmatia and Provence; he also gave careful attention to Vitruvius's books on architecture. Of his own publications, his *I Quattro Libri dell'Architettura* and *Le Antichità di Roma* were translated into many languages and provided the basis for Italian Renaissance building all over Europe. His own architectural style was strongly influenced by

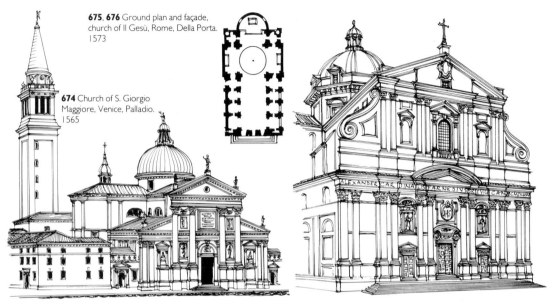

675, 676 Ground plan and façade, church of Il Gesù, Rome, Della Porta. 1573

674 Church of S. Giorgio Maggiore, Venice, Palladio. 1565

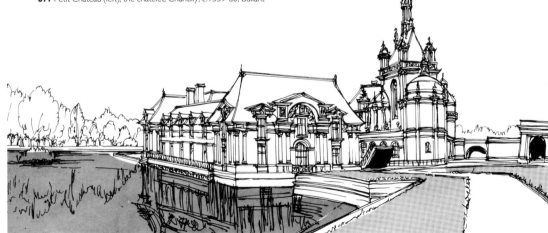

677 Petit Château (left), the châtelet, Chantilly, c.1559-60, Bullant

1550 First publication of Giorgio Vasari's *The Lives of the Most Excellent Italian Architects, Painters and Sculptors*, which describes the development of Italian art from the thirteenth to the sixteenth century

1550 The town of Helsinki founded by Gustav I Vasa, King of Sweden

1556 Archbishop Cranmer burned at the stake

1556 Publication in Basel of *De Re Metallica*, a 12 volume work on mining, metallurgy and geology which became the standard guide and textbook – especially in mining – for the following two centuries. Written by Georg Bauer (Latinized as Georgius Agricola, 1494-1555), the German scholar from Saxony, who was known as the 'father of mineralogy and geology'

1515–64 Andreas Vesalius, Flemish anatomist and physician. His great work *De Humani Corporis Fabrica*, a book of anatomical studies based upon his own experience in human dissection, became the basis of anatomical study for 200 years. The fine woodcut illustrations came from the studio of Titian

1558 England expelled from Calais, the last English possession in mainland France

1561 Philip II made Madrid his official residence in Spain and the centre of the Spanish court. It became the capital city

1561 Publication of *Observationes Anatomicae*, the work of Gabriel Fallopius. Fallopius was an Italian anatomist and physician. He is particularly known for his description

RENAISSANCE TOWARDS BAROQUE   1550 – 1600

ITALY

BELGIUM, DENMARK,
SWITZERLAND, GERMANY

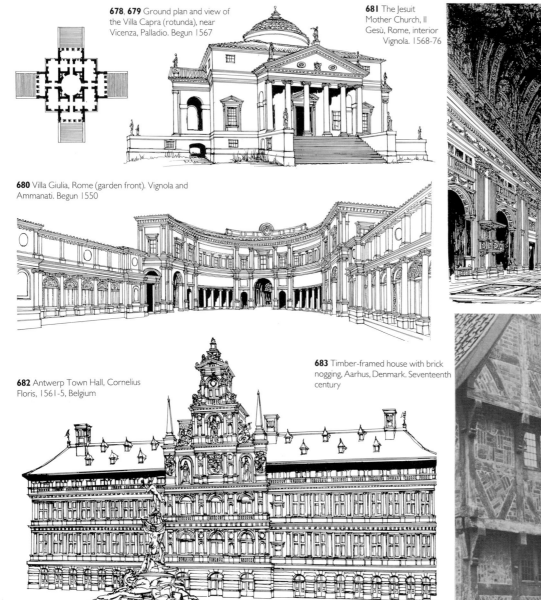

678, **679** Ground plan and view of
the Villa Capra (rotunda), near
Vicenza, Palladio. Begun 1567

680 Villa Giulia, Rome (garden front). Vignola and
Ammanati. Begun 1550

682 Antwerp Town Hall, Cornelius
Floris, 1561-5, Belgium

681 The Jesuit
Mother Church, Il
Gesù, Rome, interior
Vignola. 1568-76

683 Timber-framed house with brick
nogging, Aarhus, Denmark. Seventeenth
century

the pure classicism of Bramante, but also by the vivid Mannerism of Michelangelo and Vignola (**680**). Especially notable of his works, which became a pattern for other architects, were his Villa Capra (the Rotunda) near Vicenza (**678**, **679**), his Palazzo Chiericati in the city (**687**) and his Venetian churches (**674**).

In church design in Rome the building of the Mother Church, Il Gesù, for the Society of Jesus, which had been founded by Loyola in 1540, was a breakthrough, marking the crossroads between Mannerism and Baroque. The great church was begun in 1568 under the architect Giacomo da Vignola (1507-73). His terms of reference stated that the building must be able to accommodate a large congregation, all of whom must be able to hear and see the preacher. This was a similar need to that in post-Reformation churches of northern Europe, such as those built by Wren in the City of London after the Great Fire (p. 140-1).

Vignola designed a church with a wide, short, barrel-vaulted nave and choir, and with shallow transepts to give space and good acoustics and vision. There are no aisles or colonnades, only side chapels. To compensate for the lack of side-aisle illumination, the architect provided a large dome with a fenestrated drum, which dramatically floods the interior with light, giving a sense of space and unity hitherto unknown in the Gothic and Renaissance churches built on the Latin cross basilican plan. Il Gesù became the pattern for Jesuit churches all over Europe. The façade was completed by Giacomo della Porta (1540-1602) after Vignola's death (**675**, **676**, **681**).

After 1550, in France, several architects were developing a purer classical style based on that of the Italian Renaissance. Philibert de l'Orme, born 1520, was one of France's first professional architects. The son of a master mason, he had studied for some years in Italy, making measured, on-the-spot drawings and becoming fully conversant with the classical theme and grammar. His major publication, in nine volumes in 1569, was *Premier Livre de L'Architecture*. De l'Orme was Superintendent of the King's Buildings, and in this capacity worked at Fontainebleau; he also designed the terrace across the river at the Château of Chenonceaux. His principal contribution was the Château of Anet (1547-52), of which most of the buildings, with the exception of the gateway and the chapel, have unfortunately been lost (663).

Jean Bullant was also born c.1520. He too worked for some years in Rome. His style was more vigorous and Mannerist than that of de l'Orme and, new in France, he introduced the Giant Order to his designs on Michelangelo's pattern. He worked at the Château of Ecouen and built the châtelet, the Petit Château, at Chantilly (677), which stands on an island in the lake adjacent to the main building.

Pierre Lescot (c.1510-78) was commissioned by Francis I in 1546 to demolish the old palace of the Louvre in Paris and rebuild on modern lines. He created a new west wing and began a south wing, now part of the Cour Carrée. He created here, for the first time in France, elevations on Italian palace courtyard lines. There are three storeys in one long façade, broken only by projecting frontispieces. The theme is Italian, but the treatment French and identifiably Lescot (673).

During the fifteenth and sixteenth centuries in Italy a number of ideas were put forward for an ideal city planned on radial

684 The Capital (Campidoglio) Rome, including the Palazzo Capitolino, Palazzo del Senatore and the Palazzo dei Conservatori. 1540-1644. Designed by Michelangelo

687 Palazzo Chiericati, Vicenza, Palladio. Begun 1550

686 Palmanova. 1590

689 The Spieshof, Basel, Switzerland, c.1580

685 Filarete's design for Sforzinda

688 Scamozzi's ideal city plan

690 Heidelberg Castle, Ottheinrichsbau Wing, Germany. 1556-9

of the oviduct; the tube in the female which connects the ovary to the uterus, and which was named after him

c.1565   Introduction of tobacco into England

1568   The geographer Mercator devised his projection for the drawing of maps. In 1585 he published a book of maps, the cover of which depicted the giant Atlas supporting the world upon his shoulders. This gave rise to the use of the term 'atlas' for such a book

1558–66   Benvenuto Cellini, Florentine goldsmith and sculptor, wrote his famous *Life of Benvenuto Cellini* (published posthumously in 1728); a forceful autobiography which vividly depicted life in sixteenth-century Renaissance Italy

1550–76   The later period of Titian's work (Tiziano Vecellio), the greatest master of the Venetian school of painting

c.1570   Potatoes introduced into Europe; first in Spain, where they were being grown and eaten at this time

1546–1601   Famous Danish astronomer Tycho Brahe, who recorded details of planetary motions with a new degree of accuracy

1518–94   Tintoretto, after Titian the leading painter of the late Renaissance in Venice. Born Jacopo Robusti, he was nicknamed Tintoretto (little dyer) because his father was a dyer

1572   St Bartholomew's Day massacre of the French Huguenots of Paris

RENAISSANCE   1550 – 1600

691 The crossing. Monastery Church of the Escorial, Spain, Juan de Herrera, c.1584

693 Patio, Tavera Hospital, Toledo, Spain. 1541-79

692 Church of S. Vicente da Fora, Lisbon, Portugal, Filippo Terzi. 1582-1627

694 Detail, courtyard, Kirby Hall, England, c.1570

and/or grid lines. Antonio Averlino, nicknamed Il Filarete (1400-69), wrote a lengthy treatise (1460-4) in which he designed his ideal city which he called Sforzinda in deference to Francesco Sforza, the powerful Duke of Milan. This was a radially planned, star-shaped city enclosed within a circle (685). Several architects produced radial plans but only one was carried out (1593), that of Vincenzo Scamozzi's (1552-1616) nonagonal fortress town of Palmanova, near Venice (686). Scamozzi's own ideal city was dodecagonal in shape and contained a grid pattern layout of streets, not a radial one. This was more practical and was later more generally adopted as a guide (688).

As always, it was Leonardo da Vinci (1452-1519) who was producing drawings of ideas far in advance of his time. He was not only concerned with planning a city in an orderly, practical way, but also with segregating its wheeled traffic from its people. One of his drawings shows a city built on different levels, where the civic centre, pedestrian ways and housing were above, separated from the roads, canals and drainage beneath.

Although it was rare to build complete new cities at this time, parts, and especially centres of older cities were redesigned in a classical, symmetrical manner. Pienza has already been discussed (618 and p. 108). Other examples include the Piazza dei Signori in Verona, the Piazza San Marco in Venice and the Piazza dell'Annunziata in Florence.

One of the most influential of such Renaissance civic schemes was Michelangelo's redesigning of the Capitol Hill in Rome, the Piazza Campidoglio (684). This had been the site of the centre of

124

government since the time of ancient Rome and when, in 1538, the equestrian statue of Marcus Aurelius was moved to the piazza (under the impression that it was of Constantine), it was decided to make a worthy setting for this rare Roman monument. Michelangelo designed a piazza on trapezoidal plan, with palaces on three sides and on the fourth approach steps ascending the steep hillside from the road below. From the viewpoint of architectural history, this was the first recorded use, on palace façades, of Michelangelo's Giant Order, wherein the pilasters or columns span two storeys. This is a Mannerist innovation lending dignity and unity to a façade, later widely copied throughout the western world.

It was Juan de Herrera (c.1530-97) who established the purer form of Italian Renaissance classicism in Spain. His work, in contrast to and in reaction from the rich ornament of plateresque building, was austere, almost clinical in its plain simplicity. His most famous work was the Escorial, begun in 1559, the great monastic palace built in grey granite on the lower slopes of the Guadarrama Mountains near Madrid. This memorial to Philip II was the king's retreat from the world, displaying his asceticism and almost fanatical religiosity.

This combination of royal palace, convent and mausoleum for the kings of Spain is built in the form of a vast rectangle 670 x 530ft. The long unbroken exterior façades enclose 16 courtyards. The monastic Church of St Lawrence here was the last part to be built. The ground plan was a Greek cross (nave arm extended later). The design is extremely plain. The Doric order is used throughout and there is no colour or decoration: even the pendentives are plain (**691**).

That the purer Italian Renaissance came

695 Renaissance cloister (Gothic plateresque church behind), Convent of Christ, Tomar, Portugal, Diogo de Torralva. 1557

697, **698** Carved panelling, England

699 Doric pilaster, Longleat House, England, c.1575

696 Carved oak pilaster and panelling, England, c.1600

700 Frontispiece, Cobham Hall, England, c.1594

1577–80 Circumnavigation of the world by Sir Francis Drake

1577 Domenikos Theotokopoulos, the great Cretan painter – widely known in Italy and Spain, where he worked as El Greco – moved to Toledo where he spent the rest of his life (died 1614). In Toledo he was commissioned by Philip II to paint two works for the Escorial: the *Dream of Philip II* and the *Martyrdom of S. Mauritius and the Theban Legion*

1582 Pope Gregory XIII corrected the inaccurate calendar by deducting 10 days from it in that year. The Gregorian Calendar was gradually adopted, but it was not until the eighteenth century that northern European Protestant states (including England) did so

c.1585 Soft paste porcelain first made in Europe, from kaolinic clay, by the Medicis in Florence

1587 Drake commanded the expedition to Cadiz, where 20 ships were destroyed in the harbour – so disrupting supplies, which led to the postponement of the Armada until the following year

1588 Philip II of Spain sent his 'Invincible Armada' against England

1589 A stocking frame to machine-knit worsted hose invented by the Rev. William Lee, curate of Calverton near Nottingham. By 1598 Lee had developed a machine to knit silk stockings

c.1590 Galileo, Italian astronomer, physicist and mathematician, wrote his treatise on motion, disputing many of the theories of Aristotelian physics. This stated Galileo's

702 Strapwork plaster ceiling design. Athelhampton

701 Wollaton Hall. 1580-8

703 Hexenbürgermeister House, Lemgo. 1571

705 Tübingen, castle gateway

704 Detail, Schöner Hof, Plassenburg, Kulmbach. 1551-69

earlier to Portugal was due largely to Diogo de Torralva, who built the Church of La Graça in Evora (1527-37) but, more importantly, the beautiful Renaissance cloister at the Covent of Christ in Tomar. One of the finest of the seven (p. 112), this features Giant Ionic columns superimposed above Doric with, in between, smaller scale ordered openings (**695**).

The late sixteenth century saw in Portugal a tentative approach towards Italian Mannerism and baroque. This is first seen in the new cathedral (Sé Nova) in Coimbra, but more clearly in Filippo Terzi's S. Vicente da Fora in Lisbon (**692**). Terzi came to Portugal from Italy in 1576 and increased the momentum towards baroque. His S. Vicente has a classical façade, but the interior is based upon Il Gesù in Rome.

In northern Europe (apart from France) architecture of the Italian Renaissance stamp was rare before the seventeenth century. Renaissance classical forms – orders and ornament – were used, but in an ill-informed Mannerist way; often as all-over surface decoration, upon structures which were still fundamentally medieval. This was the case in England, the Low Countries, Germany and Scandinavia. The chief sources of information for builders in these countries came from pattern books published by designers who based their work upon Italy, but at second and third hand – from artisans of different nationalities. Influential were those of Vredeman de Vries of Holland and Wendel Dietterlin of Germany.

Flemish Mannerism was an especially important influence. Its chief monument, after 1550, was Antwerp Town Hall (**682**), which illustrates a better comprehension of classicism than earlier works, but is still singularly different from contemporary work

RENAISSANCE 1550 – 1600

in Italy. In England the Elizabethan great house was displaying similar features. More advanced were buildings such as Montacute, Kirby and Longleat, but Wollaton Hall is particularly Mannerist (**694, 696-702**). In Germany, the stepped and curved gables, strapwork and cartouches were also widely to be seen. The castles of Heidelberg and Tübingen are characteristic (**690, 703-5, 709**). Towards the end of the century, though, the Jesuit Church of S. Michael in Munich (**708**), its design based upon Il Gesù in Rome, evidenced the final emergence of a purer Renaissance form in Germany.

706 President's Gallery, Queens' College, Cambridge, c.1550

707 Little Moreton Hall, timber-framing. 1559-80

708 Interior. Church of S. Michael, Munich, Miller and Sustris. 1582-97

709 Strapwork decoration. Gateway, Tübingen Castle

proposition that bodies fell at the same speed through a given medium regardless of their weights

1594–1614 John Napier, Scottish mathematician, developed his ideas and tables of logarithms, which he had invented

Late sixteenth century In roasting food in front of a kitchen fire, the dog turnspit had become an alternative power source to the spit turned by human hand

Late sixteenth century The idea of pressing clothes by means of a mangling board and roller introduced in Europe in Scandinavia, Germany and Holland. The damp fabric was wound round the roller, which was placed on a table, then pressed by the movement of the mangling board being passed backwards and forwards over it

1600 William Gilbert, President of the Royal College of Physicians, published his *De Magnete*, which represented the findings of his years of study of electricity and magnetism. He also coined the term 'electricity' from the Greek word *electron* = 'amber'. Gilbert was Queen Elizabeth's Court Physician, for which he received a pension to enable him to carry out his researches

710 Frederiksborg Castle, Hillerød, entrance court. 1602. Rebuilding, 1861-75, after fire damage

711 S. Mary's Church, Leiden, A. van 's Gravensande. 1639-49

712 Town House, New Amsterdam, North America, c.1641

713 The Mauritshuis, The Hague, Post and van Campen. 1633

714 Detail. Leiden Town Hall, De Key. 1597-1603

As in England and Germany, it was the seventeenth century which brought a purer classical style to the Low Countries, where Dutch architecture began to emerge as the dominant force, while Antwerp declined in importance. The Dutch architectural prominence was chiefly confined to large towns, notably the political centre at the Hague and the commercial one in Amsterdam.

Two architects in particular are associated with the Dutch Renaissance of the early seventeenth century: Lieven de Key (1560-1627) and Hendrik de Keyser (1565-1621). De Key worked mainly in Haarlem and Leiden. Characteristic are the Haarlem Butchers' Guild Hall (**718**) and the town hall in Leiden (**714**). Both of these are Flemish Mannerist buildings – as shown by the ornate, tall gables and strapwork decoration – but a purer Renaissance style is to be seen in the classical fenestration and doorway design.

Much of de Keyser's work is in Amsterdam, where the city was being enlarged and developed and the famous canals – the Herengracht, Prinsengracht, Keizergracht – were being planned and dug. The terrace architecture flanking these canals has a specific, individual Renaissance character which de Keyser helped to initiate. The fully developed style is shown on p. 142.

In civic work de Keyser designed the Amsterdam Exchange and also built several churches in which, like Sir Christopher Wren later in London, he had to plan a new design suited to the Protestant faith. His Zuiderkerk (1614) and Westerkerk (1620, **717**) are traditional in plan, but have distinctive tall classical steeples which influenced Wren's later city churches (p. 141). De Keyser's Noorderkerk broke

RENAISSANCE 1600 – 1650

new ground, being centrally planned in the Greek cross form; the brick structure is quietly unpretentious and, though similar in basic form, is quite different in appearance from the domed Italian counterparts based on Brunelleschi's and Bramante's prototypes (p. 98, 116). In contrast, St Mary's Church in Leiden, though almost contemporary, illustrates the beginnings of baroque design here (711).

A style of building generally referred to as Dutch Palladian was evidenced in the Hague in the second quarter of the seventeenth century. This, as its name indicates, was strongly influenced by Palladio (p. 121) but, as with Inigo Jones's Palladianism in England, the Dutch examples are not simple facsimiles of the Italian architect's work. A notable instance of the style in Holland is the Mauritshuis, which displays all the characteristic classical features such as emphasis on the horizontal line, simple symmetry of design on the façades, rectangular pedimented windows, and Giant Order in pilaster form (713).

European colonies in North America were being founded and established in this century. Building in the English colonies, both in Virginia and New England, was mainly in timber and domestic in style: monumental civic architecture was yet to come. The Dutch influence was more clearly apparent in New Amsterdam (later New York) where, as the 1679 sketch by Danckers shows, the stepped gable, hipped roof and brick construction had crossed the Atlantic (712).

In Scandinavia, only Denmark, the nearest to the rest of Europe, had absorbed Renaissance ideas – and these came primarily from Holland, and partly from England and Germany. Thus the Flemish

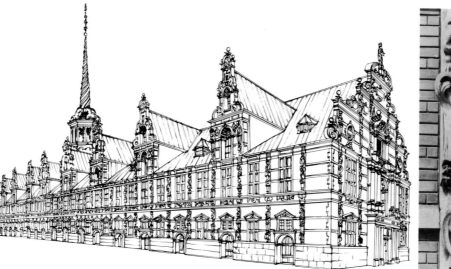

715 The Exchange, Copenhagen. 1619-30, spire 1624-5. Lorenz and Steenwinckel

716 Sculpture, The Exchange

717 Westerkerk, Amsterdam, De Keyser. 1620

718 Butchers' Guild Hall, Haarlem, De Key. 1602

1602   The Bodleian Library of the University of Oxford opened after the restoration by Sir Thomas Bodley of the book collection

1603   Death of Queen Elizabeth I

1605   Discovery of the Gunpowder Plot and arrest of Guy Fawkes

1605   Part One of Cervantes's *Don Quixote* published in Madrid

1605-6   Shakespeare writes *King Lear* and *Macbeth*

1607   Establishment of Jamestown in Virginia, the first permanent English settlement in America

1609   Galileo presented his ×9 power telescope to the Venetian Senate, an instrument which was three times as effective as the Dutch prototype. In 1610 he made an improved ×30 power telescope, with which he discovered the mountainous surface of the moon, four of Jupiter's moons and, later, the rings of Saturn

1609   First shipment of tea brought to Europe by the Dutch East India Company. Sold in London at £3 10s per pound

1610   Table forks first used at dinner tables for carrying the food to the mouth. Previously forks had been in use only to hand food to guests

1610   The English explorer and navigator Henry Hudson, on his last voyage to search for the north-east passage to the orient, entered the strait and bay which are named after him. In 1611 his crew mutinied and cast him adrift in a small boat, to starve and freeze to death

719 Zeughaus (Arsenal), Augsburg, Ellias Holl. 1602-7

720 Sculpture of S. Michael and Lucifer on façade of Zeughaus. Hans Reichle

721 Stadtkirche, Bückeburg, Hans Wolf. 1611-15

723 Entrance portico, Audley End. 1603-16

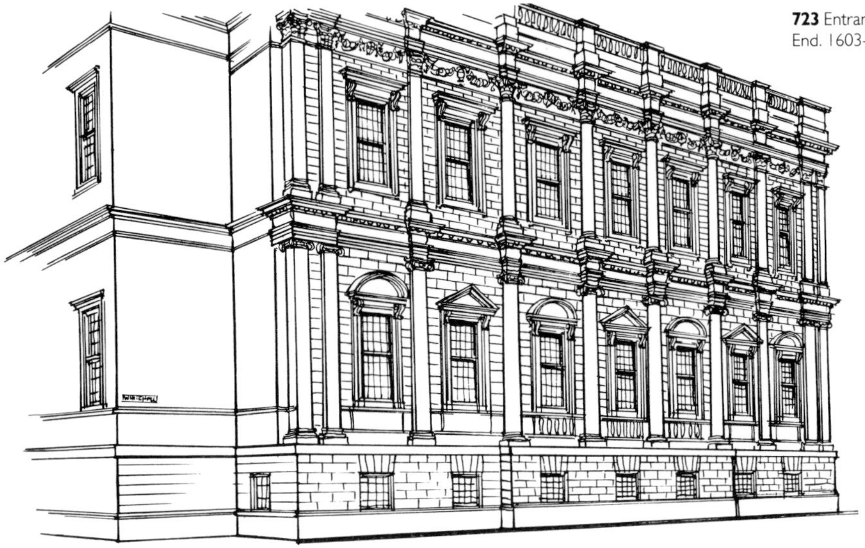

722 The Banqueting House, Whitehall, Inigo Jones. 1619-22

GERMANY

ENGLAND

Mannerist forms were paramount in the surge of building activity under King Christian IV, as may be seen in the great palaces of Frederiksborg at Hillerød (**710**) and Rosenborg in Copenhagen. The most impressive Renaissance building of this time in the city is the Exchange, constructed as a trading centre (**715**). This immensely long, two-storeyed building is on Mannerist pattern, as is evident in its gabled dormers and sculptured caryatid decoration (**716**), but the end elevations display correct classical handling in the Doric order.

A similar pattern to Holland and Denmark was instanced in England and Germany. Flemish Mannerism was still clearly seen in English Jacobean mansions, particularly in the skyline gabling and the two- and three-stage frontispiece entrances (**723, 726, 728**). By the 1630s, a plainer architectural style had developed, and Flemish brickwork had been adopted in bonding and in the stone dressings. Characteristic of such construction – and with a simpler, but still Dutch, style of gabling – is Raynham Hall (**727**).

The German equivalent is generally more richly ornamented, showing a profusion of sculptural and carved decoration, as may be seen on the town church at Bückeburg (**721**) and Wolfenbüttel church (**725**).

Of the great palaces and castles built in Germany in the years 1550-1650, Heidelberg and Plassenburg were characteristic of the later sixteenth-century work, which was a version of Mannerism (**690, 704**), but the town palace in Munich, the Residenz, started in 1550 and built over a long period, ranges round six courtyards and is more purely Italian Renaissance in style. The Antiquarian Court (1586-1600) and the Grotto Court (1581-6) are Florentine in appearance.

RENAISSANCE 1600 – 1650

A more severe classical interpretation was introduced at Augsburg by Elias Holl in his town hall (1615-20) and arsenal (1602-7). Holl's work here has much in common with Herrera's in Spain (p. 125), in that both men created an austere style of classicism apparently in reaction to the ornate forms which preceded it, an austerity far more severe than the Italian Renaissance forms which inspired them. In Augsburg the town hall fell victim to World War II (though it has now been rebuilt); but the arsenal (Zeughaus) survives (719). Both buildings have finely proportioned, dignified façades. The town hall was plainer and astylar, the arsenal is pilastered and ornamented in the centre by Hans Reichle's dynamic sculptural group (720), a notable example of the high quality school of sculpture then current in Germany.

The English counterpart of Holl in Germany and Herrera in Spain was Inigo Jones (1573-1652). A self-taught draughtsman, stage designer and, finally, architect, Inigo Jones had studied for eighteen months in France and Italy, making detailed on-the-spot drawings of ancient Roman building remains, as well as Italian Renaissance work. On his return to England in 1615 he was appointed Surveyor of the King's Works, and in this capacity was responsible for the first buildings in England designed on Italian Renaissance lines: the Banqueting House in Whitehall, built 1619-22 (722) and the Queen's House at Greenwich (1616-35). Both buildings owe much to Palladio and to Vitruvius, though neither is an exact copy but an adaptation to English taste and climate.

The example set by Italy in the sixteenth century – for planned cities or sections of cities, with elevations handled as single classical units and designed round an open

724 Aschaffenburg Castle, Ridinger. 1605-14

725 Detail. Church of St Mary, Wolfenbüttel, Paul Francke. 1604-58

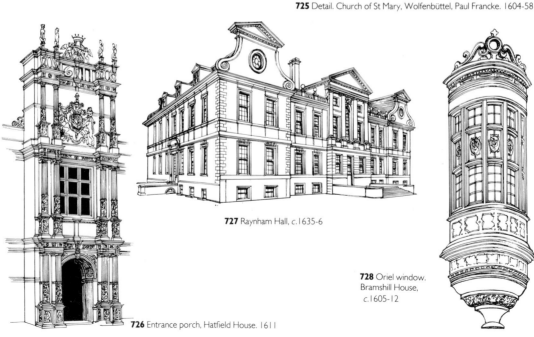

727 Raynham Hall, c.1635-6

728 Oriel window. Bramshill House, c.1605-12

726 Entrance porch, Hatfield House. 1611

1611 Publication in England of the Authorised (King James) translation of the Bible, the work of 50 of England's finest scholars

1612 Rubens painted his *Descent from the Cross*, a companion to his earlier *Raising of the Cross*, both in Antwerp Cathedral

1613 Michael Feodorovich Romanov ascended the throne of Russia and founded the Romanov dynasty

***c*.1620** Sir Robert Mansell introduced the making of plate glass into England and employed Italian craftsmen to manufacture mirrors

1620 The Mayflower sailed from Plymouth, taking the Pilgrims to the New World

1622 Richelieu made a cardinal

1571–1630 Johannes Kepler, German astronomer and mathematician. Founder of modern astronomy

1596–1650 René Descartes, French philosopher, scientist and mathematician. Founder of modern philosophical rationalism

1625–50 The box iron introduced from Holland for ironing laundered garments

1628 Publication of William Harvey's studies and discoveries on the circulation of the blood, *Exercitatio Anatomica de Motu Cordis et Sanguinis*

RENAISSANCE TOWN PLANNING   1600 – 1650

729 Plaza Mayor, Madrid, Spain, Juan Gomez de Mora, c.1620

730 Place des Vosges (originally Place Royale), Paris, 1605-12

square – were beginning to be adopted elsewhere in Europe by the early years of the seventeenth century. In Madrid, Juan Gomez de Mora (1586-1647), a follower of Herrera's style and a prolific designer, laid out the immense central square of the city, the Plaza Mayor (**729**). It is a homogeneous scheme, its four-storeyed elevations repeated all round the square; there are arcaded shops on the ground level and roof dormers at the top.

In London, in 1630, Inigo Jones was closely associated with the Earl of Bedford's scheme to lay out a square on his land at Covent Garden; the first such formal open space, lined (on two sides) with buildings of uniform and classical character, to be built in the capital.

Developments in Paris were more extensive. After years of warfare, Henry IV had begun to reconstruct the centre of the city in the last years of the sixteenth century. He envisaged planning by streets and squares, and first completed the Pont Neuf, which had been begun in 1578, and which linked the north and south banks of the Seine at the western tip of the Ile de la Cité. At this point the Place Dauphine was laid out as a well-to-do residential area (**731**). The king then planned two larger squares, the Place Royale (now the Place des Vosges) and the Place de France (**730**).

Salomon de Brosse (1571-1666) was the chief French architect of the early years of the seventeenth century. His work was crisply classical, more Renaissance than baroque, and very French. The simplicity of his designs and his fine classical detail may still be seen on the *Parlement* of Brittany in Rennes (1618), and the façade of the Church of S. Gervais in Paris (**732**).

RENAISSANCE TOWN PLANNING   1600 – 1650

De Brosse was succeeded as chief architect for the Crown by Jacques Lemercier (c.1585-1654) who, working for the king's chief minister, Cardinal Richelieu, built his château and laid out the adjoining small town of Richelieu on classical grid lines. The 'Grande Rue' of this little seventeenth-century 'new town' has survived remarkably unaltered. Lemercier's best work is the Church of the University of Paris, the Sorbonne, also commissioned by Richelieu. This is of Roman baroque design, its fine façades rising to an impressive dome (733).

François Mansart (1578-1666) was a more original architect than Lemercier, a designer of great subtlety and ingenuity who gave to French architecture a national leadership distinct from the influence of Rome. He designed several great châteaux – Balleroy in Normandy (1626) and additions to Blois (1635-8), for example. His best surviving château is Maisons-Lafitte (1642-50), the only one where the interior decorative schemes have not been lost.

Mansart's more mature style of the 1640s was more freely plastic and baroque. In 1645 he was given, by Anne of Austria, his most important commission; to build the church and restore the convent of the Val de Grâce in Paris. He provided a magnificent design, certainly his greatest work, but he was dismissed when the building was only partially erected because of his arrogance and extravagance; Lemercier completed the work (753).

The Renaissance movement, first expressed in architecture in the 1420s by Brunelleschi in Florence (p. 97), had been derived from spiritual sources. Its expression in the arts and architecture spread westwards and northwards, achieving its mature form in

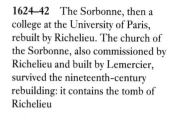

731 Ile de la Cité, Paris, the Pont Neuf. 1578-1604 and Place Dauphine begun 1607

732 Church of S. Gervais, Paris, Salomon de Brosse. 1616-21

733 Church of the Sorbonne, Paris, Jacques Lemercier. 1635

1624–42   The Sorbonne, then a college at the University of Paris, rebuilt by Richelieu. The church of the Sorbonne, also commissioned by Richelieu and built by Lemercier, survived the nineteenth-century rebuilding: it contains the tomb of Richelieu

1630   Peter Paul Rubens knighted by Charles I

1631   William Oughtred, English mathematician, published his *Clavis Mathematicae*. About this time also he invented a rectangular slide rule, an improvement on his earlier circular slide rule

1632   Anthony Van Dyck returned to England, where he was made principal painter to the king and was knighted

1632   Galileo ordered to appear before the Inquisition to defend his earlier support of Copernicus's theories on planetary motion

1633   Town of Williamsburg founded by English settlers. Became the capital of Virginia in 1699. The town has now been restored to its eighteenth-century appearance, as an example of colonial America of this period

1635   Rubens's paintings for the ceiling of the Banqueting House in Whitehall delivered to London. His fee of £3000 paid in two instalments in 1637 and 1638

1642   Rembrandt working on the painting known as *The Night Watch*

1642   Abel Tasman, Dutch navigator, discovered the Island of Tasmania (named after him) and the South Island of New Zealand

ITALIAN BAROQUE 1600 – 1650

735, 736 View and ground plan. Church of S. Carlo alle Quattro Fontane, Rome, Francesco Borromini. 1638-40

738 Church of S. Croce, Lecce, Cesare Penna. Lower part 1582, Gabrieli Riccardi. Upper part 1624

734 Detail. The Triton fountain, Rome, Gianlorenzo Bernini. 1642-3

737 Cathedral of St John in Lateran, Rome, Francesco Borromini. 1646-9

northern and western Europe in the early seventeenth century.

Meanwhile, in Italy, in reaction to the Renaissance cult of Humanism, the Counter-Reformation, also a spiritual movement, was finding its expression in art and architecture. In this turning back to the Roman Catholic Church, new spiritual values were being established, suited to the more modern current needs. The new art form – the baroque – used all media; architecture, sculpture, painting, music and literature, blended together in a dramatic manner to make the church vital and attractive to all. The movement back to the Christian Church had begun in mid sixteenth century, but its artistic expression dates from about 1590.

As with the Renaissance, the new artistic style spread outwards from Italy over two centuries but, unlike Renaissance forms, baroque design barely penetrated north of the Alps. There is no real parallel to Italian baroque in England or northern Europe. It was practised primarily by the southern, largely Latin, and Roman Catholic peoples. Baroque spread to southern Germany, Austria, Switzerland, and to Spain and Portugal.

Like Renaissance architecture, baroque is entirely classical in concept, using the orders decoratively and constructively, but it differs in its interpretation, being much freer with the use of curves, in which not only ornament but whole walls alternate sinuously from the convex to the concave. The appearance, created by a unified blend of painting, sculpture and architecture, is of vitality and movement; the whole made dramatic by the handling of the lighting from a restricted number of sources. The favourite ground plan is oval, the colour rich and the architectural forms broken and interrupted.

ITALIAN BAROQUE 1600 – 1650

Carlo Maderna (1556-1629) was one of the first of the baroque architects in Rome to break away from the academic Mannerism which had dominated architecture there during the later sixteenth century. He completed Michelangelo's nave in St Peter's and built the façade (743). In his work at S. Andrea della Valle (741) and his façade to S. Susanna (742) he further developed the trend towards baroque initiated by the builders of Il Gesù.

As well as the work being carried out by baroque architects in Rome, the style was being experimented with in many northern cities in Italy, as well as in the extreme south. The cathedrals in Bologna and the new cathedral in Brescia are two examples (739, 740), as are also Genoa University and Milan's Palazzo di Brera. In Turin, Carlo Castellamente was laying out the elegantly planned Piazza di Carlo, while in Naples Cosimo Fanzago was building churches. Apulian baroque was, as Norman had been here five hundred years earlier, a fusion of Byzantine, Arabic and Greek sources. In the small town of Lecce, the richly ornamented buildings show the dominance of Spain in the area (738, 745).

739 The New Cathedral, Brescia. Begun 1604, Lontana. Rotunda eleventh century, dome 1825

740 Cathedral of S. Pietro, Bologna, Magenta and Ambrosini. 1605

741 Church of S. Andrea della Valle, Rome, Giacomo della Porta and Carlo Maderna. 1591-1623

742 Church of S. Susanna, Rome. 1593-1605, Carlo Maderna

1642 Cardinal Mazarin succeeded Richelieu on the latter's death as chief minister to Louis XIII

1642–6 Experiments by Evangelista Torricelli, Italian scientist and mathematician, into the weight and pressure of air. He discovered that the atmosphere exerted a pressure because of its weight, and that this corresponded to a column of water just over 30ft in height

1645–50 Gradual adoption in larger homes of the weight-driven or 'gravity' mechanism for turning the spit, in cooking in front of an open fire

1649 King Charles I beheaded in Whitehall in London

1650 First coffee house in England opened in Oxford

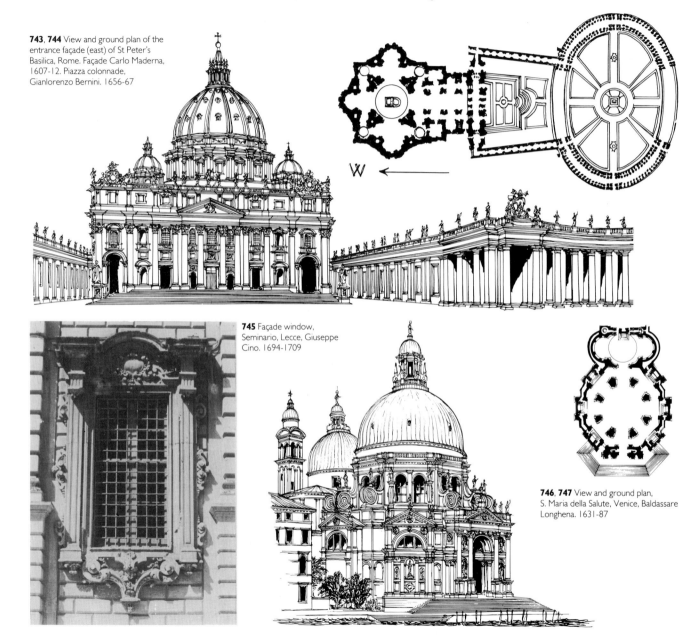

743, 744 View and ground plan of the entrance façade (east) of St Peter's Basilica, Rome. Façade Carlo Maderna, 1607-12. Piazza colonnade, Gianlorenzo Bernini. 1656-67

745 Façade window, Seminario, Lecce, Giuseppe Cino. 1694-1709

746, 747 View and ground plan, S. Maria della Salute, Venice, Baldassare Longhena. 1631-87

Michelangelo had been the genius whose works towered over the artistic world of Renaissance Italy (p. 120); Bernini was his equivalent in the era of Roman baroque. In whatever age Gianlorenzo Bernini (1598-1680) had lived, his genius would have become apparent, but his particular abilities and temperament were made to measure for the time of high baroque in Rome – which he dominated for 50 years, creating achievement after achievement with consummate ease, concentration and energy. Like Michelangelo he possessed a strong personality and was of deep religious conviction. They both lived long lives, were both masters of their own artistic circle and were painters, architects and poets – though both regarded sculpture as the most rewarding of the arts. They were both magnificent craftsmen and perfectionists. Only in temperament did they differ: Bernini was a Neapolitan, with all the charm and warmth of southern Italy; a contrast to the proud and introspective Michelangelo.

Bernini's work, whatever the medium, was dramatic and vivid; larger than life and brilliant in its handling of light and shade and mass. In architecture this is shown clearly in his piazza and colonnades fronting St Peter's Basilica (**743, 744**). These vast elliptical colonnades are symbolic of the Mother Church of Christendom, embracing the world. In their design Bernini created a precedent in that they are not, as was customary in ancient Rome, arcades – but the continuous Ionic entablature is carried immediately upon the Tuscan columns which stand four deep, 60ft high, round the piazza. Here also is Bernini's ceremonial staircase – the Scala Regia – a masterly handling of light and form which makes it one of the great staircases of the world. Even more baroque is the architect's S. Andrea al Quirinale, built typically on oval plan, and with a superb blend of lighting, colour and sculpture (**749, 750**).

In Rome, Bernini contributed extensively to secular work in palaces. His name is especially linked, though, with his painting and sculpture; his interior work at St Peter's (1624-66), and his emotionally dramatic Cornaro Chapel in S. Maria della Vittoria depicting the Ecstasy of S. Teresa (1645-52). His fountains, for example, the Triton (**734**) and those in the Piazza Navona, are especially famous (**752**).

The other great man of the Roman high baroque was Francesco Borromini (1599-1667), a very different personality; a reclusive, neurotic, unhappy man who eventually took his own life. Borromini's work was also brilliant and equally baroque, but in a different form. Despite the differences in baroque interpretation, Bernini had not challenged the basis of Renaissance classical thought. Borromini was an innovator. He evolved concepts nearer to engineering thought than sculpture, and nearer to medieval construction than Renaissance. Instead of a classical method of module design based upon the column, he preferred a division into geometrical units based on the triangle – a more medieval concept. Yet, despite this, his work is essentially baroque; especially in its sinuously curving walls and its dramatic lighting effects. Characteristic of these features is S. Carlo alle Quattro Fontane (**735, 736**) and his university church of S. Ivo alla Sapienza.

In 1646 he was asked to restore the Cathedral of Rome, St John Lateran. He was not permitted to rebuild the Early Christian basilica, so he performed the difficult task of

748 Cupola interior, S. Lorenzo, Turin, Guarino Guarini. From 1666

749, 750 View and ground plan, S. Andrea al Quirinale, Rome, Gianlorenzo Bernini. 1678

752 S. Agnese in Piazza Navona, Rome. Begun 1652 by Carlo Rainaldi, continued 1653-5 by Francesco Borromini, completed by others 1666. Foreground: Fontana dei Fiumi, Gianlorenzo Bernini. 1648-51

751 Palazzo Carignano, Turin, Guarino Guarini. 1680

1652 *Pope Innocent X* painted by Diego Velazquez (1599-1660)

1652 Cape Town founded by Jan van Riebeeck, as a supply station for the Dutch East India Company

1653 Oliver Cromwell appointed Lord Protector of England

1653 Publication of *The Compleat Angler*, a discourse on fishing by Isaak Walton

1656-7 Christiaan Huygens, Dutch mathematician, physicist and astronomer, designed the first clock accurately regulated by a pendulum. He described it in his *Horologium* published in 1658. His further research into isochronal motion was summarized in his *Horologium Oscillatorium* (1673)

1657 Otto von Guericke, German scientist and Mayor of Magdeburg, used one of his vacuum pumps in a colourful demonstration to the city intended to illustrate the immense force exerted by the pressure of the atmosphere. He showed that two teams of eight horses, each pulling in opposite directions, were not able to separate the two halves of a 20in diameter copper sphere from which air had been evacuated by his new design of pump

1657 First chocolate house was opened in London by a Frenchman. Samuel Pepys records that he first drank 'jocolatte' at a coffee house in November 1664

1660 Restoration of the English monarchy under Charles II

1660-9 The years in which Samuel Pepys kept his famous diary, which contains a million and a quarter words

753 Church of Val de Grâce, Paris. Begun François Mansart, completed Lemercier, 1645-65

754 Hôtel des Invalides, Paris, Bruant. 1671-4

755 Church of S. Louis des Invalides, Paris, Jules Hardouin Mansart. 1679-1756

757, 758 St Mary-le-Bow, London, Wren, 1670-83; St Edmund-the-King, London, Wren, 1670-9

756 West front, St Paul's Cathedral, London, Sir Christopher Wren. 1675-1710

759 St Stephen Walbrook, London, Wren, 1672-9

transforming it into a baroque church by re-clothing the interior (**737**). At S. Agnese in Piazza Navona (**752**), he designed an impressive façade, one which was to be repeated again and again all over Europe.

The most outstanding baroque architecture in northern Italy at this time was in Turin and Venice. After Emmanuele Filiberto made his capital in Turin in 1563, the city prospered for two-and-a-half centuries, and the arts and architecture reflected this importance. Carlo Emmanuele I began to lay out his new city here in 1620, planning it in streets instead of individual *palazzi* (p. 124). The architect Carlo Castellamente began building the Piazza San Carlo in 1638, and the city was further greatly extended during the seventeenth and eighteenth centuries. The chief Turin architect of this period was Guarino Guarini (1624-1683), a man whose work had much in common with that of Borromini. It was original, unusual and also medieval in its inspiration from triangles and other forms clothed in baroque. Reflecting this is his Church of S. Lorenzo, with its most original dome (**748**), and his Sindone Chapel in the Cathedral, built to house the Holy Shroud. His Palazzo Carignano in the city (**751**) is more typically Roman baroque in its undulating brick façade and central oval rotunda.

The most notable architect of Venice was Baldassare Longhena (1598-1682), who is best known for his church at the head of the Grand Canal, S. Maria della Salute; which was built in thanksgiving for the departure of the plague from the city in 1630 (**746, 747**). This is an unusual structure, in which Longhena provided an alternative approach from that of Rome. His church is a mixture of themes based on the centrally planned buildings of ancient Rome (p. 27), Ravenna (p. 29) and the Renaissance (p. 116). It is an octagonal building with surrounding ambulatory, simple on the interior, but outside dramatically baroque with its giant scrolls which, supported on the ambulatory arches, buttress the dome.

The second half of the seventeenth century was a great period for building and the visual arts in France. Under Louis XIV the autocratic régime controlled firmly which artists should receive commissions and the style they should follow but, though Louis's policies probably lost him the services of some gifted artists, he was a great builder and an enlightened, cultured patron. Charles Le Brun was appointed by the King's Chief Minister Jean-Baptiste Colbert to be in charge of the artistic activities of the Academies of France, and Le Brun brought together a talented team of original artists and craftsmen.

In architecture the style was more baroque than hitherto. This was a form never fully adopted in France. The French version was more restrained and less ornamentally exuberant, but the plastic, curving massing in buildings was seen more in the 40 years after 1660 than at any other time in French architectural history.

Louis XIV's chief architects who adapted to this style were Le Vau and J.H. Mansart. Louis Le Vau (1612-70) carried out a large number of commissions in a manner near to that of Italian baroque. Important prototypes in their individual fields are his château Vaux-le-Vicomte (762) and, in Paris on the banks of the River Seine, the Collège des Quatres Nations, which later became the Institut de France. Both are classic baroque schemes – with domes and curving façades – but articulated in a refined French manner.

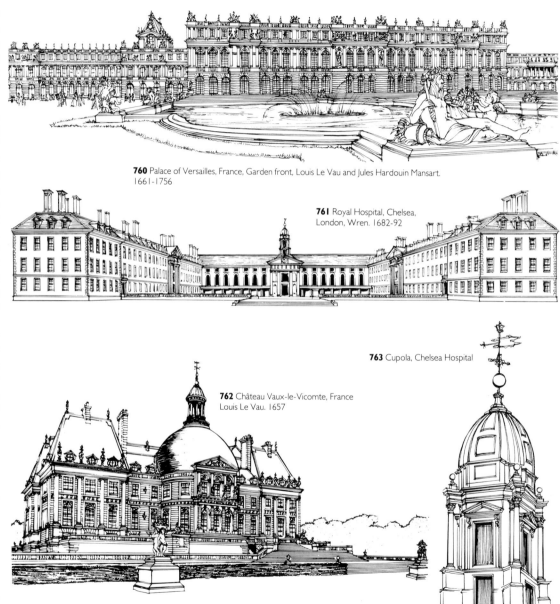

760 Palace of Versailles, France, Garden front, Louis Le Vau and Jules Hardouin Mansart. 1661-1756

761 Royal Hospital, Chelsea, London, Wren. 1682-92

763 Cupola, Chelsea Hospital

762 Château Vaux-le-Vicomte, France Louis Le Vau. 1657

1661 and 1679 Publication of *The Sceptical Chemist* by Robert Boyle, setting forth his ideas on the basis of substances. Boyle is believed by many to be the 'father of chemistry'. He was the first to separate chemistry from alchemy and, in this publication, define a chemical element

1662 Royal Charter granted by Charles II to the Society of Experimental Philosophy, which became The Royal Society, and included then in its membership Isaac Newton, Robert Hooke, Robert Boyle, Christopher Wren and John Evelyn

1664–6 The last great plague of London

1665 John Milton completed his *Paradise Lost*, which was published two years later by Samuel Simmons. The surviving original contract provided for a payment of £5 on signature with a further £5 to be paid after the sale of the first impression of 1500 copies. The payment was made in 1669. Milton's wife eventually sold her rights to the work after his death for £8

1666 Isaac Newton's early work on the theory of gravity. By 1669, in optics, he had discovered and named the spectrum

1666 Antonio Stradivari, Italian violin-maker, ended his apprenticeship with Niccolò Amati and made his first violin under his own label

1666 Great Fire of London

1669 Last diet of the Hanseatic League attended by only six cities

764 South porch. Thorpe Hall, Peter Mills. 1654-6

765 Coleshill House, Sir Roger Pratt. 1650-2

766 Grande Place, Brussels, from late seventeenth century

767 Church of S. Michael, Louvain, Willem Hesius. 1650-6

Both impressed greatly the young Wren on his visit to France in 1665.

Jules Hardouin Mansart (1646-1708), nephew of François (p. 133), had a very different approach to and style of architecture from his uncle. He became the most prolific, controversial and baroque architect of France. In Paris he laid out several squares, notably the Place Vendôme (1685-1720). At Les Invalides he built the great church of S. Louis for the King, who wanted a more impressive building than the existing chapel (**754, 755**). His best known work is at the Palace of Versailles (**760**), where he took charge in 1678 after Le Vau's death. Reluctantly, on the King's insistence, Mansart greatly enlarged Le Vau's palace, creating the famous Hall of Mirrors. His own contributions, which were more successful, included the royal chapel, the stables, the orangery and, in the park, the Grand Trianon.

In England, between 1650 and 1670, a more symmetrical and purely classical house design evolved (**764**). This was closely related to the Dutch Palladian style developed a little earlier in Holland (p. 129). Notable architects who adopted this form included Hugh May, John Webb and Sir Roger Pratt. It was Pratt who designed the prototype in England, Coleshill House (**765**).

The years 1670-1714 were dominated, architecturally, by England's most famous exponent: Sir Christopher Wren (1632-1723). One of the very few English architects to rank with the greatest of Europeans in versatility, inventiveness and perfection of craftsmanship, Wren was involved in all the great schemes of the time: the rebuilding of London's important buildings after the Fire of 1666, notably St Paul's Cathedral (**756,**

769) and the city churches (**757-9**); the naval hospital at Greenwich (**768**) and its army counterpart at Chelsea (**761, 763**); the royal palaces at Hampton Court and Kensington; extensive building at the two universities.

Yet, until the age of 30, Wren's interests were scientific. As a very young man he showed brilliance in the range and quality of his studies and researches, which he undertook in astronomy, physics, engineering and meteorology. He became Savilian Professor of Astronomy at Oxford at the age of 27 and was a founder member in 1662 of the Royal Society, in company with Isaac Newton, Robert Boyle and John Evelyn.

When, in 1663, Wren became interested in architecture, his scientific training profoundly affected his approach to architectural design and structure. All his life he retained the faculty of envisaging an extensive scheme as a whole before work commenced. He brought his mathematical ability and technical knowledge to an understanding of the roofing of large spans, sound support and buttressing, and site planning.

Wren travelled little abroad. He never visited Italy but, from a large library, he evolved from the Italian Renaissance buildings a personal, very English style, which graduated over the years from Renaissance to Mannerism to a touch of baroque.

There is a marked difference in the classical architecture of this time between Belgium and Holland. The former, as a largely Catholic area, developed a baroque style under the leadership of the Jesuits, who built many churches. In Holland the trend was similar to that in England and northern Germany. The Belgian work is mainly ecclesiastical. Typical is the Church of

768 Chapel dome and colonnade, Greenwich Hospital, begun Wren. 1699

769 St Paul's Cathedral, Wren

770 Carved wood altar rail detail. Church of S. Michael, Louvain. 1650-6

1671 English stoneware first made in England at the Fulham Pottery in London by John Dwight

1672 Temple Bar, the new stone archway which marked the boundary between the cities of London and Westminster, erected by Christopher Wren

1674 Henry Morgan, Welsh buccaneer, who had plundered Spanish ships and ports in the Caribbean, was knighted by Charles II and appointed Lieutenant Governor of Jamaica, where he lived until his death in 1688

1675 Charles II appointed John Flamsteed astronomical observer at the Royal Greenwich Observatory, at a salary of £100. The first observation was made on 19 September 1675

1676 George Ravenscroft, in attempting to produce an English equivalent of the famous Venetian *cristallo* (a clear crystalline glass developed there in the fifteenth century), succeeded in making a lead alkali glass, using lead oxide, which resulted in a heavy glass of great brilliance, ideal for cutting and polishing

1678 Publication of *The Pilgrim's Progress from this World to That which is to Come*. The book was written by John Bunyan, largely while imprisoned in Bedford County Gaol, and was fundamentally autobiographical

1679 Denis Papin (1647-c.1712), French physicist, invented the first pressure cooker. He called it 'A New Digester or Engine for softning Bones'. He demonstrated its use to

HOLLAND AND SWEDEN

SWEDEN

771 Nieuwe Kerk, The Hague, Holland, Van Bassen and Noorwits. 1665

773 Hedvig Eleonora Church, Stockholm, Sweden, Jean de la Vallée. 1656

772 Nos 364-370 Herengracht, Amsterdam, Holland, Vingboons. 1662-5

774 Summer royal palace, Drottningholm, near Stockholm. 1662-1700. Designed by Nicodemus Tessin the Elder, completed by his son

S. Michael in Louvain (**767, 770**), which is decorated internally with baroque classical features and ornament, but retains a ribbed vaulted ceiling – illustrating the reluctance in this area to relinquish late Gothic forms.

In Holland this was an active building period, more Renaissance than baroque – the latter being reserved for decoration. Most building – traditionally – continued to be in brick, with stone reserved for orders, decoration and facings. Much of the centre of Amsterdam was erected at this time, especially the terraces of tall houses bordering the famous canals (**772**). One of the chief architects was Philip Vingboons (1614-78), who built in the same basic style as had been used in the sixteenth century, but replacing the curved, stepped gables with simpler pedimented ones with swags at the sides. Giant Orders were often used, and doorways were planned in pairs. Each terrace was one architectural unit.

Dutch Palladian architecture was still in vogue, especially in the mid century. A notable example is the Amsterdam Town Hall (**775**), a prestige structure and one of the few to be built entirely of stone. Of similar style is the Maastricht Town Hall (**776**). Churches were also simple and classical, and mostly in brick. Characteristic is the new Church in the Hague (**771**) which follows the trend of de Keyser's Amsterdam churches (p. 128).

Scandinavia was still too cut off from the artistic centres of baroque Europe to develop her own individual approach to this form. On the northern fringe Norway and Finland largely went their own way architecturally, using traditional materials and building styles. Sweden and Denmark initiated building programmes under royal patronage, trying to establish cities planned and decorated in contemporary manner, but Italy was too far away for the baroque forms to arrive quickly, and the northern cities had little to offer Italian architects. In both countries work in contemporary manner was by foreign architects, chiefly French and Dutch. Typical in Denmark is the Charlottenburg Palace in Copenhagen, built 1672-83 by the Dutchman Evert Janssen. This is severe and symmetrical in brick, and characteristically Dutch Palladian.

Contemporary architecture in Sweden was more distinguished. Classical design had been developed in the first half of the century, and was consolidated in the second. This was largely due to the work of four architects, two families of father and son, both of French origin: Simon de la Vallée, who died in 1642, his son Jean (1620-96), Nicodemus Tessin (1615-81), who became city architect of Stockholm and chief royal architect, and his son, also Nicodemus (1654-1728), who continued his father's work and became Sweden's Sir Christopher Wren. These four worked initially in the Dutch Palladian idiom, but later were nearer to Roman baroque (773, 774, 777, 778).

In North America, in the English colonies, civic building was for a long time virtually indistinguishable from domestic, except in scale; but, by 1650, the meeting house was evolving into a specific style in order to fulfil its dual function, that of religious worship and secular meeting place. This was the essential building for every town. It was set in the centre for convenience and symbolism. The building design was based upon that of the English market hall, but, instead of being open-sided on the ground floor, it was enclosed to provide two storeys of internal accommodation. Above was a tall hipped roof surmounted by platform and belfry. A

775 Royal Palace (formerly the Town Hall), Amsterdam, Holland, Jacob van Campen. 1648-65

776 Tower, Town Hall, Maastricht, Holland, Pieter Post. 1658-84

777 Skokloster Castle, Nicodemus Tessin the Elder. 1646-68

778 Kalmar Cathedral, Nicodemus Tessin the Elder. 1660-73

the Royal Society in 1681. In 1690 he went on to experiment with his ideas on condensing steam to make a vacuum, of which he made a working model. It was this principle which was then made to work in later steam engines

1679 Henry Purcell succeeded John Blow as organist at Westminster Abbey and in 1682 was appointed organist at the Chapel Royal for Charles II

*c.***1680** The dodo, which inhabited the Mascarene Islands in the Indian Ocean, became extinct on Mauritius, but survived on the island of Rodriguez until about 1800

1681 William Penn, English Quaker, was granted by royal charter of Charles II a large tract of land in North America, which he named Pennsylvania after his father

1682 Edmund Halley, English astronomer, first observed the comet which now bears his name

1682 Sieur de la Salle, French explorer of North America, travelled down the Mississippi river to its mouth on the authority of Louis XIV – and claimed a great area of land for France naming it, after the King, Louisiana

1685 Revocation of the Edict of Nantes by Louis XIV, leading to a Protestant exodus from France, when over 400,000 Huguenots emigrated – chiefly to Britain, Holland, Prussia, Switzerland and North America

1685 End of the Monmouth Rebellion at Sedgemoor and execution of the Duke, illegitimate son of Charles II

1650 – 1700

779 Černin Palace, Prague, Czechoslovakia, Francesco Caratti. 1669-92

780 Façade. Cartuja Church, Jerez de la Frontera, Spain. 1667

781 Church of S. Vincente, Braga, Portugal. 1691

782 Pulpit, Garsten Abbey Church, Austria, Carlo Carlone. 1677-85

very early example was the first Boston Town House of 1657-8.

Completely different in style, materials and construction were the buildings erected in New Mexico, an area colonized by Spain and converted by the Franciscan Order. The mission buildings here were influenced by Spanish architecture, but constructed with Indian labour. The material used was adobe (sun-dried brick), built into slab-like thick walling because of the size of the bricks, some 18 x 10in. These large buildings had very small windows because of the climate. A notable surviving example (somewhat restored) is the mission church of S. Estéban at Acoma.

In the Iberian Peninsula, Portugal, in particular, was experimenting with the baroque style. By the end of the seventeenth century richly ornamented buildings were being erected and, in a number of cases, baroque façades were being added to medieval churches. Alcobaça Abbey Church is one of these, where the simplicity of the early medieval Cistercian interior contrasts markedly with the baroque façade (786). Similarly, in Oporto, the Gothic church of S. Francisco was richly re-decorated. In the villages and small towns churches built in early baroque style were more restrained in their decoration as, for example, at S. Vincente in Braga (781) and S. Pedro in Amarante.

In central Europe the Germanic influence was predominant and baroque design developed as the chief artistic expression, particularly in the central and southern regions, and in those under the influence of the Roman Catholic Church. The style transcended national frontiers and flourished equally in southern Germany, Austria, Switzerland, Czechoslovakia and,

144

further east, in Hungary and Poland. In more northern areas of Germany, as in England, Holland and northern France, the more restrained Renaissance forms prevailed.

The fully developed, characteristically baroque movement did not emerge until after 1700 (p. 148). In the previous half-century baroque architecture was being introduced mainly by architects of foreign origin, chiefly Italian. In consequence, the style was that of Roman baroque. Soon after mid century, Carlo Lurago was working at Passau Cathedral, Agostino Barelli at the Theatinerkirche, Munich, Carlo Carlone on Garsten Abbey Church and Francesco Caratti on the Černin Palace, Prague. Between 1685 and 1710 Enrico Zuccali and Giovanni Viscardi dominated the architecture of southern Germany, building in Italian baroque style; but, as time passed, this became freer and less classical and thus more Bavarian: for example, the Palace of Schleissheim, Ettal Abbey Church, or Schloss Nymphenburg. These two architects helped to set the pattern for the mature Austrian and Bavarian baroque of Fischer Von Erlach and Balthasar Neumann (785 and pp. 149-150).

783 Disentis Abbey Church, Switzerland, Moosbrugger, c.1685

784 Jesuit Church, Lucerne, Switzerland, Vogler. 1666-73

785 Dreifaltigkeitskirche, Salzburg, Austria, Fischer von Erlach. 1694

786 Alcobaça Abbey Church, Portugal. Later seventeenth century

1687   An explosion, which took place during the Venetian siege of Athens, caused serious damage to the Parthenon

1687   Publication of Isaac Newton's greatest work, *The Mathematical Principles of Natural Philosophy* (Principia), which is founded upon his three laws of motion

1689   Proclamation of William III and Mary II as King and Queen of Britain

1690   John Locke's *Essay Concerning Human Understanding*, his major philosophical work

1692   The massacre at Glencoe in Scotland by members of the clan Campbell of those of the clan MacDonald

1697   A disastrous fire which destroyed much of the remaining buildings of the Palace of Whitehall, except for Inigo Jones's Banqueting House

BAROQUE AND ROCOCO   1700 – 1750

SPAIN

SPAIN AND PORTUGAL

787 Plaza Mayor, Salamanca (town hall in centre), 1729-40, Alberto de Churriguera

788 Doorway detail. Hospicio de San Fernando, Madrid, Pedro de Ribera. 1722

789 Gable detail. Palacio Mateus, Vila Real, Portugal. Early eighteenth century

790 Pilgrimage Church of Bom Jesus do Monte, near Braga, Portugal, Cruz Amarante. 1723

Eighteenth-century architecture in Europe was predominantly classical, based for much of the time on the pattern of ancient Rome and, in the last decades of the century, upon that of Greece. But to presume that the interpretation of such classical form was uniform throughout Europe would be quite untrue. In general, in the northern parts – Britain, Northern Germany and Scandinavia – the trend was towards the more correct Roman lines, based clearly upon the precepts set by architects such as Palladio (p. 121). Further south, in areas where the Roman Catholic Church held sway, the baroque form was dominant. Thirdly, towards mid century, the French influence of rococo was felt.

Nevertheless, whatever the area and whatever the interpretation of classicism, the superbly high standard of craftsmanship was shown everywhere. This was partly due to the long centuries of evolution of classical design, of the training of craftsmen and of the technical development of means and materials. This applied equally to the handling of carving, painting, stuccowork, ceramics and metalwork. It also stemmed from the developing wealth of Europe and from the wide experience and knowledge of the patrons who were the aristocracy of the different countries. Such men travelled widely on the Grand Tour, had seen the best that Italy, above all, had produced from the *cinquecento* onwards, as well as having studied earlier work in Greece, and had collected works of art from the ancient, Renaissance and baroque worlds. They returned home, clear in their own minds about what they wished to create – and craftsmen were there in their own countries trained and ready to produce it.

Architecture in the Iberian Peninsula was overwhelmingly baroque, with some rococo decoration in the later years. Much of this baroque work is referred to as *Churrigueresque*. A particularly vigorous and ornate form, this is named after the family of three brothers and three sons of José de Churriguera (1650-1725). He worked chiefly in Castile, carving the characteristic retablos of Spanish churches in the region. Alberto (1676-1750), a younger brother and the most talented member of the family, laid out the main square of Salamanca, which is a magnificent town planning scheme (787).

Two other important exponents of the *Churrigueresque* style working in Spain were Pedro de Ribera (*c.*1683-1742) and Narciso Tomé (*c.*1690-1742). De Ribera was principal architect in Madrid, where most of his work was carried out. Typical is his centrepiece to the Hospicio San Fernando (1722-9), and his monumental Toledo Bridge, with its richly sculptured shrines (788). Tomé decorated the University façade at Valladolid (792), and was responsible for the most fantastic monument to *Churrigueresque* art, the dramatically lit *Trasparente* in Toledo Cathedral. Apart from a quantity of baroque work on Spanish cathedrals (791), the royal palaces in Madrid, that at Aranjuez and La Granja, were largely built at this time – but in these cases much of the work was by Italians (p. 145, 793).

Portuguese architecture was also richly baroque. Especially notable and characteristic are the dramatic pilgrimage churches at Lamego and Braga, where the theatrical quality of baroque architecture is extended to landscaping. Each church (790) is built on a hill top and is approached up the steep hillside by a terraced stone staircase

791 Façade. Murcia Cathedral, Jaimé Bort y Meliá. 1740-54

792 Façade. University, Valladolid, Diego and Narciso Tomé. Begun 1715

793 Mountain palace of La Granja, Spain, Garden façade, Filippo Juvara and Giovanni Battista Sacchetti. 1735-9

1701   Jethro Tull (1674-1741) devised a horse-drawn seed drill which cut rows of furrows for the seeds and sowed them therein at a suitable depth. Seeds sown by Tull's drill increased the yield eight-fold in comparison with the broadcast sowing method

1702   *The Daily Courant*, the first English daily newspaper, appeared on March 11

1703   Sir Isaac Newton elected to become President of the Royal Society, and annually re-elected until his death in 1727. The only English scientist to be buried in Westminster Abbey

1703   St Petersburg founded in Russia by the Tsar Peter the Great, as the capital of his kingdom

1709   Abraham Darby's (1677-1717) experimentation in Coalbrookdale into producing a suitable carbon fuel for smelting iron ore led to the coking of coal for this purpose

1710   The first hard paste (true) porcelain made in Europe. The German chemist Johann F. Böttger (1682-1719), who worked at the Meissen ceramics factory near Dresden, then discovered a way of making such ware. He added ground alabaster or marble to the local white clay

1710   Staffordshire potteries developed the process of making a hard, light-coloured stoneware to act as a cheaper substitute for porcelain. White-burning clay from the West Country was used, mixed with fine grit and sand

GERMANY

AUSTRIA AND GERMANY

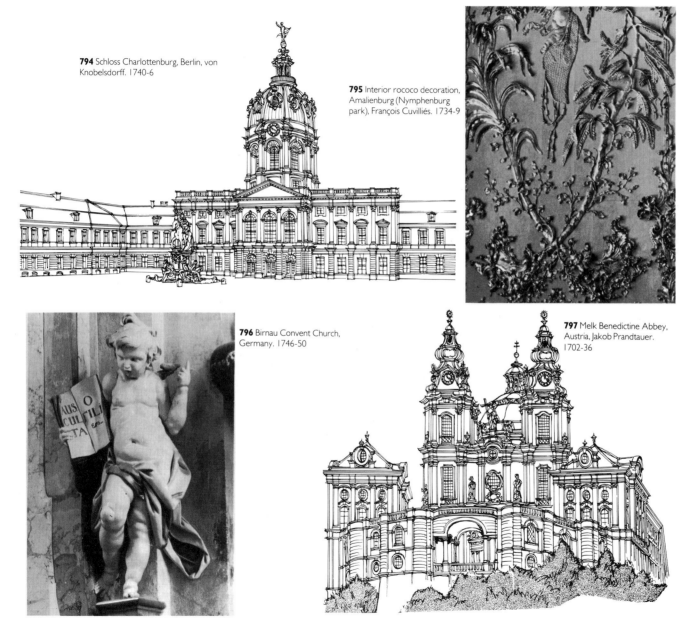

794 Schloss Charlottenburg, Berlin, von Knobelsdorff. 1740-6

795 Interior rococo decoration, Amalienburg (Nymphenburg park), François Cuvilliés. 1734-9

796 Birnau Convent Church, Germany. 1746-50

797 Melk Benedictine Abbey, Austria, Jakob Prandtauer. 1702-36

decorated all the way by finials and figure sculpture. Impressive also are the baroque palaces of Mafra and Queluz. The smaller and elegant, though more provincial, Palacio Mateus at Vila Real (**789**) is most attractive; it is depicted on every bottle of rosé wine for which the area is known.

From about 1700 the baroque style – which had been implanted in southern Germany by Italian architects (p. 145) and quickly taken up in the Vorarlberg and Switzerland by the Thumb, Beer and Moosbrugger families of architects and craftsmen building their great abbey churches (**783**, **784**) – had evolved into a mature form. It was this form which then dominated the architecture and decoration of southern Germany, Austria, Switzerland, Czechoslovakia and Hungary for the greater part of the eighteenth century.

It carried the theme of pulsating life and movement further than either the Italian or Spanish versions had done. Italian baroque, despite the undulations of alternately convex to concave curved planes (p. 134), always gives precedence to the classical structure in orders, capitals, vaults etc. The Spanish tends to obscure these by over-ornamentation (p. 147). The German achievement was to carry the baroque principle of movement to the ultimate degree. Thus, though some churches are heavily ornamented, others are restrained in the use and area of decoration. It is not in the quantity of enrichment but in the flowing, undulating, always sinuously curving architectural forms that the summit of baroque expression is obtained. Walls, vaults, capitals, piers, windows and doorways all contribute to this restless surging movement and the delicate pastel-coloured rococo ornament completes the scheme.

BAROQUE AND ROCOCO 1700 – 1750

Interiors illustrate the way in which craftsmanship in painting, sculpture and architecture, all of the highest quality, merges into one scheme of illusion and grandeur, so that it is often difficult to discern what is painted to represent three-dimensional forms and what is three-dimensional reality. Motifs are taken from nature, from plant and animal life, but the treatment is not naturalistic. The leaf, tendril or stem is stylized as part of a design. Though German rococo decoration is much more sensuous than the more delicate, subtle French prototype, both forms are sophisticated, not merely reproductions of nature's design.

Within this large area of central Europe great variations in the interpretation of the dominant baroque theme were created, by a host of outstanding architects and talented craftsmen. In the north of Germany the trend was nearer to Roman baroque: for example, Von Knobelsdorff's Schloss Charlottenburg in Berlin (**794**); though his Palace of Sanssouci at Potsdam is more lightheartedly rococo. Further south, in Dresden, Pöppelmann and his colleagues were creating a Saxon style, more extrovert and ornamental. The Zwinger* (**798**) was part of his work here on the redevelopment of the royal palace. In the central area, around Bamberg, Nuremberg and Würzburg, the leading figures were members of the Dientzenhofer family and, later, Balthasar Neumann. Three Dientzenhofer brothers were working in Germany at this time and another branch of the family created the magnificent churches in Prague (**806, 807**). Neumann (1687-

*Badly damaged in the devastating raid of 1944 but now rebuilt

798 Zwinger, Dresden, Mathaeus Daniel Pöppelmann. 1711-20

799 Aldersbach Abbey Church, Asam brothers. 1718-29

800 Staircase, Schloss Mirabell, Salzburg, Austria, Lucas von Hildebrandt. 1726

801 Karlskirche, Vienna, Austria, Johann Fischer von Erlach. 1716

1700–1730 Gesso-decorated furniture fashionable. This was a paste made from whiting and size, which was applied in successive coats to an article of furniture until the coating was thick enough to be carved or incised. The finished piece was then gilded

1710 The Statute of Anne passed the first Act of English Copyright Law

1711 The tuning fork invented by John Shore, trumpeter at the Chapel Royal

1712 Thomas Newcomen, English ironmonger (1663-1729), produced, after 15 years of experimental work, an atmospheric engine to pump out water from a colliery near Dudley Castle

c.1713 Gabriel Daniel Fahrenheit (1686-1736), Polish/German instrument maker, initiated the general use of mercury in thermometer tubes, instead of the previously used alcohol. Fahrenheit is best known for the temperature scale named after him, in which he set two fixed points: 32°, the melting point of ice and 96°, the temperature of the healthy human body. On Fahrenheit's scale, the boiling point of water was then 212°

1718 In Britain, Sir Thomas Lombe (1685-1739) patented a silk-throwing machine based upon earlier Italian models. He went on to start up a factory, water-powered from the River Derwent in Derbyshire

c.1718 Antoine Watteau, French painter (1684-1721), produced one of his last and most characteristic

802 Royal hunting lodge at Stupinigi, near Turin, Italy, Filippo Juvara. 1729-33

803 Schloss Eszterháza, Fertöd, Hungary, 1720, Erhard Martinelli. Completed 1762-6

804 Entrance doorway. Clam Gallas Palace, Prague, Czechoslovakia, Fisher von Erlach. 1707

805 Entrance hall and staircase. Royal Palace at Caserta, Italy, Luigi Vanvitelli. Begun 1752

1753) was the leading genius of German baroque in this period. His masterpiece was the Würzburg Residenz, with its superbly decorated monumental interiors. He also worked at the Palace of Bruchsal, Schloss Brühl, the Abbey Church of Neresheim and the great Pilgrimage Church of Vierzehnheiligen (**828, 832, 833**).

It was in the Bavarian south that the most characteristic baroque was to be seen. The Asam brothers were acknowledged masters in the creation in paint, plaster and marble of the illusory form. They worked for architects such as Fischer or Zimmermann, but also designed their own buildings. S. John Nepomuk in Munich is a superb example, as is Aldersbach Abbey Church (**799**).

Johann Fischer von Erlach (1656-1723) was the Bernini or Wren of Austria. Before his time Austrian baroque was largely the domain of foreign architects. Fischer von Erlach made the field entirely his own. From his Holy Trinity Church in Salzburg (**785**) – a Roman baroque church similar to Borromini's S. Agnese in Piazza Navona in Rome (**752**) – he moved on to his Vienna masterpiece in mature style, the Karlskirche (**801**). He became the official architect to the Imperial Court, working on, among other commissions, the Vienna Hofburg and the Palace of Schönbrunn. He was followed by several outstanding Austrian architects, notably Lucas von Hildebrandt and Jakob Prandtauer (**797, 800**).

By 1700 in Italy the fount of originality was drying up. Italy had led the world in classical art and architecture since 1420, un-challenged and supreme but, apart from a last flowering of work of quality in Rome, Turin and the south, Italian influence was waning in favour of dominance by French rococo and German baroque. Even the

BAROQUE 1700 – 1750

ancient origins of classicism were being challenged by Europeans travelling further and further afield on their Grand Tour, to Greece, Yugoslavia and the Middle East.

In Rome the trend was away from baroque towards a more severe and eclectic classicism. This may be seen in the monumental new façades of St John Lateran and S. Maria Maggiore. More original and rococo is the Palazzo della Consultà (**815**). In one of the other great rococo works of Rome, the Spanish Steps sweep up the steep hillside to the church which crowns its summit (**816**).

Turin was experiencing the swan song of north Italian baroque, but it was a triumphant finish. The chief architect here (**793**) was Filippo Juvara (1678-1736), a Sicilian who came north and took over from Guarini (p. 138). Juvara worked for the king, for whom he carried out a vast quantity of building in palaces, churches and town planning schemes. Particularly impressive is his hunting lodge at Stupinigi, built on grand palace scale and containing a magnificently decorated hall in rococo style (**802**). His masterpiece, the Superga, is the greatest of all the mountain churches, built on a hill overlooking the city (**808, 809**).

In the south of Italy and in Sicily vigorous, richly ornamented baroque still flourished. Luigi Vanvitelli created the vast royal palace at Caserta near Naples, summer residence of the Bourbon kings. This is a tremendous scheme with an 850ft façade and gardens which, though modelled on Versailles, extend much further – two miles up the hillside with terraces and fountains. The water for the latter comes via an aqueduct constructed by Vanvitelli from the mountains 20 miles away (**805**).

806 Church of S. Nicholas in the Old Town, Prague, Czechoslavakia, K.I. Dientzenhofer. 1732-7

807 Church of S. Nicholas, Malá Strana, Prague, Christoph Dientzenhofer. 1703-11

808, **809** View and dome interior. Basilica di Superga, near Turin, Filippo Juvara. 1717-31.

works, generally referred to as 'Enseigne de Gersaint', a signboard for his friend Edmond Gersaint, a Paris art dealer. The painting is now in the Staatliches Museum in Berlin

1719 Publication of Daniel Defoe's *Robinson Crusoe*, a novel which he based upon the autobiographical narrative of Alexander Selkirk. In 1720 Defoe published his *Journal of the Plague Year*, based this time upon the London Plague of 1665

1720 South Sea Bubble. The English speculative financial venture of the South Sea Company collapsed, causing panic and ruin for many, as well as the fall of the government

1722 Guy's Hospital, London. Built and financed by Thomas Guy, who was originally a bookseller and printer but became wealthy by financial dealing

1726 Publication of Dean Swift's satire Gulliver's Travels, under its title *Lemuel Gulliver's Travels into Several Remote Nations of the World*

1728 John Gay, English poet and dramatist, wrote his *Beggar's Opera*

1729 Johann Sebastian Bach, German composer, (1685-1750), wrote his longest work, the *St Matthew Passion*

1732 The Society of Dilettanti founded in England, as a convivial club for those with artistic interests arising from the Grand Tour. The Society gave artistic encouragement and patronage to excavations and research into the antique classical world, especially Greece. It published original papers and

BAROQUE AND ROCOCO   1700 – 1750

FRANCE AND ITALY

HOLLAND AND ENGLAND

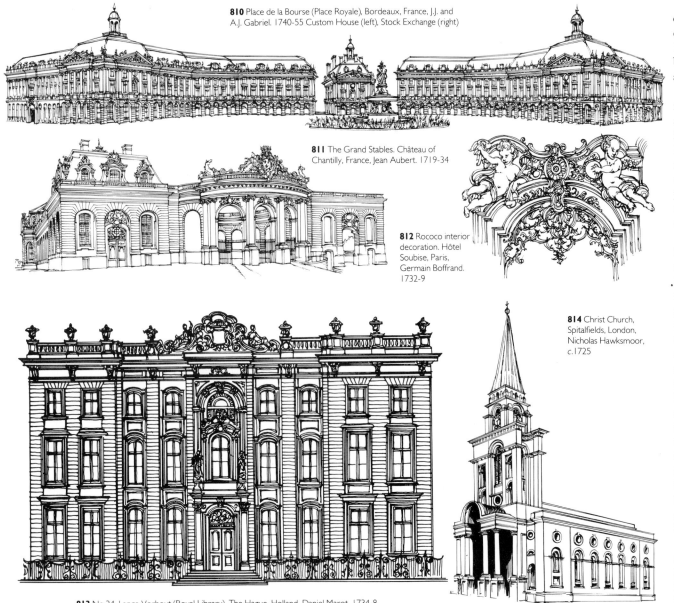

810 Place de la Bourse (Place Royale), Bordeaux, France, J.J. and A.J. Gabriel. 1740-55 Custom House (left), Stock Exchange (right)

811 The Grand Stables. Château of Chantilly, France, Jean Aubert. 1719-34

812 Rococo interior decoration. Hôtel Soubise, Paris, Germain Boffrand. 1732-9

814 Christ Church, Spitalfields, London, Nicholas Hawksmoor, c.1725

813 No.34, Lange Vorhout (Royal Library), The Hague, Holland, Daniel Marot. 1734-8

In Sicily several of the towns were almost completely rebuilt in this period after the destruction caused by the earthquakes of 1693. Catania is still largely a Sicilian baroque city, chiefly the work of the architect-planner Giovanni Vaccarini.

Louis XIV of France died in 1715 after reigning for 72 years. His prolific, vigorous architect Jules Hardouin Mansart had died in 1708. A new style was ushered in, under Louis XV, which was in reaction from the majestic imposing structures of the previous century. This style was rococo, and soon its popularity was spreading to other European countries: Germany, Austria, Scandinavia and even parts of Italy.

The style of rococo is seen chiefly in interiors and in decoration rather than structure. Exteriors were fairly plain and classical (**811**). Inside, all was lightness, elegance and gaiety. Gone were the heavy gilding, the large painted schemes, the coloured marble and the formality of the orders. Rococo architecture tended to eschew the orders. The decoration which surrounded window and door openings and enclosed ceiling and wall panelling was in lower relief and dainty, with ribbons, scrolls, arabesques, wreaths of flowers, volutes, seaweed and shells replacing the Roman classical motifs. The term rococo derives from the French *rocaille coquille*, the former appertaining to rocks, the latter to shells. Characteristic of rococo design is Boffrand's Hôtel Soubise in Paris (**812**) and Cuvilliés' Amalienburg pavilion at Nymphenburg near Munich (**795**).

Baroque forms of architecture were a rarity rather than the rule in northern Europe. A Flemish version is apparent in the Grande Place in Brussels (**766**) and Daniel Marot, a refugee Huguenot, brought a

French baroque flavour to Dutch building, as can be seen in his work at the Hague: for instance, the Royal Library (813).

In England, baroque architecture took a diverse form from elsewhere in Europe. It was a short-lived movement, emerging in the 1690s and over by 1730; the British returning to a style more suited to the national taste, a Palladianism first introduced here in the seventeenth century by Inigo Jones. The later work of Wren displayed some baroque characteristics; the west towers of St Paul's Cathedral, for example (756), and the domes and colonnades at Greenwich (p. 141), but this was a restrained, controlled baroque. As always, with Wren, his work was essentially English.

The brief flowering of English baroque came boldly, initiated by John Vanbrugh, a playwright of Flemish descent, who was commissioned at the age of 35 to design Castle Howard in Yorkshire (818). This building, like Blenheim Palace (817) and Seaton Delaval which followed it, is of a quite different form of baroque to the Italian or German. There are few curves and little voluptuousness, but the massing of three-dimensional forms is dramatic, often discordant. Vanbrugh created exciting patterns of light and shade in settings of grandeur: this cannot be termed anything other than baroque. In the early eighteenth century Nicholas Hawksmoor, in his university and ecclesiastical work (814), created his own personal style of baroque, original and different, as did also Thomas Archer.

By the early 1720s English architecture was developing along Palladian lines. The architectural pendulum was swinging back to the more correct Roman precepts of Palladio

815 Central doorway. Palazzo della Consultà, Rome, Ferdinando Fuga. 1732-7

816 The Spanish Steps, Rome, Francesco de Sanctis. 1723-5 Leading up to the Church of S.S. Trinità dei Monti from the Piazza di Spagna. Fountain: 'Barcaccia', Pietro Bernini. 1628

817 The Great Court entrance, Blenheim Palace, England, Sir John Vanbrugh. 1705-22

818 Garden front. Castle Howard, England, Sir John Vanbrugh. 1699-1712

financially supported expeditions by some of its members

1733   John Wesley's notable Oxford sermon *The Circumcision of the Heart*

1733   Invention by John Kay of the flying shuttle, a great advance in textile production in the weaving process. His son Robert invented in 1760 a multiple shuttle box, which made it possible to operate such equipment with several shuttles at once, each loaded with a weft yarn of different colour

1735   William Hogarth, English artist (1697-1764), painted his eight scenes of *A Rake's Progress*

1740   Benjamin Huntsman introduced commercially into England the wootz method of making steel. He re-melted the blister steel in closed crucibles, so producing a steel which possessed a better, more uniform, carbon content

1742   George Frederick Handel (1685-1759) gave the first performance in Dublin of his *Messiah*. It was performed in London the following year

1742   Thomas Bolsover, Sheffield cutler, observed, by accident, that with the application of heat a silver article had become fused with copper. He then developed the process which became known as 'Old Sheffield Plate', to coat buttons with silver. Joseph Hancock, in the 1750s, then perfected a method of rolling together the heated copper and silver to plate household articles

1739–47   Construction of Westminster Bridge in London. The first crossing of the Thames to be

TOWARDS PALLADIANISM 1700 – 1750

819 Church of St George, Hanover Square, London, John James. 1713-14

820 No.44 Berkeley Square, London, William Kent. 1744-5

821 Church of St Martin-in-the-Fields, London, James Gibbs. 1722

822 Fellows' Building, Cambridge, England, James Gibbs. 1724

823 Frederiksberg Palace, near Copenhagen, Denmark. 1699-1730

and away from the indigenous, yet personal concepts of Wren and the rumbustious massing of form and ornament of Vanbrugh and his colleagues.

The outstanding contribution of the English Palladian school of the eighteenth century was in country house building, where the exterior was plain, symmetrical and monumental, with careful attention paid to Roman classical proportion. What makes these great Palladian houses into master-pieces, indisputably northern European in their restraint and solidity, is their setting which is the characteristically English park-land. This represents a studied naturalness, a carefully created landscape of sweeping lawns, great spreading trees, lakes and temples, flowers and glades. This treatment is indigenous, very different from the formality of Versailles and widely copied in other parts of Europe; Russia for example.

The interiors of such Palladian houses are in marked contrast to the cool under-statement of the exteriors. Examples such as Holkham and Houghton are richly colourful and baroque in treatment. Lord Burlington, who designed Chiswick House (**827**) on the lines of Palladio's Villa Capra (p. 122 and **678, 679**), was an important leader and patron of the Palladian movement. Colen Campbell and William Kent were two of its notable architects (**820, 826**).

Until about 1730 architectural design in the British American colonies evolved by tradition, from craftsmen who brought with them to their new land the building methods and forms which they had known in Europe. In consequence there was a delay of 20 or more years before a new architectural form was adopted in America.

In the early years of the eighteenth century the Dutch Palladian form of house, of the type designed in England by such architects as Roger Pratt and John Webb, were being erected in America, and such designs were being applied also to public buildings (p. 129, 140). The architectural form was symmetrical, evincing projecting cornices, dormers in the roof and, often, a central lantern above. The sash window made its appearance, as did also the central staircase well. Coleshill House (765) was a pattern for such building, examples of which included the civic structures in Virginia's capital Williamsburg, such as the Governor's Palace and the Capitol (825).

In ecclesiastical building, knowledge of the designs of the Wren churches in the City of London (p. 140) spread in America, leading to such examples as the old North Church (1723-41) and the Old South Meeting House (1729-30), both in Boston. In both buildings the style of fenestration and steeple were based on Wren.

By 1730 books on architectural design published in Europe by notable architects were reaching America in considerable numbers. Among them were English volumes by James Gibbs and Colen Campbell, which led to versions of St Martin-in-the-Fields and Palladian houses being built (821, 822, 824).

824 Christ Church, Philadelphia, America. Begun 1727, spire 1750-4

825 The Capitol, Williamsburg, Virginia, America. 1701-15. Drawn from the Bodleian engraved plate of 1737 and the reconstruction of 1930-4

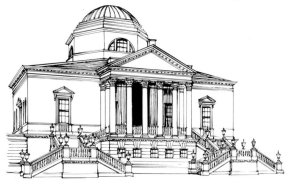

827 Chiswick House, London, Lord Burlington. 1727-36

826 The hall. Holkham Hall, England, William Kent, c.1740

built in addition to the medieval London Bridge

1745   The Frenchman Jacques de Vaucanson devised a loom to weave figured cloth, which combined the ideas of the earlier inventors in the field and took a stage further the development of a mechanism to weave a wide variety of patterned fabrics

1745   William Cookworthy (1705-80) began research into making hard paste porcelain by experimenting with Devon and Cornish Clays

1745   The Jacobite Rebellion. Charles Edward Stuart sailed from France to Scotland on 12 July, where the Highlanders rallied to him. He reached Derby in the autumn but was finally defeated on Culloden Moor 16 April 1746

1747   The first modern dictionary in the English language written by Samuel Johnson. The work was published in 1755, in two folio volumes, as *A Dictionary of the English Language* – and was accepted as the basis for all English dictionaries for at least 100 years

1750   Thomas Gray, English poet, completed his *Elegy Written in a Country Churchyard*

BAROQUE AND ROCOCO   1750 – 1800

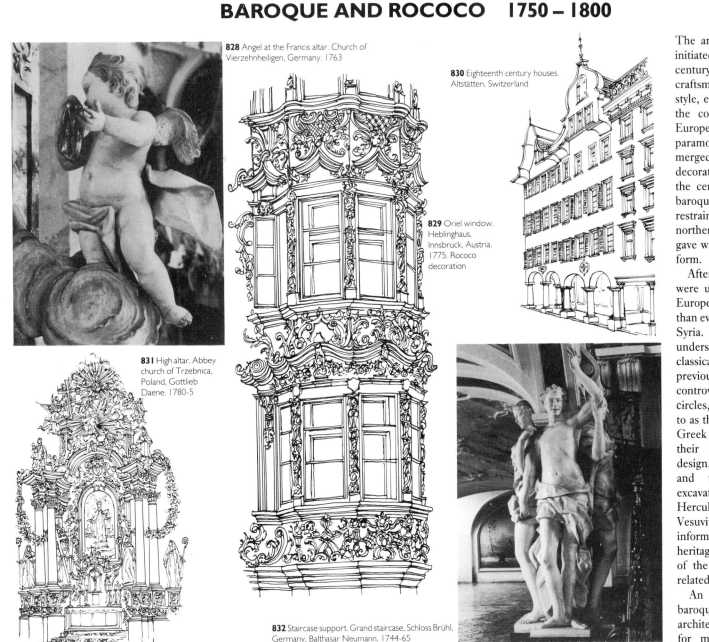

828 Angel at the Francis altar. Church of Vierzehnheiligen, Germany. 1763

830 Eighteenth century houses. Altstätten, Switzerland

829 Oriel window. Heblinghaus, Innsbruck, Austria. 1775. Rococo decoration

831 High altar. Abbey church of Trzebnica, Poland, Gottlieb Daene. 1780-5

832 Staircase support. Grand staircase, Schloss Brühl, Germany, Balthasar Neumann. 1744-65

The architectural pattern which had been initiated in the first half of the eighteenth century, of a superbly high standard of craftsmanship combined with a classical style, evolved further in the second half. In the countries of central and south-west Europe, where the baroque style had been paramount, this continued – though it was merged in some areas with a rococo decorative form. Then, towards the end of the century everywhere, the dynamism of baroque was gradually replaced by a more restrained and delicate neo-classicism. In northern Europe and America, Palladianism gave way much earlier to the Neo-Classical form.

After 1750 archaeological expeditions were undertaken by scholars from several European countries to sites further afield than ever before: to Greece, to Dalmatia and Syria. The findings were published, and understanding grew of the Greek origins of classical architecture – as well as the previously studied Roman. This led to controversy in architectural and academic circles, a situation now colloquially referred to as the 'battle of the styles', in which pro-Greek and pro-Roman factions took sides in their attitude to classical architectural design. The opening up of new classical sites and the extension of archaeological excavation at, especially, the buried cities of Herculaneum and Pompeii at the foot of Vesuvius in Italy, provided more accurate information about Europe's classical heritage, and the Neo-Classical architecture of the years 1760-1800 was then closely related to the original.

An especially bold, dynamic form of baroque maintained its strong hold on the architecture of central and eastern Europe for much of the century. In northern

BAROQUE AND ROCOCO 1750 – 1800

Germany this was nearer to Roman baroque, as may be seen in the (now restored) church of St Michael in Hamburg by Sonnini and Prey (1751-61). This brick church boasts a lofty classical steeple. Inside, the oval building, decorated in white and gold, is simply monumental; baroque only in its sinuously curving balcony which encircles the church.

Further south Balthasar Neumann's last works are the supreme achievement of Central Germany (832). His pilgrimage church of Vierzehnheiligen, built on a magnificent site on the crown of a hill (1743-72), faces Banz on the other bank of the river Main. In the tall, striking exterior the twin towers flank the curving centrepiece between. The interior is a classic German baroque masterpiece, a homogeneous blend of architecture, sculpture and painting; the ornament forming an integral part of the overall design. It is very much a pilgrimage church, the magnificent 'fourteen saints altar' dominating the centre of the nave (828, 833).

A later building is Neumann's Neresheim Abbey Church. One of his last designs, it was built after his death (1747-92) and verges on the Neo-Classical. Nevertheless the interior is still in the trend of spatial movement, based on ovals and curves, concave merging into convex. This late baroque interior illustrates clearly the master's experienced and harmonious handling of this form.

In the middle years of the eighteenth century a number of French architects were employed in Germany, especially on royal and aristocratic palaces and mansions, and these introduced a lighter rococo style of decoration. François de Cuvilliés (1695-1768) was court architect at Munich for many years, where he worked on the

834 Abbey Church of S. Gallen, Switzerland, Thumb and Beer. 1752-66

833 Pilgrimage Church of Vierzehnheiligen, Germany, Balthasar Neumann. 1743-72

835 Schloss Solitude, Stuttgart, Germany, P.L.P. de la Guêpière. 1763-7

1751–72 The great French encyclopaedia of trades and industries was compiled and published in 17 volumes of text and 11 volumes of engravings. The moving spirit behind the encyclopaedia and its first editor was Denis Diderot, French philosopher and man of letters. In editiorial work Diderot was assisted by Jean d'Alembert, and among the notable contributors was Voltaire

1753 Carl Linnaeus, Swedish naturalist, introduced the concept of binomial nomenclature for plants, published in his *Species Plantarum*. Linnaeus's code system, which greatly simplified the existing nomenclature, consisted of a Latin or Greek generic name accompanied by a descriptive term

1754 Publication by Thomas Chippendale of his *The Gentleman and Cabinet Maker's Director*

1756–9 John Smeaton built the third Eddystone lighthouse, using a strong new hydraulic cement which he had developed

1759 Voltaire (Jean François Arouet), French writer and philosopher, produced *Candide*, his most famous work – a satire upon the adventure stories of the time

1761 Publication of *The Social Contract* by Jean Jacques Rousseau

1764 James Hargreaves devised the first spinning machine, which became known as the spinning jenny. It had eight vertical spindles operated on the great wheel principle, with eight driving bands enabling eight threads to be spun simultaneously. The word 'jenny', like 'gin' or 'ginny', is a colloquialism for engine

BAROQUE AND ROCOCO   1750 – 1800

SPAIN AND PORTUGAL

836 El Pilar, Zaragoza, Spain. From 1677 Francisco de Herrera; from 1750, Ventura Rodriguez

837 Sculpture. Pilgrimage Church at Lamego, Portugal. From 1761

PORTUGAL

838 Garden front, Palace of Queluz, Mateus Vincente de Oliviera. 1758

Residenz and completed the Theatiner-kirche. Though his inspiration was French rococo, his decorative work in the Amalienburg and in the Residenz theatre evolved into a more full-bloodedly elaborate German form of this type of design. The work of another Frenchman, Pierre-Louis Philippe de la Guêpière, may be seen in the country palace of Schloss Solitude near Stuttgart (1763-7). This has a baroque theme, but its central oval room is decorated in rococo manner (**835**).

Extensive building in baroque and rococo styles continued in Switzerland, Austria, Czechoslovakia, Hungary and Poland, until the last decade of the century. For example, the abbey church of S. Gallen boasts a classic baroque exterior in the Vorarlberg tradition (**834**) while, at Innsbruck, the Heblinghaus is elegantly decorated all over the exterior in rococo design (**829**). The high altar of the abbey church at Trzebnica illustrates the richness of Polish baroque workmanship (**831**).

In the Iberian Peninsula architects continued to design in baroque form until the later eighteenth century. Baroque façades, or alternatively a complete baroque re-clothing, were added to earlier cathedrals and churches. The most impressive of these is the baroque dress given to the famous pilgrimage church at Santiago de Compostela, the Romanesque building created in honour of St James at the end of one of the greatest of all medieval pilgrimage routes (p. 44). The baroque re-clothing was carried out largely between 1738 and 1749 by Fernando Casas y Nuova, though the north side was not completed until after 1770 and then was in more Neo-Classical form. Baroque façades were also added to Jaèn and Murcia Cathedrals (1750-4) (**791**). Cadiz is the only completely baroque cathedral in Spain. It was begun in 1722, but was not completed until 1853.

In the last decades of the eighteenth century baroque design was gradually abandoned in favour of a less ornamented classicism of greater purity. One of the chief leaders of this movement was Ventura Rodriguez (1717-85). His work at the immense cathedral in Zaragoza – Nuestra Señora del Pilar – is characteristic (836). The building had been designed in 1677 by Francisco de Herrera and was intended to be baroque throughout; however, it was not completed. Rodriguez took over and worked there from 1753-66, clothing the interior in a Neo-Classical manner. Other, more severely classical cathedrals include those at Vich and at Lugo.

In Portugal a more light-hearted baroque tempered with rococo was typical of this half of the eighteenth century, and a number of fine examples survive. Notably, there is the pilgrimage church at Lamego (837, 839) and the Lisbon summer palace at Queluz (838, 841). This, the work of Mateus Vincente de Oliviera, is no Versailles or La Granja, but has an elegant rococo charm set in beautiful gardens.

France's most important contribution to architecture in this period was in extensive town planning schemes (p. 164). Apart from these, this was not a great time for church building in France and England, but in the surviving examples the stylistic trend was, as in secular building, towards a symmetrical, more monumental classicism. This is evidenced in Jean Servandomi's S. Sulpice in Paris (1733-45), and in the Madeleine church in Besançon built in 1766.

The outstanding church of the time is a pure example of Neo-Classicism: the

839 Pilgrimage Church of Nossa Senhora dos Remédios, Lamego, Portugal, Niccolò Nasoni. 1750-61

840 Basilica da Estrêla, Lisbon, Mateus Vincente. 1779-90

841 Gateway sculpture, Palace of Queluz. 1758

1768 Joshua Reynolds, leading English portrait painter, was unanimously elected to be first President of the newly founded Royal Academy of Arts

1768 Richard Arkwright invented a spinning frame which made use of rollers to draw out the rovings before being passed to the spindle. His frame required greater power than then produced by a human operator, so he designed it to be geared to a horse mill. In 1769 the invention was adapted for use with water power and became known as the water frame. Among Arkwright's other important textile machinery inventions was his carding machine of the 1770s

1770 *The Blue Boy* painted by Thomas Gainsborough, famous English portrait and landscape artist

1770 Joseph Priestley recommended the use of rubber as a pencil eraser. In England it became known as india rubber because the substance was cultivated and utilized in the West Indies, and by South American Indians

1774–5 In England Joseph Priestley discovered oxygen by heating mercuric oxide, calling it 'dephlogisticated air'. It was the French chemist Antoine Lavoisier who named the gas and recognized its role in combustion, publishing his paper on combustion in 1777

1776 First use in Britain of the French method of casting plate glass, in the new casting hall at St Helens

1776 Boulton and Watt made their first full-size steam (atmospheric) engine

CLASSICISM   1750 – 1800

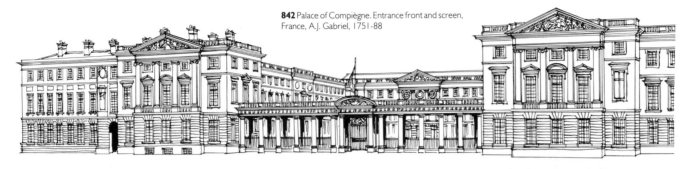

842 Palace of Compiègne. Entrance front and screen, France, A.J. Gabriel, 1751-88

FRANCE AND ENGLAND

843 The Panthéon, (S. Geneviève), Paris, begun 1757 J.G. Soufflot. Neo-Classicism

844 Pedestal and urn, Saltram House, England, Robert Adam. 1779-80. Neo-Classicism

Panthéon in Paris (**843**). Begun in 1757, it was designed by Jacques Germain Soufflot and dedicated to S. Geneviève, the patron saint of Paris. The building became a pantheon at the time of the Revolution and great Frenchmen are buried here: Voltaire, Mirabeau, Rousseau, Victor Hugo and many others.

The Panthéon is a supremely classical building, very plain and pure, based on its namesake and prototype in Rome (p. 19) but, being an eighteenth-century structure, the dome, which stands upon a drum fenestrated to light the interior, is carried by pendentives in turn supported on the four great crossing piers (see pendentive construction on p. 31). Soufflot had intended columns to carry the pendentives, but he died in 1780 before the church had been completed and his successor, Rondelet, was responsible for the piers. It was he also who experimented here with the then fairly new concept of concrete reinforced with metal for his construction purposes. Rondelet used a metal reinforced mortar and rubble aggregate.

The Panthéon is a centrally planned church on Renaissance lines (p. 116). It is built on Greek cross plan, with the dome over the crossing. The building exterior is very plain; only the great Corinthian portico provides a focal decorative feature. Inside, the dome is coffered, and coffered saucer domes cover the four arms of the cross. The lantern and pendentives are painted.

In England a new generation of Palladian architects continued the work of this school which, under the leadership and patronage of Lord Burlington, had established a revival of the precepts of Palladio, especially in country house building. During the 1750s and early 1760s architects such as Sir Robert

CLASSICISM   1750 – 1800

Taylor, James Paine and John Carr (847) continued to build in the Palladian manner, creating such houses as Heveningham Hall, Denton Hall and Wardour Castle.

From 1760 onwards the leader in this tradition of Roman classical architecture was Sir William Chambers, the designer of Somerset House in London (1778-86). All his life Chambers was a staunch adherent of the Roman cause and designed, in strictly Roman classical form, work of the highest standard and finest proportions. Apart from Somerset House, Chambers was responsible for the town house in Piccadilly (Melbourne House 1770-4) and the mansion near Edinburgh (Duddingston House 1762-8).

In England the years 1760-1800 are, however, primarily noted for the introduction and establishment of Neo-Classicism, a style initiated by the Scottish architect Robert Adam and taken up by several other important architects such as James Wyatt, Thomas Leverton and Henry Holland.

Robert Adam spent nearly four years travelling and studying architecture in France, Italy and Dalmatia. He returned to Britain in 1758, set up practice in London, and for over 30 years poured out a tremendous number of very varied and very personal designs. He was an eclectic, using many classical sources: Imperial Roman as at Syon House, Republican Roman from Pompeii and Herculaneum as in his so-called 'Etruscan' rooms at Osterley House and 20 St James's Square, and Diocletian Roman as at Bowood House. He was, though, no copyist but an innovator. He blended his ideas culled from so many sources into a style personally 'Adam': romantic, elegant, restrained and of the highest quality of craftsmanship and design

845 No.20, St James's Square, London, Robert Adam. 1772. Neo-Classicism

846 The Orangery, Heveningham Hall, England, James Wyatt. 1790-1800. Neo-Classicism

847 Fairfax House, York, England, John Carr of York. 1770. Palladianism

848 Dining Room, Syon House, England, Robert Adam. 1761-70. Neo-Classicism

1779 Samuel Crompton devised a machine for spinning which became known as the spinning mule, as it was a cross between Hargreaves's spinning jenny and Arkwright's water frame. The mule produced finer, softer yarns than before. At first hand-operated with 30 spindles, it was soon enlarged to take up to a thousand, and was operated by water power

1783 War of American Independence ended with the Treaty of Versailles, when Britain recognized the independence of the American colonies

1786 Dr Edmund Cartwright designed and made the first successful power loom for weaving greater widths of cloth. This loom, which he patented, could be operated by horses, water or steam

1789 The storming of the Bastille in Paris and the start of the French Revolution

1789 George Washington became first President of the United States of America

1789 Soda first successfully and commercially produced from salt by the French scientist Nicholas Le Blanc

1790 Joseph Marie Jacquard devised the loom, which bears his name, to weave complex patterns without the need for a drawboy. The jacquard loom makes use of a punched card system, in which the cards pass over a perforated prism. Needles are then pressed by a spring against this so that some pass through the card holes. Each needle controls one warp thread, lifting it as required.

CLASSICISM 1750 – 1800

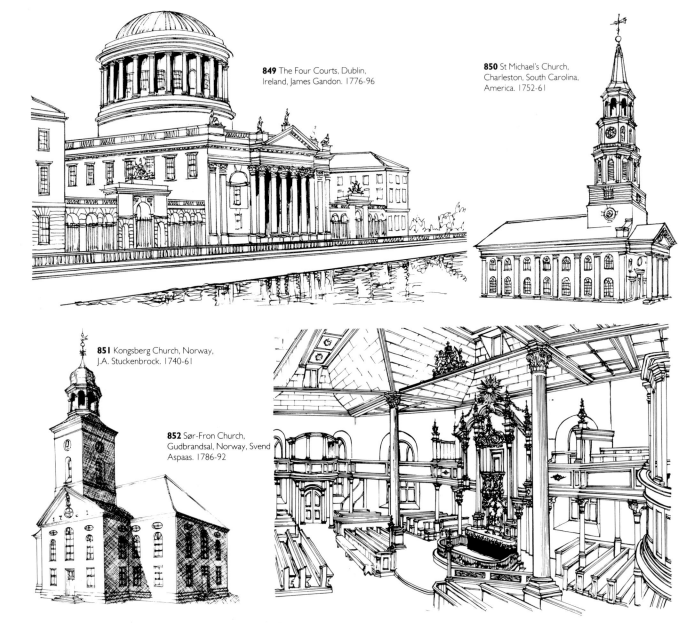

849 The Four Courts, Dublin, Ireland, James Gandon. 1776-96

850 St Michael's Church, Charleston, South Carolina, America. 1752-61

851 Kongsberg Church, Norway, J.A. Stuckenbrock. 1740-61

852 Sør-Fron Church, Gudbrandsal, Norway, Svend Aspaas. 1786-92

(844, 845, 848). He gauged unerringly what the aristocratic owners of houses in Britain would want at this time, and he used this intuition to combine architectural themes derived from his own European studies *in situ* with those of other men – such as Robert Wood's drawings of Palmyra in Syria.

Adam was immensely successful. Nearly all the wealthy men in Britain employed him to enlarge and redecorate their houses. Two disadvantages for him arose from this. Most of his clients already possessed great mansions and/or town houses, so he rarely had the opportunity to design from scratch. Secondly, his very success led to widescale plagiarism of his designs, a fact which particularly irritated him.

Robert Adam created a new form of classical design, one of world-wide influence, especially in America, Russia and France. He was convinced by his research in Europe that the ancient Romans had never abided by rigid rules such as those which the Palladians followed, but had adapted their classical orders to need and scale. Adam did this too. He would take an order, recreate its proportions and decoration, alter the accepted rulings and the result would have the essence of the source material.

Palladianism came to Ireland in the 1730s and flourished for several decades. The influence of Lord Burlington, an Irish as well as an English peer, seems certain – though exercised from a distance. The local aristocracy absorbed the Palladian ideals from England, and many fine public buildings were erected in Dublin and other cities. The earliest of these was the Parliament House in Dublin (now the Bank of Ireland), built 1728-39 by Edward Lovat Pearce. Earlier still came the first great stone Palladian mansion, at Castletown in Kildare, built for the Speaker 1725-30.

The Roman classical tradition continued in the 1760s under the influence of Chambers, who contributed the design (1759) for the charming and perfect Palladian little pavilion, the Casino, at Marino near Dublin. James Gandon (1743-1823) had worked as a young man in Chambers's office in London, but spent much of his later life in Ireland, where he was responsible for a number of public buildings in Dublin which are amongst the finest in the city. Two are particularly notable and both occupy prime sites along the banks of the River Liffey: the Custom House 1781-91 and the Four Courts building 1776-96 (**849**). Both are powerful, domed structures, strictly Roman classical, but less rigidly Palladian than earlier works. The dome and drum surmounting the Custom House, indeed, closely resembles Wren's more baroque treatment at Greenwich (p. 141).

In the late 1770s Adam-style neo-classicism came to Ireland, and there are a number of elegant town houses in Dublin, as well as larger country mansions, which reflect his style of low relief stucco decoration in white against a coloured background, mahogany doorcases, and fine wrought iron staircases, balustrades and fanlights.

After 1750, a steady stream of architectural books became available in America. In the English colonies these were mainly English publications – Leoni, Kent, Campbell, Gibbs – but Serlio and Palladio also appeared. The professional architect was a rarity until the late eighteenth century, so the books served as an important guide. Inevitably, architectural style followed (with a delay in time) the current English pattern. For example, the third quarter of the century saw the building by the Anglican Church of

853 The State House, Boston, Massachusetts, America, Charles Bulfinch. 1795-8

854 Cliveden, Germantown, Pennsylvania, America, Benjamin Chew. 1763-4

855 Stiftsgården Palace, Trondheim, Norway. 1774-8

Jacquard first established his loom in 1801, for use in the French silk industry

1791 Luigi Galvani, Italian physiologist, published his observations upon the effects of atmospheric electricity upon the muscular responses of frogs. He had found that muscular contractions were induced whenever the moist tissues of the frog were in contact with two differing metals, such as iron and copper. He put forward his theory that animal tissues generate electricity. It was Volta who drew the correct conclusion that the electricity was generated by the contact of two dissimilar metals and that this was then passed on to the frogs

1793 King Louis XVI of France condemned to death by the Convention and guillotined

1794 Eli Whitney, American inventor and manufacturer, patented his cotton 'gin'. This was an attempt to mechanize the hitherto manual process of cleaning raw cotton on the plantations of America, and so reduce costs. In a rotating cylindrical cage the cotton seed pods were broken up and the seeds and pods fell out through a mesh leaving the cotton behind. A current of air was then blown through the cotton to remove dirt particles. By 1794 Eli Whitney's cotton gin had been improved from his original invention. It was horse-driven, so that one man controlling the operation replaced the 50 required on the earlier equipment

1796 Edward Jenner, English physician, first used his cowpox vaccine against smallpox on an

FRANCE, DENMARK AND ENGLAND

BELGIUM AND SCOTLAND

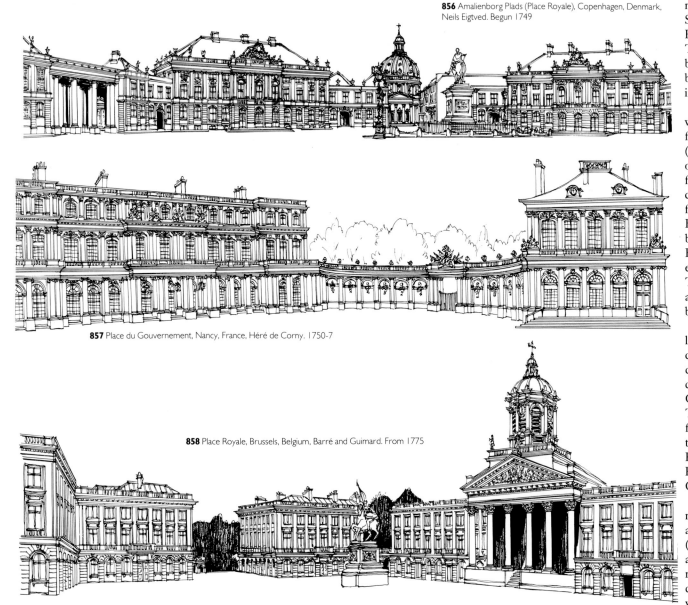

856 Amalienborg Plads (Place Royale), Copenhagen, Denmark, Neils Eigtved. Begun 1749

857 Place du Gouvernement, Nancy, France, Héré de Corny. 1750-7

858 Place Royale, Brussels, Belgium, Barré and Guimard. From 1775

many 'Gibbs' designs, particularly St Martin-in-the-Fields, though Wren and Hawksmoor were still an inspiration (**850**). The traditional colonial house continued to be built for some time, based on Pratt (**854**), but mansions nearer to Palladianism were increasingly being erected.

It was the late 1780s before the Adam style was introduced, but it became very fashionable after that. Charles Bulfinch (1763-1844) was one of the early architects of note. He was self-taught and did not at first accept professional fees, but he gained considerable knowledge and experience from the years which he spent studying on a European Grand Tour. One of his early buildings was the Massachusetts State House in Boston, in which he combined elements from Chambers, Adam and Wyatt. The concept of a central dome which he adopted here set a pattern for public buildings in America for years to come (**853**).

France had taken over from Italy leadership of civic planning earlier in the century, and several of these extensive city-centre developments survive, such as the central squares in Rennes (1734-43, J.J. Gabriel) and The Place Capitole in Toulouse (1750-3, Cammas). One of the finest European mid-century schemes is in the centre of Nancy, where the octagonal Place Stanislas connects via the tree-lined Place Carrière with the Place du Gouvernement (**857**).

The architectural style of these layouts is mainly baroque or rococo, but from *c*.1760 architects such as Servandomi and Soufflot (pp. 159-60) were initiating the movement away from curves towards the more monumental symmetry of neo-classicism. The chief architect in the field of town planning was Ange-Jacques Gabriel (1698-1782).

TOWN PLANNING   1750 – 1800

Together with his father Jacques-Jules Gabriel, he was responsible for the fine redevelopment in Bordeaux, especially the Place de la Bourse (**810**). He went on to work in Paris, where he built the École Militaire in the Champs de Mars (1751-68), and the imposing twin palaces in the Place de la Concorde (1761-70). Gabriel was also responsible for the rebuilding of the Palace at Compiègne (**842**).

Elsewhere, of particular note, is the ambitious street layout of the Amalienborg in Copenhagen (**856**) and the Place Royale in Brussels (**858**), both large-scale baroque schemes. In Britain terrace architecture was developed chiefly for town house design, beginning with the work in Bath by John Wood and his son (**859**), and taken up by Robert Adam in London and Edinburgh (**861**).

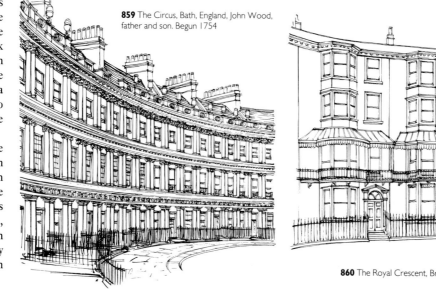

859 The Circus, Bath, England, John Wood, father and son. Begun 1754

860 The Royal Crescent, Brighton, England. 1798

eight-year-old boy – James Phipps. Two months later Jenner innoculated the boy with smallpox, but the child failed to develop the disease. Jenner published in 1796 a case-by-case history of his experimental use of the vaccine. Its publicity quickly led to a widespread use of vaccination

1798   John Dalton, English scientist, wrote the first scientific account of colour blindness. He himself suffered from the red-green type which later became known as Daltonism

1800   Count Alessandro Volta, Italian scientist, announced his discovery of the 'voltaic pile', the first source of constant-current electricity. Volta's 'pile' consisted of a stack of alternating zinc and silver plates, separated by cardboard sheets soaked in brine

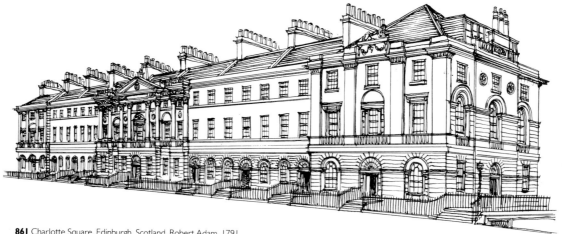

861 Charlotte Square, Edinburgh, Scotland, Robert Adam. 1791

1800 – 1830

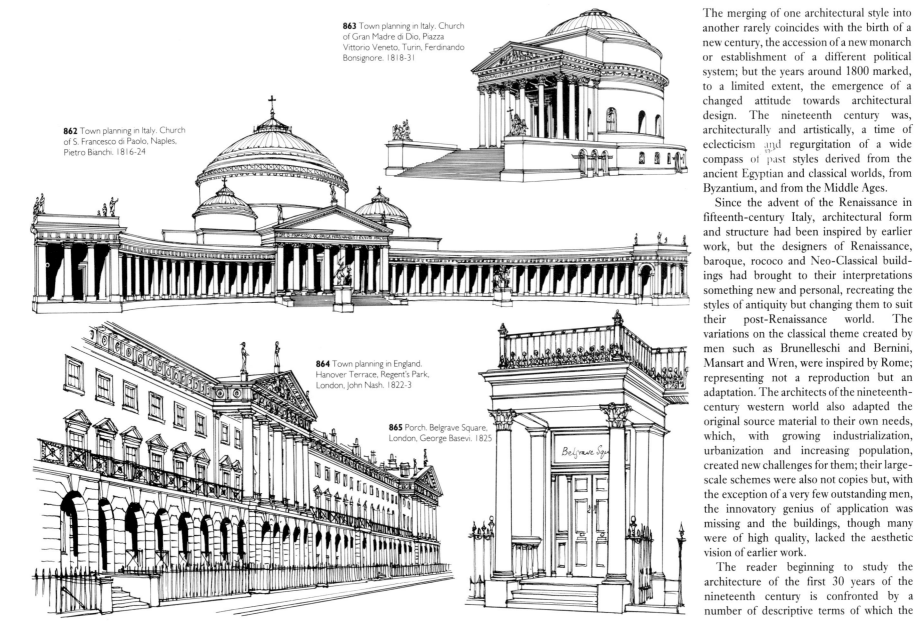

863 Town planning in Italy. Church of Gran Madre di Dio, Piazza Vittorio Veneto, Turin, Ferdinando Bonsignore. 1818-31

862 Town planning in Italy. Church of S. Francesco di Paolo, Naples, Pietro Bianchi. 1816-24

864 Town planning in England. Hanover Terrace, Regent's Park, London, John Nash. 1822-3

865 Porch. Belgrave Square, London, George Basevi. 1825

The merging of one architectural style into another rarely coincides with the birth of a new century, the accession of a new monarch or establishment of a different political system; but the years around 1800 marked, to a limited extent, the emergence of a changed attitude towards architectural design. The nineteenth century was, architecturally and artistically, a time of eclecticism and regurgitation of a wide compass of past styles derived from the ancient Egyptian and classical worlds, from Byzantium, and from the Middle Ages.

Since the advent of the Renaissance in fifteenth-century Italy, architectural form and structure had been inspired by earlier work, but the designers of Renaissance, baroque, rococo and Neo-Classical buildings had brought to their interpretations something new and personal, recreating the styles of antiquity but changing them to suit their post-Renaissance world. The variations on the classical theme created by men such as Brunelleschi and Bernini, Mansart and Wren, were inspired by Rome; representing not a reproduction but an adaptation. The architects of the nineteenth-century western world also adapted the original source material to their own needs, which, with growing industrialization, urbanization and increasing population, created new challenges for them; their large-scale schemes were also not copies but, with the exception of a very few outstanding men, the innovatory genius of application was missing and the buildings, though many were of high quality, lacked the aesthetic vision of earlier work.

The reader beginning to study the architecture of the first 30 years of the nineteenth century is confronted by a number of descriptive terms of which the

ITALY AND ENGLAND

ENGLAND

meaning is not instantly clear; for example, Greek Revival, Neo-Classicism, Romantic Classicism, Gothic Revival. The first and last of these are straightforward but Romantic Classicism (a term coined in the twentieth century) appears to be a contradiction in itself. How does it differ from Neo-Classicism?

The great majority of buildings of the years 1800-1830 were constructed, as they had been for 200 years, in classical style. This form had long been based on the antique world of Rome. Since the mid eighteenth century, extensive archaeological studies in Greece and the Middle East had introduced the severer, plainer form of Greek classical architecture to western Europe and, in reaction to the extrovert and decorative boldness of baroque design, architects had veered toward a more restrained interpretation of both Greek and Roman sources: this severe and elegant style we refer to as Neo-Classical.

From the later 1790s this form was gradually succeeded by what is now called Romantic Classicism, and this interpretation differs according to the country concerned and the individual architectural designer. In general the work was more picturesque and dramatic than previously, and more elaborately decorated. After 1800 the model was frequently Greek classical architecture, creating bold, clear buildings utilizing the Greek Doric order, the column fluted and without base and – less often – the Greek Ionic order. Such buildings were to be seen all over western Europe. An early example was the Brandenburg Gate in Berlin (**870**), the first – and one of the finest – of such Doric ceremonial gateways, which became so characteristic of Romantic Classicism. Planned as the entrance to the city and the

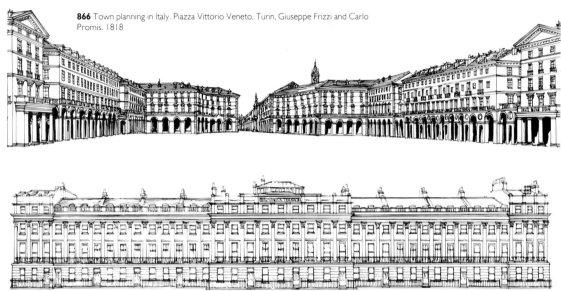

866 Town planning in Italy. Piazza Vittorio Veneto, Turin, Giuseppe Frizzi and Carlo Promis. 1818

867 Town planning in England. Brunswick Terrace, Hove. Sea front, Wilds and Busby. 1825

868 Interior of the Bank of England, London, Sir John Soane, c.1800

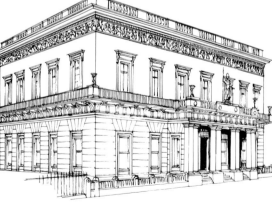

869 The Athenaeum Club house, London, Decimus Burton. (Later top story has been omitted) 1829-30

1801 First public demonstration of gas for lighting and heating took place in Paris at the Hôtel Seignelay. The gas was generated from a distillation of wood, a process developed by Phillipe Lebon, a French engineer who, three years later, was mugged and died in the Champs-Elysées

1801 John Dalton, English chemist, propounded his atomic theory in which he suggested that matter consists of tiny indivisible atoms, that in an element all atoms are identical, and that atoms from different elements have different weights

1801 Union of the Irish Parliament with that of Britain

1802 Richard Trevithick, English mining engineer, built a high pressure steam engine which developed a pressure 10 times that of the atmosphere

1804 William Blake, English poet and visionary, wrote *Jerusalem*

1804 Napoleon Bonaparte became Emperor of France

1805 Completion of the great Pont-Cysylltau aqueduct in the vale of Llangollen in North Wales, which carries the Shropshire Union Canal over the River Dee. This 1000ft long structure, with stone piers and iron superstructure, was designed by Thomas Telford

1805–27 Publication of the Waverley Novels by Sir Walter Scott, Scottish poet and novelist

1807 Part of Pall Mall in London illuminated by piped gas manufactured from coal

1790 – 1830

870 Brandenburg Gate, Berlin, K.G. Langhans. 1789-93

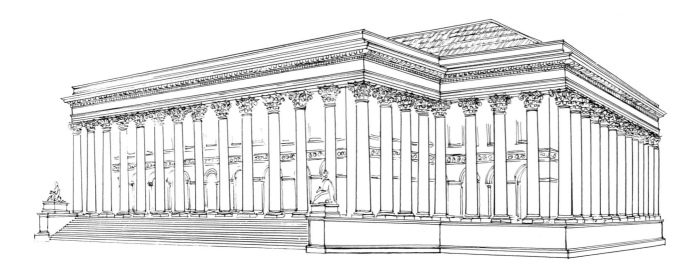

871 The Bourse, Paris, A.T. Brongniart. 1808-15, enlarged 1902-3

great boulevard Unter den Linden, this gateway, based on the Propylaea on the Acropolis of Athens (**35**), is sadly now the symbol of the dividing wall between East and West Berlin.

Among the many examples of this Greek form elsewhere are Schinkel's great achievements in Berlin, his Altes Museum (**872**), Neue Wache (**873**) and his Schauspielhaus (1819-21). Karl Friedrich von Schinkel (1781-1841) was Germany's finest architect in the first half of the century, a man of international stature, as was Soane in England. Also in Germany is von Klenze's Walhalla, an impressive hill temple design; in Denmark, Hansen's Copenhagen Cathedral (Vor Frue Kirk, **885**); in America, the Philadelphia bank (**888**) and in England, Inwood's St Pancras Church, Nash's Carlton House Terrace, Soane's Moggerhanger (**887**) and Wilkins's Downing College, Cambridge.

Romantic Classicism took several other forms. In Italy, naturally, the inspiration was Rome (**862, 863, 866**). In France, its birthplace, the simpler early forms changed under the aegis of Napoleon's First Empire towards a richer and monumental Roman Imperial style. Among the well known structures of this time in Paris are the Arc de Triomphe de L'Etoile (**874**), the Bourse (**871**) and the Madeleine (**875**).

In England there were several versions of this form. Sir John Soane (1753-1837) developed his highly individual architectural style which, stripped of all superfluous ornament, relied on pure lines and simple, fine proportions. His inspiration was multi-centred: classical, Byzantine, Oriental. In his interiors of the Bank of England, where he was architect from 1788-1833, his spatial handling, lighting and almost linear

1800 – 1830

treatment were superb (868). His churches and houses showed a similar originality of approach (880, 881, 887).

Also characteristic of England at this time were the essays into the Picturesque and the early development of the Gothic revival. John Nash (1752-1835) initiated several forms of Picturesque design, in his castellated mansions, rural cottages and, more flamboyantly for the Prince Regent, in his Indo-Chinese exotica at the Royal Pavilion in Brighton.

Other English architects were experimenting with a revival of the medieval genre, the asymmetrical and the Gothic. Whereas in Italy the classical form of architecture had never died out, with the result that Gothic design never really took hold; in England it was medievalism which survived – albeit as a submerged style – during the seventeenth and eighteenth centuries, while classicism held the field. During the eighteenth century a literary, picturesque form of Gothic appeared, spasmodically attempted by men of such different approach as Hawksmoor, Vanbrugh, Horace Walpole, Adam and Wyatt (p. 153, 161, 162) then, towards 1820, a more seriously archaeological attitude developed. Gothic designs were incorporated into university rebuilding and extensions: for example Wilkins at King's College and Corpus Christi, and Rickman and Hutchinson at St John's, all in Cambridge (878). In 1817 Thomas Rickman (1776-1841) published his description and nomenclature of the styles of English medieval architecture and, during the 1820s, Gothic was being utilized, tentatively at first, in a more correctly archaeological manner: St Luke's Church in Chelsea was a prototype, displaying greater understanding of medieval construction and handling (884).

872 Altes Museum, Berlin, Karl von Schinkel. 1824-8

873 Neue Wache, Berlin, Karl von Schinkel. 1816

874 Arc de Triomphe de L'Etoile, Paris, J.F.T. Chalgrin and others. 1806-37

875 The Madeleine Church, Paris, Pierre Vignon, 1806-12

1810 Peter Durand took out a patent for canning food in tin-plated iron cans packed with heat-sterilized food

1811 The Prince of Wales became Prince Regent

1812 Napoleon began his retreat from Moscow in October. Of a great army, a mere 30,000 survived to reach Germany

1812 Charter granted to the Gas, Light and Coke Company

1814 The steam-driven cylinder printing press, designed in 1811 by the German Friedrich König, first used to print the *Times* newspaper

1815 Defeat of Napoleon at Waterloo. Exile to S. Helena

1815–16 Sir Humphry Davy, English chemist, invented the miner's safety lamp, which was called after him

1815 John McAdam, Scottish engineer, became surveyor-general of the Bristol Road Trusts and began rebuilding 180 miles of road there on the basis of his own methods, which later gave his name to the macadam system of road surfacing

1816 The British government purchased the sculptures from the Acropolis of Athens (the Elgin Marbles) from Lord Elgin, who had earlier paid the Turkish government for them while he was British ambassador to Turkey

1818 Publication (posthumously) of *Persuasion*, Jane Austen's last complete novel

1818 Friedrich Krupp, German manufacturer, built an iron and steel plant at Essen – the foundation of the

1800 – 1830

AMERICA

ENGLAND

876 Catholic Cathedral, Baltimore, Benjamin Latrobe. 1805-18

877 Unitarian Church, Quincy, Massachusetts, Alexander Parris. 1828

878 Screen and gateway. King's College, Cambridge, William Wilkins. 1822-4

In Europe developing industrialization and technology brought increased wealth, an acceleration of urbanization and an increase in population. Schemes of urban renewal – especially in city centres – of domestic and civic building, became urgently necessary. This was, logically, more marked in the most advanced industrialized areas: in parts of Italy and Germany, in England and in France.

In Italy this was predominantly in the north, in Turin and Trieste (pp. 166-7). The seventeenth- and eighteenth-century tradition of urban planning by streets and squares in Turin (p.138, 151) continued, and the city centre expanded outwards. The House of Savoy had always lent a French flavour to Turin civic architecture, and the great squares and wide arcaded business and shopping streets laid out in the early nineteenth century were characteristic. Notable is the vast Piazza Vittoria Veneto (**866**), which debouches from the arcaded Via Po towards the river; the vista is terminated by the church of Gran Madre di Dio, built to commemorate the re-establishment of the Savoy monarchy after the end of the Napoleonic occupation (**863**). Also large-scale and most successful is the different church design of S. Francesco di Paolo in Naples (**862**), a highly eclectic composition, its centrepiece based on the Pantheon (**107**) and its colonnade on Bernini's St Peter's (**743**).

Between 1800 and 1860 the centres of several major cities in Germany were rebuilt and laid out in extensive schemes, notably Berlin, Munich and Karlsruhe. The work of Langhans and Schinkel in Berlin has already been referred to (pp. 168-9). In Munich three outstanding architects redesigned the city centre. Up to 1830 two of these, Karl von

Fischer (1782-1820) and Leo von Klenze (1784-1864), were working here. Fischer laid out the Karolinenplatz in 1808. Von Klenze's chief contribution at this time was in a pure, somewhat severe, scheme for the vast Königsplatz. He designed a sculpture gallery on the left to balance a picture gallery opposite, then completed the scheme, in 1846-63, with a central Propylaeon derived from that on the Athenian acropolis (35 and p. 11).

In France the Revolution brought architectural construction to a halt. In addition, areas of city centres as well as individual buildings were devastated. In Paris, from 1806, Napoleon managed to get a building programme started, though much of the work was not completed until after his death. This is in French Romantic Classical style. Notable schemes and buildings include the Rue de Rivoli (1802-35) by Percier and Fontaine, the extensions to the Louvre and the Arc du Carrousel (based on that of Septimius Severus in Rome), the Palais Bourbon (1807) by Poyet on the bank of the Seine (now the Chamber of Deputies) and the completion of Gabriel's Place de la Concorde scheme with the building of the church of the Madeleine, designed for Napoleon in 1808 by Pierre Vignon, originally as a temple of glory (875).

In England, separated geographically from the Continent and so involved to a much lesser extent in war and revolution, the enterprise in town planning was less in the field of city-centre reconstruction and more in domestic urban renewal and expansion. The movement had begun early in the 1740s in Bath, where John Wood and his son initiated the laying out of stone terrace architecture in Palladian style (p. 165 and 859). Many architects followed suit in Bath,

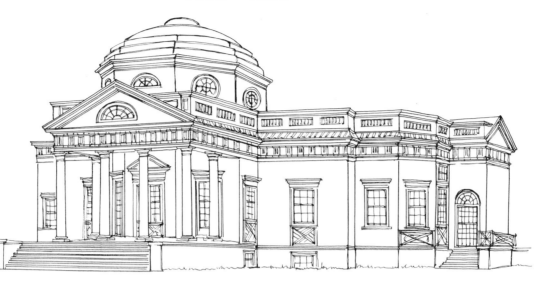

879 Monticello, Virginia, Thomas Jefferson. Remodelled and enlarged 1796-1809

880 St John's Church, Bethnal Green, London, Sir John Soane. 1826-8

881 St Mary's Church, Wyndham Place, London, Sir Robert Smirke. 1823-4

later internationally famous steel and armament works

1819 Peterloo massacre at Manchester

1819 Publication of the first two cantos of *Don Juan* by Lord Byron, English poet and satirist

1821 John Constable, English landscape painter, painted the *Hay Wain*

1822 Louis Daguerre, French co-inventor with Charles Bouton of the Diorama – a popular theatrical spectacle showing large views painted on a semi-transparent canvas, the realistic effects being produced by transmitted light

1822 Charles Babbage, English mathematician, made his first small calculating machine, which could rapidly and accurately perform mathematical calculations

1822 On the Island of Chios, during the Greek War of Independence, the Turks slaughtered in reprisal about 20,000 of the population of some 100,000, and sold nearly 50,000 into slavery. In 1824 the French painter Eugène Delacroix depicted the massacre

1823 Statement made by James Monroe, President of the United States, that the USA would regard any interference in the internal affairs of American States as an unfriendly act: a statement subsequently known as the Monroe Doctrine

1823 Ludwig van Beethoven, German composer, completed his ninth symphony, in which the last movement was a choral setting of Friedrich von Schiller's *Ode to Joy*

1800 – 1830

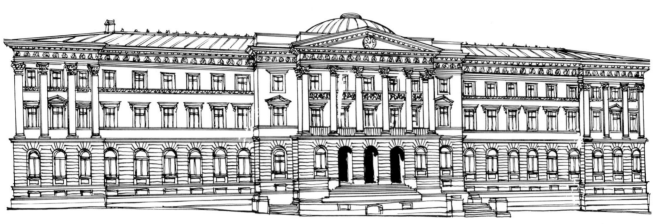

882 Senate House, Senate Square, Helsinki, Finland, Carl Ludwig Engel. 1818-22

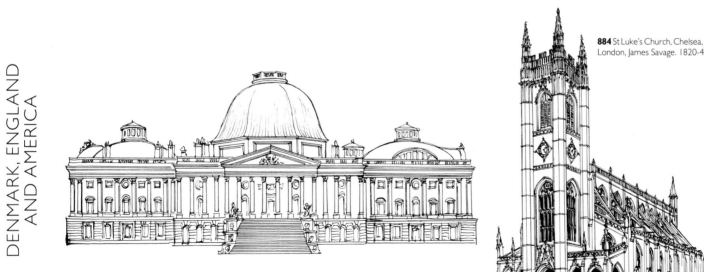

883 The United States Capitol, Washington D.C., as in 1830, Benjamin Latrobe and Charles Bulfinch. 1793-1830

884 St Luke's Church, Chelsea, London, James Savage. 1820-4

in London, in Edinburgh and, in the nine-teenth century, in the developing spa and seaside leisure resorts such as Cheltenham and Tunbridge Wells, Brighton and Hove (**860**). The style changed gradually from Palladian to Neo-Classical (**861**, **867**) to Romantic Classical and, in the 1840s, to Gothic (p. 169).

It was natural that England, the leading industrialized nation, should build more extensively in urban areas, particularly for the wealthier members of society. John Nash's famous Regent's Park and street scheme, begun in 1812, was the prime example of this. Work continued into the 1830s and other architects, such as Decimus Burton, were employed (**864**, **869**). It was also a natural corollary that the founder of the first modern-style building firm, Thomas Cubitt (1788-1855), should be an Englishman. In the 1820s Cubitt established a system of employing all craftsmen (architects too) needed for his extensive new building projects in London on a permanent wage basis, and providing continuous work for them on large-scale, high quality speculative building – a revolutionary idea at the time. Many examples of his work survive in the streets of St Pancras, Belgravia and elsewhere (**865**).

By the 1790s in America, after Independence, an architecture still influenced by Europe – but resulting more from architects studying antique classicism directly *in situ* – was slowly being established. Thomas Jefferson (1743-1826), although funda-mentally a Palladian, was influenced by French classicism from his four years in Europe. In 1785 he based his design for the Virginia State Capitol at Richmond on the Roman temple, the Maison Carrée in Nîmes (**112**). His remodelling of his own house of

Monticello of 1796 shows greater independence and sophistication (879). In his University of Virginia in 1817 he used the Pantheon in Rome as a model.

After 1800 several notable emigrés from Europe introduced a more professional standard of architecture and the current Romantic Classical style to America. Chief of these was the English-born Benjamin H. Latrobe (1764-1820), who had been a pupil of S.P. Cockerell and emigrated in 1796. His first important building, the Bank of Pennsylvania in Philadelphia, was Greek inspired, though its large central hall was covered by a saucer dome.

In his Baltimore Cathedral Latrobe displayed his affinity with the thoughts of Soane and Schinkel, evidenced (especially in the interior) in the extreme simplicity, fine proportions and restrained detail (876). By 1803 Latrobe had become architect to the building of the United States Capitol in Washington, working with Thornton – who had earlier won the competition to design the building. The interiors are largely Latrobe's. In 1817 he resigned and Charles Bulfinch (p. 164) took over and designed the dome. The present dome, a famous Washington landmark, was built in 1855 (p. 176). Two of Latrobe's pupils, Robert Mills and William Strickland, continued to build in Romantic Classical style (888).

886 Town hall, Hamina, Finland, Carl Blaesingh. 1798. Tower, Engel, 1840

885 Copenhagen Cathedral, Denmark, C.F. Hansen. 1810-29. Marble sculpture, Thorvaldsen

887 Moggerhanger House, England, Sir John Soane. 1806-11

888 Second Bank of the United States, Philadelphia, William Strickland. 1818-24

1823 The waterproof fabric called mackintosh patented. It was named after the inventor Charles Macintosh, Scottish chemist, who cemented two fabric thicknesses together with rubber dissolved in naphtha

1824 Joseph Aspdin, Yorkshire builder, took out a patent for a product which he called Portland Cement. He named it thus in the hope that the material would become accepted as a substitute for Portland stone

1824 The invention by Henry Berry of a safer, partly automatic, box for ignition. The instantaneous light box had become available earlier in the century. It contained the materials for ignition by means of the chlorate match. The box contents comprised the matches, tipped with a mixture of chlorate of potash, sugar and gum arabic, a small bottle of vitriol (sulphuric acid), candles and a holder. Utilizing such means of ignition in a bedroom on a dark morning was a dangerous proceeding. In Henry Berry's box the stopper on the bottle remained in place as long as the lid was closed. When it was opened, a string on a pulley lifted the stopper and supplied one drop of vitriol only to one match head

1827 Publication by Georg Simon Ohm, German scientist, of his famous Law, which established the relationship between voltage and current strength, and led to the concept of electrical resistance

FERROVITREOUS CONSTRUCTION 1830 – 1870

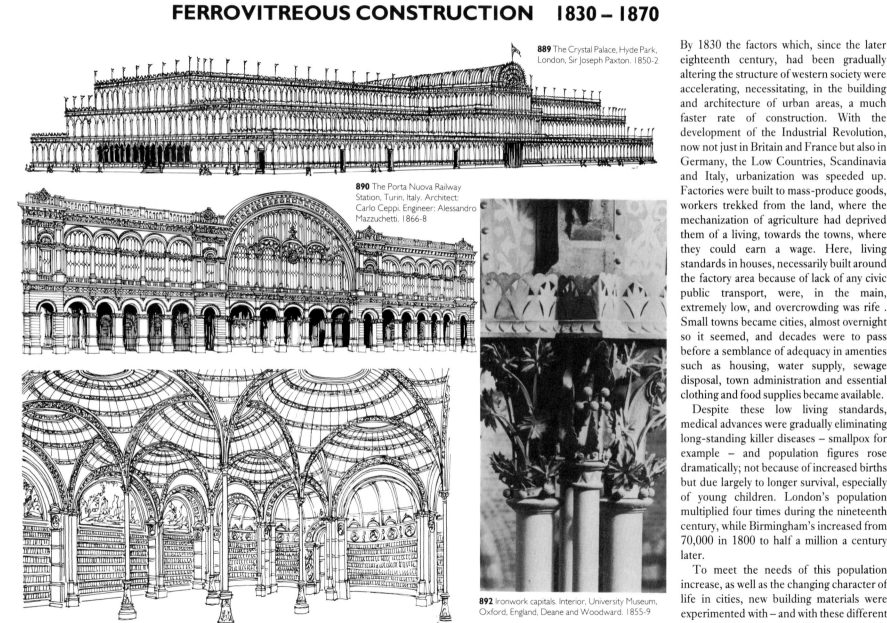

889 The Crystal Palace, Hyde Park, London, Sir Joseph Paxton. 1850-2

890 The Porta Nuova Railway Station, Turin, Italy. Architect: Carlo Ceppi. Engineer: Alessandro Mazzuchetti. 1866-8

892 Ironwork capitals. Interior, University Museum, Oxford, England, Deane and Woodward. 1855-9

891 Reading room. Bibliothèque Nationale, Paris, H.P.F. Labrouste. 1862-8

By 1830 the factors which, since the later eighteenth century, had been gradually altering the structure of western society were accelerating, necessitating, in the building and architecture of urban areas, a much faster rate of construction. With the development of the Industrial Revolution, now not just in Britain and France but also in Germany, the Low Countries, Scandinavia and Italy, urbanization was speeded up. Factories were built to mass-produce goods, workers trekked from the land, where the mechanization of agriculture had deprived them of a living, towards the towns, where they could earn a wage. Here, living standards in houses, necessarily built around the factory area because of lack of any civic public transport, were, in the main, extremely low, and overcrowding was rife. Small towns became cities, almost overnight so it seemed, and decades were to pass before a semblance of adequacy in amenties such as housing, water supply, sewage disposal, town administration and essential clothing and food supplies became available.

Despite these low living standards, medical advances were gradually eliminating long-standing killer diseases – smallpox for example – and population figures rose dramatically; not because of increased births but due largely to longer survival, especially of young children. London's population multiplied four times during the nineteenth century, while Birmingham's increased from 70,000 in 1800 to half a million a century later.

To meet the needs of this population increase, as well as the changing character of life in cities, new building materials were experimented with – and with these different methods of construction. The most notable advance in both of these fields was the

FERROVITREOUS CONSTRUCTION   1830 – 1870

adoption of iron and glass, used separately at first but, increasingly as time passed, together. This ferro-vitreous type of construction, as it is called, had been made possible by technical advances in both materials which had been taking place since the later eighteenth century, but which accelerated in the mid nineteenth.

Iron had been regarded as a durable, utilitarian material since the Middle Ages, first hammered into wrought iron and later, with the development of improved blast furnace design and consequent higher temperatures, poured molten into moulds to give cast iron. The switchover to coal as a smelting fuel in the early seventeenth century because of diminishing timber supplies caused technical problems, but after Abraham Darby's experiments in England from 1709, which showed that the coal must first be coked to give satisfactory results, iron was increasingly used for the construction of bridges and factories to house heavy machinery. Two vital further advances were due to John Wilkinson, the great ironmaster, who, in 1776, installed a Boulton and Watt steam engine in his Shropshire works, so improving the power potential, and also Henry Cort who, in 1784, introduced the action of puddling; this was a process of stirring the molten iron which freed it from impurities, so rendering it less brittle.

The way was then clear for an extensive use of iron in building for railings, balconies, staircase balustrades then, later, structurally, for supporting columns, whole staircases, galleries and roofing. England was the leader in this development, and famous achievements include the Iron Bridge at Coalbrookdale over the Severn (1779), Nash's 'Chinese-style' staircase in the Royal Pavilion at Brighton (1818), Hopper's fan-

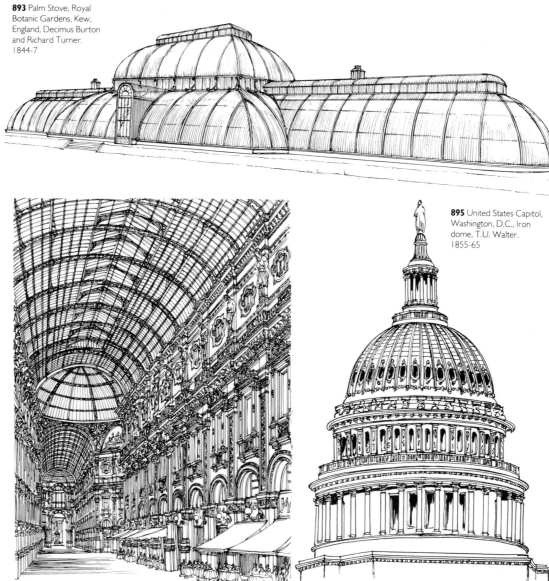

893 Palm Stove, Royal Botanic Gardens, Kew, England, Decimus Burton and Richard Turner. 1844-7

895 United States Capitol, Washington, D.C., Iron dome, T.U. Walter. 1855-65

894 Galleria Vittorio Emmanuele II, Milan, Italy. Architect: Giuseppe Mengoni. 1865-77

1830   The opening of the Liverpool and Manchester Railway, begun earlier by George Stephenson

1830   The first satisfactorily functioning single thread chain stitch sewing machine invented by Barthélemy Thimmonier, a French tailor, to sew army uniforms

1831   Michael Faraday, English physicist, achieved the first successful magnetic induction of electric current, an experiment which he described to the Royal Society in London on 24 November

1831   The construction of London Bridge completed by John Rennie to his father's design

1832   Early trial in England by Sir Marc Brunel of reinforced concrete. In building his Thames Tunnel, Brunel used hoop iron to reinforce brick and cement arches

1832   Chance Bros of Birmingham began to manufacture sheet glass. In 1851 the firm supplied the 900,000 sq.ft of this glass for the construction of the Crystal Palace

1833   Joseph Aloysius Hansom, designer of Birmingham town hall (1830), became known for his invention of the 'Patent Safety Cab', later to become the hansom cab

1833   Abolition of legal slavery by the British. William Wilberforce, philanthropist and abolitionist, who had fought so hard to outlaw slavery, died just a month before the Act was passed through Parliament

1837   Accession of Queen Victoria

1838   Joseph Mallord William Turner, English landscape and seascape artist, painted his *The Fighting Téméraire* and, in 1844, *Rain, Steam and Speed*. Both paintings illustrate his great interest at the time in the changes being brought about by the Industrial Revolution

ENGLAND, GERMANY, ITALY

FRANCE, ENGLAND

896 Canale Grande layout, with Church of Antonio di Padova at end of vista, Trieste, Italy, Peter von Nobile. 1826-49

897 Milner Square, Islington, London, Gough and Roumieu. 1841-3

898 Lonsdale Square, Islington, London, R.C. Carpenter. 1838-42

899 Place de l'Opera, Paris, de Fleury and Blondel, 1858-64. The Opera House (Académie Nationale de Musique), J.L.C. Garnier. 1861-74

vaulted conservatory in Carlton House in London (1811-12), and the work of the great engineers of the day – such as Telford's suspension Menai Bridge in Wales (1819-24).

The second half of the nineteenth century saw the increasing use of iron for heavy structural work. Beams for floors and roof trusses were manufactured which would withstand considerable loads in railway stations, civic and industrial buildings. In 1848 James Bogardus (1800-74) in New York created his first four-storyed factory structure of iron piers and lintels. He went on to undertake more ambitious urban buildings using iron, and others followed his example for factories, department stores and apartment blocks. In Britain in 1851, at Balmoral Castle, the Prince Consort ordered a pre-fabricated iron ballroom. At Saltaire, much of the new textile mill was constructed of iron (p. 193 and **901**). Iron was used more and more extensively for roofing, as it was deemed to be more fireproof than the earlier wood and stone or brick structures. Thus Barry, when building the new Palace of Westminster in London to replace the original one destroyed by fire in 1834, used iron joists and roofing plates (**902**). Similarly, in the USA, Walter used iron to build the new dome for the United States State Capitol in Washington in 1855 (**895**).

Advances in technique and practice were simultaneously making the production of suitable, larger panes of glass available at a lower price than previously. During the nineteenth century a number of factories were established to manufacture cast plate glass, a process earlier developed by the French, in which molten glass was run directly on to a table where it was rolled out. This was a faster process, and produced

URBAN DEVELOPMENT AND DESIGN   1830 – 1870

lustrous glass, but, due to its contact with the table, it was costly – as it still had to be ground and polished. A cheaper, thinner glass process was developed on the Continent from the old cylinder method. Called sheet glass, this was ideal for glazing, and much larger panes could be produced than formerly.

The employment of glass and iron together was widely developed during the nineteenth century. At first the chief use was for conservatories and glasshouses. Notable in England were Paxton's Great Conservatory at Chatsworth (1836, now demolished) and, still surviving, the Palm Stove at Kew (**893**). This remarkable structure is 362ft long and comprises 45,000 sq.ft of greenish glass. Inside, a decorative iron spiral staircase gives access to an upper gallery from where tall plants may be closely viewed.

It was soon realized that iron and glass together were ideal for use in structures such as railway stations (**890**), for example, Cubitt's Kings Cross in London (1851-2) and Duquesney's Gare de L'Est in Paris (1847-52). Also great ferro-vitreous coverings were erected over important public buildings: London's Coal Exchange by Bunning (1846-9, now demolished), Sydney Smirke's reading room at the British Museum (1854-5) and, more famous, the one by Labrouste at the Bibliothèque Nationale in Paris (**891**).

Iron and glass continued to complement each other as the century advanced. As both quality and quantity of steel production dramatically improved, steel more frequently replaced iron for structural purposes. In many European cities great undercover shopping arcades and galleries were built where people could stroll, chat at café tables,

900 Königsbau, Max Josefsplatz, Munich, Germany, Leo von Klenze. 1826-33

901 Salt's textile mill, Saltaire, England, Lockwood and Mawson. 1851-3

902, 903 The Palace of Westminster, London (**902**) as seen from the river Thames and (**903**), the Clock Tower, Sir Charles Barry and A.W.N. Pugin. 1836-65

1838   Publication of *The People's Charter*, the basis of Chartism. The charter demanded six particular reforms which included universal male suffrage and the secret ballot

1839   The French government purchased the daguerrotype process from the inventors, Louis Jacques Mandé Daguerre and his late partner Nicéphore Niépce

1840   Samuel F.B. Morse, American inventor, devised the code for sending and receiving messages which bears his name

1840   Professor Justus von Liebig, German organic chemist, inaugurated the modern approach to plant nutrition and later turned his attention to animal nutrition, analysing the chemical composition of food required for healthy growth

1841   Thomas Cook, English travel agent, arranged his first excursion by the new railways – from Loughborough to Leicester – for a temperance group

1841   William Henry Fox Talbot refined his calotype process. Unlike Daguerre's photographic process, in which there was no negative, Fox Talbot's calotype method produced a negative from which prints could be mass-produced

1842   Sir John Bennet Lawes, English agricultural chemist, founded the world's first chemical fertilizer factory, which manufactured his superphosphate fertilizer

1843–4   Alexandre Dumas wrote his novel *The Three Musketeers*

1844   Charles Goodyear in America patented his process of vulcanization of rubber, which increased its elasticity and strength

CLASSICAL DESIGN 1830 – 1870

ENGLAND, FRANCE AMERICA

ENGLAND, GERMANY FINLAND

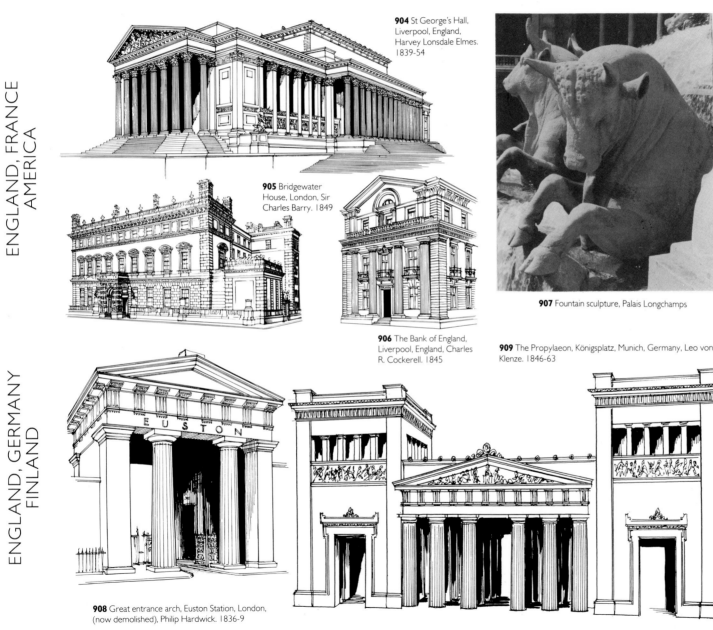

904 St George's Hall, Liverpool, England, Harvey Lonsdale Elmes. 1839-54

905 Bridgewater House, London, Sir Charles Barry. 1849

906 The Bank of England, Liverpool, England, Charles R. Cockerell. 1845

907 Fountain sculpture, Palais Longchamps

908 Great entrance arch, Euston Station, London, (now demolished), Philip Hardwick. 1836-9

909 The Propylaeon, Königsplatz, Munich, Germany, Leo von Klenze. 1846-63

or window-gaze. The Galleria Vittorio Emmanuele II in Milan is a superb surviving example (**894**).

By the 1840s, in order to supply the extensive building needs, methods of mass-production of parts and pre-fabrication were being experimented with. The most famous early example of a completely pre-fabricated building was the Crystal Palace, a ferro-vitreous structure erected in Hyde Park in London for the Great Exhibition of 1851. Designed by Sir Joseph Paxton (**889**), such an immense structure – 1848ft long, 408ft wide and over 100ft high – could not possibly have been erected in the short time available by traditional means. The Crystal Palace, so dubbed by Punch, was a landmark in construction in its day for its size and speed of construction. Parts were standardized, made in quantity and assembled on site.

The work of city-centre re-planning, with open spaces lined with imposing buildings and connected by wide thoroughfares, continued in this period, the style varying according to country and date. In Italy the classical form persisted, characterized by the waterfront area development of the Canale Grande in Trieste. Palace façades line the water's edge, while at the head is another Pantheon (**896**). In Munich von Klenze completed his Grecian layout in the Königsplatz (**909**) and, in the 1830s, von Gärtner laid out the long boulevard Ludwigstrasse in the severe, round-arched manner of local Romantic Classicism (*Rundbogenstil*), typified by his university elevations and twin-towered Ludwigskirche (**914**). In England terraced squares of town housing continued to be built, especially in London; the style merging from classical into Gothic (**897, 898**).

CLASSICAL DESIGN 1830 – 1870

The finest urban schemes of the third quarter of the nineteenth century were in Paris and Helsinki. The main layout of the centre of nineteenth-century Paris is the product of the Second Empire. Napoleon I had little time to establish his ideas for urban renewal here, and it fell to his nephew Napoleon III to expand his projects. Under von Haussmann and his colleagues the Grandes Boulevards of Paris were laid out with their *rond-points* and flamboyant buildings set at significant places. The schemes were extensive, the quality of work high, the façades along the boulevards homogeneous and imposing. An urban masterpiece was created. In general, the individual buildings are not outstanding; it is the whole which is impressive. The structures are of stone or stucco-faced, with shops at ground level, flats above, covered by mansard roofs. The roofline is even, the fenestration uniform. The whole is classical, often neo-baroque. Of especial note is the *rond-point* of the Etoile, laid out by Haussmann, its buildings by Hittorff; here 12 roads radiate from the earlier, centrally placed arch (874). Particularly flamboyant and successful is the Avenue and Place de l'Opéra, with its famous opera house setting a pattern for capital cities all over Europe (899).

Outside Paris, a neo-baroque layout of great magnificence is the Palais Longchamps at Marseilles (910). The monument constitutes an imposing entrance to the park, set into the hillside, with a central sculptured cascade (907) flanked by sweeping staircases and curving colonnades which terminate at each side in classical blocks.

In 1812 the Russian Tsar Alexander I decided to set up a new Finnish capital at Helsinki: a site nearer to Russia (the old

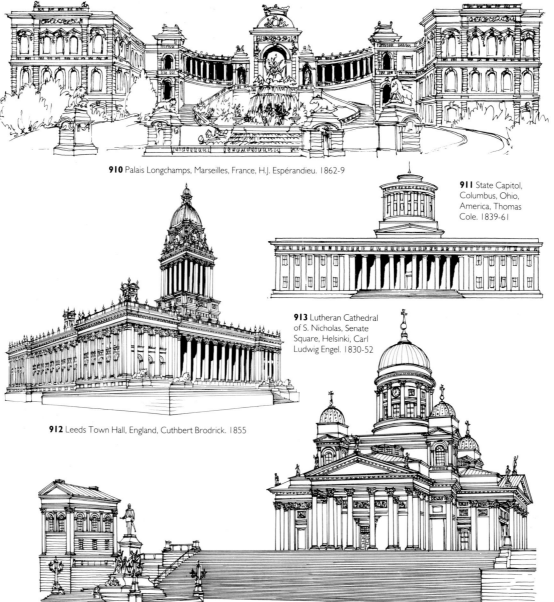

910 Palais Longchamps, Marseilles, France, H.J. Espérandieu. 1862-9

911 State Capitol, Columbus, Ohio, America, Thomas Cole. 1839-61

913 Lutheran Cathedral of S. Nicholas, Senate Square, Helsinki, Carl Ludwig Engel. 1830-52

912 Leeds Town Hall, England, Cuthbert Brodrick. 1855

1845 Victor Marie Hugo, French poet, novelist and playwright, began his fictional social study *Les Misères*, later known as *Les Misérables*

1845 *Tannhäuser*, the opera by the German composer Richard Wagner, performed in Dresden

1846 Marriage of Elizabeth Barrett to Robert Browning

1847 Publication of *Wuthering Heights* by Emily Brontë

1848 First discovery of gold in California

1848 Brigham Young led the first company of Mormon pioneers 1100 miles from Illinois to settle in Salt Lake Valley in Utah

1848 Publication of the *Communist Manifesto* by Friedrich Engels and Karl Marx

1851 The Opera *Rigoletto* by Giuseppe Verdi, based upon Victor Hugo's *Le roi s'amuse*

1854 Invention of the kerosene lamp in America

1854 Boers founded the Republic of the Orange Free State in South Africa

1855 After the cholera epidemics of 1849 and 1853, Sir Joseph Bazalgette appointed engineer to the new Metropolitan Board of Works, to rebuild London's sewage system

1855 Invention of the bunsen burner, named after the German chemist Robert Wilhelm von Bunsen. In this burner air was mixed with the gas before ignition, so giving a hotter, and therefore brighter, flame

1855 Development of the safety match by Johan Lundstrom of Sweden. In this he divided the chemical constituents between the

914 Ludwigskirche, Munich, Germany, Friedrich von Gärtner. 1829-40

915 Exeter College Chapel, Oxford, England, Sir George Gilbert Scott. 1864

916 Petrikirche, Hamburg, Germany, de Chateauneuf and Fersenfeld, 1843-9

917 Smithsonian Institution, Washington D.C., James Renwick Jnr. 1848-9

918 Detail ornament, Palace of Westminster

capital was at Turku) and further from Swedish influence. At that time Helsinki was only a small fishing town of some 4000 inhabitants. Alexander decided on an imposing, classical city, the civic centre to be one homogeneous layout. The architect was the German Carl Ludwig Engel (1778-1840), a colleague of Schinkel. He came to Finalnd and stayed for the rest of his life, some 25 years.

According to the Tsar's wishes, Engel made Helsinki into a fine capital city, magnificently laid out on monumental lines, homogeneous but also varied. The city has been added to over the years, but the original layouts are unaltered and well cared for: they are unforgettably impressive. The chief of these is the great Senate Square, measuring 560ft by 330ft, dominated by the vast Lutheran Cathedral (**913**), built on a great podium and approached via an impressive flight of steps. Other buildings round the square include the Senate House, the University and its library.

The style of architecture during these 40 years was extremely varied but entirely derivative, ranging from Italian Renaissance and baroque to Byzantine, Romanesque and Gothic. Areas where the classical tradition was strongest – Italy and much of France for example – built little in Gothic. Northern Europe and America used all styles, in general reserving monumental classicism for civic and palatial work (**895, 904-6, 908, 911, 912**) and medieval styles for ecclesiastical and university building.

Romantic Classicism lasted a long time in Germany. The Grecian form was most generally adopted in the 1830s, as in von Klenze's Propylaeon in Munich (**909**). He also experimented with the Renaissance Florentine palace style, with severe

ROMANESQUE AND GOTHIC DESIGN   1830 – 1870

rusticated façades and stress upon the horizontal line; a form inspired by the Pitti Palace (p. 107 and **900**). From the late 1830s a round-arched style was widely adopted. Called in Germany the *Rundbogenstil*, this was a form of Romantic Classicism, owing much to both the classical and Romanesque arch. It was particularly to be seen in the 1830s(**914**). While *Rundbogenstil* was a particularly German approach, Romanesque architecture provided inspiration elsewhere on the Continent, and in England, America and Norway, where Oslo (then called Christiana) was being developed as a capital city; the Parliament building (1866) is typical.

The revival of Gothic design was most marked in England, though it was gradually taken up also in northern Europe and America. First initiated as a literary, then theological movement, by the 1840s it had also become more archaeological. The most outstanding building of the first half of the century is the Palace of Westminster, rebuilt in Perpendicular Gothic style after the fire of 1834 (**902**, **903**). The Gothic Revival in Britain was at its height between 1855 and 1885, when the style (mainly of thirteenth- and fourteenth-century inspiration) was used to design railway stations, hotels, buildings for education, country houses and churches (**915-23**).

919 Trinity Church, New York City, Richard Upjohn. 1839-46

920 Manchester Town Hall, England, Alfred Waterhouse. 1869-77

921 St Marie's Church, Derby, England, A.W.N. Pugin. 1838-9

922 Window, Scarisbrick Hall, England, designed Pugin. From 1837

923 Church of S.S. Mary and Nicholas, Wilton, England, Wyatt and Brandon. 1840-6

match head and the striking surface on the match box, so markedly reducing the chances of spontaneous combustion

1856 In England William Henry Perkin made the first aniline dye, which he called mauveine

1856 Henry Bessemer in England designed his converter, which helped to revolutionize steel-making

1858 The Englishman Charles Frederick Worth set up his own fashion house in the Rue de la Paix in Paris. The House of Worth was the first couture salon to use live mannequins to display its creations and, with his flair for elegance and originality of design, Worth acquired a monopoly of dressing the wealthy aristocrats of Europe

1859 Publication of *On the Origin of Species* by Charles Darwin

1859 Successful drilling for oil in Pennsylvania marked the beginning of the modern petroleum industry

1860 Giuseppe Garibaldi and his 'Thousand' captured Sicily and Naples in the struggle for the unification of Italy

1861–5 The American Civil War and the abolition of slavery

1865–9 Count Leo Tolstoy, Russian novelist and philosopher, wrote *War and Peace*

1867 Publication of *Das Kapital* by Karl Marx

1867 Joseph Monier in France patented a method of reinforcing concrete with wire mesh

ROMANESQUE AND GOTHIC STYLE   1870 – 1900

924 Vondelkerk, Amsterdam, Holland, P.J. Cuijpers. 1870

925 Terracotta capitals of main doorway, Natural History Museum, London

926, 927 St Augustine's Church, Kilburn, London, J.L. Pearson. 1870-80

928 The Natural History Museum, London, Alfred Waterhouse. 1873-9

ENGLAND, GERMANY, AMERICA

ENGLAND AND GERMANY

The revival of all forms of medieval and classical architecture continued everywhere until after 1900. Gothic design was rare in Italy and, in France, Spain and Portugal, reserved primarily for church building. Elsewhere the Gothic Revival proceeded apace; the style was used in most forms of architecture, regardless of purpose. The English form of High Victorian Gothic, evidenced in the work of men such as Scott, Street, Waterhouse, Pearson and Butterfield, was adopted widely in North America, Germany, the Low Countries and Scandinavia.

This movement, stemming from its literary eighteenth-century beginnings, was firmly established in England by the 1840s, then, widely publicized by the writings of Pugin and Ruskin, and supported strongly by Ecclesiologists who favoured the Middle-Pointed or fourteenth-century form of Gothic design, it became internationally influential. During the 1870s a tremendous quantity of tall, elaborate Gothic structures were erected: railway stations, hotels, universities, churches and town halls. Typical English examples include Scott's St. Pancras Hotel (1865-75) and Street's Law Courts, both in London (**929**), Pearson's Truro Cathedral (1879-1910) and many churches (**926, 927**), and Butterfield's Keble College, Oxford (1868-82). Polychrome brickwork, further enriched with terracotta relief ornamentation, was widely adopted.

In the New World such colourful decoration could be seen, for instance, in the Museum of Fine Arts in Boston (1870-6), Holy Trinity Church in New York City (1873) and in the Memorial Hall at Harvard University (1870-8). Characteristically Gothic, soaring, crocketed spires, rich carving and coloured window glass appeared in many countries. In New York City James Renwick had begun St Patrick's Roman Catholic Cathedral in 1859. In Canada the Parliament House in Ottawa was erected by 1867. In Germany, Munich boasts an elaborate and lofty town hall (**930**). On Vienna's Ringstrasse, von Schmidt built the city's new town hall (1872-83) and, nearby, in 1856-79 rose Ferstel's twin-towered Votivkirche – a smaller, slenderer Cologne Cathedral (**464**). In Amsterdam the Dutch architect P.J. Cuijpers built a number of churches (**924**) and was responsible for two vast Gothic structures, the Central Station (1881-9) and the Rijksmuseum (1877-85). From the exterior the buildings are so similar that it is not easy to know which was intended to house trains and which paintings. On closer inspection, however, the museum is appropriately ornamented with panels of sculpture and ceramic decoration. Sweden's chief re-creator of the medieval heritage was Helgo Zettervall, as energetic a medieval cathedral restorer as Scott in England and Viollet-le-Duc in France. His Church of Oskar Frederik in Gothenburg is a characteristically polychrome example of the 1870s.

From the 1870s other periods of medieval architecture were also being revived. Several architects in different countries were using the round-arched Romanesque form as a model, but creating widely differing inter-pretations. Alfred Waterhouse's Natural History Museum is a richly ornamented English example (**925**, **928**). In Boston Henry Hobson Richardson was establishing his reputation for bold structural use of this style in his Trinity Church (**931**), its west portico based upon that of S. Gilles du Gard (**350**). In Berlin the church built at the head

929 The Law Courts, London, G.E. Street. 1868-80

931 Trinity Church, Boston, USA, H.H. Richardson. 1873-7

930 Neues Rathaus, Munich, Germany, G.J. von Hauberrisser. 1867-74

932 Kaiser-Wilhelm Gedächtniskirche, Berlin, Franz Schwechten. 1891-5

1869–70 *Twenty Thousand Leagues under the Sea* written by the French novelist Jules Verne

1870 Growth of the open-hearth method of steel-making: by 1900 it had become the predominant process

1870 Introduction of celluloid, an early plastic, then used chiefly for billiard balls and collars

1871 Performance of *Aida* in Cairo, opera written by Giuseppe Verdi in belated celebration of the opening of the Suez Canal

1871 The unification of Germany. At Versailles the Deutsches Reich declared: Wilhelm of Prussia became First Emperor, and Bismarck Imperial German Chancellor

1870-90 Edgar Degas, French painter, developed his mature style and became known for his studies of women, particularly dancers

1871 The Great Fire of Chicago, which destroyed a large proportion of the city buildings

1875 William Gilbert and Arthur Sullivan brought together by Richard D'Oyly Carte, manager of the Royalty Theatre, to write and compose the first of their comic operas – *Trial by Jury* – for which they became famous

c.**1875** The combine, a machine combining the actions of harvesting and threshing, used on farms in California; it was drawn by a team of horses

1875 Georges Bizet composed *Carmen*, his most famous opera

1875–7 Count Leo Tolstoy wrote *Anna Karenina*

1876 Melville R. Bissell of Grand Rapids, Michigan, was granted a patent for his carpet sweeper

1876 The 'Last Stand' of George

CLASSICAL DESIGN 1870 – 1900

AUSTRIA, FRANCE, ITALY, ENGLAND

BELGIUM, FRANCE, ITALY

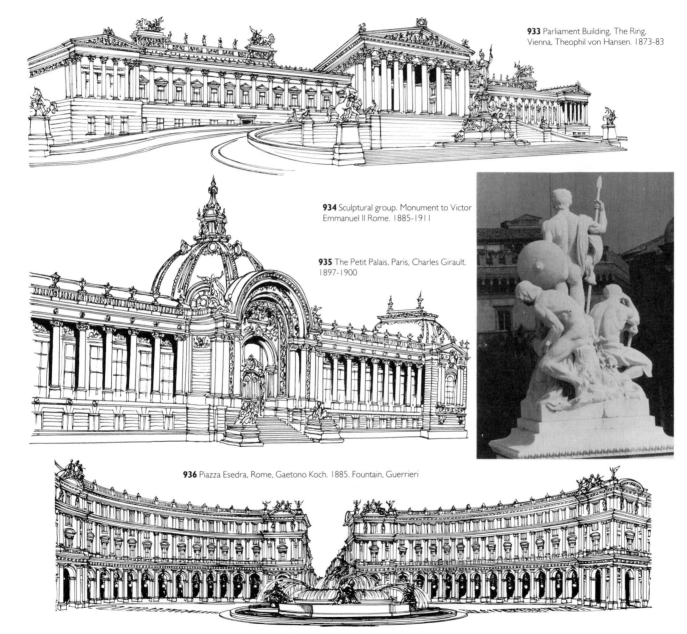

933 Parliament Building, The Ring, Vienna, Theophil von Hansen. 1873-83

934 Sculptural group. Monument to Victor Emmanuel II Rome. 1885-1911

935 The Petit Palais, Paris, Charles Girault. 1897-1900

936 Piazza Esedra, Rome, Gaetono Koch. 1885. Fountain, Guerrieri

of the Kürfürstendamm, in honour of Kaiser Wilhelm I and the unification of Germany (**932**), was a revival of German Rhineland Romanesque design, as typified by Worms and Mainz Cathedrals (**370, 371**). In Paris, in contrast, the great Church of Sacré Coeur began in 1874 to rise on the hill of Montmartre, a controversial and arresting building inspired by the Church of S. Front in Périgueux.

Classical design was primarily reserved for civic planning and important urban structures. This was particularly so in the building up and extension of three capital cities: Rome, Berlin, Vienna. Especially in the first two of these, much of this work was in a monumental baroque style; large-scale and weighty.

After the unification of Italy, Rome became the new capital and King Victor Emmanuel commissioned some suitable imposing schemes. The Piazza Esedra is the most successful (**936**), its façades sweeping round in quarters of a circle at the head of a new boulevard, the Via Nazionale, which itself contains some impressive classical buildings: for example, Piacenti's Palazzo delle Belle Arti (1878-82) and Koch's Banca d'Italia (1889-92). Most overpowering of all, dominating the Piazza Venezia, indeed the whole city, is the great marble monument to Victor Emmanuel. Dubbed *La Torta Nuziale* (wedding cake) by the Romans, this gleaming structure represents the essence of this period in all European nations; it is imperial, dramatic, richly sculptured. Dedicated to King and Country, it stands for sentiment and sacrifice, a true monument of its age (**934**).

At the same time, Kaiser Wilhelm I was laying out his new capital of a unified Germany in Berlin. Typical is Wallot's neo-baroque Reichstag (1884-94), now restored from the fire of 1933 and World War II damage. At the other end of the Unter den Linden is the also restored, similarly styled Cathedral, by Raschdorf, with its imposing façades and great central dome (1894-1905). Even more monumentally weighty is the Palace of Justice in Brussels (**939**). In contrast, *fin de siècle* baroque building in Paris was lighter and more elegant: for example, the Grand and Petit Palais structures (**935**).

After Napoleon III's Paris (p. 179), the most extensive and impressive nineteenth-century development of a capital city took place in Vienna. On Franz Josef's accession in 1848 this was still small and medieval. Its fortifications were destroyed and the Emperor created the famous Ringstrasse which, with the Danube Canal, completely encircles the medieval city. The 'Ring' took 30 years to build, from 1858-88. In scale the structures are homogeneous. In style they vary, according to date, from Hansen's Grecian Parliament Building (**933**) to von Hasenauer's Hofburg (**938**), the Opera House and Burgtheater, and the large but more pedestrian museums in the Maria Theresienplatz (1872-81). Several of the larger structures are in Gothic style (p. 183).

Contemporaneously with the medieval and classical eclecticism just described evolved a splintered minority movement, contributed to by architects all over the western world, who were endeavouring to design in a new way; one less derivative and shackled to the past. With the development of the use of new materials, notably iron, glass and concrete, such a movement might have been expected to arise earlier but, despite a multiplicity of ideas and experiments, these nineteenth-century

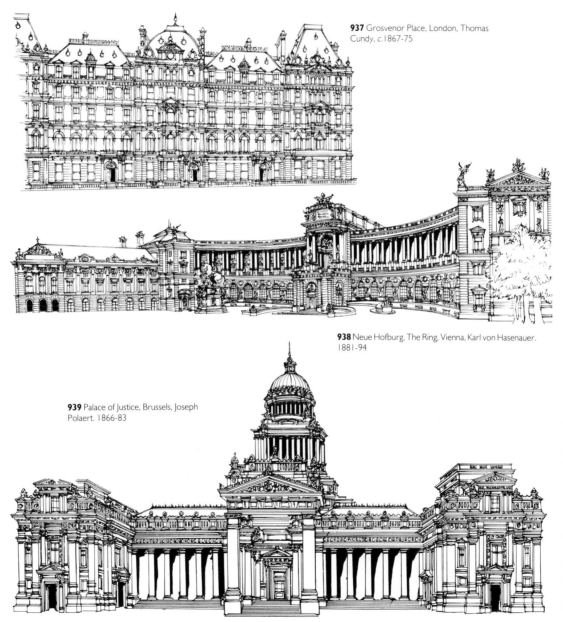

937 Grosvenor Place, London, Thomas Cundy, c.1867-75

938 Neue Hofburg, The Ring, Vienna, Karl von Hasenauer. 1881-94

939 Palace of Justice, Brussels, Joseph Polaert. 1866-83

A. Custer, American Army officer, against the Sioux at Little Bighorn

1876   Karl von Linde, German professor of thermodynamics, introduced an ammonia compression system of refrigeration

1876–8   Excavation by Heinrich Schliemann of Mycenae and, later, Tyrins (p. 7)

1877   Thomas Alva Edison produced his talking machine which he called a phonograph, on which he recorded his recitation of *Mary had a little lamb*. The machine had a tin-foil covered brass drum on one side, to which was fitted a recorder with mouthpiece, diaphragm and stylus. On the other was a similarly designed reproducer

1877–85   Louis Pasteur, French scientist, in his studies of diseases, notably anthrax and rabies, established the germ theory of disease and laid the foundations of the science of immunity by injection and vaccination

1878–9   Manufacture of the first incandescent carbon filament electric lamps by Joseph Swan and Thomas Alva Edison, working independently in England and America

1879   The first shipment of refrigerated meat arrived in England from America in satisfactory condition

1879   *A Doll's House* written by Henrik Ibsen, Norwegian playwright

1879   Sir William Crookes devised an early glass cathode ray tube

1879–80   Fyodor Dostoyevsky wrote his last novel, *The Brothers Karamazov*

1880   Heinz introduced canned baked beans in the USA

940 Tassel House, Brussels, Baron Victor Horta. 1892-3

943 Glasgow School of Art, Scotland, Charles Rennie Mackintosh. 1897

941 14-16 Hans Road, London, C.F.A. Voysey. 1891

942 First Alliance Assurance Building, London, Norman Shaw. 1882

944 Whitechapel Art Gallery, London, C. Harrison Townsend. 1900

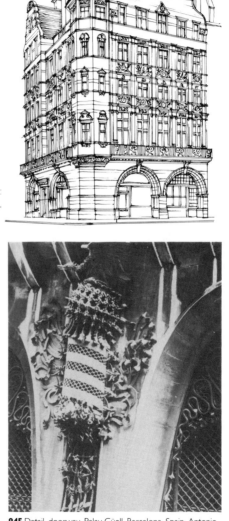

945 Detail, doorway. Palau Güell, Barcelona, Spain, Antonio Gaudí. 1885-9

attempts to design differently were hesitant and unsure. Outside the USA there was little evidence of understanding of the structural possibilities endemic in such new materials. Certainly the buildings erected in this way provided a basis or jumping-off ground for twentieth-century work, but at the time many of them appeared to be blind alleys.

The earliest group of designers searching for a new architectural form tended to look backwards rather than forwards. They were reacting from over-decoration, monumentality and polychromy, returning to the simpler vernacular forms of architecture which had been prevalent in their own countries in an earlier age. The back-to-craftmanship approach inspired by an abhorrence of urbanization and the machine age, initiated by William Morris in England and taken up later in the Arts and Crafts Movement, strongly influenced English architects such as Norman Shaw and Philip Webb. Shaw, in particular, successfully designed in a wide variety of past styles, using traditional materials and techniques (**942**).

In other lands architects were similarly experimenting with the plainer, traditional past. I.K. Clason in Sweden, for instance, in his Nordiska Museet in Stockholm (1890-1904), in which he revived the seventeenth-century Danish palace design. In the USA H.H. Richardson was building his bold, plainly decorated masonry libraries (in Quincy 1880-3) and at Harvard (1878-80) using Georgian brickwork. In the 1880s he developed a masonry style using large hewn blocks and almost no decoration, creating buildings of powerful, finely proportioned form; the granite Allegheny County Jail in Pittsburg (1884-8) is one such building. His masterpiece, a commercial structure, was erected in Chicago, the Marshall Field

Wholesale Store (**951**). Constructed of granite and stone, here was an immense, grandiose structure, superbly built and utilizing an up-to-date iron skeleton construction inside the bearing masonry walling.

In the last decades of the century architects such as C.F.A. Voysey in England and C.F. McKim and Frank Lloyd Wright in America were designing plain and spreading low houses. Though traditional materials were being used, the designs were more than plainer versions of past vernacular building. In Voysey and Wright were two of the founders of modern architecture, creating new and different forms, though still inspired by past traditions (**941, 948, 949, 983, 984**).

Equally original were two greatly contrasting architect-designers: the Spaniard Gaudì and the Scotsman Mackintosh. Both men are often considered to be part of the Art Nouveau scene; that aesthetic, romantic, ephemeral movement which manifested itself in many countries of Europe in the late 1880s, but which had burnt itself out by 1914 (**940, 947** and p. 191). Although there are tenuous connections in the designs of both men with mainstream Art Nouveau, the work of each was so personal as to defy categorization.

Antonio Gaudì (1852-1926) was a Catalan, and most of his work was carried out in and around Barcelona. His career stems from the 1870s, when he turned away from Neo-Classicism to a personalized Neo-Gothic. In total contrast is his fantastic 'unfinished' cathedral-temple dedicated to the Holy Family (**946**) to which he devoted his life from 1883 onwards. Another unmistakably Gaudì *oeuvre* is his Güell palace, with its parabolic-arched doorways

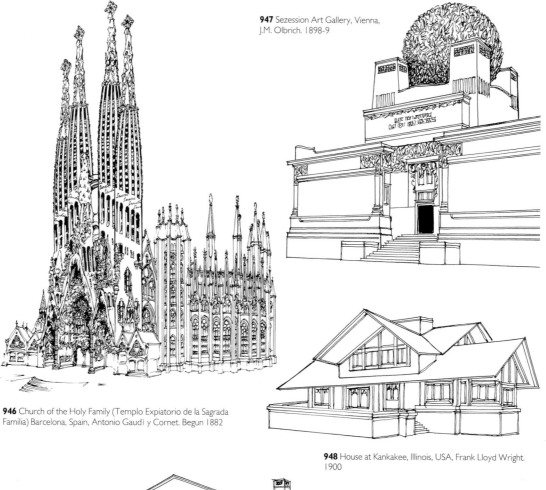

947 Sezession Art Gallery, Vienna, J.M. Olbrich. 1898-9

946 Church of the Holy Family (Templo Expiatorio de la Sagrada Familia) Barcelona, Spain, Antonio Gaudì y Cornet. Begun 1882

948 House at Kankakee, Illinois, USA, Frank Lloyd Wright. 1900

949 House, Bristol, Rhode Island, USA, McKim, Mead and White. 1887

1880 Auguste Rodin, French sculptor, commissioned by the French government to design a pair of doors for a projected museum of decorative arts in Paris. Rodin worked on this project for the rest of his life (he died in 1917). Known as the 'Gates of Hell', the work represented Rodin's personal view of man's spiritual relationship to life

1882 Edouard Manet, French painter, exhibited his *Bar at the Folies Bergère* at the Salon in Paris

1883 Foundation of the Fabian Society, named after the Roman general Fabius Cunctator

1884 Morton's patent Steam Washer made in Glasgow: one of the early washing machines with the means of heating water

1884 General Gordon killed on the steps of the governor-general's palace in Khartoum, after a 317-day siege by the Mahdists. Two days later a British force relieved the city

1885–6 The incandescent gas mantle devised by the Austrian Carl Auer von Welsbach. This was a mantle of knitted cotton which he impregnated with a solution of rare earth oxides. When the cotton mantle burned away, a skeleton of the material retained its form. The mantle represented an immense advance in the level of illumination and in the convenience of gas lighting

1885–7 Working independently, the Germans Gottlieb Daimler and Karl Benz made automobiles powered by internal combustion engines

1887 Nikola Tesla, Yugoslav-born American inventor of the induction A.C. motor, applied for the patent. This was the first step in providing small motors to drive household equipment, and in the early decades

THE BIRTH OF THE SKYSCRAPER 1870 – 1900

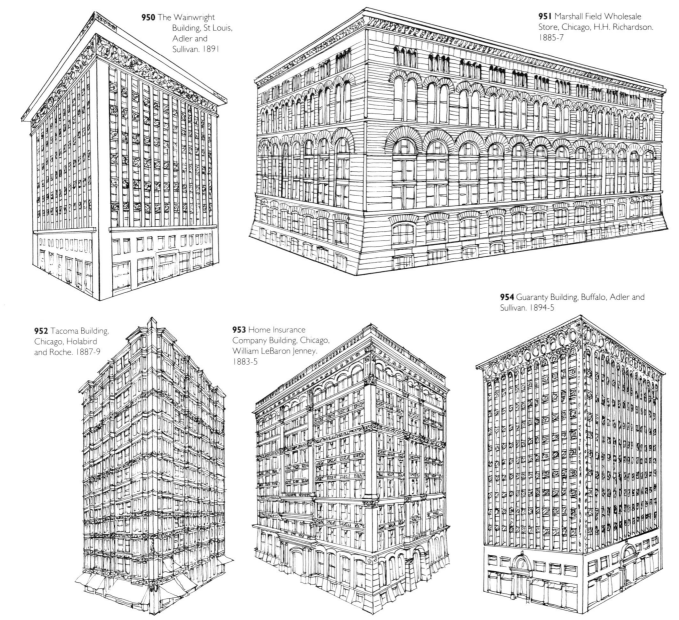

950 The Wainwright Building, St Louis, Adler and Sullivan. 1891

951 Marshall Field Wholesale Store, Chicago, H.H. Richardson. 1885-7

952 Tacoma Building, Chicago, Holabird and Roche. 1887-9

953 Home Insurance Company Building, Chicago, William LeBaron Jenney. 1883-5

954 Guaranty Building, Buffalo, Adler and Sullivan. 1894-5

and decorative iron grilles (**945**).

Charles Rennie Mackintosh (1868-1928) also broke dramatically with nineteenth-century eclecticism, but his personal form of design was rooted in Scottish architectural traditions. In this period the Glasgow School of Art was his masterpiece (**943**); an austere, almost functionalist building which looks forward into the twentieth century.

The nineteenth-century skyscraper was the American contribution to urban architectural development. Here the high-rise building form was conceived and named. By the 1880s conditions were ripe for this type of office development; in the big cities, notably New York and Chicago, steeply rising land values provided the incentive to build high and the structural means to do so had become available.

The two factors which made skyscraper building possible were the lift and the steel-framed structure. The latter had been developed much earlier in Europe, originally in England, where cast iron framing was used for factories, mills and warehouses, later combined to become ferro-vitreous construction (pp. 174-5). The stumbling block to building high was the need to transport personnel from floor to floor. As early as 1849 William Johnston had erected his seven-story Jayne Building in Philadelphia, but this was regarded as the limit until Elisha Otis (1811-61) adapted the age-old hoist for passenger use, by developing a safety mechanism of spring-controlled pawls in case the rope should break. This was in 1852.

In the 1870s the first elevator buildings (as they were then called) were erected. They were between seven and ten storeys high and, stylistically, were Neo-Classical or Neo-Gothic, built of stone and/or brick, with iron framing. A pacesetter in this type of design was Post's Western Union Building in New York City (**955**).

The next essential development to enable buildings to rise above ten storeys or so was the steel-framed structure. Until the early 1880s tall buildings up to this height were erected on traditional load-bearing lines but, to rise still higher, they required impracticably thick walls at base in order to carry the load above. It was the emergence of the load-bearing metal framework, structurally independent of the external walling, which made the true skyscraper possible. An early landmark in this development was the Home Insurance Building in Chicago (**953**). In this, Jenney devised an iron and steel framework of columns, lintels and girders. This building was quickly followed by the fully developed steel skeleton construction of the Tacoma building in the same city (**952**), where the walls were merely cladding.

The skyscraper had arrived, but it was still eclectic in design (**981**). It was Louis H. Sullivan (1856-1924) who, moving forward from the treatment and structure of Richardson's Chicago warehouse (**951**), built his elevations to stress the steel-framed construction rather than to clothe it as had his predecessors. In his Wainwright (**950**) and Guaranty Buildings (**954**) continuous pilasters accented the vertical lines of the framework. By the 1890s Price was developing the skyscraper design further; his 21-storey Surety Building pointed the way to the columnar block (**956**).

956 American Surety Building, New York City, Bruce Price. 1895

955 Western Union Building, New York City, George B. Post. 1873-5

of the twentieth century these were fitted to vacuum cleaners and washing machines

1892–4 Claude Monet, leader of Impressionism in France, painted his Rouen Cathedral series, showing the lighting and colour of the building at different times of day

1895 First performance of *The Importance of being Earnest* by Oscar Wilde

1896 *La Bohème*, opera composed by Giacomo Puccini, first performed in Turin

1897 The building of the Glenfinnan viaduct in the Scottish Highlands which carries the railway from Fort William to Mallaig. Constructed by Robert McAlpine, with 21 massive concrete arches, this is an early use of this material on such a scale

1890s Introduction by the gas companies of the prepayment slot machine system, which brought gas cooking within reach of the poorer members of the community. The coin used was one penny

ART NOUVEAU AND TRADITIONAL ARCHITECTURE   1900 – 1920

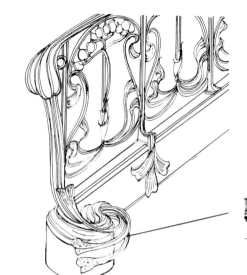

957 Staircase, Louis Majorelle, *c.*1900. Bronze and wrought iron. Majorelle Factory, Nancy, France, Art Nouveau style

958 'Heathcote', Ilkley, England, Sir Edwin Lutyens. 1906. Classical style

959 Marischal College, Aberdeen, Scotland. Entrance façade. A. Marshall Mackenzie. 1905. Gothic style

960 Inveresk House (Morning Post), London, Mewès and Davis. 1906-7. Classical style

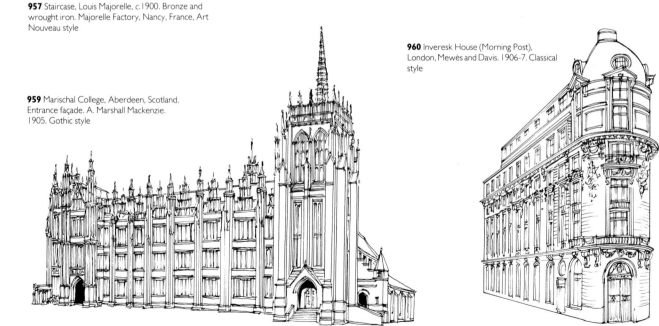

Until 1900, architecture in Europe had been based upon two fundamental styles: classical and Gothic (or medieval). The ancient cultures of Greece and Rome had evolved the classical pattern. Byzantine and Romanesque were partially derived from them; then there developed a medieval style which we call Gothic. The Renaissance rediscovered the classical world, the baroque, rococo and Romantic Classicism reinterpreted the theme until, finally, in the nineteenth century, came an eclecticism of these forms, successively and almost indiscriminately.

The twentieth century is different. Modern architecture makes use of new methods of construction, of materials and, thus, different proportions. It makes the architect freer – although he does not always use this freedom wisely – to design in a totally different manner from that circumscribed by the traditions of the past. In the later nineteenth century in the USA architects such as Adler and Sullivan experimented in this way, using concrete and steel-framing, to build high and on a large scale (p. 188), but in Europe where, traditionally, a huge, low-cost labour force was still available, where cities were old and established and where population increase had been less rapid, the need to build fast – using modern methods of construction – was not apparent until after World War I.

Over the western world as a whole there were therefore in the years 1900-1920 four basic architectural trends. There was Art Nouveau, showing the desire of designers for something new; then secondly and most commonly, a continuation (though in a simplified manner) of traditional Gothic and classical forms; thirdly a plainer, less eclectic approach, though still using traditional materals and proportions; and lastly, the early prototypes of genuine modern architecture.

Art Nouveau, as the style is called in England (after the shop of that name which opened in Paris in 1895 to sell merchandise of non-derivative design) was a decorative rather than architectural movement, though some of its exponents created notable buildings. It was an attempt to break away from eclecticism, representing a deeply-felt striving to design something new, but backward-looking in that it shied away from the current trend towards industrialization. It was an extension of the ideas of Ruskin and Morris, based upon a return to the craftsmanship of a smaller population in a pre-industrial age; it could not last.

Art Nouveau began as a decorative movement in book illustration, textiles, glassware and furniture: it was primarily successful in interior decoration. Predominant motifs displayed a nostalgic affinity with rococo design in undulating plant forms, flames, moving waves and abstract shapes. The work was linear rather than three-dimensional. Decoration soon extended to coloured glass, faïence and stucco. In architecture, metal and glass were favourite materials (**957**). Characteristic and outstanding in the earlier work was the contribution of Victor Horta in Belgium (**940**), and Olbrich and Wagner in Vienna (**947**), where Wagner was designing his decorative Majolika Haus (1898-9). In Paris, Guimard was working on his Metro Stations and Wagner was doing the same for the Vienna Stadtbahn.

Britain was on the fringe of the movement, contributing, for example, Townsend's Whitechapel Art Gallery (**944**), but more characteristic and important were Mackintosh's Glasgow tea rooms – interiors

961 Casa Castiglione, Milan, Italy. Giuseppe Sommaruga. 1903. Art Nouveau style.

963 Liverpool (Anglican) Cathedral, England. Sir Giles Gilbert Scott. 1903-78, Gothic style

962 Case Milà, Barcelona, Spain. Antonio Gaudi. 1905. Art Nouveau style

964 Iron gate. Nashdom Abbey, England, Sir Edwin Lutyens. 1910

CIVIC AND DOMESTIC PLANNED ARCHITECTURE 1900 – 1920

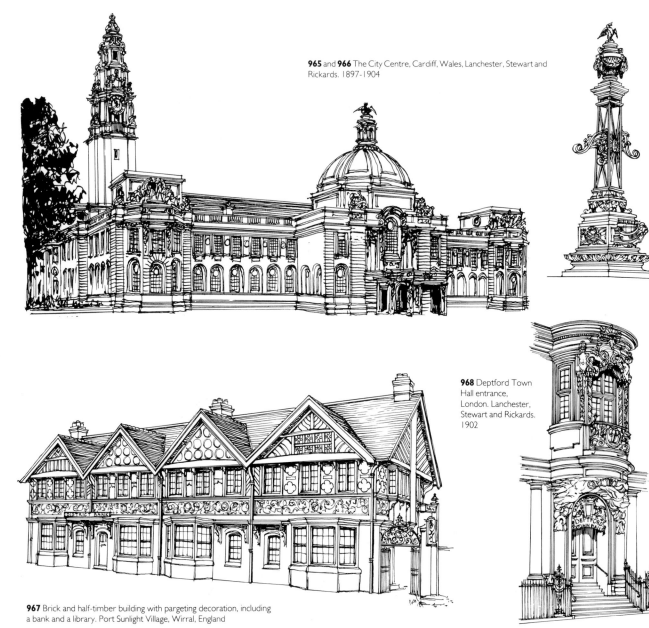

965 and **966** The City Centre, Cardiff, Wales, Lanchester, Stewart and Rickards. 1897-1904

968 Deptford Town Hall entrance, London. Lanchester, Stewart and Rickards. 1902

967 Brick and half-timber building with pargeting decoration, including a bank and a library. Port Sunlight Village, Wirral, England

which he designed in the years 1897-1904. The approach in Italy and Spain was more extrovert, as in Sommaruga's work in Milan (**961**) and in Gaudì's Barcelona apartment blocks (**962**), the façades of which are plastic in appearance, undulating and full of movement.

Many architects, indeed the majority, continued to design in an eclectic manner, maintaining the tradition of the late nineteenth century. This was especially so in England where, although steel-framing had been introduced early, as in the Ritz Hotel in Piccadilly and Inveresk House – the Morning Post Building (**960**) also in London – the exterior cladding remained classical, and apparently unrelated to the internal structure. Both buildings were designed in the French manner in 1906 by the firm of Mewès and Davis. Not dissimilar, but rather more modern, is Kodak House (now the Gallaher Building) in Kingsway – designed 1911 by Sir John Burnet. An early example of a reinforced concrete framework clad in granite is the Royal Liver Building in Liverpool (1908), by Walter Thomas.

More traditional still are the Edwardian Baroque works of the firm of Lanchester, Stewart and Rickards, closely modelled on the Paris buildings of the Grand and Petit Palais (p. 185). The Cardiff City Centre development contains the chief of these, where the architects were responsible for the City Hall and Law Courts (**965**, **966**): a magnificent layout completed in 1904. The same architects built Deptford Town Hall in London (**968**) and the Central Hall in Westminster (**971**). The Gothic tradition is represented by such structures as Marshall Mackenzie's immense, granite Perpendicular-style granite Marischal College in Aberdeen (**959**) and Scott's Liverpool

Cathedral. He won the competition here to build the Anglican Cathedral in 1903 – an imposing Gothic building in red sandstone – though it was not completed until 1978 (**963**).

Maintaining the classical tradition were Sir Aston Webb (**972**) and, outstanding British architect of the first half of the twentieth century in England, Sir Edwin Lutyens (1869-1944). The country house practice established by Lutyens from the late nineteenth century had shown him following the Norman Shaw tradition in designing in a varied, vernacular manner. From about 1905 his work became more classical, as at Heathcote in Ilkley (**958, 964**). It was after 1920 that Lutyens turned to the extensive civic and commercial schemes which confirmed his reputation in the inter-war years.

In the middle years of the nineteenth century in Europe, attempts were made to alleviate the slum conditions endemic in industrial towns and provide better housing, greater convenience and an improved working environment for the increasing population. Ideas and practical schemes to do this were being produced in a number of countries by philanthropists, visionaries and architects with a sense of social purpose. A pacemaker among these was the industrialist Krupp at Essen in Germany – closely followed by Salt in England, who created Saltaire, a new town on the banks of the river Aire in Yorkshire, to which he brought his Bradford textile mill workers (**901**). Such men built ideal townships for their workers, with housing, shops, hospital, clubs and schools and other amenities near the factories. These were the forerunners of the Garden City and New Town concepts of the twentieth century.

969 Central Square, Hampstead Garden Suburb, London. Architect for the square Sir Edwin Lutyens. Begun 1906

970 The Free Church in Central Square

971 The Central Wesleyan Hall, Westminster, England. Lanchester and Rickards. 1906-12

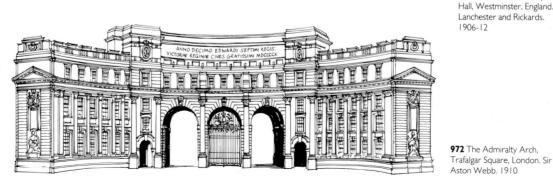

972 The Admiralty Arch, Trafalgar Square, London. Sir Aston Webb. 1910

their first powered flight in their flying machine

1903   Henry Ford founded the Ford Motor Company in the USA

1903–4   *The Cherry Orchard*, by the Russian dramatist Anton Chekhov, written and performed

1904   Invention by Sir John Ambrose Fleming of the thermionic vacuum tube, later of vital importance in making possible the development of radio-telephony

1905   Columnar radiants introduced in the design of gas fires

1905   Albert Einstein, German physicist, published his special theory of relativity

1906   *The Doctor's Dilemma*, play by George Bernard Shaw

1907   J. Murray Spangler devised the first vacuum suction clearner fitted with a small electric motor. He sold the rights to a successful firm of saddlers who, with the growing interest in America for motor cars, found this affecting their leather saddle trade, so were looking for a new venture to invest in. They developed Spangler's machine and marketed it in 1908. This was the first electrically powered, upright domestic vacuum clearner with exterior dustbag. It was an instant and continuing success. The firm was W.H. Hoover.

1907–11   George Macaulay Trevelyan produced his masterpiece, the trilogy on Garibaldi

1909   Sergei Pavlovich Diaghilev launched his Ballet Russes in Paris

1910   First performance of Igor Stravinsky's *Firebird* in Paris

TOWARDS MODERN ARCHITECTURE   1900 – 1920

NORWAY, SWEDEN, FINLAND

FINLAND, ENGLAND, HOLLAND, SWEDEN

973 Tampere Cathedral, Finland. Lars Sonck. 1902-7

974 Engelkbrekt Church, Stockholm, Sweden, L.I. Wahlman, 1906-14

976 Helsinki Railway Station, Finland, Eliel Saarinen. 1904-14

975 Heal and Son, department store, London, Smith and Brewer. 1914-37

In the 1870s a different type of housing experiment was planned in London. At Bedford Park, a dormitory suburb was created where high-standard vernacular-style houses were built round a church and general stores. In 1906 the theme was taken further, when the Garden Suburb Trust was founded to build a high quality architectural layout at Hampstead. The architect for the central area of the new Garden Suburb was Lutyens, who created a symmetrical scheme in brick on simplified classical lines (**969, 970**).

Expanding upon Sir Titus Salt's ideas, several industrialists were creating their own model housing estates – not dormitory suburbs, but self-contained communities. The finest of these in Britain was that laid out by Lord Leverhulme in the Wirral in Cheshire, across the Mersey from Liverpool. Around the Lever factory, built in 1888, several notable architects contributed houses, schools, banks, shops, an inn, hospital, fire station, library and club, in high quality structures of varied but vernacular form and materials (**967**).

The proto-modern school of architecture, the third style of the years 1900-1920, was considered to be modern indeed in the mid century, but is now re-assessed as being traditional in modern dress. The work cannot be termed classical or Gothic, but the majority of buildings erected in this 'modern' form, in Scandinavia and Holland especially, employed traditional materials (most commonly brick but also stone) and methods of construction and, for all their elegant simplicity, displayed traditional proportions and scale.

The chief architect of this school in England was still C.F.A. Voysey (1857-1941, p. 187). His style was personal and non-

TOWARDS MODERN ARCHITECTURE 1900 – 1920

eclectic. He appreciated the vernacular tradition but developed an individual approach, on an intimate scale, displaying subtlety and quality in a practice chiefly devoted to domestic design (**984**).

In Holland Hendrik Berlage (1856-1934) was the leader of the national school. In the last years of the century he abandoned his traditional style of work and moved towards a more dynamic approach. Characteristic are his Amsterdam buildings of the Exchange (**980**) and his Diamond Workers' Union Building (1899-1900). This 'Amsterdam school', thus projected, flourished under other architects in the years 1912-23. Agressively bold and original is Van der Meij's Scheepvaarthuis (dock offices) of 1913, while his assistants de Klerk and Kramer set the pattern in the city for original designs in the great housing estates of the time: the Eigen Haard Estate, begun 1917, and that of De Dageraad (**1004**). Built in brick, five to six storeys high, these displayed unusual curved forms and simple decoration incorporated into the long blocks, which avoided any feeling of monotony.

In Scandinavia there was an energetic school of high quality building in modern traditionalism, ranging from Martin Nyrop's Copenhagen Town Hall (1892-1902) to the elegant Stockholm City Hall by Ostberg (**985**) and the Masthugg Church in Göteborg (**979**). The most original architect of the time – designing in this manner but in a more dramatic and rugged masonry block form – reminiscent of Richardson in the USA (p. 186), was Lars Sonck (1870-1956), Finnish architect of Tampere Cathedral (**973**, **978**), Kallió Church in Helsinki (1909-12) and most Richardsonian of all, his Telephone Exchange in the same city (1905).

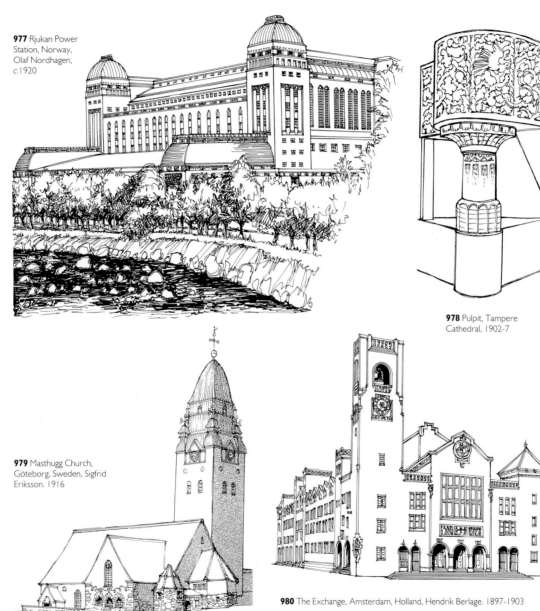

977 Rjukan Power Station, Norway, Olaf Nordhagen, c.1920

978 Pulpit, Tampere Cathedral, 1902-7

979 Masthugg Church, Göteborg, Sweden, Sigfrid Eriksson. 1916

980 The Exchange, Amsterdam, Holland, Hendrik Berlage. 1897-1903

1910 First known use of radio in apprehending a murderer, when Hawley Harvey Crippen was arrested in Quebec, after the Captain of the ship of which Crippen and Ethel Le Neve had travelled to Canada wirelessed a description of the couple to London

1910–13 *Principia Mathematica*, one of the most important and original works on the history of mathematics, written by Bertrand Russell and A.N. Whitehead

1911 Tungsten filaments in general use for manufacturing filament electric lamps, thus replacing the earlier carbon and tantalum filaments

1912 C.R. Belling devised an element for electric fire heating in which the wires were wound round a fire-clay former

1912 Self-service food stores opened in the USA

1912 The White Star liner Titanic sank on her maiden voyage after colliding with an iceberg, with a loss of more than 1500 lives

1912 Robert Falcon Scott, with his companions Lt Bowers and Edward Wilson, died in the Antarctic in a snowed-up tent on the Ross ice shelf after reaching the South Pole

1914 28 June. Assassination of the Archduke Franz Ferdinand and his wife at Sarajevo

1914 Britain entered World War I on 4 August

1914 The Kelvinator household refrigerator marketed in Detroit. It was at first powered by steam, later by electric motor

1916 Margaret Sanger, American

THE EMERGENCE OF MODERN ARCHITECTURE 1900 – 1920

ENGLAND, GERMANY, USA

USA, SWEDEN, GERMANY

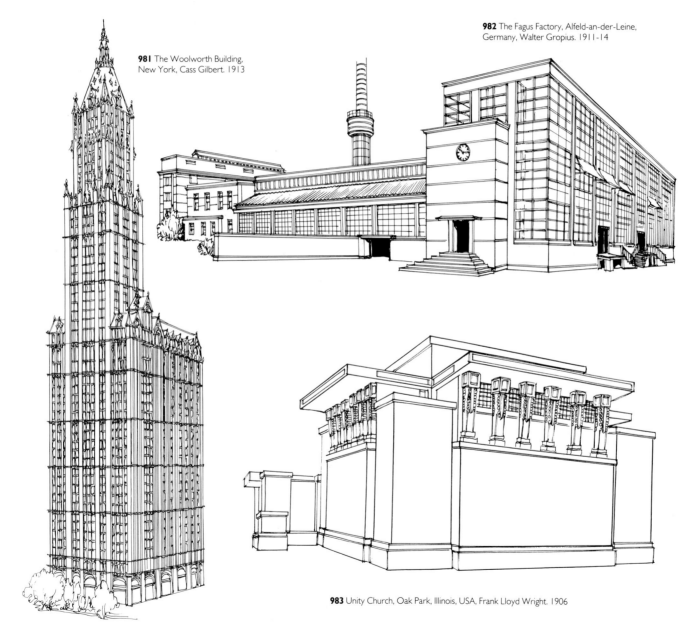

982 The Fagus Factory, Alfeld-an-der-Leine, Germany, Walter Gropius. 1911-14

981 The Woolworth Building, New York, Cass Gilbert. 1913

983 Unity Church, Oak Park, Illinois, USA, Frank Lloyd Wright. 1906

By 1900 a few architectural innovators in several countries were experimenting successfully with new forms of construction, often using less traditional materials and producing designs which aesthetically reflected such an approach. Most notable of these men were Frank Lloyd Wright in the USA, Auguste Perret in France, Adolf Loos in Austria and Peter Behrens in Germany.

American architects had a head start over their European colleagues as they developed and consolidated the achievements already made in the late nineteenth century by Richardson, Sullivan and Wright himself (p. 187). Frank Lloyd Wright (1869-1959) had begun by working with Sullivan, and in a career of nearly 70 years, which began after he set up practice on his own in 1893, he became the most important figure in the modern architectural scene in America. His career developed in three different phases, the first of which, up to World War I, was spent mainly designing houses which became known (as so many were built in the Midwest of America) as 'prairie houses'. These were low and spreading, with gently sloping rooflines, built in traditional materials in warm rural colours blending softly into their setting (**948**). Wright, however, was also interested in the possibilities of reinforced concrete, and in 1906 he built his church at Oak Park entirely of this material (**983**).

Even more interested in experimentation with the material was Auguste Perret, who concentrated from early in his career on the use of ferro-concrete and the types of design which would be most suitable for its employment. His best known structures date from the inter-war years (p. 204), but of innovatory and notable interest is his house in the Rue Franklin in Paris of 1903, which shows in its stark vertical and horizontal members the framework of the construction.

From Vienna Adolf Loos was building up a large practice designing houses in reinforced concrete in Austria, France, Switzerland and Czechoslovakia, though he also created some superb interiors, in particular finished with polished marbles and metals: the Kaïtner Bar in Vienna of 1907 illustrates this.

Peter Behrens in Germany was developing the combined use of steel, glass and concrete in original schemes of industrial architecture. A turning point in his career was his appointment in 1907 as architect and consultant to AEG, the Berlin electrical company. His surviving turbine factory in the city (1909) was a breakthrough in the design of functional architecture in modern materials (986). In 1913 he built the large AEG plant at Riga, and became in great demand for industrial work, designing in Düsseldorf and Frankfurt.

There were others producing interesting work which was verging upon the modern approach. In Sweden Wahlman's Engelbrekt Church in Stockholm (974) broke new ground with its tall, elegant tower and internally, the great brick parabolic arches of the vault. Also in Scandinavia, Eliel Saarinen was Finland's leading architect of the day before his departure for the USA. More traditional and not dissimilar from Sonck's work is his National Museum in Helsinki (1905), but his chief work is his railway station in the city (976), a large, clean-lined structure. Among the many such great railway termini erected in Europe at this time was Stuttgart Railway Station (987) – one of the most uncompromisingly modern, though built with traditional block courses of material.

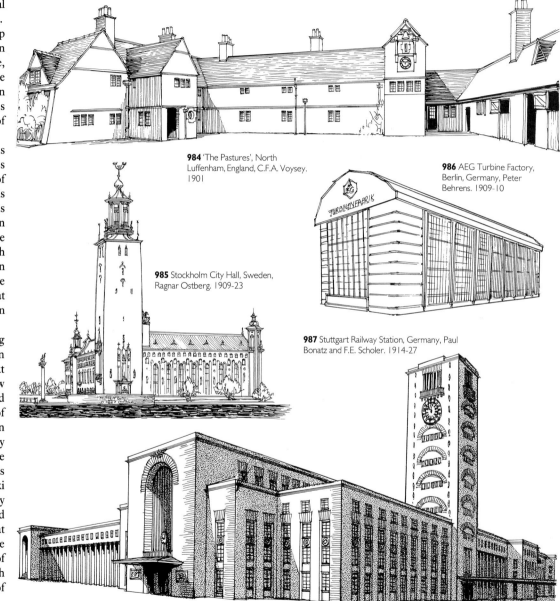

984 'The Pastures', North Luffenham, England, C.F.A. Voysey. 1901

985 Stockholm City Hall, Sweden, Ragnar Ostberg. 1909-23

986 AEG Turbine Factory, Berlin, Germany, Peter Behrens. 1909-10

987 Stuttgart Railway Station, Germany, Paul Bonatz and F.E. Scholer. 1914-27

advocate of birth control, opened the first birth control clinic in Brooklyn. She had coined the term a few years earlier

1916 Battle of the Somme in France, began on 1 July, in which over a million men died

1917 The October Revolution in Russia and takeover by the Bolsheviks

1917 Ernest Rutherford, New Zealand born physicist, became the first man to change one element into another when he bombarded nitrogen atoms with alpha particles, converting them into oxygen

1918 8 July. Nicholas II, last Tsar of Russia, executed by Bolsheviks at Ekaterinburg

1918 11 November. Armistice and end of World War I

1918–19 Influenza pandemic in which many millions of people died

1918–20 Plasterboard employed as a replacement for plaster ceilings due to a shortage of plasterers after the War. The plaster panels consisted of a layer of gypsum plaster sandwiched between sheets of strong paper

1919 Treaty of Versailles between the Allies and Germany

1919 C.R. Belling marketed his small electric cooker, the 'Modernette'

1919 Observations of the total eclipse of the sun agree with predictions made using Einstein's Theory of Relativity

TRADITIONAL ARCHITECTURE IN MODERN DRESS   1920 – 1945

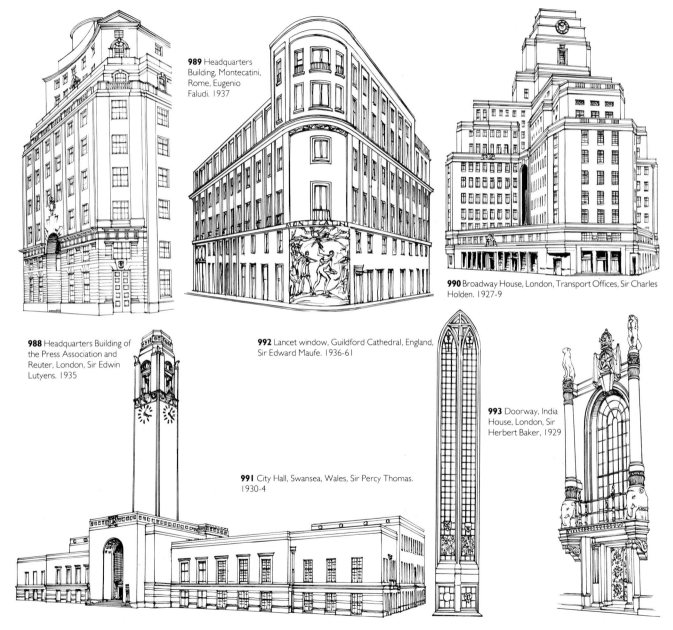

989 Headquarters Building, Montecatini, Rome, Eugenio Faludi. 1937

990 Broadway House, London, Transport Offices, Sir Charles Holden. 1927-9

988 Headquarters Building of the Press Association and Reuter, London, Sir Edwin Lutyens. 1935

992 Lancet window, Guildford Cathedral, England, Sir Edward Maufe. 1936-61

993 Doorway, India House, London, Sir Herbert Baker, 1929

991 City Hall, Swansea, Wales, Sir Percy Thomas. 1930-4

Between the two World Wars modern design and construction in architecture gradually evolved in Europe and America, but such work remained a minority of the total. The bulk of construction continued to be traditional in materials, means and style. No longer could much of this building be termed classical or Gothic – it was often severely plain and nondescript – but neither was it forward-looking. Frequently it was a vacuous form of eclecticism – a negation of the past, yet shackled to it.

Characteristic of this type of building in France are the Paris schemes of the Palais de Chaillot (**994**) and the Museum of Modern Art (**997**); the latter is fronted by a colonnade of featureless columns supporting an even more characterless 'entablature'. In Scandinavia, typical are Copenhagen's Broadcasting House (1937-45, Lauritzen), Helsinki's Parliament Building (1927-31, Sirén) and Göteborg's layout of City Concert Hall, Art Museum and Theatre (1923-35, Eriksson and others) in Sweden. Rather more interesting are the Lucerne churches by Metzger and Dreyer of S. Charles and S. Joseph (**1003**) of 1933 and Bartning's Berlin church (**1000**).

Some good quality work based more closely on past styles includes the Gruntvig Church in Copenhagen (**999**), while Lutyens in England built some fine civic structures (**988**), such as Britannic House in London. Classicism of a plainer type is represented by **989-91**, **993**, **996** and **1001-2**. In America, skyscrapers also were subject to backward glancing, even if the structure was of modern steel-framing: for example, (**998**) and the City Hall in Los Angeles (1928, Austin, Parkinson and Martin).

In the early years of the twentieth century a number of schemes were put forward to plan new ideal cities. Expanding upon the idea which had been considered in Italy for the *cinquecento* (p. 124), these more modern plans were seeking to accommodate the needs and convenience of the urban industrial society, segregating traffic from pedestrians and industry from leisure pursuits. Leonardo da Vinci and suggested such a plan (p. 124). This was taken up by the Italian Antonio Sant'Elia (1880-1916) who, fascinated by certain aspects of technology, planned cities for Italy. His *Città Nuova*, projected in 1914, was exhibited in Milan. It envisaged skyscrapers, pedestrian precincts and traffic moving on overhead roadways at two or three different levels. Saint'Elia was killed in action in 1916 but his drawings have survived, as have his ideas. In France, Tony Garnier (1867-1948), thinking on similar lines, designed his *Cité Industrielle*. He also envisaged and illustrated, before the World War One, flat-roofed buildings supported on *pilotis*, constructed with steel-framing end-clad with glass, as well as an extensive use of concrete.

These were all drawing board projects, but the separation of pedestrians and vehicles was experimented with in the USA in Radburn, New Jersey just after World War One. It was not until the 1950s in most countries that traffic pressures forced a more serious consideration of the problem (p. 211).

To provide better accommodation for increased populations and city expansion, extensive housing schemes were put into effect in many countries. These comprised housing estates or dormitory suburbs, as well as Garden Cities where industry and commercial, educational, medical, leisure and administrative facilities were provided within the periphery of the planned area.

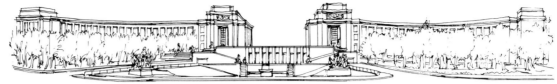

994 Palais de Chaillot, Paris, Carlu, Boileau, Azema. 1937

995 Central Railway Station, Milan, Italy, Eugenio Montuori. Begun 1931

996 Via Roma, Turin, Italy, Marcello Piacentini. 1938

997 Sculptural decoration on exterior of building. Museum of Modern Art, Paris. 1937

TRADITIONAL ARCHITECTURE IN MODERN DRESS   1920 – 1945

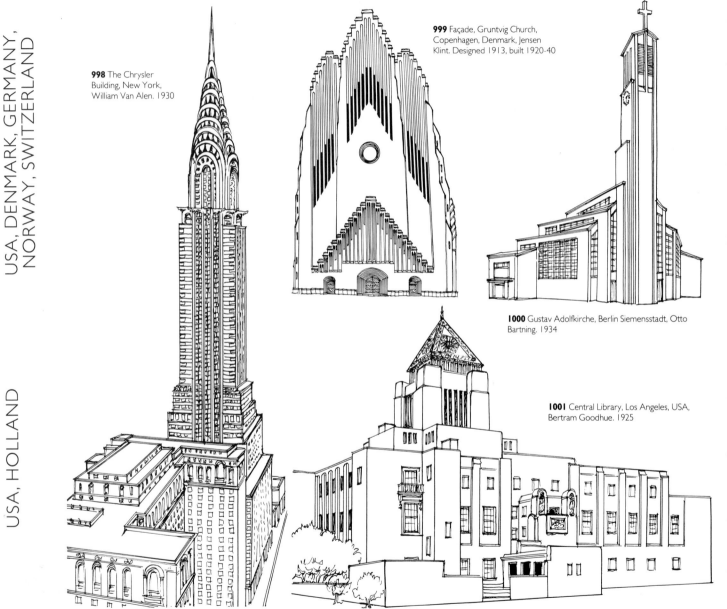

998 The Chrysler Building, New York, William Van Alen. 1930

999 Façade, Gruntvig Church, Copenhagen, Denmark, Jensen Klint. Designed 1913, built 1920-40

1000 Gustav Adolfkirche, Berlin Siemensstadt, Otto Bartning. 1934

1001 Central Library, Los Angeles, USA, Bertram Goodhue. 1925

Some of these schemes were built on traditional architectural lines with traditional materials. Typical of these were the English Garden Cities at Welwyn and Letchworth, which provided houses with gardens. The Continental pattern tended towards living in large blocks of flats with communal gardens. The brick-built estates of this kind in Amsterdam have already been referred to (p 195 and **1004**). In London, Lutyens designed a low-cost scheme of flats in 1928, built of grey bricks and Portland stone to give a chequerboard pattern to the buildings.

In Germany and Holland a number of architects were initiating a new type of design for such estates, which were laid out with long, thin blocks constructed in standardized units in severely plain treatment. Prototypes of this more modern approach included Gropius's Siemensstadt of 1930 in Berlin and the Weissenhof experiment in Stuttgart (1927), to which a number of leading architects contributed: Mies van der Rohe, Le Corbusier, Behrens, Gropius. Oud's modern housing estate at the Hook of Holland (1926-7) was also influential.

Modern architecture is a term which has been universally applied to the twentieth-century style which developed spontaneously in several European countries from 1918, and which has culminated in the current buildings of glass, concrete and steel based on module construction, which are erected all over the world.

The term International Style was coined in the 1930s to express the fact that this modern building type transcended frontiers and was being adopted on both sides of the Atlantic and beyond. This was not just because it spread as an architectural style but because, more fundamentally, the social structure in so many countries created a need for buildings which could be produced at a cost and a speed which such methods made possible.

It was not only that there existed a deep desire on the part of architects and designers for a change of style. The pressure was engendered by two more vital factors which created the catalyst for a complete stylistic break with the past. One was the nineteenth-century population explosion which, together with the effects of industrialization, made urgently necessary an increased rate of building for all purposes. The second, later factor was the widescale destruction caused by two World Wars which necessitated the rebuilding of whole towns as well as individual sites. This need greatly hastened technical developments of new improved materials and means of construction, so making it possible to erect large scale schemes more cheaply by mass-production methods. The combination of these factors has, since 1945, brought about a transformation in building which has killed for ever the architectural industry founded on individual craftsmanship.

It was a paradox of the inter-war years in Europe that so many of the original thinkers and designers, the men who possessed the courage and initiative to defy established traditions, were nationals of countries which submitted to totalitarian régimes; a type of government which rendered it impossible for such architects to retain integrity in their work. Such countries were, notably, Germany, Italy and Russia. The architects emigrated, were imprisoned or submitted to dictatorship.

The greatest national loss of architectural talent was in Germany. Here, by 1920, was developing an architectural school of vigour and originality which was attracting men of

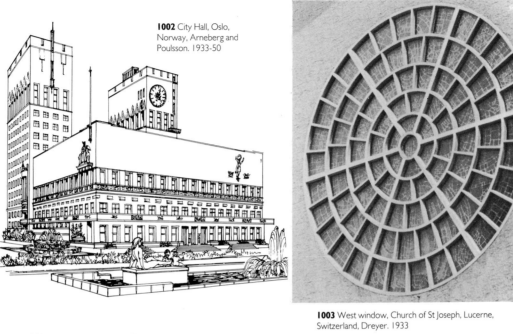

1002 City Hall, Oslo, Norway, Arneberg and Poulsson. 1933-50

1003 West window, Church of St Joseph, Lucerne, Switzerland, Dreyer. 1933

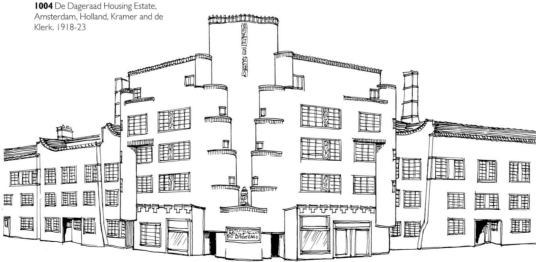

1004 De Dageraad Housing Estate, Amsterdam, Holland, Kramer and de Klerk. 1918-23

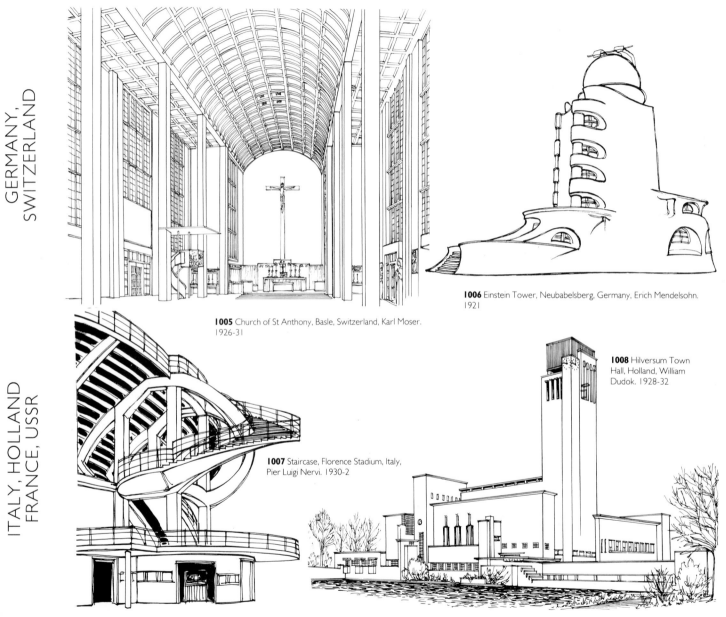

GERMANY,
SWITZERLAND

ITALY, HOLLAND
FRANCE, USSR

1005 Church of St Anthony, Basle, Switzerland, Karl Moser.
1926-31

1006 Einstein Tower, Neubabelsberg, Germany, Erich Mendelsohn.
1921

1008 Hilversum Town
Hall, Holland, William
Dudok. 1928-32

1007 Staircase, Florence Stadium, Italy,
Pier Luigi Nervi. 1930-2

great ability, dedicated to the new form of
architectural expression. By 1933 most of
these had emigrated, chiefly to Britain *en
route* for the USA. Two of the best known of
these – Walter Gropius (1883-1969) (**982**)
and Mies van der Rohe (1888-1969) (**1023**,
1037) – were successively Director of the
Bauhaus, that famous and influential school
of art at Dessau, for which Gropius had
designed the purpose-built structures and
which was dedicated to the interrelationship
between the various arts and crafts – many of
which were vital to architecture. With the
growth of National Socialism the Bauhaus
finally closed its doors in 1932.

Of particular interest in German
architecture of the 1920s was the
development of Expressionism. This was a
movement derived from contemporary art in
which dramatic forms and curves (as in
parabolic arches) predominated, though
angular shapes were also incorporated into
the designs. Notable examples of this style
included the extensive scheme designed by
Peter Behrens for I.G. Farben in Höchst
(1920-4), Hans Poelzig's Grosses
Schauspielhaus in Berlin (1919) (a most
striking interior, its ceiling resembling the
stalactites depending from a cave roof), Fritz
Höger's dramatic Chilehaus in Hamburg
(**1009**) and Domenikus Böhm's church of
S. Engelbert at Cologne-Riehl (1931-3).

Erich Mendelsohn (1887-1953) came to
England in 1933, where he went into
partnership with the Russian emigré Serge
Chermayeff. Together they designed De la
Warr Pavilion at Bexhill (**1016**).
Mendelsohn also produced one of the most
unusual Expressionist buildings: the
Einstein Tower (**1006**). This physical
laboratory and observatory, purpose-built
for Professor Einstein's research work, was

MODERN ARCHITECTURE 1920 – 1945

intended to be constructed in poured cement – but in the event was made of brick faced with stucco. Mendelsohn was also responsible for the pace-setting Schocken department stores in Stuttgart (1926) and Chemnitz (1928), as well as Berlin's Columbus Haus (1929-31).

In the USSR younger architects in particular saw the post-revolutionary years as an opportunity to introduce a new architectural style fundamentally suited to socialism. In the years 1925-32, under State finance and control, several architects (with little contact possible with the west) began empirically to design more modern structures within the framework of the needs of Soviet society. A leader in this was Konstantin Melnikov (1890-1974) who became known for his workers' clubs; multi-purpose buildings comprising facilities for leisure, education and entertainment (**1012**).

In Italy, in the early 1920s, it was Giuseppe Terragni (1904-43) who led the modern school. In 1926 he helped to found the *gruppo sette*, seven architects who joined the modern movement. They were all young and inspired by the Bauhaus project and work in the USA. Terragni's work included the Casa del Fascio (1932-6) and an apartment block (**1014**), both in Como, and some flats in Milan in the Corso Sempione (**1015**). Sadly, his career was cut short by his death in World War II. Among his colleagues were Pagano, Ridolfo and Michelucci (**1013**). All their work illustrated the modern trend, but incorporated the use of traditional Italian materials such as marble.

French architecture was dominated in these years by the Swiss architect Charles Edouard Jeanneret (1888-1965), usually known as Le Corbusier, who with Frank Lloyd Wright became a great world leader of the modern architectural movement. By

1009 Chilehaus, Hamburg, Germany, Fritz Höger. 1923

1010 Window detail, Chilehaus

1012 Workers' club, 'Club Rusakov', Moscow, Konstantin Melnikov. 1925-6

1011 Swiss Pavilion, Cité Universitaire, Paris, Le Corbusier. 1931-2

1933 27 February. The burning of the Reichstag in Berlin.
23 March. The establishment of the Third Reich

1933 Concentration camps set up in Germany

1933 The 'New Deal' initiated by Franklin D. Roosevelt, 32nd President of the United States, to counter the effects of the Great Depression

1934 Mersey Tunnel in Liverpool opened by King George V

1935 Death of T.E. Lawrence (Lawrence of Arabia) as a result of a motorcycle accident

1935 Sir Robert Watson-Watt, Scottish physicist, developed his radiolocation equipment to a degree of accuracy and sensitivity which enabled him to patent his radiolocater; it was this which formed the basis of the radar used in wartime Britain

1935 Greta Garbo, Swedish actress, appeared in the title part in the film of Tolstoy's *Anna Karenina*

1936 Publication of *Gone With the Wind* by Margaret Mitchell, American novelist. The book made publishing history, setting a sales record of 50,000 copies sold in one day, and one and a half million copies in its first year of publication

1936 2 November. The BBC began transmitting from Alexandra Palace, the first regular public television service in the world

1937 Pablo Picasso painted *Guernica*, the mural allegory portraying the Spanish town bombed in the Civil War

1937 The largest rigid airship ever built, the German Hindenburg, burst into flames at Lakehurst, New

MODERN ARCHITECTURE   1920 – 1945

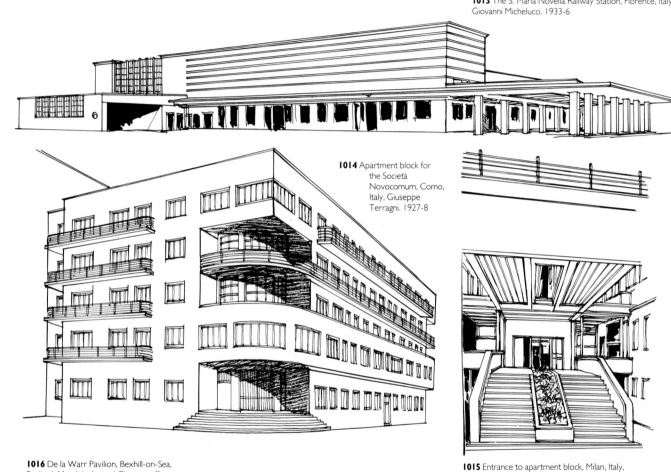

1013 The S. Maria Novella Railway Station, Florence, Italy, Giovanni Michelucci. 1933-6

1014 Apartment block for the Società Novocomum, Como, Italy, Giuseppe Terragni. 1927-8

1015 Entrance to apartment block, Milan, Italy, Giuseppe Terragni. 1934-5

1016 De la Warr Pavilion, Bexhill-on-Sea, England, Mendelsohn and Chermayeff. 1935-6

1920 he was becoming established as an architect with advanced original ideas, very much of the 'Functionalist school'.

The need for a building to be designed suitably for its purpose had always been a tenet of good architecture, though this had, to a certain extent, been lost sight of in the decades of nineteenth-century eclecticism. The theme of the 'Functionalists' went further. It stressed the structural qualities of the building but left it bare of decoration. They were intrigued by the new technology in engineering and the shapes there evolved: cones, cubes, spheres, cylinders. They repeated such forms endlessly to facilitate cheaper production.

Le Corbusier specialised in low-cost housing in flats and estates. He envisaged the housing unit as a 'machine for living in'. Extraneous and unnecessary features were stripped away leaving a plain, flat-roofed structure. He evolved the piloti system. Pilotis were free-standing reinforced concrete piers upon which the building stood (**1011**). The rectangular box on stilts has been with us ever since. Le Corbusier was absorbed in the social problems of housing people in cities and developed these ideas in his book *Urbanisme*, published 1925.

One of the major materials used by the modernists was reinforced concrete. In France Eugène Freyssinet had pioneered its industrial use in his great parabolic-vaulted airship hangar at Orly in 1916. In Italy the engineer Pier Luigi Nervi (b. 1891) was continuing its use in his hangars at Orvieto and Ortebello, and at the earlier stadium in Florence (**1007**). August Perret (p. 196) built his church at Le Raincy (**1017**) in this material. Here he covered the wide, light interior with a segmental vaulted roof carried solely on slender reeded columns while the walls, carrying no load, were composed of pre-cast concrete units filled with coloured glass. This design, which created unimpeded vision and hearing from the altar to the entire congregation, became a prototype for churches for decades all over Europe as at, for example, Moser's Basle church (**1005**).

Elsewhere in Europe and the USA the convenience and structural possibilities of the material were being exploited. In Wright's 'Falling Water', the Pennsylvania house which exemplified his belief that a building should belong to its landscape, he cantilevered a series of concrete slabs out from the bedrock over a waterfall (**1019**). In quite different vein the firm of Tecton designed the famous and sculptural penguin pool in London Zoo (1933).

Like concrete, the concept of the glass curtain wall, so characteristic of architecture since 1950, stemmed from earlier origins. The first true example is believed to be the Hallidie Building in San Francisco, built 1918 by Willis Polk, while Gropius's Fagus Factory (**982**) introduced the concept to Europe. A limited use was made of this here in the inter-war years – and to a much greater extent in the USA – but its ubiquity belongs to the post-1945 era.

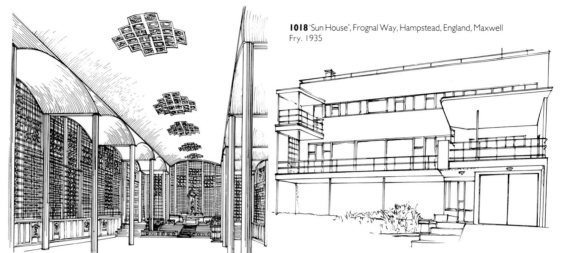

1018 'Sun House', Frognal Way, Hampstead, England, Maxwell Fry. 1935

1017 Church of Notre Dame, Le Raincy, France, Auguste Perret. 1922-3

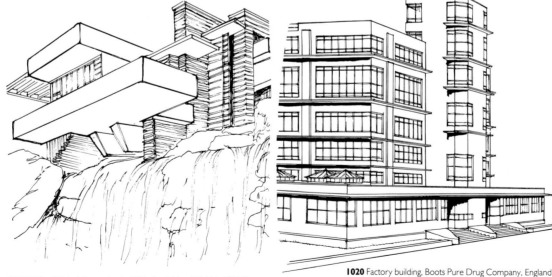

1019 'Falling Water', Pennsylvania, USA, Frank Lloyd Wright. 1936-7

1020 Factory building, Boots Pure Drug Company, England, Sir Owen Williams. 1938

Jersey with a loss of 36 lives

1938 29 September. The Munich Pact. Neville Chamberlain returned to England proclaiming that his concession had brought 'Peace in our time'

1938 George Biro of Hungary made the first effective ballpoint pen

1939 3 September. Britain declared war on Germany

1939 *The Dancing Years*, musical play by Ivor Novello

1939 Archaeological find made in Suffolk of the Sutton Hoo ship burial. This was the grave of a seventh-century king of East Anglia, and consisted of the remains of an ancient timber ship laden with treasure

1939 Nylon thread, developed in the Du Pont laboratories in the USA between 1927 and 1938 at a cost of 27 million dollars, first made into stockings

1939 Igor Sikorsky, Russian-American aeronautical engineer, developed the first American helicopter capable of sustained flight and adequate control

1940 Discovery of the Lascaux Caves in France, which contain magnificent prehistoric paintings

1941 First flight made by an aircraft powered by Frank Whittle's jet engines

1942 The world's first atomic reactor was constructed on the racquets court of the sports stadium of Chicago University; the controlled chain-reaction started on 2 December. The leader of the team of scientists who took part in the experiment was Enrico Fermi, expatriate Italian physicist

1945 – 1955

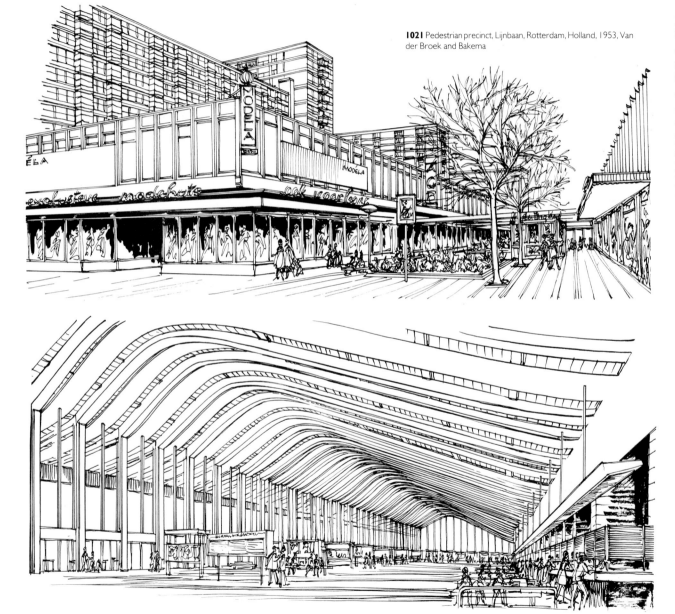

1021 Pedestrian precinct, Lijnbaan, Rotterdam, Holland, 1953, Van der Broek and Bakema

1022 Central railway station, 'Termini', Rome, 1947-51, Eugenio Montuori

In the years since 1945 all architecture has become 'modern', notably in its methods of construction and in materials used. At the same time, and related to this, the pace of building has increased phenomenally, partly due to the urgent need to replace war-destroyed structures and partly to house, educate, administer and entertain a growing population accustomed to expect a rising standard of living. The style of architecture has also become truly international: the high-rise towers, the housing estates, the civic centres, hotels and university buildings are familiar to all western nations.

The result of this vast quantity of similar construction has been a feeling created in the minds of people of a boring monotony, a sensation particularly deeply experienced in the 1970s, after over 20 years of fevered urban construction. The monotony stems partly from the sheer quantity of work, but also from the need to erect quickly which, in turn, has meant using the cheapest ways of mass-producing and erecting buildings. Since 1970-5 many lessons have been learnt, particularly with regard to the use of high-rise structures for housing and the resultant problems of safety, social deprivation and vandalism.

Internationalism in architecture has not, however, meant quite the same type of buildings being put up everywhere, and national traditions have soon made themselves apparent; based, as they always have been, on climate, material resources, mode of living and economic necessity. In the 1950s, for example, countries with an advanced steel industry – the USA, West Germany, Britain, for instance – tended to utilize steel-frame construction based on the rectangular block, which was then curtain-walled or faced. In Italy and Spain, on the other hand, where steel was less readily available, there was greater emphasis on the use of ferro-concrete which could be made into parabolic curves and vaults. Glass curtain-walling was clearly less suited (until more recent times) for use in a hot, sunny climate – and here the traditional desire for colour led to mosaic and ceramic facing for concrete surfaces.

Improved cummunications and travel facilities led to the leading architects of the world being responsible for creating buildings in quite different areas from those in which they practised. This resulted in, for example, a Le Corbusier *Unité d'Habitation* block in West Berlin, a Mies van der Rohe glass and steel National Gallery in the same city (**1037**), an Alvar Aalto brick student hostel block at MIT (**1025**), an engineering contribution from Pier Luigi Nervi at St Mary's Cathedral in San Francisco (**1047**), and Richard Rogers experimenting with Hi-Tech in the Pompidou Centre in Paris.

Immediately after the War, Italian civic and commercial building design was more varied and imaginative then elsewhere (**1022, 1030, 1040**). Sponsored by large companies which set an example – Olivetti and Pirelli for instance – architects succeeded in blending new materials and methods, such as concrete, with traditional Italian facing materials like marble and mosaic. West Germany was slower off the mark; cities lay in ruins and the economy was bankrupt. By the 1960s, however, original and interesting buildings were being erected (**1036, 1046**). The most remarkable post-war school of architecture was in Finland, where the promise of originality shown in the 1930s has blossomed since 1950. The Finns have adapted their modern architecture to

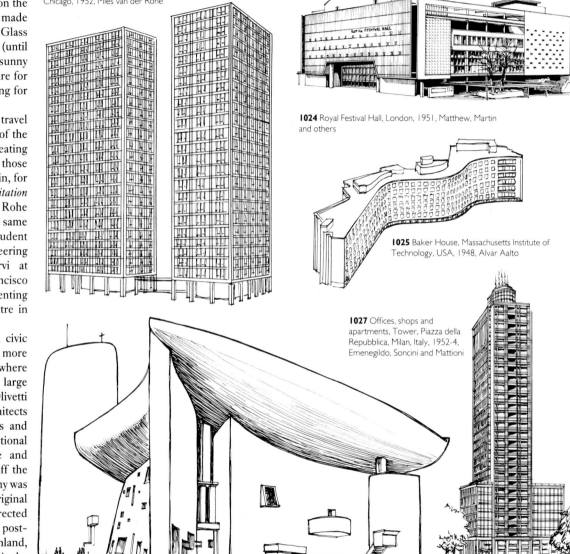

1023 Lake Shore Drive apartments, Chicago, 1952, Mies van der Rohe

1024 Royal Festival Hall, London, 1951, Matthew, Martin and others

1025 Baker House, Massachusetts Institute of Technology, USA, 1948, Alvar Aalto

1027 Offices, shops and apartments, Tower, Piazza della Repubblica, Milan, Italy, 1952-4, Emenegildo, Soncini and Mattioni

1026 Church of Notre Dame du Haut, Ronchamp, France, 1950-5, Le Corbusier

1945 Foundation of the United Nations Organisation

1945 16 July. Test explosion of the first plutonium bomb at Alamogordo in New Mexico

1945 6 August. Uranium 235 bomb exploded over the Japanese city of Hiroshima. On 14 August the Japanese government surrendered and World War II ended

1945 The film *La belle et la bête* (Beauty and the Beast) shown: a surrealistic version of the fairy tale by the French artist and writer Jean Cocteau

1945 First electronic digital computer built at the University of Pennsylvania in America; it weighed $29\frac{1}{2}$ tons

1946 Winston Churchill coined the phrase 'Iron Curtain' to describe the barrier of distrust between Western Europe and the countries dominated by the USSR

1946 The Play *The Winslow Boy* by Terence Rattigan, English playwright

1947 Production of the play *A Streetcar named Desire* by Tennessee Williams, set in New Orleans and about the American South

1947 Discovery of the Dead Sea Scrolls in 11 caves in the cliffs of Qumran, the manuscripts of which include the oldest known copies of Old Testament Scriptures

1947 English translation of Carlo Levi's novel *Cristo si è fermato a Eboli* (Christ stopped at Eboli), an account of the desperate poverty and backwardness of the forgotten area of Lucania in southern Italy which Levi himself experienced between 1935 and 1936 when he was exiled there because of his anti-Fascist views

USA, ITALY, FRANCH, PORTUGAL

DENMARK, ENGLAND AND ITALY

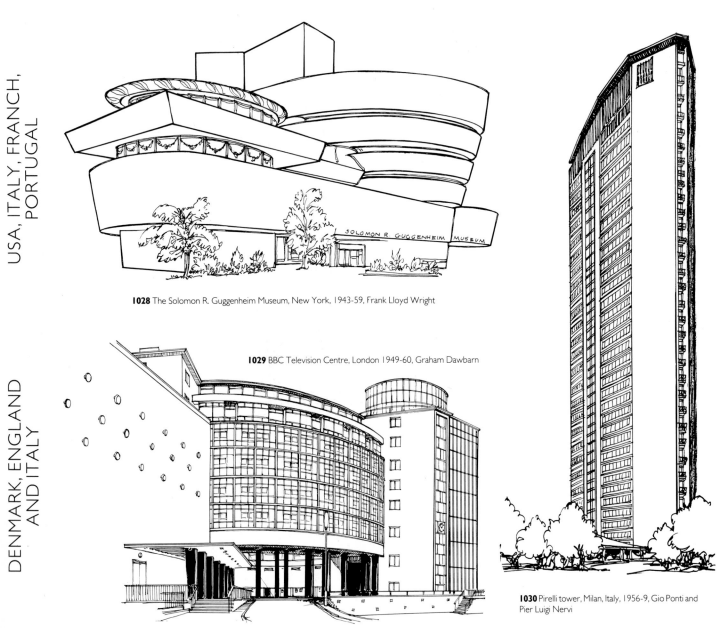

1028 The Solomon R. Guggenheim Museum, New York, 1943-59, Frank Lloyd Wright

1029 BBC Television Centre, London 1949-60, Graham Dawbarn

1030 Pirelli tower, Milan, Italy, 1956-9, Gio Ponti and Pier Luigi Nervi

suit their difficult climate and to blend into – not obtrude upon – their landscape. The standard of originality of design, suitability for purpose and high quality of finish in such a quantity of post-War building has been remarkable for such a large country and so tiny a population (**1038, 1041**).

Technological research has gradually solved the problems met earlier in the century in the use of the chief materials of modern architecture: glass, concrete, steel and plastics. As early as 1918 in San Francisco Willis J. Polk had introduced the 'curtain wall' of steel and glass which, hanging in front of the building's constructional framework, separates this from the cladding (p. 205).

Since then, and especially since 1945, glass curtain-walling has become ubiquitous, employed particularly on high rise structures but also for buildings of few storeys. The development of the float glass process in England by Pilkington has made available larger panes of pristine transparency, which has been most helpful for this purpose. The notable problems of using glass for curtain walling – the difficulty of adequate sealing together of the panes, the chill factor of the material and, conversely, the heat problem from direct sunshine, as well as the sensitivity of the users of the building to being on view to passers-by – have now been largely solved. Silicone sealants are truly waterproof. Double-glazing units with nitrogen filling the space between the sheets have dealt with the chill factor. Sun-reflecting coating has reduced the glare and air-conditioning controls the cooling of the interior atmosphere. One-way and coloured glass have made it possible to sheath the whole building, giving the occupants a light airy atmosphere yet retaining their privacy.

American architects such as Ludwig Mies van der Rohe (1886-1969) and Philip Johnson (b.1902) developed the widescale use of the curtain wall of panes of glass held by steel or aluminium mullions, both for low-level houses and skyscrapers. In more recent times, with new sealants, buildings may be totally clad in glass on curved as well as flat planes, as at Norman Foster's Willis Faber Headquarters in Ipswich of 1972 and the John Hancock tower in Chicago of 1970 by Skidmore, Owings and Merrill. Changing weather conditions can totally alter the appearance of such buildings from reflecting the exterior world to becoming almost invisible. At night, when illuminated from within, the interior scene comes alive (**1023, 1030, 1037, 1052, 1053**).

Once technology had made possible the elevator, the steel-frame construction and varieties of cladding from stone and concrete to terracotta and glass, American architects moved ahead to develop the theme of the city skyscraper, varying the form and increasing the height until, in 1932, the Empire State Building rose 85 storeys into the New York City skyline. For many years there was a nostalgic backward glancing in architectural style, as in the Gothic detailing of the Woolworth Building of 1913 (**981**) and in the Art Nouveau capping of the Chrysler Building of 1930 (**998**), but after this time the Americans accepted the modern characteristics inherent in the skyscraper form, passing through the juke-box phase (McGraw-Hill Building, 1932) to the grouping of the towers (Rockefeller Centre 1932-40).

After the War the 1950s witnessed a renewed wave of skyscraper building in the USA, and the slab became the mode. As long

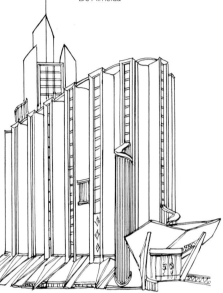

1031 Church of Notre Dame, Royan, France, 1954-9, Guillaume Gillet

1032 Detail. Sculpture on Discovery Monument, Belém, Portugal, 1960, Sculptor De Almeida

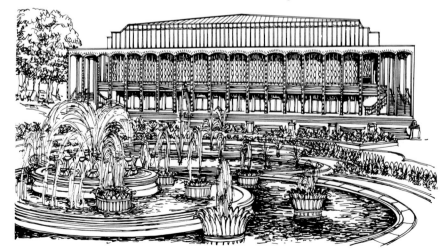

1033 Concert hall, Tivoli, Copenhagen, Denmark, 1956, Hans Hansen and Fritz Schegel

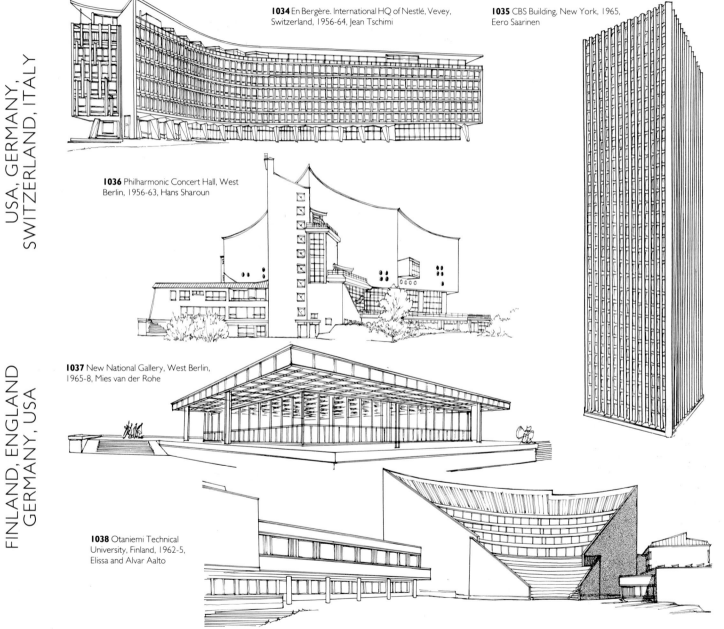

USA, GERMANY, SWITZERLAND, ITALY

FINLAND, ENGLAND GERMANY, USA

1034 En Bergère. International HQ of Nestlé, Vevey, Switzerland, 1956-64, Jean Tschimi

1035 CBS Building, New York, 1965, Eero Saarinen

1036 Philharmonic Concert Hall, West Berlin, 1956-63, Hans Sharoun

1037 New National Gallery, West Berlin, 1965-8, Mies van der Rohe

1038 Otaniemi Technical University, Finland, 1962-5, Elissa and Alvar Aalto

ago as 1919 in Berlin Mies van der Rohe had suggested a 20-storey tower sheathed in glass as a vertical-sided slab without set-backs. Examples of such towers were now being erected, among the pacesetters the United Nations Secretariat (1947-50, Wallace K. Harrison), Lever House (1950-2, Skidmore, Owings and Merrill) and the Seagram Building (1958, Mies van der Rohe and Philip Johnson), all in New York City.

Not all these skyscrapers were intended for office accommodation. Mies van der Rohe, the most prolific of the German Bauhaus architects who emigrated to the USA (p. 202), became known not only for excessively plain buildings pure in line but for buildings constructed from fine materials superbly finished and, often, containing luxury apartment accommodation, such as his Lake Shore Drive flats in Chicago (**1023**). Reaction in the 1960s and 1970s led to the use of alternative cladding materials, as in Eero Saarinen's CBS Building (**1035**), using grey granite vertical columns extending unbroken from top to bottom, attempts to break away from the slab into chunky boxes with set-backs and, in the 1980s, a return to nostalgia with the Telephone and Telegraph Building (**1050**).

Europe only adopted the skyscraper with enthusiasm after 1945 and the 1950s and 1960s were the decades of slabs being erected in the major cities everywhere to provide accommodation for housing and offices. Since 1970-5 enthusiasm has waned in respect of housing provided in this form.

Attempts were made after the War to deal with the problems of rebuilding the shattered towns, with increasing urbanization of populations and with the rapidly increasing flow of vehicular traffic in towns. In Britain the New Towns Act of 1946 provided for 20 such towns to take the overspill from large cities, especially London. Such new centres were intended to be self-sufficient in industry and services and were not to be built adjacent to exisiting conurbations. On the whole these, and later developments, have been successful.

In Scandinavia, untouched by the War, the garden cities of Vällingby and Farsta near Stockholm in Sweden had been established early. The theme was similar but the towns soon appeared to be shabby and old-fashioned. Much more successful and imaginative was the satellite town of Tapiola begun in 1952 eight miles from Helsinki. The layout comprises a large artificial lake with swimming pools and fountains and, behind it, service facilities. The mixed housing development is pleasingly planned and naturally sited to take advantage of the ·wooded landscape.

Not dissimilar is the new satellite town of Reston in Virginia in the USA, 18 miles from Washington. Like Tapiola it has a large artificial lake, wooded areas and houses which are planned informally to blend into the natural landscape. An important feature of Reston is its stress upon segregation of pedestrian from motor traffic, a safety factor achieved by laying out new roads and paths at different levels.

The European prototype of the city pedestrian precinct was the Lijnbaan of 1953-4, laid out in the destroyed centre of Rotterdam in Holland (**1021**). Later, West Germany widely adopted the idea when rebuilding her shattered northern cities: Essen, Düsseldorf, Bremen, Hamburg, Hanover. In later years, when both public and commercial interests had shown their approval, the segregation scheme was adopted in Munich and, in Italy, in Verona.

1039 Art and Architecture Faculty Building, Yale University, USA, 1961-3, Paul Rudolph

1041 Kaleva Church, Tampere, Finland, 1964-6, Paatelainen and Pietilä

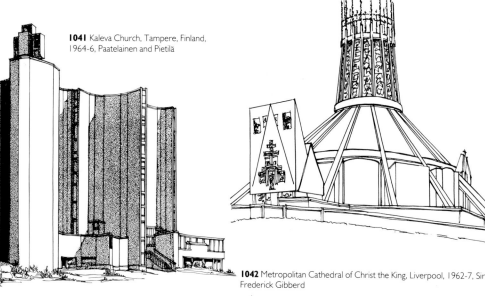

1040 Palace of Labour, Turin, Italy, 1960-1, Pier Luigi Nervi

1042 Metropolitan Cathedral of Christ the King, Liverpool, 1962-7, Sir Frederick Gibberd

operating and the first photographs taken

1949 Bonn became the (provisional) capital of the Federal Republic of Germany

1950-1 The Korean War

1952 First successful detonation of a hydrogen bomb carried out on Eniwetok Atoll

1954 Final defeat of France at Dien Bien Phu in North Vietnam, which ended the eight-year long unsuccessful attempt to retain French control of Indochina. The second Indochina War – the Vietnam War involving the Americans – began in 1957

1955 Experimental service of colour television began in Britain

1955 ICI introduced their polyester textile fibre which they called Terylene; the bulked form of this was Crimplene

1956 Soviet tanks entered the city of Budapest to crush the infant rebellion against Soviet rule

1957 Bronze group depicting the 25ft high figure of St Michael the archangel in conflict with the Devil modelled by the British sculptor Jacob Epstein, to be set against the walls of the new Coventry Cathedral by Sir Basil Spence which was consecrated in 1962

1958 1 January. The European Economic Community began to operate

1958 General de Gaulle elected President of the Fifth Republic of France by a 78% vote of the electoral college

1958 Publication of *Our Man in Havana* by the British writer Graham Greene

1965 – 1973

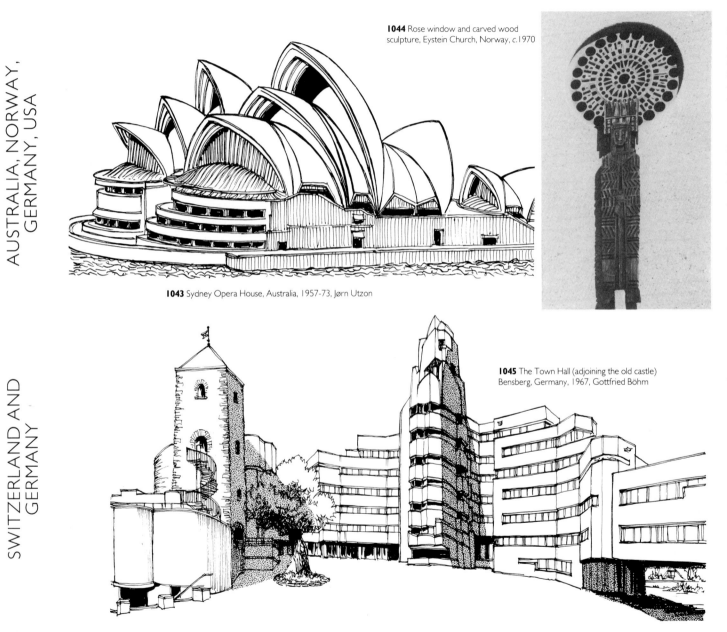

1044 Rose window and carved wood sculpture, Eystein Church, Norway, c.1970

1043 Sydney Opera House, Australia, 1957-73, Jørn Utzon

1045 The Town Hall (adjoining the old castle) Bensberg, Germany, 1967, Gottfried Böhm

Since 1945 the most ubiquitous material in use has been concrete. Technical advances had made high tensile steel and high quality concrete available and the infinite variety of form that can be achieved with prestressed reinforced concrete has been explored to the full.

The pacesetter, soon after the War, was Le Corbusier, who utilized the material in its most overt naked form – as in his Unité d'Habitation theme which exemplified his pre-war theories on low-cost ideal housing (p. 204). In Marseilles, where the first Unité was erected 1946-52, this single, immense rectangular block, carried on pilotis, contained 350 flats as well as shops and various communal facilities: a machine for living in, indeed.

From this structure and others inspired by it was coined the term 'brutalism', an English language derivation from the French *béton brut*, meaning concrete in its raw, natural state. A fashion developed for this, many architects impressed by this stark uncompromising material representing, it was felt, an honesty of structure and fabric. In the 1950s and 1960s many examples were built in different countries, for instance: Paul Rudolph's Art and Architecture Faculty at Yale University in America, Denys Lasdun's University of East Anglia and the GLC Architects Departments' Queen Elizabeth Hall and Hayward Gallery on London's riverside, both in England, Le Corbusier's Dominican Convent of La Tourette at Eveux-sur-l'Abresle in France, Brütsch's Catholic church at Buchs in Switzerland, and Helmut Striffler's Church of the Atonement at the site of the Nazi concentration camp at Dachau in Germany (**1031, 1036, 1039, 1045, 1048, 1054**).

Concrete as a material also lends itself to

expressionist and sculptural forms of architecture, to curves and arches, vaults and shells. Many architects experimented with the material in this way, using it in its natural form unadorned or facing it with other materials. The pacesetter in this field was Pier Luigi Nervi, the Italian engineer who had already established a reputation for originality and versatility in such work in the 1930s (p. 204). He went on after the War to design his stadia and exhibition halls in Rome and Turin, using steel and pre-cast concrete (**1040**), then continued, creating a brilliant range of shapes and structures for all purposes (**1047**). Early in this field also was Le Corbusier, with his highly personal and remarkable pilgrimage church of Notre Dame du Haut at Ronchamp in France (**1026**) while, in America, the now elderly Frank Lloyd Wright was completing his Guggenheim Museum in New York (**1028**).

As the drab weathering effect became apparent on so many raw concrete buildings a few years after erection, boredom and distaste set in from both patrons and general public. It then became customary, at least for the more costly prestige buildings, to face the curving concrete forms with ceramic tiling. There are many interesting examples of structures of this kind, notably a number of Finnish buildings such as Kaleva Church at Tampere (**1041**) and the world famous Opera House in Sydney in Australia (**1043**).

Various methods have evolved since 1945 to speed up building construction and so reduce costs. Modular design has been generally adopted, wherein an overall three-dimensional unit of measurement is used; so ensuring the accurate fitting of all building parts of whatever material and wherever or by whomsoever manufactured.

Prefabrication, extensively utilizing

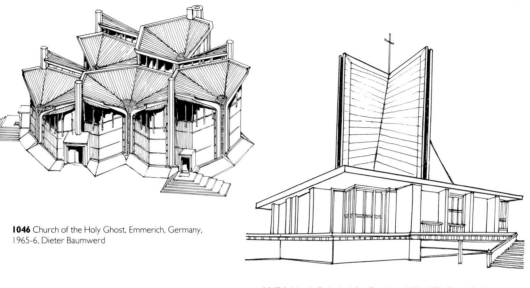

1046 Church of the Holy Ghost, Emmerich, Germany, 1965-6, Dieter Baumwerd

1047 St Mary's Cathedral, San Francisco, USA, 1971, Pietro Belluschi and Pier Luigi Nervi

1048 Church of St Anthony, Lichtensteig, Switzerland, 1968-70, Walter Förderer

1959 Microwave cooking, in which food is cooked by very high frequency (short) radio waves (such VHF waves first developed for radar purposes during World War II) introduced into Britain from America

1960 First laser action obtained in the USA by Theodore Maiman, using a ruby crystal which emitted pulses of red light lasting 1/1000th of a second. In 1961 a continuously operating gas laser was developed at the Bell Telephone Laboratories there

1960 OPEC (Organization of Petroleum Exporting Countries) formed by Iran, Iraq, Kuwait, Saudi Arabia and Venezuela to stabilize crude oil prices and establish uniform export policies among its members

1962 Cuba missile crisis brings USA and USSR to the verge of war

1963 22 November. Assassination of John F. Kennedy, President of the USA, in Dallas, Texas

1963 The Berlin Wall built by the East Germans to seal off the Western part of the city

1965 Death of Sir Winston Churchill

1965 Earlybird, first satellite to be launched into space for commercial communications purposes

1966 Chairman Mao instigated the 'Great Proletarian Cultural Revolution' in China

1967 The Six Day War between Israel and Egypt

1967-75 Egypt closed the Suez Canal to shipping, forcing foreign ships to be re-routed round the southern tip of Africa

1968 21 August. Half a million troops of the Warsaw Pact countries

USA AND GERMANY

USA, ENGLAND AND JAPAN

1049 Entrance forecourt, Staatsgalerie, Stuttgart 1977-84, Stirling and Wilford

1050 American Telephone and Telegraph Company Headquarters, New York, 1978-83, Johnson and Burgee

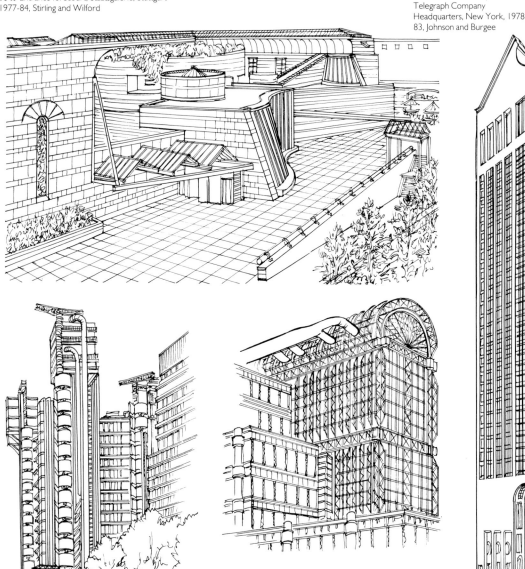

1051 Lloyds Headquarters, City of London, 1980-6, Richard Rogers

factory-made units, has become standard practice, as is also on-site casting and assembly. One development from this has been the architectural capsule design, in which the units may be added to, subtracted or replaced, so producing a living, changing architectural form. Habitat '67, designed by Moshe Safdie for the Montreal Expo 1967, illustrated the potential of this idea. This was a prototype design composed of pre-fabricated concrete living units fitted together like a child's building brick project, each secured in place by a vertical steel cable. The Nakagin apartment tower in Tokyo, designed by Kisho Kurokawa in 1972, pursues a similar theme. Here the steel box capsules containing office or housing suites are suspended from two fixed concrete service cores (**1056**).

Technology, particularly in the form of plastics, has offered further possibilities leading to the so-called Hi-Tech structures. The geodesic dome devised and exhibited at the US Pavilion in Montreal in 1967 by R. Buckminster Fuller makes use of balloon acrylic panels held in an aluminium framework. The concept was to provide a weather-proof, controlled environment within such domes. Another important plastics advance is glass reinforced plastic, known as GRP. This material may be moulded into large wall and roof panels which lend themselves to sculptural architecture as in, for instance, James Stirling's Olivetti Training Centre (**1055**).

Hi-Tech then moved towards the metal framework theme, a kind of architectural meccano, such as that established by Richard Rogers in his Paris 'Beaubourg' (officially entitled the Centre National d'Art et de la Culture Georges-Pompidou), which was completed in 1977 and has since proved immensely popular with Parisians. In November 1986 H.M. The Queen officially opened Rogers's newer structure, the Lloyds Headquarters in the City of London (**1051**). In gleaming silvery stainless steel, polished aluminium and smooth grey concrete, this unusual building displays its domestic functions on the exterior in a profusion of heating and ventilating pipes as well as its glass-walled observation lifts. From the central atrium rises the latter-day 'Crystal Palace' hall in glass and lacework steel.

Is this the trend for the decades ahead or will nostalgia for the past, which is rising in reaction to such designs, prevail? Although the desire for a return to 'buildings of human scale and of classical proportions' is understandable, it seems unlikely that, in terms of needs and costs, it can be practicable for large structures. The reality will probably be a middle way, utilizing modern means yet, hopefully, evidencing versatility and sympathetic imagination.

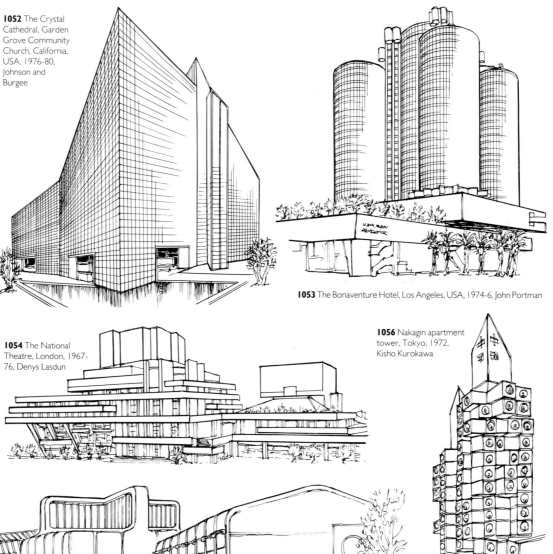

1052 The Crystal Cathedral, Garden Grove Community Church, California, USA, 1976-80, Johnson and Burgee

1053 The Bonaventure Hotel, Los Angeles, USA, 1974-6, John Portman

1054 The National Theatre, London, 1967-76, Denys Lasdun

1056 Nakagin apartment tower, Tokyo, 1972, Kisho Kurokawa

1055 Olivetti Training Centre, England, 1969-73, James Stirling

invaded Czechoslovakia in order to halt the process of liberalization which had been set in train by Alexander Dubček and his colleagues

1969 20 July. The two American astronauts Neil Armstrong and Edward Aldrin were the first human beings to set foot on the surface of the Moon

1971 Britain adopted a system of decimal currency, the last of the major nations which had not previously done so

1971 Introduction of the microprocessor by the Intel Corporation of Silicon Valley in California

1973 Yom Kippur War in the Middle East leads to a sharp rise in the price of oil and economic problems in the west

1974 As a result of the Watergate scandal, Richard Nixon became the first American president to resign

1976 Concorde, the first supersonic passenger aircraft, built by a consortium of British and French firms, went into service in January

1977 24 July. King Juan Carlos I opened Spain's first freely elected parliament for over 40 years

1979 Margaret Thatcher became Britain's first woman prime minister

1984 Assassination of Indira Gandhi, Prime Minister of India

Dictionaries and encylopaedias

COLVIN, H.M., *A Biographical Dictionary of British Architects, 1600-1840,* John Murray, 1978

CURL, J.S., *English Architecture: an Illustrated Glossary,* David and Charles, 1977

ENCYLOPEDIA AMERICANA

ENCYLOPEDIA BRITANNICA

FLEMING, J., and HONOUR, H., *The Penguin Dictionary of Decorative Arts,* Allen Lane, 1977

FLEMING, J., HONOUR, H., and PEVSNER, N., *The Penguin Dictionary of Architecture,* Penguin, 1977

HARRIS, J. and LEVER, J., *Illustrated Glossary of Architecture, 850-1830,* Faber and Faber, 1966

LAMPUGNANI, V.M., Ed. *Encylopaedia of 20th Century Architecture,* Thames and Hudson, 1983

PLACZEK, A.K., Ed. *Macmillian Encylopaedia of Architects* (4 vols.), The Free Press, 1982

RICHARDS, J.M., Ed. *Who's Who in Architecture from 1400 to the Present Day,* Weidenfeld and Nicholson, 1977

YARWOOD, D., *Encylopaedia of Architecture,* Batsford, 1985

General

ANDREWS, W., *Architecture in America,* Thames and Hudson, 1960

BRUNSKILL, R.W., *Traditional Buildings of Britain,* Gollancz, 1982

BRUNSKILL, R., and CLIFTON-TAYLOR, A., *English Brickwork,* Ward Lock, 1977

CICHY, B., *Great Ages of Architecture,* Oldbourne, 1964

CLIFTON-TAYLOR, A., *The Pattern of English Building,* Faber and Faber, 1972; *English Parish Churches as Works of Art,* Batsford, 1974

CLIFTON-TAYLOR, A., and IRESON, A.S., *English Stone Building,* Gollancz, 1983

CONDIT, C.W., *American Building: Materials and Techniques from the beginning of the Colonial Settlements to the Present,* University of Chicago Press, 1968

COOK, O., *The English House Through Seven Centuries,* Whittet Books, 1983

COPPLESTONE, T., Ed., *World Architecture,* Hamlyn, 1963

FINTEL, M., Ed., *Handbook of Concrete Engineering,* Van Nostrand Reinhold, 1974

FLETCHER, B., *A History of Architecture,* The Athlone Press, 1975

FOSTER, M., Ed., *The Principles of Architecture,* Phaidon Press, 1983

GARDINER, S., *An Introduction to Architecture,* Leisure Books, 1983

GIROUARD, M., *Life in the English Country House,* Yale University Press, 1978; *Cities and People,* Yale University Press, 1985

GLOAG, J., and BRIDGEWATER, D., *History of Cast Iron in Architecture,* Allen and Unwin, 1948

GOMBRICH, E., *The Story of Art,* Phaidon, 1972

HARVEY, J., *Cathedrals of England and Wales,* Batsford, 1978

JONES, E., and WOODWARD, C., *The Architecture of London,* Weidenfeld and Nicholson, 1983

JORDAN, R.F., *European Architecture in Colour,* Thames and Hudson, 1961

JONES, E., and ZANDT, E. VAN, *The City: Yesterday, Today and Tomorrow,* Aldus Books, 1974

KOSTOF, S., *A History of Architecture,* Oxford University Press, 1985

LLOYD, N., *History of the English House,* The Architectural Press, 1975; *A History of English Brickwork,* Antique Collectors' Club, 1983

MUMFORD, L., *The City in History,* Secker and Warburg, 1961

NORWICH, J.J., Ed., *Great Architecture of the World,* Mitchell Beazley, 1975

NUTTGENS, P., *The Story of Architecture,* Phaidon Press, 1983; *The World's Great Architecture,* Hamlyn, 1980

PEVSNER, N., Founding Ed., *The Buildings of England, Ireland, Scotland and Wales,* (many vols.), Penguin Books; *An Outline of European Architecture,* Penguin, 1961

RAEBURN, M. Ed., *Architecture of the Western World,* Orbis Publishing, 1980; *An Outline of World Architecture,* Octopus Books, 1973

RICHARDS, J.M., *800 Years of Finnish Architecture,* David and Charles, 1978

ROTH, L.M., *A Concise History of American Architecture,* Harper and Row, 1979

SAUNDERS, A., *The Art and Architecture of London,* Phaidon, 1984

SIMPSON, F.M., *A History of Architectural Development,* new edition in 5 vols, Longmans, from 1982

SITWELL, S., *Great Houses of Europe,* Weidenfeld and Nicholson, 1961; *Great Palaces of Europe,* Weidenfeld and Nicholson, 1964

STANLEY, C.C., *Highlights in the History of Concrete,* Cement and Concrete Association, 1979

WATKIN, D., *A History of Western Architecture,* Barrie and Jenkins, 1986

YARWOOD, D., *The Architecture of Britain,* Batsford, 1980; *The English Home,* Batsford, 1979; *English Interiors,* Lutterworth Press, 1984; *The Architecture of Europe,* Chancellor Press, 1983; *Outline of English Architecture,* Batsford, 1977; *The Architecture of Italy,* Chatto and Windus, 1970

The ancient classical world

AKURGAL, E., *Ancient Civilisations and Ruins of Turkey,* Mobil Oil Türk A.S., Istanbul, 1970

BOËTHIUS, A., *Etruscan and Early Roman Architecture,* Pelican History of Art Series, Penguin, 1978

HODGE, P., *The Roman House,* Longman, 1977

LAWRENCE, A.W., *Greek Architecture,* Pelican History of Art Series, Penguin, 1983

RICHTER, G.M.A., *Greek Art,* Phaidon, 1959

WARD-PERKINS, J.B., *Roman Imperial Architecture,* Pelican History of Art Series, Penguin, 1981; *Roman Architecture,* Abrams, New York, 1977

WHEELER, M., *Roman Art and Architecture,* Thames and Hudson, 1964

Early Christian and Byzantine

KRAUTHEIMER, R., *Early Christian and Byzantine*

Architecture, Pelican History of Art Series, Penguin, 1981

STEWART, C., *Byzantine Legacy*, Allen and Unwin, 1959

TALBOT RICE, D., *Art of the Byzantine Era*, Thames and Huson, 1963

Pre-Romanesque and Romanesque

CONANT, K.J., *Carolingian and Romanesque Architecture*, Pelican History of Art Series, Penguin, 1979

VERSONE, P., *From Theodoric to Charlemagne: A History of the Dark Ages in the West*, Methuen, 1967

Medieval

ANDERSON, W., *The Rise of the Gothic*, Hutchinson, 1985

FRANKL, P., *Gothic Architecture*, Pelican History of Art Series, Penguin, 1962

HARVEY, J., *The Gothic World*, Batsford, 1950; *Gothic England*, Batsford, 1948

SITWELL, S., *Gothic Europe*, Weidenfeld and Nicholson, 1969

WEBB, G., *Architecture in Britain in the Middle Ages*, Pelican History of Art Series, Penguin, 1956

1550 – 1800

BEARD, G., *The Work of Sir Christopher Wren*, Bartholomew, 1982; *The Work of Robert Adam*, Bartholomew, 1978; *The Work of John Vanbrugh*, Batsford, 1986

BLUNT, A., *Art and Architecture in France 1500-1700*, Pelican History of Art Series, Penguin, 1957; Ed., *Baroque and Rococo Architecture and Decoration*, Granada, 1982

DOWNES, K., *Vanbrugh*, Zwemmer, 1977; *Hawksmoor*, Zwemmer, 1979; *The Architecture of Wren*, Granada, 1982

FLEMING, J., *Robert Adam and His Circle*, Murray, 1962

GUINESS, D., and SADLER, J.T., *The Palladian Style in England, Ireland and America*, Thames and Hudson, 1976

HARRIS, J., *The Palladians*, Trefoil Books, 1981

HEMPEL, E., *Baroque Art and Architecture in Central Europe*, Pelican History of Art Series, Penguin, 1965

HOOK, J., *The Baroque Age in England*, Thames and Hudson, 1976

KUBLER, G., and SORIA, M., *Art and Architecture in Spain and Portugal 1500 – 1800*, Pelican History of Art Series, Penguin, 1959

MURRAY, P., *The Architecture of the Italian Renaissance*, Batsford, 1963

PALLADIO, A., *The Four Books of Architecture*, Dover Publications, New York, 1965

SCULLY, V., *American Architecture and Urbanism*, Thames and Hudson, 1969

SERLIO, S., *The Five Books of Architecture*, Dover Publications, New York, 1982

SITWELL, S., *British Architects and Craftsmen 1600 – 1830*, Batsford, 1948

SUMMERSON, J., *The Classical Language of Architecture*, Thames and Hudson, 1983, *Architecture in Britain 1530-1830*, Pelican History of Art Series, Penguin, 1969; *Georgian London*, Barrie and Jenkins, 1962

WHIFFEN, M., and KOEPER, F., *American Architecture 1607-1976*, Routledge and Kegan Paul, 1981

WITTKOWER, R., *Architectural Principles in the Age of Humanism*, Academy Editions, 1977; *Palladio and English Palladianism*, Thames and Hudson, 1974; *Art and Architecture in Italy 1600-1750*, Pelican History of Art Series, Penguin, 1965

YARWOOD, D., *Robert Adam*, Dent, 1970

The nineteenth century

BEAVER, P., *The Crystal Palace*, Hugh Evelyn, 1977

BOSSAGLIA. R., *Art Nouveau*, Orbis, 1973

BRADLEY, I., *William Morris and His World*, Thames and Hudson, 1978

BRIGGS, A., *Victorian Cities*, Odhams Press, 1963

CLARK, K., *The Gothic Revival*, John Murray, 1952

CROOK, J.M., *The Greek Revival*, John Murray, 1972

HAMLIN, T., *Greek Revival Architecture in America*, Dover Publications, New York, 1964

HITCHCOCK, H. RUSSELL., *Architecture, Nineteenth and Twentieth Centuries*, Pelican History of Art Series, Penguin, 1982

HOWARTH, T., *Charles Rennie Mackintosh and the Modern Movement*, Routledge and Kegan Paul, 1977

MIGNOT, C., *Architecture of the Nineteenth Century in Europe*, Rizzoli, New York, English Translation 1984

RICHARDS, J.M., and MARE, E., *The Functional Tradition in Early Industrial Buildings*, The Architectural Press, 1958

RICHARDSON, M., *Architects of the Arts and Crafts Movement*, Trefoil Books, 1983

WADDELL R., Ed., *The Art Nouveau Style*, Dover Publications, New York, 1977

The twentieth century

BANHAM, R., *The New Brutalism*, The Architectural Press, 1966

BENEVOLO L., *History of Modern Architecture*, Routledge and Kegan Paul, 1971

GOLDBERGER, P., *The Skyscraper*, Allen Lane, 1982

GROPIUS, W., *Scope of Total Architecture*, Allen and Unwin, 1956

JENCKS, C., *Late-Modern Architecture*, Academy Editions, 1980

KIDDERSMITH, G.E., *The New Architecture of Europe*, Penguin, 1962

KULTERMANN, U., *New Architecture of the World*, Thames and Hudson, 1966

LE CORBUSIER, *Towards a New Architecture*, The Architectural Press, 1970; *The City of Tomorrow*, The Architectural Press, 1971; *The Modulor*, Faber and Faber, 1977

MACFADYAN, D., *Sir Ebenezer Howard and the Town Planning Movement*, Manchester University Press, 1970

PEVSNER, N., *The Sources of Modern Architecture and Design*, Thames and Hudson, 1981; *The Pioneers of Modern Design*, Penguin, 1982

RICHARDS, J.M., *An Introduction to Modern Architecture*, Penguin, 1956

SUDJIC, D., *New Architecture: Foster, Rogers, Stirling*, Thames and Hudson for the Royal Academy of Arts, 1986

WHITTICK, A., *European Architecture in the 20th Century*, Leonard Hill Books, 1974

WINGLER, H.M., *Bauhaus*, MIT Press, 1980

GLOSSARY

The bold references in brackets refer to figure numbers of illustrations.

Abacus   The top member of a capital, usually a square or curved-sided slab of stone or marble (**31**)

Abutment   The solid mass of masonry or brickwork from which an arch springs or against which it abuts.

Acanthus   A leaf form used in classical ornament (**51**).

Acropolis   A city upon a hill. A Greek term usually implying also some fortification (**35**).

Acroteria   Blocks resting upon the vertex and lower extremities of a pediment to carry carved ornament (**22**).

Agora   A Greek word for the open-air meeting place to be found in city centres which was used for the transaction of business and which included a market-place, shops, business premises and stoas (**39**).

Alcázar   A Spanish word for a castle or fortress.

Ambulatory   A passage or aisle giving access in a church between the choir with high altar and the exterior apse (**491**).

Antefixae   Carved blocks set at regular intervals along the lower edge of a roof in classical architecture (**70**).

Anthemion   A type of classical ornament based upon the honeysuckle flower (**53**).

Apse   Semicircular or polygonal termination to a church, most commonly to be found on the eastern or transeptal elevations (**270**).

Arabesque   Classical ornament in delicate, flowing forms, terminating in scrolls and decorated with flowers and leaves (**845**).

Arcade   A series of arches, open or closed with masonry, supported on columns or piers (**347**).

Architrave   The lowest member of the classical entablature (**118**).

Arcuated construction   Wherein the structure is supported on arches (**131**).

Arris   The vertical sharp edges between flutes on a column or pilaster (**33**).

Articulation   The designing, defining and dividing up of a façade into vertical and horizontal architectural members.

Ashlar   Hewn and squared stones prepared for building.

Astragal   A moulding at the top of a column and below the capital (**407**).

Astylar   A classical façade where an order is not used.

Atrium   In domestic ancient classical building, an open courtyard surrounded by rooms (**81**). In Early Christian and Byzantine churches a colonnaded entrance court (**150**). Atria are sometimes incorporated into modern ecclesiastical or domestic designs.

Attic   In Renaissance and later classical architecture an upper storey above the cornice (**899**).

Baldacchino   A canopy supported on pillars set over an altar or throne.

Barbican   Outer defence to a city or castle. Generally a double tower over a gate or bridge (**462**).

Barrel vault   A continuous vault in semicircular section like a tunnel (**282**).

Basilica   In Roman architecture a hall of justice and centre for commercial exchange. This type of structure was adapted by the early Christians for their church design. It was a rectangular building usually with an apse at one end. Internally it was divided into nave and aisles by columns not piers and these supported a timber roof. There were no transepts. The basilican plan has continued in use for centuries, though somewhat modified. It is especially to be seen in Italy and France (**90, 154**).

Cantilever   A specially shaped beam or other member – for example, a staircase tread – which is supported securely at one end and carries a load at the other, free end or with the load distributed evenly along the beam. A cantilever bracket is used to support a cornice or balcony of considerable projection. The cantilever principle is widely used in bridge design.

Capital   The crowning feature of a column or pier (**85**).

Caryatid   Sculptured female figure in the form of a support or column (**34**).

Cella   The enclosed sacred part of a Roman temple (**74**).

Centering   A structure, usually made of wood, set up to support a dome, vault or arch until construction is complete (**129**).

Chevet   Term given to a semicircular or polygonal apse when it is surrounded by an ambulatory from which radiate chapels (**376**).

Chevron ornament   Romanesque decoration in zig-zag form.

Cimborio   Spanish term for lantern or fenestrated cupola (**553**).

Clerestory, Clearstory   The upper story of a church usually pierced by windows (**466**).

Coffer   A panel or caisson sunk into a ceiling, vault or dome. Most commonly the coffer is octagonal in shape and decoratively carved (**124**).

Conch   The domed ceiling of a semicircular apse (**165**).

Console   A decorative scrolled bracket used in classical architecture to support a cornice (**50**).

Corbel table   A projecting section of wall supported on corbels (carved blocks of stone or wood) and generally forming a parapet.

Cornice   The crowning member of the classical entablature.

Coupled Columns   In classical architecture, where the wall articulation is designed with the columns in pairs.

Crocket   A projecting block of stone carved in Gothic foliage on the inclined sides of pinnacles and canopies (**470**).

Crossing   The central area in a cruciform church where the transepts cross the nave and choir arm. Above this space is generally set a tower or cupola.

Cruciform   A ground plan based upon the form of a cross.

Curtain wall   In modern architecture this term is in general use to describe an external non-loadbearing wall, composed of repeated modular elements generally of glass in metal framing (**1023**).

Cusp Point forming the foliations in Gothic tracery (**476**).

Cyclopean masonry Walling composed of immense blocks of stone as seen in building at Tyrins or Mycenae. Named after the mythical Cyclopes (**10**).

Cyma A moulding in a section of two alternative curves – either *cyma recta* or *cyma reversa* – used especially in classical architecture (**50**).

Domical vault A groined or ribbed vault where the diagonal groins or ribs are semicircular in form, so causing the centre of the vaulted bay to rise higher in the centre than the side arches, as in a low dome.

Domus A Roman town house (**79**).

Dosseret A deep block often placed above the Byzantine capital to support the wide voussoirs of the arch above (**83**).

Drum The circular or poly-sided walling, usually pierced with windows, supporting a dome (**181, 188**).

Echinus A curved moulded member supporting the abacus of the Doric Order. The curve resembles that of the shell of a sea urchin after which it is named (*echinos* = sea urchin in Greek) (**33**).

Engaged Column One which is attached to the wall behind it.

Entablature The continuous horizontal lintel made up of mouldings and supported by columns characteristic of classical architecture (**27-30**).

Entasis Taken from the Greek term for distension, is a carefully and mathematically calculated convex curving along the outline of the column shaft. It is designed to counteract the optical illusion which gives to a shaft bounded by straight lines the appearance of being concavely curved. In Greek work the column sides appear to be straight, so slight is the entasis. In later (especially nineteenth-century) work the entasis is often overexaggerated, appearing convex.

Fillet A narrow flat band which divides mouldings from one another. It also separates column flutes (**118**).

Finial Ornament finishing the apex of a roof, gable, pinnacle, newel, canopy, etc. (**513**).

Flèche French term for a slender spire commonly found over the crossing in a Gothic church (**421**).

Flute Vertical channelling in the shaft of a column (**32**).

Forum The Roman place of assembly for markets, temples, courts of justice etc. (**88**).

Frieze In classical architecture, the central section of the entablature. In a room, the decorative strip along the upper part of the walls (**28**).

Frontispiece The two- or three-stage entrance feature applied to the principal façade of a court or building (**666**).

Giant Order Used in Mannerist, baroque and later classical architecture where the order spans two storeys of the façade (**684**).

Greek cross plan A cruciform ground plan in which all four arms of the cross are of equal length.

Guilloche Classical ornament in the form of an intertwined plait.

Guttae Small cones under the mutules and triglyphs of the Doric entablature (**33**).

Hall church One where the vaulting height of the entire building interior is the same. Such a church has, therefore, no triforium or clerestory. Most commonly found in medieval church design in Italy, Germany and Scandinavia (**524, 549**).

Hypocaust An underfloor chamber of brick or stone, constructed in ancient Roman buildings for central heating purposes. Hot air in the basement furnace passed through wall flues to heat all the rooms (**130**).

Insula Roman multi-storey tenement block (**103**).

Intercolumniation The space between columns (**22**).

Intersecting vault Where two vaults, either of semicircular or of pointed section, meet and intersect one another at right angles. The most usual instance is at the crossing of a church where the transepts cross nave and choir.

Lantern Structure for ventilation and light. Often surmounting a dome or tower (**576**).

Latin cross plan A cruciform ground plan where the nave is longer than the other three arms.

Lierne From the French *lier* (= to tie). A short intermediate rib in Gothic vaulting which is not a ridge rib nor rises from the impost (**477**).

Lintel The horizontal stone slab or timber beam spanning an open and supported on columns or walls (**10**).

Loggia Open-sided gallery or arcade.

Machicolation A parapet in medieval fortified buildings with openings between supporting corbels for dropping missiles upon the enemy (**548**).

Manoeline Portuguese decorative architectural style of the early sixteenth century, named after Dom Manoel I (**643**).

Metope The space between the triglyphs of a Doric frieze. Often decorated with sculptured groups or carved ornament (**33**).

Modillion A scrolled bracket as a console, but set horizontally not vertically.

Module A unit of measurement by means of which the proportions and detailed parts of a building may be regulated. In classical architecture the column shaft diameter (or half diameter) was so used. In the twentieth century Le Corbusier proposed a system of measurement based upon the proportions of the human male figure; he called the system *Le Modulor*. The module is essential to modern mass-produced building parts.

Monolithic column One whose shaft is made of one piece of stone or marble in contrast to one made up in hollow drums.

Mozarabic A style of architecture in medieval Spain named after the Mozarabs – Christians owing allegiance to a Moorish king but allowed to practise Christianity (**252**).

Mutule Blocks under Doric cornices from which guttae depend (**33**).

Naos Chamber in a Greek temple containing the cult statue (**23**).

Narthex In a Byzantine or Early Christian church, a vestibule extended transversely across the western end of the building, separated from the nave by a screen or wall and set apart as an area for women and penitents. Also known as an antenave or antechurch and as a galilee (**145**).

Orchestra The circular area in a Greek theatre where the chorus danced and sang (**37**).

Pediment In classical architecture, the triangular low-pitched gable above the entablature which completes the end of the sloping roof. Pediments are also used as decorative features above doors, niches and windows. In Renaissance, Mannerist and baroque work these may be broken, open, scrolled or segmental (**107, 815**).

Pendentive Spherical triangle formed by the intersecting of a dome by two pairs of opposite arches, themselves carried on piers or columns (**168, 180**).

Peristyle A row of columns surrounding a temple, court or cloister, also the space so enclosed (**22, 80, 616**).

Piano nobile An Italian Renaissance term meaning literally the 'noble floor'. In classical building it is the first and principal floor.

Pilaster A column of rectangular section usually engaged in the wall.

Pilaster strip Low relief vertical strips with the appearance of pilasters but with only decorative purpose (**245**).

Pilotis A term in modern architecture derived from the French word for pile or stake. Popularized by Le Corbusier in his designs for flats and houses supported on such piles (**1011**).

Plateresque A form of rich surface ornament in Spanish architecture used in both Gothic and Renaissance building. The term is derived from *plateria* = silverwork (**644**).

Podium A continuous projecting base or pedestal.

Pozzolana A substance used in Roman concrete building. A volcanic ash found in quantity in the volcanic areas round Rome and Naples and named after the town of Pozzuoli near Naples. When mixed with lime from the local limestone, pozzolana helped to form an exceptionally hard concrete to which base was added brick and travertine fragments.

Propylaeum An important entrance gateway in Greek architecture as, for example, the entrance to the Athenian acropolis (**35**).

Putto From the Italian word meaning child, used to describe the cherubs in sculpture, especially in baroque architecture (**796**).

Retablo An altar piece, or the framing of enclosing painted panels above an altar. A Spanish term used in Spanish architecture.

Relieving arch A relieving or discharging arch or slab is constructed to prevent the weight of masonry above it from crushing the lintel stone below.

Rotunda A building of circular ground plan often surmounted by a dome. A circular apartment (**107, 125**).

Rustication A treatment of masonry with sunk joints and roughened surfaces. Used in classical architecture.

Set-off Sloping or horizontal member connecting the lower and thicker part of a wall with the receding upper part (**399**).

Shaft The column of an order between the capital and base.

Spandrel Triangular space formed between an arch and the rectangle of outer mouldings, as in a doorway. Generally decorated by carving or mosaic.

Squinch Arches placed diagonally and corbelled out across the internal angles of a tower to convert the square form into an octagonal base which supports an octagonal or circular drum (**57**).

Stave church Medieval stave or mast churches of Scandinavia constructed in self-contained units. The walls, the stave screens, rest upon timber sleepers but do not take weight or thrust. This is taken upon the skeleton framework of poles (masts) which are set into the timber ground sills, then attached to the staves (**449**).

Strapwork A form of ornament using straps of decoration intertwined and forming panels. The straps are flat with raised fillet edges. Used in plaster decoration of ceilings and walls in Renaissance work, especially in Flanders, Germany, England and Poland (**702, 709**).

Stucco An Italian word for decorative plaster. The Italian *stucco duro* was the hard plaster used by Renaissance craftsmen which, in addition to lime and gypsum, contained powdered marble.

Stylobate The platform upon which the columns of a Greek temple stand (**20**).

Tholos A circular classical temple (**25, 26**).

Tierceron An intermediate rib in Gothic ribbed vaulting which extends from the vault springing to the ridge rib (**423**).

Trabeated construction A structure composed of horizontal lintels and vertical posts (post-and-lintel) as in Greek architecture (**19**).

Tracery The ornamental stonework in the head of a Gothic window (**475, 476**).

Transept The arms of a cruciform church set at right angles to the nave and choir. Transepts are generally aligned north and south.

Triforium The first floor intermediate stage of a medieval church between the nave arcade and the clerestory. The triforium is usually arcaded and may have a passage behind which extends all round the church at this level (**310**).

Triglyph The blocks cut with vertical channels which are set at regular intervals along the frieze of the Dorc order (**33**).

Trumeau A French term which refers to the pier between two openings or, more commonly in Gothic architecture, to the pier dividing a large portal into two parts (**378**)

Tympanum The face of a classical pediment between its sloping and horizontal cornice mouldings; also the area between the lintel of a doorway and the arch above it. Tympana are generally carved and/or sculptured (**361, 414**).

Undercroft A chamber partly or wholly below ground level, generally in a medieval building. In a church this would be a crypt, in a house or castle it would be used for storage.

Vault An arched covering.

Vaulting bay The rectangular or square area bounded by columns or piers and covered by a stone vault (**423**).

Vaulting boss A carved decorative feature set over the intersections of a ribbed vault to hide the junctions (**423**).

Vault springing The point at which the vault ribs spring upwards from the capital, corbel or arch impost (**586**).

Volute A spiral or scroll to be seen in Ionic, Corinthian and Composite capitals (**84, 85**).

Voussoir The wedge-shaped blocks which comprise an arch (**61**).

INDEX

Buildings are generally listed under the names of towns or villages and persons under the surname. Illustration references are printed in **bold** type.

222

223

4/93 BG

DEMCO